An Accident

Paul J.J. Welfens

An Accidental Brexit

New EU and Transatlantic Economic Perspectives

palgrave
macmillan

Paul J.J. Welfens
European Institute for International
   Economic Relations (EIIW)
University of Wuppertal
Wuppertal, Germany

ISBN 978-3-319-58270-2   ISBN 978-3-319-58271-9   (eBook)
DOI 10.1007/978-3-319-58271-9

Library of Congress Control Number: 2017940595

This Palgrave Macmillan imprint is published by Springer Nature
The registered company is Springer International Publishing AG
The registered company address is: Gewerbestrasse 11, 6330 Cham, Switzerland

Preface

The historical referendum on European Union membership was the second such event to take place in the United Kingdom since 2014—when the Cameron government organized the Scottish independence referendum. In an obvious way, a referendum in a Western country invites all voters of the respective country to indicate their view on a critical topic and may be dubbed the ultimate expression of democratic decision-making. Thus, one should expect careful preparation on the side of government and a lively debate between the pro and con sides. At first sight, the British EU referendum of 2016 was indeed organized according to this logic, but upon closer inspection one can easily understand how unprofessional the information campaign of the Cameron government had actually been. Under normal circumstances, with the expected referendum standards applied, the outcome of the referendum would have been—as will be shown—52.1% in favor of Remain. The reality was decisively different for several reasons, as we shall see, with a 51.9% majority in favor of Brexit—a historical result on June 23 which one may argue represents a surprising and hardly legitimate decision for leaving the European Union: an accidental Brexit. That is the title of this book, and it is not easy to consider that the United Kingdom, with the benefit of a history of hundreds of years of rational decision-making in many key economic and political fields, should be characterized by a Brexit majority which is not the result of a solid decision-making procedure. Supporters of the Leave campaign will have a different view, but the facts presented here cannot be dismissed. In the end, the readers—and the British people—will have to decide how convincing the arguments of the political economy analysis presented are.

For the world economy, the UK's final decision on EU membership is crucial as the UK represented about 2.3% of the global economy in 2015 (based on purchasing power parity real income data from the World Bank), the EU27 stood for 14.5% in the same year. As regards the EU, Brexit clearly means a weakening of the European Union as the UK accounts for about 18% of EU28 Gross Domestic Product (GDP); for the UK, it could mean that its share in world GDP will fall below 2% as we shall see. The long-term Brexit effects will mean a weaker UK, probably a weaker EU, and a US gaining enhanced access to London, but simultaneously losing influence in Brussels. China's global role will be reinforced beyond its 17.3% share in world income in 2015, notably ahead of the US with 15.7%.

In a nutshell, the subsequent analysis is not difficult to understand, but many important details can only be explained in the book's individual chapters. On June 23, 2016, a majority of British voters decided to leave the EU, and this historical decision is an interesting development in and of itself; for an international economist, however, this is not necessarily a starting point to write a thought-provoking book: even if one might argue that the Brexit vote was rather unexpected by many observers. Among the key drivers for this study were, as a first point, the disorderly nature of the referendum: with the Cameron government commissioning Her Majesty's Treasury to prepare a 200-page study on the long-term benefits of the British EU membership and the cost of a potential Brexit, respectively, but then not mentioning the key finding of a 10% income loss in the extensive government information brochure sent to all households—thus undermining any chance for Cameron's almost certain victory in the EU referendum. Who is responsible for this unprecedented "Treasury-gate" in London and other surprising developments? One rather strange element including confusing conjectures from the side of government was the anti-EU migration debate, with immigration portrayed to be a large economic and fiscal burden for the UK. What about the facts that show the opposite and why did the Cameron government not present these key facts to the British population? Should a democratic government be interested in facts? What is the motivation for a government to use very misleading rhetoric? What made many British voters so concerned about immigration dynamics beyond the economic aspects—obviously, the fear of a rising number of refugees from Islamic countries played a role along with the perception that immigrants from countries with different religious and cultural backgrounds are not easily integrated in the Internet age in which certain young immigrants can come under the online influence of radical religious leaders based abroad (the integration of immigrants thus seems to become more difficult and the traditional tolerance of modern Western countries seems to be weakening: the open society could become mentally rather more closed in a period of globalization). A third element of the motivation for this book was the fact that the European Commission had organized neither a professional monitoring of the run-up to the historical UK referendum nor ensured that Mr. Juncker, President of the European Commission, gave a pro-EU speech in London or Birmingham; rather, the US President Obama gave a speech in which he supported the EU integration project in the British capital. What is wrong with the EU? Inefficient regional policies, over-regulation, a lack of leadership? More than this. A fourth element was the desire to understand whether or not the May government's promise to conclude new free trade treaties—after Brexit—would generate the high growth impulses promised; in 2016, the Leave campaign even created the impression that the UK could prosper as a free trade leader in a renewed Commonwealth. The answer to such promises is clear-cut. A fifth motivation concerns the apparently very low short-term negative output effects of the referendum, and this naturally leads to the question about the medium- and long-term effects of Brexit: could leaving the EU come at zero cost? Certainly not, and it will be explained why this is the case and also that the effects involve not only the UK, but also the EU27, the US, and hence the world economy in the long run.

While finalizing the preface at the University College London and in a café close to St. Paul's Cathedral on March 3, 2017, I contemplated the first drastic foreign policy and trade policy changes associated with Trump's victory in the presidential elections in the United States. Considering the information from Washington DC, Brussels, Berlin, Paris, and London through a theoretical economic lens, there was indeed an important question that to some extent is explored in this book: can the Global Britain project of the May government—with emphasis on free trade and free capital flows plus economic stability—really work in a situation characterized by the sudden weakening of the international institutional architecture with global international organizations such as the World Trade Organization and the Bank for International Settlements being actively dismantled by a protectionist and anti-multilateral Trump's administration—which Prime Minister May has deliberately chosen to be the UK's preferred partner? The book is also ultimately concerned with necessary EU reforms, including an overhaul of the Eurozone, the candidate countries for which are still chosen on the basis of the so-called convergence criteria, but not on the basis of the complementarily important optimum currency area literature. This is unwise, and not modifying the EU catalogue of Eurozone admission criteria would be irresponsible. As regards the speed of necessary EU reforms, one should not have the illusion that slow adjustments will work to stabilize the EU since with Brexit, the Trump victory in the US and the ongoing growth of China, there are at least three dynamics which require reforms to simultaneously be energetic and careful. The 2017 EU Commission's White Paper on the Future of the EU is not very convincing here. While it is true that EU integration problems are quite difficult, for every disease there is a cure.

There is also the new question of whether or not people in EU countries would support innovative elements of European integration and whether or not pent-up problems within the EU could be resolved? How will EU member countries react to the twin challenges of Brexit and Mr. Trump's election victory in the US? Given the fact that a majority of elderly voters in the UK are against British EU membership—according to exit polls after the referendum—and taking into account the graying of the EU's other societies, will it suffice to mobilize more young people in EU countries to express public support for the European integration project? What are the key benefits of a "neo-EU" that would be more in line with the challenges of the twenty-first century and that could expect a broad majority in all countries of the EU? What could help to maintain EU integration as a role model for other regional integration schemes—and what implications does the new phenomenon of disintegration (assuming Brexit will be implemented in 2019) have for Europe, the US, and the world economy? The analytical challenge of a broader UK–EU27–US perspective on certain issues is not easy, but in the twenty-first century, no international analysis of economic dynamics is complete without considering the role of China in the politico-economic adjustment process. As regards the latter, only a few thoughts can be developed here, but in some fields, even a trilateral view of US, Europe, and Asia is important.

The June 2016 British referendum was a historical event, despite actually being the second EU referendum to be held in the United Kingdom, the first, in 1975, resulted in a clear pro-EU majority. For many observers, the result was rather unexpected, and it brought about a rapid change in the government of the UK, with Theresa May becoming the new Prime Minister. This was followed just a few months later by the also rather surprising success of Donald Trump in the US presidential election. One of the first actions of the newly-elected President Trump was to declare that the US would withdraw from the Trans-Pacific Partnership (TPP), a Pacific-area free trade agreement concluded by 12 countries—including Japan, Australia, Vietnam, Mexico, and Canada—Trump had already threatened that he would also withdraw from the North American Free Trade Agreement (NAFTA) and was eager to engage in only bilateral trade negotiations in the future. With the UK leaving the European Union, and the US moving away from TPP and NAFTA, the two leading historical, liberal, Western economies, which were world powers in the nineteenth and twentieth centuries, have now become leaders of disintegration. Strangely enough, the Australian Prime Minister has suggested that the US should remain a part of the TPP project—or the 11 partner countries might consider asking China to come on board. With the election of Trump and the Brexit referendum, the Western world and indeed the wider global community have changed enormously. Interestingly, the protectionist Mr. Trump received Mrs. May as the first international visitor after his inauguration. Prime Minister May is the leader of British global trade liberalization—she presented her country as the Global Britain in her Brexit speech of January 17, 2017—suggesting the referendum had given her a pro-globalization mission.

The question of the legitimacy of the 2016 referendum is one issue, the other big question is to what extent Parliament will be involved. The Supreme Court in London has decided that authorization to trigger Article 50 of the Treaty of the European Union—and thus to declare the UK's intention to leave the EU—will need majority support in Parliament; Mrs. May initially wanted to write her exit letter without prior consent from Parliament. The Supreme Court's decision does not strengthen Mrs. May's position, and her decision to visit the White House in January 2017 might also raise some doubts: does the country of David Ricardo and Adam Smith, the pioneering free trade economists, really want to take sides with the neo-protectionist Donald Trump whose international economic policy agenda is so strange?

As the new Prime Minister, Theresa May emphasized in her speech in January 2017 that her government aims at a 'hard' Brexit, which means leaving not only the EU and the single market, but also saying no to a customs union that would require the UK and the EU27 to impose joint import tariffs. Instead, future economic relations between the EU and the United Kingdom should be framed within a bilateral free trade treaty; and not much time is left for achieving a political deal between London and Brussels. The pro-Brexit majority in the referendum came as rather a surprise to many observers, but as is shown in this study, this majority was in fact contrived, since the Cameron government in its 16-page information brochure, which was sent to all households, did not mention the Treasury's finding that leaving the European Union would bring a real income loss of 10%. Had British voters been aware of this important fact, the result—according to standard UK popularity functions—would actually have been a 52% majority in favor of Remain. Thus, one may conclude that there is no legitimacy behind Brexit unless one considers the government's suppressing of crucial information for voters a natural element of politics. It can be argued that a disorderly referendum should not be the basis for a historical political change.

Strangely, the Treasury study was presented to the public just a week after the government had sent out the info brochure to households in England. As the Brexit majority is artificial, one may argue that many of the conclusions drawn from the referendum are to some extent rather far-fetched. One could also ask why a Parliament that knows about the very dubious circumstances surrounding the referendum would follow the spurious result of said referendum.

The world owes British philosophy and scientific development a debt of gratitude for the modern approach of science which is based on observation, modeling, and empirical studies. All this dates back to the sixteenth century and Sir Francis Bacon who was an influential English philosopher, statesman, jurist, scientist, and author—he also served as Attorney General and Lord Chancellor of England. In his judicial approach to reality, Bacon called on scientists and indeed others to not only come up with new ideas and conjectures, but to always show supporting evidence for conjectures made; self-deception was to be avoided, carefully observing the facts and reality, respectively, should help in gathering the critical evidence required. Scientists and politicians who mislead themselves or others would not be held in high esteem by Francis Bacon, nor do they respect the old school of empirical methodology developed in the United Kingdom. Against this background of modern progress from 1700 to 2000, the run-up to the British referendum of 2016 looks particularly strange.

Some observers of the referendum have argued that immigration was a key issue for voters and a determinant of their behavior, but this is indeed only partly true as expert analysis suggests. Did EU immigration really represent a critical burden on the UK for many years prior to the referendum? Perceived developments and newspaper reports in the tabloid press is one thing, statistical facts and the careful analysis of experts is quite another. The Organisation for Economic Co-operation and Development (OECD), a professional international organization, has shown that the EU immigrants' participation rate in the UK labor market has exceeded the British average and that immigration has actually created a surplus for the government budget; a Bank of England Staff Paper based on careful empirical research finds that immigration has put significant downward wage pressure on one category only in the labor market—unskilled workers in the services sector. The annual UK population growth rate from EU immigration amounted to only 0.2%, and all this amounted to an excessive burden for the world's fifth largest economy?

For decades, the EU has combined the liberalization of markets with a growing global trade and investment flow orientation, plus social policy. What the adequate balance of these elements should be has been viewed in very different ways in various EU countries. The UK supported the development of the EU single market—an institutional innovation which was successful enough to encourage the ten Association of Southeast Asian Nations (ASEAN) countries to start their own single market in 2015/16. The liberalization approach of the Western world, which has inspired so many regions in the global economy to follow steps toward the opening-up of markets and increased competition, is now facing a double stress test since both Brexit and the election of Donald Trump in the US stand for new approaches that contradict the traditional models of Western success. By leaving the EU, the UK will have less liberal trade and capital flows than before, while in the US, President Trump made trade protectionism and barriers to foreign direct investment (FDI) outflows a hallmark of his election campaign. As Mrs. May, arguing in favor of a Global Britain, has declared her strong interest in cooperating with Mr. Trump's protectionist government, there will be a new transatlantic political odd couple.

While Mrs. May's speeches often seem to follow the spirit of Adam Smith, who published his famous book on Economics in 1776, the year of US independence, Mr. Trump's speeches echo a very different approach that sometimes sounds like Mercantilism, the politico-economic ideology of the early eighteenth century that brought international conflicts through the obsession of many countries to all achieve a current account surplus which, of course, is logically impossible.

The EU needs to reform regardless of the result of a British referendum (including of a potential second referendum in 2018). While some EU approaches were useful, other policy elements were doubtful, e.g., overregulation in many fields—but not in financial markets and banking, respectively. This book makes various suggestions for EU reforms, and it also presents some fresh thoughts on how the historically decisive Transatlantic Banking Crisis could be overcome in a sustained manner—a topic that is of key interest to both European and North American readers. This analysis discusses whether or not Brexit is the starting point of a protracted politico-economic crisis in Europe and whether or not major changes in transatlantic relations should be expected from Brexit dynamics. The study shows that Brexit does not mean simply moving back to a situation akin to pre-1973 and undoing part of the free trade networks in Europe.

As a European economist with good links to both leading British and US universities and to many international organizations, I have tried to put key pieces of information on Brexit together—and I certainly agree that in the end, it is for the British voters to decide for or against EU membership. At the same time, I should like to argue that it is only fair to present critical reflections on a debate which is historical but often not careful enough to take into account the key facts. Political systems and government in Western democracies have always had a tendency to respond to certain political movements and to not only rely on hard facts, statistics, or expert views. Rarely, however, have OECD countries' governments had much success when reality is largely ignored. Here, the EU28 has a broad responsibility not only for European economic and political dynamics but for global developments as well. It is hoped that this book will contribute some enlightenment to a confusing Brexit debate in Europe and beyond and it is clear that the EU28 has broad responsibility not only for European economic and political dynamics but for global developments as well.

Many observers of Great Britain would surely agree with the estimation that the country, which is known for being rich in tradition, the source of many important inventions, historic achievements, an advanced political system, and a high level of economic dynamism worldwide, is perceived as a leading light in Western Europe and as a shining example of democracy. However, this makes the massive policy failures in the run-up to the referendum on EU membership on June 23, all the more incredible. One may anticipate that Brexit will take place in early 2019—indeed it would have to take place before spring 2019 since elections to the European Parliament will take place at that time. Whether or not Scotland will then seek to hold a new independence referendum and break away from the UK is an open question. However, one cannot rule out that there will be a second referendum on British EU membership—and the result might be in favor of Remain. This, in turn, would bring new adjustment costs to the United Kingdom. The announcement of the President of the EU Commission, Jean-Claude Juncker, not to stand for a potential future re-election, as he is afraid that the Brexit negotiation will lead to further EU disintegration, is a signal that there are considerable tensions among the EU27 which could yet break apart. This statement, of February 2017, is an indication of a lack of EU leadership. The view expressed by Mr. Juncker, in an interview with a German radio station, that "the other EU 27 don't know it yet, but the Brits know very well how they can tackle this…They could promise country A this, country B that and country C something else and the end game is that there is not a united European front") stands in stark contrast to the expectations of Prime Minister May as expressed in her Brexit Speech on January 17, 2017, in Lancaster House, when she said "I know that this—and the other reasons Britain took such a decision—is not always well understood among our friends and allies in Europe. And I know many fear that this might herald the beginning of a greater unraveling of the EU. But let me be clear: I do not want that to happen. It would not be in the best interests of Britain. It remains overwhelmingly and compellingly in Britain's national interest that the EU should succeed".

My first research activities with British colleagues—from Hertford College/Oxford University—began in the 1990s and were focused on the energy and telecommunications sectors, fields which were deregulated in the United Kingdom early and sensibly, faster than was the case in other EU countries. Further, EU-related research projects followed (which included colleagues from the University of Birmingham and, later, the University College London), and British economists and indeed foreign economists at British universities, respectively, certainly enjoy a high level of respect across the globe. It would be most regrettable if this kind of cooperation with colleagues from these universities should, in the longer term, be made more difficult due to Brexit.

With regard to the preparation of the manuscript for this publication, I would particularly like to thank my research team for their technical assistance: Ms. Evgeniya Yushkova, Mr. Arthur Korus, Mr. Samir Kadiric, Mr. Fabian Baier, Mr. Tristan Feidieker, and, with special

gratitude, Ms. Christina Wiens at the EIIW. Without the excellent edi-
torial support of Mr. David Hanrahan, this English version of the book
would not have been published so quickly. I am thankful for discussions
with Cillian Ryan, Nottingham Trent University, and grateful to Andrew
Mullineux from the University of Birmingham for his critical comments.
For an exchange of ideas on Brexit, I also wish to thank Jackson Janes,
the Director of the American Institute for Contemporary German Studies
(AICGS)/Johns Hopkins University, who published my short, and with
the benefit of hindsight essentially accurate, Brexit analysis on the website
of the AICGS (Advisor Section) prior to the referendum on March 30,
2016. The author bears sole responsibility for this book and its contents.
Finally, on the occasion of my June 27 TTIP-related presentation before
the Congressional Research Service, Washington DC, many questions
were forthcoming which influenced the selection of topics for the present
study. What does Brexit mean for the United Kingdom, for Germany, for
France, other countries in the EU, and indeed the entire world economy?
How dramatic could the fall-out of the negative disintegration dynamics
be for the Eurozone? What national and EU-level reform measures are
urgently needed—this study (a shorter version of my German-language
book *Brexit aus Versehen*, November 2016; with some updates that
include, of course, US–UK and US–EU perspectives after the Trump election) provides new and important answers. The focus is, of course, limited
to some key issues and topics, but one may emphasize that this study is an
attempt to close an important analytical gap in the literature and in the
public debate in the UK, the EU, and the USA—as well as elsewhere.

Wuppertal and London   Paul J.J. Welfens
March 2017
President of the European Institute for International
Economic Relations (EIIW) at the University of Wuppertal
And
IZA Research Fellow, Bonn and Non-resident Senior
Research Scholar at AICGS/Johns Hopkins University, Washington DC
And
Alfred Grosser Professorship 2007/2008
Sciences Po, Paris

Contents

List of Figures

List of Tables

1

Introduction

The decision taken in the British referendum on June 23, 2016, to leave the European Union (EU) is the biggest shock to European integration since the founding of the Communities on January 1, 1958: with the negative outcome of the referendum in the United Kingdom (UK), the EU has entered its first phase of disintegration and to some extent the first serious integration crisis. The decision for the UK to leave the EU can be described as an 'accidental Brexit,' an unplanned exit brought about as a result of policy failures and a chaotic referendum, for which Prime Minister Cameron bears responsibility, as will be shown herein. With a hugely inconsistent and, with regard to the main effects of leaving the EU, lacking information policy vis-à-vis the electorate and the unprofessional preparations for the EU referendum on June 23 in the various constituent parts of the UK, Cameron grossly contradicted his own speech at his party conference in Birmingham (2010): "A sense that politics shouldn't be so different from the rest of life, where rational people do somehow find a way of overcoming their disagreements." The extremely poor, inadequate information policy of Cameron in relation to the Brexit referendum made the political referendum into something

© The Author(s) 2017   1
P.J.J. Welfens, *An Accidental Brexit*,
DOI 10.1007/978-3-319-58271-9_1

which diverges from the rest of life, where rational people can overcome their differences in a sound and reasonable manner.

It shall be made clear how the planned UK exit from the EU amounts to an accidental Brexit, which may sound strange; however, the indications and facts which will be presented herein are clear. The British government sent a 16-page information booklet (HM Government 2016a) to households in the UK which did not contain a single important number from the report of Her Majesty's Treasury (HM Government 2016b) on the long-term benefits of EU membership and the costs of Brexit, respectively: a threatened 3–10% loss of income as a result of Brexit is one figure which every head of government with a sense of responsibility would, in the event of a historic EU referendum, have shared with the population of their country. The 16-page government info booklet was sent to households in England shortly before the date when the report was presented to Parliament on April 18; in the other constituent nations of the UK, the government-sponsored information was first sent to households in the week from May 9, however still not one single figure from the 201-page official analysis which featured hugely important economic findings. While one may have no doubt that well-educated, high-income Britons got the message of the Treasury Report in indirect ways (i.e., through the traditional media or the internet), most workers and very many pensioners—both groups which were largely in favor of Brexit—most likely had no adequate information on this. It is stunning to read the government's 16-page referendum information brochure and not find one simple sentence: "The Treasury Report on the long-run benefits of European Union membership indicates that the UK's leaving of the EU will mean that the average British voter will lose the equivalent of about one month's income." Not making the Treasury Report's key findings broadly available to all voters in the UK was unfair—and indeed totally inadequate from the side of the Cameron government. If 750,000 of those who voted for Brexit had switched to remain having received this information, the UK would still be in the EU. At the bottom line, the timing of the Treasury study's publication one week after the sending out of the government's referendum information brochure is very strange and needs to be explained.

The whole situation seems so curious, that Miss Marple herself would not be surprised if she were to discover that anti-EU elements within the British government were responsible for the misinformation with regard to the referendum. That Cameron's team did not recognize the mistakes and inadequacies relating to information is unjustifiable: an unprecedented political failure in the UK in just the second national referendum in the history of the country.

In the absence of a formal written constitution, the duties and responsibilities of a British government with regard to information are unclear, but 2,000 years of development in terms of European rationality suggest that the electorate should not be asked to prematurely cast a ballot in a referendum if the most important figures are not, at the very least, officially available to government or, better still, made available to the public by government. To the best of this author's knowledge, nobody has thus far commented critically on this de facto violation of the rules in the field of best practice/good practice when it comes to organizing a referendum, neither in the UK nor the EU27 or the US. In 2014, as the integrity of the UK was at stake and the government was attempting to prevent the exit of Scotland, that is prior to the Scottish Independence Referendum taking place, Prime Minister Cameron provided the public and households, respectively, with the crucial economic information in a timely manner; in 2016, however, this was not the case. Instead of the relevant information being provided to voters almost four months before the actual vote, only two months were allowed, instead of distributing a government brochure with information regarding the expected loss in income as calculated by HM Treasury, 16 pages of text and photos were sent out without a single figure from the Treasury's analysis.

In the short term, the UK may, following the referendum on EU membership, first be troubled by recessionary forces; however, the UK, by announcing an exit from EU, appears as a disruptive factor in Europe and at the same time has new room for maneuver. The May government will determine to utilize new free trade agreements, as there is a threatened high drop in income which needs to be compensated for somehow: in the long term, this drop equates to the average Briton losing circa 8% of income due to Brexit, and in terms of 2016 this would be like foregoing on one's December wage. This extremely important piece of information was, however, not known to most British voters in advance of the actual vote on June 23, 2016. In light of this, how should the result of the referendum really be viewed? Where is the British and European debate on this issue?

The economic logic of Brexit suggests a plus for London in terms of globalization as a driver of growth and, in particular, that the UK should strive for a free trade agreement with the United States. Meanwhile, Germany and France are halfway to scuttling the Transatlantic Trade and Investment Partnership (TTIP)—the planned transatlantic free trade project between the EU and the US that alone threatens in the medium term to encourage other EU member states to move towards the exit. They could follow London's lead, with a view to their own national interest vis-à-vis free trade with the US, and realize a "growth dividend." Even in the case of a skeptical US approach to free trade under the Trump administration, there should be a large willingness in Washington to conclude a liberalization agreement with European countries.

EU disintegration, that is the shrinkage of the EU, is a threat in various ways: the conflict about who should in future bear the burden of the UK's net contribution of circa £7.6 billion Pounds Sterling (or circa $9.4 billion US Dollars)[1] alone could lead to the next EU exit referendum in one of the main contributing member states. With its economic power reduced by almost one-fifth and with anti-EU parties emerging or expanding in an ever growing number of countries, the EU has no chance of survival in the longer term, if it cannot adapt institutionally and with regard to its primary objectives, that is to reinvent itself as a sustainable, future-oriented, and attractive Neo-EU. If it cannot, Europe will revert to an instable state, reminiscent of the late nineteenth century, with one major difference—along with the US as economic powerhouse, in the twenty-first century Europe will face global pressure, including from a dominant China.

The fact that a majority of British voters voted for Brexit, that is for the UK to leave the EU, despite expert warnings regarding a long-term reduction in income of 3–10%, demands closer attention—the rationality of western, or at the very least of British, politics has been called into question by the referendum. There are clear indications that Brexit is the result of a political miscalculation by Prime Minister Cameron, and that Mr. Cameron himself had, paradoxically, contributed to the majority in favor of Brexit, as can be shown. The European Commission, in turn, let itself be blinded by a Eurobarometer survey from May 2016, which showed only 36% of Britons with a negative attitude towards the EU—at a supranational level, results which were based upon methodologically sound surveys were lacking and therefore Brussels was without a fundamental requirement for successful governance.

Brexit has triggered adjustment pressures in the UK and the EU27, but also in Hong Kong and in other Asian countries. Furthermore, there is widespread astonishment in the US, many Asian nations, and even further afield that the electorate in the UK voted for an exit from the EU in a referendum which, however, is non-binding on either Parliament or government. The question was not a Yes/No on accession to the EU, as was twice the case in Norway's (with a negative result both times) referenda. This time, the question was Yes/No on withdrawal from the EU after circa 43 years.

It is obvious that the West, following its victory in the Cold War and in the competition of the economic systems since 1991, the year of the collapse of the Soviet Union, has gone through a variety of crises, which range from the Banking Crisis, via the Euro Crisis and the Refugee Crisis, to Brexit. In Beijing and Moscow, the diagnosis with respect to the EU is as follows: we have always regarded EU integration as a less than promising concept, much more important is national politics; in this way, however, national politics and nationalism will be stronger than before and may again become the dominant approach in the world.

The EU of today must come to terms with a potentially existential crisis; however, this trend could affect other integration clubs of the global and economic system tomorrow. On the one hand, there is no big doubt that Great Britain (here taken to be synonymous with the UK for the sake of simplicity) can be reinvigorated economically through a withdrawal from the EU as the market economy system offers efficient adjustment mechanisms; the political system must, like the citizenry, come to grips with the negative welfare effects. On the other hand, the

EU27 is certainly capable of managing regional integration without the UK. However, the British exit after more than 40 years of membership will weigh heavily, economically speaking, it is a political and economic shock for continental Europe, and furthermore raises the question of how the negative economic effects of the UK and the EU27 will interact: from an economic point of view, the negative effects of both will be mutually amplifying which is not indicative of smart cooperation. Whereas at the 'Group of Twenty'—i.e., G20—Summit in Brisbane in 2014, promises were made regarding the raising of real income by 2% by the year 2018, it can be expected that Brexit, with effects for both the UK and for the EU27, will cause more than a 2% long-term reduction in income in the EU28. It will not only be the G20 who will be critical of the UK, Germany, France, and Italy.

Moreover, Brexit is a historical turning point, which can lead to a spiral of EU disintegration in certain circumstances—which could return Europe to the late nineteenth century. The then rivalries of the great European powers resulted in an international arms race and led to the First World War. A relatively complicated arrangement based upon a balance of power operating between independent nation states, as once conceived by Otto von Bismarck, did not function as a system of peace for very long. Only the EU, following yet another world war, could deliver such a system, in conjunction with supranational institutions and an EU philosophy of cooperation. With Brexit happening, the twenty-first century seems to be unexpectedly threatening for Europe.

Conflict over the future EU budget will soon follow Brexit. Who should take on the responsibility for the British net contributions from 2020 and what budget cuts are appropriate? Only after the UK's exit from the EU will the country see a dampening of the growth of real income and there will also be a negative impact on the EU27. In contrast, the short-term effects in terms of production will be relatively minor, although short-time work in some firms can be expected. The reactions of the financial markets are already, in the short term, quite significant. Here, the changing expectations following the result of the referendum play a role. Furthermore, economic volatility indicators on the financial markets have risen since Brexit and there are negative Brexit-related effects as far away as Asia (Asia Times 2016).

Long-term instability and new conflicts threaten the European continent, and it is totally unclear what the European Commission together with the EU member states and the European Parliament want to do to counteract this development. At the highest political levels, one does not hear much from Brussels about an EU crisis in the public sphere, the internal discussion, however, is a very different one; more than a few EU civil servants have a skeptical view of the functioning of the European Commission and the European Council, which represents the relevant "governments" of the member states. Informally, Brexit is indeed a pressing issue and is officially an important topic for working groups of the European Commission. The European Central Bank has also established a special working group on Brexit.

The EU, as was strikingly shown by the 2014 British report on EU competencies, is tremendously complex. While the citizens can only barely recognize the institutions, the functioning of the institutions is broadly incomprehensible. Since 2010, everyone can see that the once powerful EU Commission has little influence beyond its many actions and directives with which the actors in the economy are all too often overly regulated. One can hardly argue that the EU brings clear and comprehensible benefits for its citizens, with certain exceptions, for example the ever cheaper cross-border mobile telephony. In the field of telecommunications, the European Commission made significant liberalization efforts with the market deregulation in 1998. During the first decade, many had thought that the Eurozone was functioning well; however, since the Euro Crisis fewer and fewer share this view. The acid test for any institutional innovation is, of course, not the honeymoon phase, but the stormy periods which follow, the latest of which began in the United States with the collapse of the Lehman Brothers bank on September 15, 2008; however, no matter where the troubled times have their origins, a monetary union must be able to function and ride out the storm. That was not the case between 2010 and 2015, and the confusing chorus of critics from the field of economics did not improve matters for either the public at large, or for the politicians. As unexpected as the Euro Crisis was for many, the result of the UK referendum on EU membership came as a complete surprise to most people in Europe and indeed worldwide: the financial markets were also wrong and the British betting firms to boot. Do we still understand the international system and Europe, respectively? What went wrong?

Brexit was a possibility since 2013, when Prime Minister Cameron promised a referendum on the EU membership of the UK. Many studies were carried out in 2015 and during the first half of 2016 which focused on Brexit. If one has experience in EU integration analysis and is familiar with international economic topics, one can draw many conclusions from the Brexit decision based on the aforementioned studies, explain the market reactions, and highlight the most important reform options with regard to Brussels and selected EU member states. This is what the present book aims to do. At the same time, as the British withdrawal from the EU did not come as a complete surprise to this author—see my Brexit contribution for the AICGS/Johns Hopkins University from the end of March 2016 (Welfens 2016a)—and because prior to the referendum there were already numerous studies on relevant issues in the context of Brexit, the main aspects of the debate are not difficult to emphasize. To the aforementioned studies belong contributions from the European Institute for International Economic Relations (EIIW), of which the focus of analysis for over two decades has been the process of European integration and indeed integration dynamics worldwide. On a side note, this author also correctly outlined the most relevant and important points regarding the Euro Crisis about 18 months before the crisis actually erupted in the spring of 2010 in his book *Transatlantische Bankenkrise*—translated as The Transatlantic Banking Crisis—(p. 158ff.), the manuscript for which was dated October 2008 (Welfens 2009).

With regard to Brexit, scenario analyses are naturally also required. The present analysis can, on a theoretical and empirical basis, highlight many new and important connections and explain a particular sequence of adjustment problems for both the UK and Europe: culminating in a series of depreciations of the Pound in the short and medium term. It cannot be overlooked that Brexit is a massive historical speculative failure by Cameron and is indicative of a limited rationality on the side of the British political system—which has usually been the subject of much praise. The policies of Cameron vis-à-vis the referendum were filled with contradictions, to put it mildly, and in the immigration debate, which one could describe as completely dishonest, Theresa May stood by his side as a Home Secretary.

If, however, there are economists and commentators who seek to portray the economically absurd Brexit as something very positive—for example that the British exit is a step towards more freedom—this is evidence of a lack of knowledge about the British reality as well as the continued dissemination of naivety and ignorance, which previously led the western world into a massive banking crisis.

One can certainly question the role of President of the Commission Juncker. He would definitely have followed with interest the pro-EU membership speech of US President Obama in London—although he himself did not travel to London. The European Commission showed a peculiar and irresponsible carelessness in the run-up to Brexit and Berlin and Paris were no less surprised by the referendum, with the result that Brexit was commented on in a very unanimated fashion, which automatically diverted attention from the necessary EU reforms. Should and can European politics be so unmoved by the loss of a major member country, which accounts for almost one-fifth of the EU economy? It is evident that Brexit has reinforced anti-EU forces in every country in Europe. That need not be a permanent development.

The present study also formulates possible problem-solving approaches for Germany and the EU28/27, in order to emerge from the Brexit predicament relatively unscathed. It is crucial for all groups in society to understand the historical turning point which is Brexit; to appreciate its enormous potential for destabilization—and, naturally, to be able to react appropriately in order to prevent the destabilization of the Europe and to push for sound reforms. Brexit is revealing and strange, as it shows to observers across the globe how clueless 'old Europe' is and how even the prospect of high economic losses did not hinder political adventurism; not in 2016 in the UK, and possibly also not in the case of Brexit Mark II in another country in the near future.

In 2013, the British Conservative Prime Minister David Cameron, in order to fend off critics within his own party and competition from the right-populist United Kingdom Independence Party (UKIP), announced that he would hold an EU referendum. The question which was the subject of the referendum was should the UK leave the EU, that is "Brexit", or whether the UK should remain in the EU. Following a short campaign in spring 2016, and in light of the compromise reached in Brussels by Cameron regarding the limiting of social protection for immigrants, the Prime Minister recommended a vote against Brexit to the public. This recommendation was also given by over 1,000 top managers from large firms and banks in the UK, dozens of economists, bishops as well as prominent figures from the field of culture. The majority of voters, however, did not follow Prime Minister Cameron's call on June 23—despite support for Cameron's position of staying in the EU coming from the Liberal Democrats and the social democratic Labour Party. The gulf between the UK's electorate and the elites was simply too wide since the Banking Crisis. If a referendum had been held on the question of the 'abolition of zebra crossings'—with a recommendation for the Cameron government for zebra crossings to be retained for safety reasons—then it is possible that a majority would still have voted for their abolition.

To not have appreciated the extent of this sentiment in his own country, and also having made EU immigration into an anti-EU argument through his own policies and a lie regarding the burden of immigration—an objectionable policy element for a head of government, as former German Chancellor Helmut Schmidt stressed to me in a conversation in Paris a number of years ago—represents a double failure on the part of David Cameron. The British regent, King George III, who once carelessly and needlessly lost the North American colonies—the present day United States, which has since often dominated the UK—was just as short-sighted and injudicious as Prime Minister Cameron.

Over 60% of Germans regret, according to opinion polls (*Politikbarometer*), the planned British withdrawal from the EU. This can, in part, be deemed an operational accident of the Cameron government; however, the Brexit decision also reflects the circumstances that the EU had over time become relatively less important to the UK as a trading partner and that the EU is not sufficiently in concordance with the twenty-first century: this century is, to put it frankly, Asian, digital, and innovative. The EU, with the exception of efforts regarding digital modernization from the European Commission, does not embody these key points in its agenda. In terms of free trade negotiations with Asian countries, apart from Singapore and Vietnam (although that agreement has yet to be ratified), the EU has little to offer, in contrast to the US which has a signed agreement with Pacific Rim countries—mostly Asian—since 2015: the Trans-Pacific Partnership (TPP), which, however, now needs to be reevaluated considering the Trump administration. The EU countries took the opportunity of the TPP initiative a number of years ago to complain that the US was neglecting the EU, after which the US offered to begin negotiations on TTIP. Currently, however, TTIP is hardly supported by Germany and France, and since Brexit even less so than before, which further weakens the EU and raises questions about international policy dynamics in the coming years. The EU is not an institutionally sound and convincing answer to the opportunities and challenges of the twenty-first century. Despite the digital agenda, the EU is obviously much too slow-moving. That the EU brings considerable economic and political advantages is clear. However, this is a little-known fact.

The EU was a good response to the then serious economic and political challenges faced by the founding members in 1957—a revival of trade and growth in western Europe, the embedding of the Federal Republic of Germany in a network of countries; however, the old EU is not capable of acting decisively, and despite the single market its attraction is only limited: with an antiquated mixture of intergovernmental agreements by the member states and federal political elements, namely the European Commission, the EU Court of Justice and a European quasi-Parliament which has no tax-raising powers and a peculiar permanent grand coalition; it is not particularly innovation-friendly and is democratically weak. The Parliament is far removed from the principle of elections, that of one man, one vote—for example in the case that the population of Germany rises by one million, and that of Greece drops by one million, the former should gain one seat in the European Parliament while the latter lose one seat. Here, it is a matter of democracy, power, and rationality.

Brexit creates adjustment difficulties for the UK, but almost just as many for the Eurozone and the EU27 countries, which are also losers due to Brexit and which after the UK's exit will carry almost 20%

less weight economically in terms of international negotiations. The interest rate differentials in the Eurozone will grow further, and Greece and Portugal will again experience higher adjustment pressures; the Eurozone, which was created too early and without a political union, will encounter new problems. In one area, Brexit could help the Eurozone, namely that interest rates in Europe will, because of the new British low-interest rate policy, remain unusually low for the years to come: that will help both the state and corporate sectors, which are the principal debtors in every country. It will also bring redistribution effects for many homebuyers and property investors, who can refinance the loans on their properties which were taken out some years ago at historically low interest rates. Germany will benefit further due to the safe haven effect, that is the risk aversion which will encourage investors from across the globe to invest in Germany—but also in France (and the US, Switzerland, and even in the UK). This benefit will be offset by the fact that the negative side effects of ultra-low interest rates will partly weaken the national economies of the West, through ever less profitable banks.

One can only find Prime Minister Cameron's complaint about too much immigration strange taking the International Monetary Fund's (IMF) Discussion Note 16/07 on Eastern European migration into account. The UK was not even among the top five Organisation for Economic Co-operation and Development (OECD) destination countries in terms of Eastern European emigrants and also, economically speaking, the country was only average in terms of migration. That the financial markets in the UK and worldwide seemed sure that there would be no Brexit also contributed to the result. The appreciation of the Pound Sterling before the referendum signaled to undecided voters that one did not need to reflect too much on the costs of Brexit; if, on the other hand, the financial markets had assumed a Brexit and therefore had brought about a massive depreciation of the Pound and a collapse in share prices before June 23, the Brexit vote would, paradoxically, not have happened. In fact, the financial markets, with their false assessment of the Brexit vote, also contributed to EU disintegration. Prior to June 23, almost nobody was interested in the report of the economic costs of Brexit from the Cameron government which came far too late in April 2016. Moreover, with regard to the UK and the world economy, the IMF has written in the conclusion of their June 19, 2016, update of the World Economic Outlook that "The outcome of the UK vote, which surprised global financial markets, implies the materialization of an important downside risk for the world economy."

It is important for Germany and Europe, and indeed the world economy, to understand the effects of Brexit and view them in the right context. The present study aims to contribute to this endeavor on the basis of theoretical and empirical findings, as well as new simulations which highlight the short-, medium-, and long-term effects of the vote on June 23, 2016. The short-term effects will impact foreign exchange rates as well as share prices, interest rate responses, and the agenda setting of the economic policies of the UK and the EU. The medium-term impacts relate to income and job-market effects. In the longer term, the issue is a global shift in the balance of forces between Europe, the US, and China and/or Asia, along with effects on international organizations and the world economy, which has been destabilized since the Banking Crisis. By exploring the arguments from the various sides in relation to Brexit, one can arrive at a differentiated viewpoint. This standpoint is, however, only partially useful for an analysis of the future: from there, the new key actors in the government in London, based on their earlier positions—i.e., before the referendum—can be better classified in terms of political strategy, or where it is about the learning process.

Some anti-EU arguments of various British politicians, including from Prime Minister John Major's former Europe Minister David Davis, were worthy of consideration. Mr. Davis should now, as part of Theresa May's cabinet, negotiate the UK's withdrawal from the EU, so it is all the more important to analyze his Brexit position and to draw attention to the contradictions which will lead the British government into difficulty sooner or later. An analysis of the speeches and texts from Mr. Davis in the months prior to the Brexit referendum shows comprehensive reflections on Brexit and, in part, also plausible arguments for a UK exit from the EU. Did Mr. Davis have an understanding of the fact that Brexit could set in motion a disastrous process of EU disintegration, the negative dynamics of which, in Europe and globally, will in the end greatly impact the economic and political development on the UK itself? David Davis and Prime Minister May, and indeed other leading British politicians, will be aware that from the point of view of voting behavior, the Brexit referendum was not only about the issue of EU membership. The interests, which played a role in the decision of the electorate, can also be validly classified according to New Political Economy just as the information policies of various actors. That the UK should decide on leaving the EU in the same year as the ten nations in the Association of Southeast Asian Nations (ASEAN) were in the first year of a single market—based upon the example of the EU—is also noteworthy.

When it came to the Brexit referendum, the majority of British voters voted against the parliamentary majority, ended British cooperation in the EU project of integrating the peoples of Europe, and apparently proclaimed a new era of self-determined British sovereignty: the end effect is clearly much greater than a simple No to the EU, and it represents a British (primarily English) rejection of broad international policy cooperation and in part also a vote against the globalization of the economy. This is particularly true of older voters, who appeared to indulge in nostalgic dreams about a return to former British greatness—outside the EU and with a strengthened relationship with the Commonwealth—while the voting pattern of younger voters in the UK clearly showed a pro-EU integration sentiment within that group.

Meanwhile, David Davis was clearly intending, after Brexit, to actually lead the UK towards more globalization and not less. This results in new contradictions in British politics. Furthermore, one can point out that Jeremy Corbyn, as leader of the Labour Party, had only half-heartedly campaigned against Brexit, as even the EU with its single market seemed to him to be too influenced by economic liberalization—what a delusionary approach: the new government in London will, free of EU limitations, certainly seek to engage in globalization with a renewed speed. This is sure to happen as the government will want to avoid the years of sluggish growth which clearly threaten the UK following Brexit.

On the other side of the English Channel, almost immediately following the referendum decision, Germany and France attempted to emit political signals relating to less globalization, at the very least hinting at an end to the EU–US negotiations in the area of TTIP, despite the fact that that would be a large political and economic mistake, as TTIP would bring the EU27 about 2% in real income growth. That would mean, taken together with the direct negative effects of Brexit of a circa 1% loss in real income, a total loss in income of approximately 3% which the withdrawal of the UK could entail, directly and indirectly: circa £76 billion ($93 billion) for Germany, that is about £3,400 per four-person household ($4,150). Brexit will cost the entire EU27 about £255 billion/$311 billion (and that has negative repercussions for the UK, which would reduce real income even more). Nevertheless, the President of the European Commission could not bring himself to hold a pro-EU speech in London. If one takes a long-term income loss of 9% as a result of Brexit, then that would mean a loss of about £212 billion for the UK ($259 billion)—also assuming that the UK will have concluded a free trade agreement with the US. In London, there will not be the hesitancy and egocentrism which were visible in Berlin and Paris, where there was relatively little support for TTIP even before the June 23 referendum. The EU27, and Brussels, Berlin, and Paris, respectively, could soon find themselves in an extremely odd position. Should the UK have a transatlantic free trade agreement by 2020, and not the EU, one will know who has failed.

Cameron's approach to uniting the Conservative Party using the strategy of a referendum on EU membership and hoping for a broad British acceptance of EU integration has, with the Brexit decision, completely failed. The second largest economy in the EU will—following a badly organized referendum—with, in part, strange and counterfactual claims from prominent Brexit supporters—leave the EU after almost 45 years of membership. This will considerably damage the UK economically, but also the EU and the entire western world: 1–2% of global output is foreseeable as a cost of Brexit. That Boris Johnson could for many weeks with his Brexit campaign bus misleadingly portray British gross contributions to the EU budget, without the EU Commission ever commenting on this, is peculiar; the Commission did not even conceive a digital and real information campaign for the 1.6 million Britons living in other EU member countries. One cannot defend EU integration in this manner, with this approach disintegration will spread in the EU, and six decades of work on integration and the EU itself will come to nothing.

The EU and the Eurozone, respectively, have obvious weaknesses which contributed to the mood surrounding Brexit. With a rational and vertical political organization of the EU, the head of the Eurosceptic party UKIP, Nigel Farage, would never have been able, with his political attacks on the Conservatives, to force Prime Minister Cameron into holding a referendum on the EU. This aspect has not been discussed; however, this contradiction will be revealed herein. A new perspective on the Brexit debate, which will be shown here, is that the anti-immigration component of the Brexit campaign was in fact stirred up by Cameron's government: huge budget cuts to central government transfers to local authorities—as a result of the large government deficits which followed the Banking Crisis—created the image of a crisis in terms of public services in cities and towns across the UK: a shortage in the supply of local services and long waiting times in the National Health Service became obvious; however, the cause for these, in many towns, was perfidiously laid at the door of immigrants from the EU in the political debate. Prime Minister Cameron and (then) Minister May simply looked on without uttering one word to explain the reality of the situation.

The low level of rationality of the government was also made clear as Cameron promised to limit immigration to 100,000, when he knew that in the EU single market, with its four freedoms, there was no possibility of controlling EU migration in this way without much opposition: over two decades had passed since the beginning of the single market on the January 1, 1993, and yet Cameron was making promises which were untenable from the outset. In reality, the number of EU immigrants to the UK rose between 2014 and 2015 from 100,000 to circa 150,000. If a country wishes to join the EU, it must in the context of the Copenhagen Criteria be capable of withstanding the pressures of being in the EU single market; the UK, which joined in 1973, was, according to Prime Minister Cameron, not in fact able to do so. In how far the referendum was really a vote on EU membership or whether it became simply an outlet for voters to express their anger at the political establishment is still unclear and here a weakness of referenda was exposed. One thing is clear, that on June 23 a majority of the electorate cast their votes against further British cooperation within the EU for perhaps the next century.

In many commentaries, the pro-Brexit decision of the electorate is portrayed as a sort of puzzle, and that one can merely take it as a clear protest vote by the British and draw the relevant conclusions in relation to EU reforms. The majority for Brexit is, however, not a puzzle, if one had seen it as an allegory for the answer to the following examination question: how would the majority vote in a referendum on the possible exit of their county from X, if (a) the head of government of that country speaks out against an exit, but a third of his cabinet is in favor; (b) the key economic points regarding an exit are only made available, in a less than comprehensible form, just nine weeks before the vote; (c) the government, by cutting transfers to local authorities by 35%, creates the impression of the undersupply of local services in towns and cities and this, in combination with the Prime Minister's anti-immigration rhetoric, leads to immigration from the X-Community being turned into a scapegoat; (d) the basic knowledge amongst the citizens in the country regarding X lies under 49%—and that even on the day after the referendum, the second most asked question on Google in the referendum country is: what is the integration club X, the membership of which we just voted on? The answer is not a puzzle, and the answer is an accidental Brexit. With a sound, timely supply of information from the government, a normal level of EU knowledge amongst British voters, and less cuts to the central government transfers to local authorities, it can be ruled out that a Brexit majority would have carried the day. Brexit is a political error by the British democracy, which with the Brexit referendum reached a new low in terms of rationality since 1950. Marian Bell, a former member of the Bank of England's Monetary Policy Committee, said in a Sky News interview following Brexit that, from her point of view, the Brexit majority was a chance result.

Brexit is an impulse for the UK to move towards slower output growth in 2018, together with a serious decline in property prices, which threatens to destabilize private pension schemes—which are widespread in the country. One may, however, point out that Donald Trump's economic program for the US could help the UK to avoid a downturn in 2017/18, since the combination of corporate tax cuts previously announced and expansionary fiscal policy will translate into a real appreciation of the US Dollar and thus a depreciation of the British Pound. This will raise the British inflation rate and thus indirectly reduce real wage rate growth; at the same time, export growth will increase and import growth will decline so that an improved current account position (net of international transfers) will contribute to higher GDP growth in the UK.

Property plays an important role as an insurance investment in the UK. Sinking property prices, falling levels of new construction activities, rising unemployment rates, low investment, a growing budget deficit, falling share prices, and a massive depreciation of the Pound can be expected in the medium term as a result of the decision in the referendum to leave the EU. That stock markets will rise in the future as a result of the ultra-low-interest rate policy of the Bank of England and the US stock market boom is not a contradiction here.

Whether the UK itself will disintegrate, as a result of Scotland's wish to remain in the EU and seek its own full independence from London, remains to be seen. Prime Minister Cameron could end up emulating the Greek King of Lydia, Croesus, who faced the Persians in battle in 542 BC. Croesus had previously consulted the Oracle of Delphi on his chances of success. The answer from the Oracle was "If you cross the Halys, you will destroy a great empire" and the Lydian King took this as evidence of his coming victory against the Persian King, Cyrus the Great. With his forces, Croesus crossed the river Halys, which marked the boundary between the two foes, and invaded Cappadocia, today a region in Turkey, but he lost on the field of battle against the Persians and, in doing so, also the Greek dominions in Asia Minor; the capital of Lydia was eventually captured by the Persians and the Kingdom of Lydia itself ceased to exist in 541 BC. There were already skeptics of British membership of the European Communities as early as the 1960s, in particular France's President De Gaulle who would not agree to British applications to join; basically because he feared that the Britons had too weak a pro-European attitude.

The UK, which France under President De Gaulle initially did not want to accept into the EU—he allowed two British attempts to join, in

1963 and 1967, to fail—eventually did join along with Denmark and Ireland in 1973 and now, on the basis of a referendum in 2016, will leave: a shock for the EU on one hand, and a result of the policies of the Conservative Party in the UK on the other hand. For many years, Prime Minister Cameron never really intervened to counter the extreme criticisms of the EU which were commonplace in the important UK print media. Furthermore, due to a weakness in the institutional framework of the EU, the anti-EU UKIP was allowed to grow over time. This failure in how the EU is constructed also enables the growth of radical, right-wing populist parties in other countries. It can be shown that certain EU mechanisms have strengthened in particular the position of radical and populist parties such as UKIP, the Alternative for Germany (or AfD, its German acronym) in Germany, or the Front National in France over many years.

As a European economist, I present here my view on the referendum and on the Cameron government's referendum preparations, while also looking into the implications of a Brexit for both the UK and Europe plus the world economy—what I can offer to the reader is a careful analysis and, based on this, possible scenarios at the end; political conclusions will have to be drawn in the UK and in the EU, after an enhanced debate. Following the publication of the German edition of my book, the US presidential elections took place and therefore I have chosen to add in this, the English edition, an extended chapter discussing the US views on Brexit and on transatlantic economic relations, respectively.

With a knowledge of EU history and the theory of integration, one should not underestimate the international destabilizing impact of the Brexit referendum. That in the current relatively good economic situation of western Europe, a majority of the electorate in the UK decided for a withdrawal from the EU—against all advice from governments, experts, leading business figures, and supposedly influential intellectuals—indicates the political instability in Europe, a possibly disastrous incapability of important countries to engage in peaceful economic cooperation and achieve sustainable economic prosperity in the age of globalization. In contrast to this, the US still appears in the early twenty-first century, despite some problems and over 200 years of national history, to be vibrant and relatively stable. The fact of the US' higher growth rate in terms of real income, an advantage of about 10% over the EU between 2008 and 2015, alone is a warning signal for the EU and its members. However, few countries seem to be genuinely prepared to reform and policy interventions are also in the wrong areas.

The fact that governments in Berlin and Paris, as well as the European Commission itself, were taken by surprise by Brexit shows a lack of analytical capabilities. That the financial markets and the British bookmakers also did not anticipate Brexit shows serious misjudgment on the side of economic actors. This indicates that there will be a temporary further loss of trust in the western economic system: the old confidence that rational decisions shape the economies and politics of western democracies and market economies, respectively, will be weakened, and with that also the trust in stability and prosperity.

With the British vote for leaving the EU, it was made clear that a politically instable European integration community of 28 countries can basically be subjected at any time to a populist or opportunist withdrawal by a member. In the process of the Brexit vote, the UK, unlike the Republic of Ireland, did not have an effective independent referendum commission to provide objective and factual information to citizens. On the contrary, the pro-Leave groups often resorted to unreliable and far-fetched campaign promises and the referendum was influenced by eccentric millionaires such as Arron Banks, a man who imported concepts regarding the development of digital networks for campaign purposes from the US and who bankrolled the Leave.eu campaign—making it available to supporters of Brexit free of charge. State limits on the financing of campaigns of both groups in the referendum were blatantly circumvented.

Not only are the UK and the EU destabilized, but other integration clubs will also suffer from the destruction of the aura surrounding EU integration, which for decades has been an example of both growing membership and deepening integration. After decades of the Latin American integration group Mercosur and the important integration club ASEAN having sought to emulate the EU, Brexit also creates disintegration impulses in other parts of the world.

EU integration must be reconsidered. Questions need to be raised of a political union and deepened EU integration, respectively, however not as a simple continuation or further development of the EU as it is now. In a first step, the clock on excessive regulation from Brussels should be turned back and only on the basis of certain reforms can the course be set towards a political union. Naturally, there are also those who argue that the EU should permanently revert to being a simple free trade area. Considering globalization dynamics and the geopolitical situation, whether less EU is a sensible framework for Europe in the longer term remains a matter of debate.

There are some valid reasons behind the British voting to leave the EU, whereas the quite significant advantages of integration for the UK also play a role. Furthermore, the bad reputation which the EU self-generated in the course of the Euro and Refugee Crises also contributed—and the government of the Federal Republic of Germany is just as culpable here as the European Commission itself. The idea that the EU is capable of surviving in its current construction can be categorically ruled out, and increasingly the question needs to be asked of how EU integration can be best organized in the twenty-first century in order to be a sustainable project going forward.

The subsequent analysis begins with the actual Brexit decision itself (Part I), followed by an exposition of the effects of the decision in Europe and the world economy (Part II), an explanation of EU developments (Part III) and an overview of a possible scenario and consequences for the future, respectively, (Part IV). In light of the unique British Brexit vote, it is appropriate to reassess the fundamental concepts of the advantages, problems, and perspectives of EU integration and to discuss reasonable institutional reforms.

In a failed feat of political speculation, Prime Minister Cameron, with his referendum promise of 2013 which was motivated by challenges within his own party, led his country at the end of June 2016 into a period of short-term political chaos; in doing so, he also destabilized the EU27 group of countries. The opportunist Boris Johnson, former Mayor of London, who spearheaded the anti-EU faction's 'Vote Leave' campaign—was, at the end of June, left seeming quite bewildered and at a loss despite his successful campaign; however, as the Secretary of State for the Foreign and Commonwealth Office (effectively the UK's foreign minister) in the new government under Theresa May he will in fact, in the end, play an important role. He will not, however, be able to negotiate easy access to the EU single market. Considering that up to 45% of UK exports go to the EU, the UK needs access to the single market, which will not be simply available free of charge. Here, cooperation between the EU and the UK will continue.

The main challenges for the May government and the EU Commission, respectively, are as follows in the medium term: (1) coming to an agreement on the UK's exit bill and (2) finding an EU–UK agreement for British EU market access and for EU27 market access to the UK. As regards EU27 countries, the challenge will be to show that medium-term growth is higher than for the EU27 in the first decade post-Brexit when the UK's leaving of the EU could reduce the annual growth rate by about 0.5% for many years. Without such an EU growth advantage vis-à-vis the post-Brexit UK, the pressure in some other EU countries to launch additional X-EXITs will rise. Major reforms in Italy and France are obviously needed and might indeed be implemented. At the same time, the EU is facing immigration pressure from North Africa and Arab countries plus Afghanistan and it is not clear whether or not the EU can find an adequate answer for the new challenges in the field of immigration and refugee crises. The political situation with Turkey in particular is getting more complex. The US under President Clinton pushed hard for Turkey to get the status of an EU candidate country in 1999—after the Kosovo War in which Turkey provided strong military support for US and NATO forces, respectively. Eighteen years later, however, Turkey is still far removed from the EU's shared political values and new tendencies in Ankara to blend autocratic tendencies with a broad religious zeal make the situation tense and a dialogue difficult (even though Poland, with its strong emphasis on Catholicism, seems to follow a similar approach under the conservative PiS government). As political convergence has become difficult in Europe, political integration projects look more complex than previously. That EU integration, however, could really be rolled back was not anticipated by many. With Brexit, this new challenge is on the table.

The British capital is a political center as well as being a global financial center which indeed has served as a financial center for all EU28 countries so far. The one passport solution for banks made this possible and a very competitive environment has contributed to a dynamic City. If there is no "equivalence" solution for banks in the UK with respect to EU27 market access, the globally leading financial center of London will face dramatic adjustment pressure. Mrs. May's prospects to get a good deal here look fairly modest, although one should not rule out a compromise in the EU–UK agreement that brings several sectoral free trade agreements.

The European Commission should be wise enough to enact some of the (strictly speaking, no longer politically binding) negotiation results reached with the Cameron government in early 2016 relating to EU single market deepening since this would bring a 2–3% increase of output in the EU: with an emphasis on the digital single market and the liberalization of services. The May government's key challenges will be to cope with Scotland's demand for a new independence referendum and to get a double agreement with the EU by late 2018. Moreover, government must have enough budget flexibility once British output growth should decline considerably, probably in 2019. This could bring internal tensions in the government since Mrs. May already intervened in relation to Mr. Hammond's public announcement in mid-March 2017 that the self-employed would have to pay higher contributions into the social security system. No. 10 Downing Street rebuked this announcement by the Treasury because it ran contrary to the Conservative Party manifesto pledge not to increase tax rates and social security contributions. The implication is that the deficit–GDP ratio will remain higher in the medium term than initially planned by the Treasury. The public deficit–GDP ratio could further increase if there is (net) outward migration of EU migrants living in the UK after 2019, since EU immigrants are net contributors to the British government budget. If the UK does not get a good deal by 2018, some EU migrants will move back to continental EU countries—and many possibly from England, Wales, and Northern Ireland to Scotland and the Republic of Ireland. The old UK could lose half of these 3.5 million immigrants within a decade or so and this would weaken long-run growth considerably. If the US Dollar should have a period of strong depreciation in the medium term, the UK could be in recession.

One may emphasize that there is no new special Economics for Brexiteers; for example, the standard gravity equations for trade and foreign direct investment, respectively, are still valid and this holds for the UK, the EU27 as well as the US. Equally, there is no new approach in International Economics in the field of free trade and the conjecture of the Trump administration that the US has been a victim of the World Trade Organization is totally unconvincing—with the US winning 75 of the 79 US-related disputes at that organization. Populist forces might push for a "Geocentric Paradigm in Economics" which would mean an ideologically-framed analysis in contrast to the traditional theoretical and empirical approaches (and one cannot exclude that strong religious and populist groups in the US, Poland, Hungary, and other EU countries, plus Turkey, may one day ban evolutionary biology and Darwin's historical insights; perhaps, a fight against heliocentric physics could be the next step). The implication of policy which is not based on sound scientific analysis will be a rise of disappointing results and an even fiercer struggle of government to control the media in one form or another—with Poland (via Beata Mazurek, the spokeswoman of the PiS party) already providing a strange example as the government in Warsaw is fighting foreign ownership of media companies since such ownership is allegedly depriving the public of the 'right news'—in the US, the wording of the Trump administration has been that fake news can only be prevented if the ownership of the New York Times, for example, would change. The rationality of the Western world is at stake since 2016 and it is unclear who will win the coming political debates and elections in key countries, respectively. Part of the Western world's disorientation is caused by the need to adjust to the biggest opening up of an economy in history, namely China whose meteoric increase in terms of the British and US imports of manufacturing goods is quite remarkable—in the US, China's share in manufacturing imports has increased from 4.5% in 2001 to 23.1% in 2011, and US manufacturing employment has declined between 2000 and 2007 by 18.7% (figures based on Acemoglu et al. 2015). No active labor market policy has been developed in this context in the US and in the UK the finding is similar: with active labor market expenditures per person unemployed being only about a quarter of the respective figure in Germany. That this "adjustment overstretch" on the side of workers in the manufacturing industry in the US and the UK results in a strong upswing of support for populist movements is not surprising. Unfortunately, Economics has thus far not developed the concept of adjustment overstretch in any meaningful way although psychology suggests that human beings will change attitudes considerably during periods of massive economic stress.

It also seems clear that with respect to the UK's option to leave the EU, very few economists support Brexit and the same can be said about US economists' support for Mr. Trump's international economic policy approach and the new anti-multilateralism proclaimed in Washington, DC. The fact that the US prevented the ministers of finance and central bank governors at the Group of Twenty (G20) meeting in Baden-Baden in March 2017 from proclaiming support for global free trade is shocking: the high US capital outflows, including foreign direct investment flows, have as a mirror aspect a negative current account balance (imports of goods are higher than US exports) and the apparent inability of the Trump administration to understand key economic insights is strange.

It is still not certain that the process of Brexit will be completed, as the economic disadvantages which the UK—if that union even continues to exist—would experience due to leaving the EU are clear: temporary disadvantages, such as an economic downturn and a massive currency devaluation, on one hand, and restrained economic growth in the long term on the other, are quite conceivable. For the EU27, there may also be slower economic expansion and even a reduced influence globally: for example, in shaping the globalization of the world economy. One can also presume that another effect of Brexit will be that TTIP, the proposed EU–US free trade agreement, will not be concluded.

In Germany, the political leadership on TTIP-related matters is lacking, and in the absence of the usually strong liberalization quartet, that is Germany–UK–the Netherlands–Denmark, it will be extremely difficult politically to ratify a TTIP Agreement in the EU. Here, it should be noted that in the rather bitter confrontations between Trump and Clinton during the course of the US presidential election campaign, it became apparent that in the US there also appears to be reduced political support for international free trade agreements. The Trump administration will not implement the Trans-Pacific Partnership, between the US and 11 other countries from the Pacific region, but TTIP is likely to remain on the US agenda and a transatlantic US–UK mini-TTIP could be realized rather easily once the UK has left the EU.

The EU will need to consider a sustainable reduction in terms of regulatory interventions in the economy, but also about how it can make its projects more visible to citizens and indeed how to implement large projects with professionalism. Simultaneously, however, increased political integration is also required in certain areas: climate change and protection, infrastructure and defense spending, and in relation to taxation and redistribution. Large EU reforms will be considered, but it would be wise to critically assess its present position. Since 2007, EU member states have largely been focused on themselves, and thus the huge challenges posed by the world economy, in particular by the rise of the ASEAN countries and China, have barely registered in political circles and, therefore, the question of necessary reforms in the EU will in the future be asked on the basis of both of these developments. In facing this question, the EU27 must take care not to undermine and weaken itself, on the one hand, and to remain a capable actor internationally, on the other.

Only a few days after the Brexit referendum, the French Prime Minister Valls called for an end to the EU–USA free trade negotiations. His comments reflect the fears of a government with poor economic policies of its own, of a government of the country that for almost three decades has had a youth unemployment rate twice that of Germany, and three times that of Switzerland, and the anxiety of a politician vis-à-vis globalization. There is a threat that the West could stumble into a crisis of meaning. The US presidential elections of 2016 were widely interpreted as showing that people with a fear of globalization had voted for Donald Trump. However, the DHL Connectedness Index 2016 has shown that US citizens in recent surveys on globalization and internationalization, respectively, have overestimated the degree of internationalization generally and by large orders of magnitude (Ghemawat and Altman 2016). The Obama administration obviously did not communicate in a meaningful and effective way the true facts on the intensity of

US internationalization. It seems that post-truth perceptions are a problem in both the US and in the UK. The economic consequences of Brexit are looked at closely within this book, as are the background of how the referendum came to pass and the broad surprise at the result which was reflected by financial markets, betting firms in the UK and many experts. Six weeks prior to the vote, I suspected that the vote would indeed be close-fought which could end with a narrow victory for the Remain camp. In a March 30, 2016, text on Brexit, which I wrote for the AICGS/Johns Hopkins University, I discussed a hypothesis in the opening section which has since proven to be a prescient, that for certain reasons the pro-Brexit camp could receive a majority in the referendum (Welfens 2016a).

That the EU will no longer be able to continue to tread the same path appears obvious. However, it remains unclear what a reasonable direction for reform actually is. A not insignificant number of people are calling for less integration, claiming that Brexit can be seen as a rebuttal to too much integration—including many anti-EU Euroskeptic groups in other EU member countries, who have long campaigned against Brussels wielding too much power. The opposite position must not simply be a call for more EU integration; a certain differentiation is certainly feasible and this should, with a solid economic foundation, entail steps toward a Euro political union and, at the same time, less EU regulation. However, that alone will not be a solution, as the problem remains that weaknesses of national politics systematically lead to protest votes and, from this perspective, without a limit on inadequate policies at a national level, no sustainable EU integration can be expected. If the EU27 countries do not draw the logical conclusions from this, the EU will enter a period of continuing disintegration and Europe as a whole into political conflicts and serious social and economic problems. Europe will find itself in a situation similar to the late nineteenth century, with huge power rivalries between the larger European countries—including Russia—and, as was the case then, countries spending 4% of GDP on military expenditures, which would be roughly double the defense spending of EU member states in 2016.

The North Atlantic Treaty Organization (NATO) is also weakened by Brexit, and the US will play a greater role within the organization, as the hitherto indirect US leadership of NATO, which to date has been achieved on the basis of a close cooperation with the UK, will no longer function as before—the US will need to establish a more direct leadership role. At the same time, the new Trump administration will put heavy pressure on most EU countries, that is those which are also NATO member countries, to considerably raise military budgets.

Germany's relative economic importance in the EU will increase after the withdrawal of the UK. The relative German weighting will rise in mathematical terms, as with Brexit the EU will lose about one-fifth of its Gross Domestic Product. Germany and France will become increasingly dependent on each other in terms of leadership in, and of, the EU. Italy, following a decade of stagnation, will be stronger than before and—together with France—will want to exert more influence within the EU. The new EU could be more protectionist and could try to adopt a bigger role in the economy than that of the regulatory body which it has largely been to date, a development which many firms—sometimes totally justifiably—reject, viewing it as the EU overstepping the mark. A federal EU following Brexit is conceivable: one possible design could include an independent EU income tax, a limited EU unemployment insurance, and an EU Social Market Economy in general. It remains to be seen how this discussion, and indeed the EU itself, will develop, and what suggestions are capable of garnering majority support. If the EU27 wishes to thrive alongside the globally dominant US and China, which could once again double its GDP by 2029, one thing is certain—the old EU cannot be the benchmark going forward.

The EU has a viable core, key institutions, a tradition of liberalizing trade, capital flows, and intra-EU migration, a long history of city networking among EU member countries and of students studying abroad in the Erasmus program; for several years, the EU has, as an institution, been participating in G20 meetings and it has a history of actively negotiating free trade treaties. The first attempt to set up a joint Western European defense institution failed in the 1950s, and a new approach has been adopted in 2003, but no distinctive new profile has emerged as NATO remains the dominant institution in this area. The EU has partly been active at a global level in the field of climate policy and this makes sense to a large extent and facilitates international negotiations considerably. However, the European Commission suffers from rather weak legitimacy and a lack of influence—compared to EU member countries whose power was reinforced during the Euro Crisis—and, as a consequence, the Commission has started to finance many big, non-governmental organizations (e.g., Friends of the Earth Europe, with more than 50% of their budget coming from Brussels for several years). This has backfired on the EU's ability to deliver results in foreign trade policy since it was influential non-governmental organizations in Germany and France that almost killed the EU–US negotiations on TTIP—and here the UK could justifiably raise the question: what is wrong with the EU?

So far, no tradition has developed of the President of the European Commission making official visits to the US, China, Russia, India, or other countries, after his/her election unless there is a G20— or even a 'Group of Seven/Eight,' i.e., G7/G8—meeting. With Brexit, a further retreat of leading EU policymakers might occur and some naïve form of new economic nationalism could emerge in EU countries—few international policy challenges could be handled successfully by a large majority of EU countries acting in an individual capacity. However, this in itself is not a strong argument for membership of the EU policy club which should indeed deliver net benefits to the member countries and its citizens within a system that is transparent, efficient, and simple enough to be understood by voters everywhere. The theory of fiscal federalism is useful for designing a new EU which creates a better division of power than the current assignment which leaves the supranational EU too small on the one hand and too bureaucratic on the other to be broadly convincing to voter majorities in all countries. Finally, it is unclear why the ability of the European Commission to come up with some self-critical reflections after Brexit is so weak and why the desire to mobilize international intellectual resources to suggest much needed institutional innovations in the era of globalization is rather limited. More innovations should be mobilized in the graying societies of the EU—not an easy challenge.

Wuppertal and London, March 2017.

Note

1. Please note, that the Bank of England's Daily Spot Rates as of January 3, 2017—the first business day of 2017—is used to make conversions from Euro figures to Pound Sterling and US Dollars: £0.8484/€1 and $1.034/€1, i.e., £1/$1.22. The same rates are used throughout this book. Conversions are rounded for simplicity.

References

Acemoglu, D. (2015). *Import Competition and the Great U.S. Employment Sag of the 2000s*. UBS Center Working Paper Series No. 13. University of Zurich.

Asia Times. (2016). Asia won't be immune to Brexit vote, Online Edition, 20 June.

Ghemawat, P., & Altman, S. (2016). DHL Global Connectedness Index 2016, The state of globalization in an age of ambiguity. Available at http://www.dhl.com/content/dam/downloads/g0/about_us/logistics_insights/gci_2016/DHL_GCI_2016_full_study.pdf.

HM Government. (2016a). The best of both worlds: The United Kingdom's special status in a reformed European Union, London, February 2016. Available at https://www.gov.uk/government/uploads/system/uploads/attachment_data/file/502291/54284_EU_Series_No1_Web_Accessible.pdf.

HM Government. (2016b). Why the government believes that voting to remain in the European Union is the best decision for the UK, London. https://www.gov.uk/government/uploads/system/uploads/attachment_data/file/515068/why-the-government-believes-that-voting-to-remain-in-the-european-union-is-the-best-decision-for-the-uk.pdf.

Welfens, P. J. J. (2009). *Transatlantische Bankenkrise*. Stuttgart: Lucius.

Welfens, P. J. J. (2016a). British Referendum pains and the EU implications of Brexit, AICGS-Beitrag/Brexit. http://www.aicgs.org/issue/british-referendum-pains-and-the-eu-implications-of-Brexit/.

Part I

The Referendum Process and Politico-Economic Aspects

2

Brexit: A Campaign and a Fatal Communication Disaster

Great Britain has lost an empire and has not yet found a role. The attempt to play a separate power role apart from Europe, a role based on a 'special relationship' with the US and on being the head of a 'commonwealth' which has no political structure, unity, or strength—this role is about played out.

Dean Acheson, former US Secretary of State, in famous speech
at West Point, 1962

This above all: to thine own self be true, And it must follow as the night the day, Thou canst not then be false to any man.

William Shakespeare, Hamlet (Act I, Scene 3)

June 23, 2016, will forever be an important date in British history as on that day the historical Brexit referendum was held. The referendum resulted in a 51.9% majority in favor of the United Kingdom (UK) leaving the European Union (EU) which seems to be a rather clear result. It thus reversed both the decision of the Conservative Party-led Heath government to join the European Economic Community (EEC) in 1973 and the subsequent referendum on that membership in 1975, which had resulted in a two-thirds majority in favor of maintaining that EEC membership. The

© The Author(s) 2017
P.J.J. Welfens, *An Accidental Brexit*,
DOI 10.1007/978-3-319-58271-9_2

referendum of 2016 could have dramatic consequences for the UK and the EU, which is facing the situation of a major member country having held a popular vote to give up EU membership for the first time. The EU, which celebrates 60 years of development in 2017, might not only face the UK's leaving of the community in 2019, but could also face a new situation in that the US, for the first time since the end of the Second World War, is no longer supportive of EU integration; this is the implication of Donald Trump's public support for Brexit in mid-2016. Exactly why EU disintegration would be in the interest of the US is difficult to understand.

The UK is the EU's second-largest economy, accounting for 18% of the European Union's Gross Domestic Product (GDP) and 13% of its population. Choosing a referendum, often considered the highest form of democratic decision-making, suggests a desire to apply a high-quality democratic tool to an important question and indeed a standard referendum—organized with care and decided by a clear majority—can resolve complex issues in a decisive way. Mr. David Cameron, the Prime Minister with responsibility for organizing this referendum (during his time as head of government he had already organized the 2014 referendum on the question of Scottish independence), chose to have a referendum for several reasons and he declared from the outset that his government was in favor of Remain. However, the referendum was in fact won by the Brexit majority, and the result seemed to be a clear indication that British voters really wanted the UK to leave the EU. But is it?

In her first speech as Prime Minister at a Conservative Party Conference—in Birmingham on October 2, 2016—Theresa May expressed the desire of the British government to start EU–UK negotiations no later than March 2017 so as to complete the largely unexpected Brexit process by spring 2019. In the words of Mrs. May: "Even now, some politicians—democratically elected politicians—say that the referendum isn't valid, that we need to have a second vote…others say they don't like the result, and they'll challenge any attempt to leave the European Union through the courts…But come on. The referendum result was clear. It was legitimate. It was the biggest vote for change this country has ever known. Brexit means Brexit—and we're going to make a success of it…We will invoke Article 50 no later than the end of March next year." This book will show, however, that the referendum is lacking in both legitimacy and clarity: that the result was in fact not clear at all. It was not the biggest vote for change in the history of the UK but an accidental Brexit vote, stemming largely from the chaotic situation regarding information and communication in the UK in the weeks before the referendum, the responsibility for which lies squarely with the Cameron government. By employing standard economic and econometric analysis, one can arrive at the finding that the result of an orderly, well-organized referendum on June 23 would have been a majority of roughly 52% for Remain. That the actual vote ended with a Leave majority is down to two key tragic and irresponsible figures: Mr. David Cameron as Prime Minister and Mr. George Osborne as the head of Her Majesty's Treasury—this will be shown in the first part of this book. As Sir Francis Bacon might have argued four centuries ago, there is no evidence that the referendum was organized in a way that is consistent with minimum Western information standards—thus, contrary to Prime Minister May, one may indeed question if Brexit really means Brexit.

This is one key analytical element which this book explores and in addition it raises doubts about the claims that Brexit could be an economic success. Mrs. May's mantra is an ill-founded, contradictory conjecture; Brexit could perhaps be a success for the Conservative Party and Mrs. May or indeed some investor groups, but that it could be an economic success for the UK and its people is very unlikely. The further conjecture of Mrs. May in Birmingham that the UK would never again give away so much sovereignty as it allegedly had until 2016, particularly that verdicts of the European Court of Justice would no longer be binding on the UK, is illustrative of a new British government approach—that is a willingness to undermine international law and to effectively destroy common institutional capital in the EU. That the UK could get easy access to the EU single market in future when the British government says that it does not want to accept verdicts of the European Court of Justice in single market matters is inconceivable. However, the more Mrs. May pursues a hard Brexit, as she suggested was her government's goal in her Brexit speech on January 17, 2017, the higher will be the economic costs for the UK (HM Govt 2017). Moreover, to suggest that the politico-economic power of an "independent" UK would be much greater than that of a UK which is still an

EU member, and benefitting from the support of four times the UK's economic power, is strange. In the twenty-first century, with China and the Association of Southeast Asian Nations (ASEAN) becoming new powerful mega players on world markets, the idea of going back to a nationalist UK runs counter to research, facts and real British opportunities and abilities. It is clear that a UK outside the EU may very well get some satisfactory solutions to certain issues on its own or as a permanent shadow state of the US, but in a broader view—looking at all key policy fields, issues and topics—this is an unconvincing view.

How big was the power of the UK in the EU? From an analytical perspective, one can use concepts from game theory—such as the Shapley Value or the Banzhaf Index. The latter measures the power of a country in an integration club with majority requirements in a rather simple way: look at the number of cases of all potential coalitions of countries where the respective country, here the UK, can change a 'losing' or minority coalition group into becoming a 'winner' or majority group simply by aligning itself with the group. With the exception of the field of tax policy, where unanimous voting is required for a decision to be made, there are various fields of economic policy (and other policy areas) where the UK enjoys a relatively high power status: it is in a position—due to the high number of votes that the UK has in weighted majority decision-making in the EU—to change a losing coalition into a winning coalition in many cases—giving the UK an effective deciding vote. Moreover, together with Germany, the Netherlands, and Denmark, it used to have a blocking minority so that certain protectionist measures could be avoided—thus the whole EU28 remained on a liberal trading track for decades. In the future, the post-Brexit UK will no longer sit at the table in Brussels. Instead of being able to cast the second highest number of votes in decisions being made by qualified majority in the EU, the British government in London will have to call on Berlin or Paris or The Hague in order to have its interests represented by proxy while decisions are being made at the EU table. On paper, the UK has more autonomy, but in effective power terms, Brexit actually means a critical loss of power.

That the UK could gain from leaving the EU is not a very convincing idea. Such a conjecture is all the more unlikely since the British withdrawal is likely to destabilize the EU27 (which is roughly four times the economic size of the UK). How could the UK benefit from a political maneuver that amounts to a serious destabilization of its main trading partner? More instability in continental Europe will further undermine the potentially weakened union in Great Britain. It is also clear that other integration areas will watch the new disintegration dynamics in the EU with a critical interest, while powers in geographical proximity to the EU28 will most likely consider reinforcing their own positions in the international arena.

Among the early reactions of economists to Brexit—disregarding the German (longer) edition of this book (Welfens 2016c), which was published in November 2016—was the book by Baldwin et al. (2016) which carefully looked at some initial key findings and core options for Brexit policy. Critical forum contributions in the Journal *International Economics and Economic Policy* were offered by Ryan (2016), Welfens (2016b) and James (2016a). Harold James, the renowned Princeton historian, argued that Brexit was not a sensible decision and also that the referendum undermined the power of the British Parliament which traditionally is the key political institution of the UK. In my own contribution, I not only explained the key information blunder of the Cameron government, which greatly undermines the referendum's legitimacy, but also emphasized that the EU will need broader reforms which should bring less regulation but also—for the Eurozone—a political union. Cillian Ryan has argued that there is no economic theory which would be a convincing basis for expecting welfare benefits from Brexit.

In 2016, the EU28 was still the biggest single market in the world—with some 515 million inhabitants and a GDP of about $17,000 billion. The European Union traces its roots back to integration steps taken during the 1950s, when the UK, at first, stood on the sidelines. At that time, the UK was a member of the European Free Trade Association (EFTA) which had been created by Denmark, Switzerland, Portugal, Sweden, and the UK in 1960. In 1986, Finland joined, with Liechtenstein and Iceland also later coming on board. Within EFTA, there were no tariffs on trade within that community; while as regards external tariffs, each member country had an individual import tariff list. This was different in the case of the European Union where countries had agreed upon forming a Customs Union in which free trade within the EU was combined with a common external tariff. Free trade in an economic community stimulates intra-community trade and thus economic gains from specialization—this is a welfare-enhancing trade creation effect. Trade with outside countries is somewhat reduced (a trade diversion effect), however, if enhanced intra-community trade and enhanced foreign direct investment flows linked to the creation of the integration clubs raises real incomes sufficiently, the effect will be a rise of imports from third countries as well. Hence, the trade diversion effect could be rather limited in the long run and regional integration clubs could, under certain circumstances, contribute to reinforcing global trade liberalization.

The specific trait of the EU is that it has a joint external tariff. It is clear that agreement on such a joint tariff policy is a field of cooperation among member states and demonstrates vis-à-vis trading partners (i.e. third parties) that the community of European countries had achieved a basic consensus with regard to foreign trade policy. In effect, the common foreign trade policy became a trait of EU integration; a joint tariff policy means efficiency gains compared to a situation of individual import tariffs. The 1960s witnessed a certain rivalry between the EU and the EFTA, but the European Union grew increasingly attractive to many EFTA countries—mainly because the economic heavyweights of continental Western Europa were participants in that community. Over time, most EFTA countries eventually joined the EU—including the UK and Denmark—who along with Ireland joined the EU in 1973. With Brexit, Europe seems to move backwards to the 1970s and possibly even further back.

After more than four decades of UK integration in the EU, the British referendum of 2016 has brought the chapter of uninterrupted EU expansion to an end. The traditional political wisdom, which held that the European Union could overcome any crisis and continue relatively unscathed on a journey towards further development and expansion, has been soundly refuted. The Brexit crisis reinforces anti-EU political parties in many EU countries and at the same time it seems that the economic benefits of EU integration were not sufficiently strong to convince the roughly 17 million voters who said no to EU integration. However, this is a popular misreading of Brexit, the information background of which has not been critically discussed so far.

Besides a strong nominal and real depreciation of the British Pound, there were no serious negative effects on the UK economy in 2016 and many observers might have the view that Brexit will have no impact on the economic welfare of the people of the UK. This, however, is a misleading view since the main dynamics will not unfold before the UK government's official 'divorce' letter to the European Commission and the EU27 partners has been sent to Brussels. At the Birmingham Conservative Party Conference in late 2016, Prime Minister May announced that this letter—required by Article 50 of the EU Treaty— would be sent to Brussels no later than the end of March 2017. As regards the long-term economic impulses of Brexit, the main effects will become visible once it is clear under exactly what conditions the UK will regain access to the EU single market—which would stand for 430 million people in 2020. The more restricted this future access will be, the larger the negative output effects of Brexit. In addition to these aspects, one should be careful not to ignore the stabilizing interventions of the Bank of England—cutting the interest rate to a record low in the weeks after the referendum—and the government, respectively. To the extent that the Trump administration's first two years bring an economic upswing for the USA and a real appreciation of the US Dollar, there are also new export opportunities for the UK, and this should help to stabilize British output dynamics.

If the UK should leave the EU in 2019 on the basis of the Brexit referendum held in June 2016, then to some extent the obvious question is where is the UK headed? Will Great Britain really go it alone in the twenty-first century? That is hard to imagine. On the other hand, the UK could attempt to found a sort of enhanced EFTA ("EFTA+"), and with that the EU would face two difficulties: with the exit of the UK, the EU would have lost almost 20% of its economic weight; furthermore the UK, its second-largest EU member state (as of 2016), is large enough in the event of Brexit to attract other dissatisfied EU countries to follow it. The EU will not be able to defend itself against that eventuality via some sort of EU–UK trade and cooperation agreement. From an economic perspective, one may argue that competition for members between EFTA+ and EU27 could be a framework for achieving an efficient integration process in Europe. This, however, is not very likely, rather EU disintegration dynamics are likely to be the dominating phenomenon. Moreover, it is obvious that the UK could consider options for attracting new members to EFTA+ including by offering effective subsidization by means of transfer payments and of military or political support arrangements to would-be members. The key issue here is the question of what the UK stands to gain from a destabilized continental Europe—obviously not really much.

Incidentally, these elements were highlighted in the run-up to the Scottish independence referendum in 2014 in a UK government information brochure (HM Govt 2014b) which explained that within the British union, Scotland is a recipient of de facto net transfers worth £1,400 (ca. $1,700) per capita from England, that as a constituent part of the union Scotland enjoys both military and political protection, as well as that Scottish citizens enjoy advantages worldwide via the services of UK embassies. In the event of an integration competition with the EU, the UK could potentially, and at least initially, employ considerable financial resources, as with Brexit circa £8 billion/$9.8 billion (or 0.4% of UK GDP in 2014 terms) in annual contribution payments to the EU have become available in terms of public finances. To look at the EU budget contribution of 2015 is misleading since this contains a one-off effect of cumulated postponed British contributions over several years— reflecting an upward revision of the UK's GDP. However, part of these former annual net contributions to the EU will be needed for future new contributions to the EU in a deal to give Great Britain access to the EU single market. Keeping Scotland in the UK will have a price tag as well and this, together with a small rise in the military budget, is likely to erase any major net budget gain for the UK: with the UK outside of the EU, the weaker EU27 and indeed the whole of Europe will be much more exposed to military pressure from Russia and other sources of instability so that a rise of the military expenditure-GDP ratio in the medium term is rather likely.

In the event of Brexit, the European integration project will once again be called into question, a situation which will create unrest in Europe. This will put the EU under pressure, but whether the EU and its member states can undertake smart and timely reforms is unclear. Russia and China, as well as the US, will consider the smaller EU as a weaker political and economic actor and thus new pressures on the EU27 on the world stage could quickly emerge. This option already weakens the politico-economic position of the EU27.

At the same time, the UK is facing another potential Scottish independence referendum once it has become clear how good or bad British access to the EU single market will be. Once the finer details of a future EU–UK treaty are known, the debate about Scottish independence, and an independent Scotland's membership of the EU, will likely emerge and cause serious divisions—again undermining the stability of the UK for some time and weakening, disregarding the outcome of the debate, the union of England, Scotland, Wales, and Northern Ireland. Getting the same critical referendum on Scottish independence back on the political agenda within a few short years is not a normal situation.

In a statement released prior to the Scottish independence referendum ("Scottish Referendum: Our place in the world," published on April 28, 2014 [HM Govt 2014a]) in a section on the EU, and sent to voters as a brochure, the British government explained to voters:

> We are a member of the EU on terms which would be hard to negotiate again. Thanks to our influence and long-term negotiations, the UK has unique terms for our membership of the EU. This includes keeping the UK pound and the ability to control our own borders and immigration policy. The UK's rebate means that the average Scottish household saves between £750 and £1,470 per year between 2014 and 2010 on the cost of EU membership (PJJW: that is between $915 and $1,795 per year). If Scotland leaves the UK it would need to start formal negotiations to join the EU as a new member state—a lengthy and costly process.

It will be difficult to assess prior to 2025 what Brexit will actually entail. The actual UK withdrawal is expected to occur before the European elections in 2019. Certainly, it would be strange indeed if the UK government was still negotiating a withdrawal from European Union while also holding elections for the European Parliament. If such a situation would occur, a strong vote for pro-EU parties could undermine the

signal of the 2016 referendum in an opaque way. The economic adjustment processes for the UK and the EU27 would take about a decade
and this period will be shaped by reduced growth dynamics as by then
the negative economic effects of EU disintegration would have been felt.
Facing the pressure of a reduced growth rate, the British government is likely to implement internal pro-growth reforms and push
for a series of new trade treaties for the UK. Leaving the European
Union means that the UK would lose privileged access to about 50
countries to which British exports have so far enjoyed favorable access
under the EU umbrella. While some free trade arrangements with
certain Commonwealth countries, including Canada and Australia,
would probably be relatively easy to achieve, these trade relations are
not decisive for the UK in quantitative terms. With obvious hesitancy
on the part of Germany and France regarding the envisaged EU–US
Transatlantic Trade and Investment Partnership (TTIP) venture, the
opportunities for a UK–US agreement on a transatlantic free trade project should not be difficult to exploit: a UK–US TTIP is not only quite
important for the UK but would also be quite attractive for the US,
since the British market represents 25% of US exports to the EU28.
Moreover, US investors represent, via production by US subsidiaries in
the UK, about 6% of British GDP and for British economic development it will be quite important to have closer UK–US economic relations once the economic relations with continental Europe have been
weakened through Brexit. Based on BEA data (see Table 2.1), it is
obvious that the US multinationals' direct output impact in the UK
is rather large, namely about three times the figure for France, just

Table 2.1 The GDP share generated by US subsidiaries in Europe (and selected European countries)

Country	2009 (%)	2010 (%)	2011 (%)	2012 (%)	2013 (%)	2014 (%)
EU	3.00	2.98	3.01	3.22	3.01	3.16
France	1.94	1.90	1.91	1.87	1.87	1.94
Germany	2.55	2.50	2.46	2.36	2.36	2.47
UK	6.58	6.31	6.09	5.84	5.84	5.75

Source BEA database and WDI database. EIIW calculations: *Note* data is taken from all Majority-Owned Bank and Non-Bank under two and a half times the figure for Germany and almost double the European Union average. Hence, if one considers the findings of Francois et al. (2013) that reducing transatlantic FDI barriers will raise employment in US subsidiaries by 11%, one may conclude in a simplified analysis—assuming that output would also be raised by the same percentage—that British output could be raised by about 0.7% if a transatlantic UK–US TTIP could be achieved along the lines originally envisaged for the bigger EU–US TTIP project.

At the same time, it is clear that Franco-German doubts in the field of TTIP considerably undermine growth prospects for many EU countries, including—paradoxically—Germany and France themselves. Jungmittag/Welfens (2016) have calculated, based on a panel data analysis of 20 EU countries looking at knowledge dynamics in the context of cumulated foreign direct investment inflows, researchers employed and per capita income, that for Germany one would expect about 2% long-run real income growth from TTIP. Brexit, in combination with British initiatives for new free trade agreements, will certainly put the EU27 under pressure. Whether or not a pro-free trade initiative will really raise British GDP sufficiently enough to counterbalance negative EU disintegration impulses remains to be seen and will be discussed subsequently.

Neither the UK nor the EU27 will be in a position to simply adopt a 'wait-and-see' attitude in the field of trade liberalization, since the world's largest economy, China (measured by purchasing power parity GDP) could roughly double its GDP again by 2029 assuming growth rates of 5%. The traditional logic of the EU integration process would normally be in favor of TTIP, since the history of the EU itself consists of so many favorable integration dynamics that political support for a transatlantic deal should be strong. This holds even if one would have to engage in difficult negotiations with the US about issues surrounding investor-state dispute settlement and the fact that foreign investors should get a privileged framework for settling disputes with governments in host countries—at least if it proceeds according to US wishes and negotiation priorities. Before we turn to the particular circumstances of the Brexit referendum, it is worth briefly recalling some key aspects of the history of EU integration and highlighting some core issues of integration dynamics.

EU Integration Approaches in a Historical Perspective

The idea of European integration emerged over centuries and gained in terms of political importance following the end of the First World War; however, no real political progress was made; despite some impulses in the middle of the 1920s—with Aristide Briand and Gustav Stresemann as the respective foreign ministers of France and Germany—it was not possible to launch Franco-German reconciliation and concurrent economic and political cooperation. The Second World War and its over 50 million dead followed. Only after 1945—with the support of the US via the Marshall Plan and aid for a new European Payments Union—was it possible by the early 1950s for a concrete integration project to emerge, namely the founding of the so-called Montanunion, that is the European Coal and Steel Community (ECSC) in 1952, where Luxembourg became home to the political headquarters of the institutions of the ECSC. The European Communities—which later became the European Union—were founded in 1957, the founding members of which were the member states of the ECSC: Germany, France, Italy, Belgium, the Netherlands, and Luxembourg. At that stage, the UK had no wish to participate. While Winston Churchill had called in his 1948 speech in Zürich for the establishment of a "united states of Europe," he was expressly suggesting European integration without the UK—the position of power of which he saw as being most likely as the head of the Commonwealth—that is in close connection with the former British colonies.

It is interesting to read the Leave campaign websites and find there the idea that the UK should again strive for a great international role—after Brexit—in the context of a more active Commonwealth strategy. This leaves open obvious two questions:

- Will a new Commonwealth strategy of the UK be welcomed by other Commonwealth member countries?
- Could a new British Commonwealth strategy create major benefits for the UK?

The UK joined the EEC under Conservative Prime Minister Edward Heath in 1973, but after he suffered a defeat in the next general election, it was the Labour Party that raised critical questions about British membership and obtained some additional concessions in negotiations with Brussels and the EU, respectively. It was a Labour government, under Harold Wilson, which organized a first referendum in the UK on EU membership in 1975, which resulted in a two-thirds majority in favor of remaining a member. Under Prime Minister Cameron, the second British referendum—in 2016—brought a very different result. David Cameron became Prime Minister in a coalition government in 2010 and only following his successful re-election in 2015— with a clear majority for the Conservative Party in parliament—could Cameron form a strong and stable government. However, he viewed the large number of Conservative EU critics as a problem: one year previously, the anti-EU United Kingdom Independence Party (UKIP) had secured 28% of the vote in European Parliament elections. The leader of UKIP, Nigel Farage, was himself once a member of the Conservative Party and had campaigned, as a Member of the European Parliament, for 17 years for a UK exit from the EU. Following his victory in the 2015 national elections, Cameron wanted to neutralize the anti-EU forces within his party—by means of a prompt and hopefully successful EU referendum. Prime Minister Cameron had already announced in 2013 that should he be re-elected, he would hold a referendum on the UK's EU membership. On February 20, 2016, the British newspaper, *The Guardian*, reported that Prime Minister Cameron had decided on June 23 the same year as the date of the referendum—the vote was scheduled to be held following the, at least from the UK's point of view, successful negotiations with the EU. These negotiations had secured a special role for the UK within the EU into the future—including limitations on how immigrants from EU countries could benefit from the British social welfare system and certain clarifications about Britain's role as a non-Eurozone country, and in turn Cameron supported continuing membership of the EU; furthermore, leaving the EU would mean endangering the UK's economic and national security. According to *The Guardian*, Cameron said "We are approaching one of the biggest decisions this country will face in our lifetimes: whether to remain in a reformed EU or to leave. The choice goes to the heart of the kind of country we want to be and the future we want for our children" (Mason et al. 2016).

There was an official grouping of Brexit supporters (the "Vote Leave" campaign) and an official—that is recognized by the state—pro-EU group, namely "Britain Stronger in Europe" (formally: the In Campaign Ltd.). Over the course of four months, these organizations, and indeed other lobby and interest groups, mobilized the voters for the referendum on June 23. In this book, the term "Leave campaign" is intended to be a catch-all phrase for all those who backed Brexit. Additionally, from the side of a fractured cabinet—with six ministers publicly supporting the Brexit side—came a government information and mobilization campaign (supplying information to households, see appendix). Prime Minister Cameron was massively involved in the campaign, however with little persuasiveness and the campaign lacked a certain level of credibility; possibly because for many years Cameron's speeches as Prime Minister had indicated that he was the head British Tory critic of the EU. Despite Cameron calling for a Remain vote, the six pro-Brexit ministers in his cabinet were allowed to remain in government even though the great electoral winner, David Cameron, could have dismissed these ministers rather easily; certainly, there would have been an inner party conflict within the Conservative Party, but at least a clear direction for the government campaign would have been visible. Despite very close opinion poll results, Cameron's side was still extremely confident that they would win the referendum; not even the financial markets, in the two weeks prior to the referendum, seemed to believe that a pro-Brexit majority would emerge—there was an appreciation of the Pound Sterling. The betting firms, often seen as extremely accurate predictors, also foresaw a pro-EU majority in the vote in the referendum. Both the financial markets in the run-up to the referendum—particularly during the two weeks before June 23—and punters on the street were betting on a vote to remain in the EU as was indicated by the implied probability of a Remain vote according to the betting companies. The opinion polls did indicate a narrow outcome, but the wisdom of capital markets suggested a clear Remain result. Thus came the surprise news in the early morning of June 24 that there had actually been a pro-Brexit majority of 51.9%.

Key European Issues in the Eyes of Voters

According to Opinium Research surveys (as reported in *The Guardian* (2016)), the main themes in relation to Brexit were immigration and problems regarding the National Health Service (NHS)—indirectly caused by waiting times which were also connected to the number of immigrants—having been cited by more than 50% of respondents. In answer to the question on the three most important topics related to Europe out of the following: the relationship between the UK and EU, economic issues, poverty problems, the housing market, poverty/inequality, low wages, and unemployment, respondents were able to give multiple responses.

However, when asked for the "three most important issues for you and your family," then the most common responses were the NHS (50%); the economy, low wages, and immigration (each with over 20%); the relationship between the EU and the UK; the housing market; the education system; and poverty/inequality. Here, one can discern that the huge cuts imposed by the Cameron governments on transfers to local government and the budget of the NHS were perceived as the major problem. The issue of rising rents is not an EU-related problem, but is indicative of deficits in terms of British construction policies with regard to residential properties. In relation to poverty, inequality, low wages, unemployment, and the education system, Cameron's governments imposed cutbacks and allowed a doubling of tuition fees after the Banking Crisis—again, the EU is not involved. European Parliament elections are known to have often served a scapegoat function in the sense that voters are less likely to voice concerns about critical EU politics, but rather want to indicate frustration about national policies; here the British referendum clearly also faced the problem that the voting decision was overloaded with domestic issues that were not really related to the question asked on the voting day, which was:

Should the United Kingdom remain a member of the European Union or leave the European Union?

Fighting poverty and providing affordable high-quality education are not really EU policy fields. It is, however, true that the Transatlantic Banking Crisis of 2008/09 brought enormous increases in terms of university tuition fees (raising fees by a factor of two or three). Government budget deficits after the Banking Crisis had been so high—initially above 10% of GDP—that the Cameron government desperately considered all kinds of revenue raising and cost cutting measures. The referendum result seemed to indicate broad frustration with key elements of Cameron's economic policy and faced with a referendum result, which was in large part a protest vote against his government, Prime Minister Cameron quickly stepped down.

After several rather chaotic days, a new Prime Minister was selected with the Tory nomination of Mrs. Theresa May, former Home Secretary, as new party leader of the Conservatives. Among the key promises of her government, Mrs. May indicated that she wanted a society and economic system which would deliver benefits not only for a few people but for everybody. This all sounded as if Mrs. May had carefully listened to the voters' priority list mentioned above. However, as regards the upcoming new policies of the May government, it is already quite clear that they will not result in less inequality and poverty, but rather inequality will become more pervasive as the government will push for more economic globalization through pursuing more far-reaching free trade agreements. That is not to say that free trade agreements would not generate economic benefits through real aggregate income gains, however, as Jaumotte/Lall/Papageorgiou (2008) have shown, the interplay of trade globalization, technological progress—with an emphasis on an expansion of information and communication technology—and financial globalization is reducing international per capita differences across countries, but is also raising the skilled wage premium in all industrialized countries. Given the poor record of British active labor market policies over many years—with the UK spending about a quarter of what Germany spends per person unemployed—one cannot expect that the British government will have a convincing package of measures to handle the envisaged accelerated globalization that will be an indirect consequence of Brexit in the UK.

What were the main arguments of the Leave versus the Remain campaign? In a paper of the US Congressional Research Service, one can find the following list (Mix 2016) which is included as an excerpt here:

- the EU has eroded national sovereignty by shifting control over many areas of decision-making from national leaders to Brussels;
- the EU lacks democratic legitimacy and accountability because many of its decisions are made behind closed doors by non-British and/or unelected officials;
- EU bureaucracy and regulations stifle the UK's economic dynamism;
- the UK would be better off freed from the EU's rules and regulations and able to focus more on expanding ties to growing and dynamic emerging economies elsewhere;
- the UK's contributions to the EU budget are too expensive;
- high levels of immigration to the UK from Central and Eastern Europe mean fewer jobs and lower wages for British citizens; and
- Brexit would have a minimal effect on security cooperation and defense issues because the UK would remain a leading member of NATO.

Arguments for a continuance of UK membership of the EU include the fact that

- membership is essential for the UK's economic fortunes, as half of the UK's exports go to the EU "single market";
- EU membership serves as a launchpad for the UK's global trade;
- Brexit would mean losing out on the benefits of the prospective US–EU comprehensive free trade agreement, the Transatlantic Trade and Investment Partnership (T-TIP);
- the EU has many shortcomings, but the UK is "better off fighting from the inside";
- EU membership gives the UK a stronger voice and more influence in foreign policy;

- the EU has important transnational security dimensions, and Brexit would "divide the West," weakening its ability to deal with threats such as terrorism and Russian aggression; and
- Brexit is a "leap in the dark," with uncertain consequences and no clear vision of what a post-EU future would look like.

So, in the end, it seems to be clear that the UK, the sixth largest economy in the world, was heading towards a historical decision with many important key issues to be decided in a referendum that had been on the political radar since 2013.

A Majority for Brexit

Just four months after the referendum was announced in the UK, a slim majority of just 51.9% voted against continued UK membership of the European Union, where primarily older voters and voters from the English industrial midlands tended to vote strongly in favor of an exit: in other words, for Brexit. Northern Ireland, Scotland, and London, on the other hand, delivered relatively clear pro-EU majorities. With the exception of London, most English regions returned a pro-Brexit vote. Beyond the regional perspective, there is a clear distinction between younger and older generations, the elderly being in favor of Leave. For the younger generations with a clear pro-EU majority, the non-binding referendum stands for a bitter result as their desired European future seems to be clouded by the coming Brexit. After it had become clear that the Brexit referendum had gone disastrously wrong for Prime Minister Cameron, he announced his decision to step down—the new Prime Minister should be chosen by October 2016, and only then should the new incoming leader of government trigger Article 50 of the Lisbon Treaty and in doing so convey to the EU its official intention to withdraw from the Union. A chaotic next couple of weeks followed until July 13 when the new Prime Minister, Theresa May, assumed office. She declared "Brexit means Brexit, and we're going to make a success of it." How this success is going to happen remains as yet unclear, as will be pointed out later, since Brexit will not be easy to implement nor are there many valid arguments which suggest that Brexit will be a success story in economic terms. The winning margin of Leave over Remain was 1.3 million votes. One strange finding on the day after the referendum was the spike in Google's trend statistics which showed a massive increase in EU-related questions being entered in the search engine in the UK. The second most frequent EU-related question was "What is the EU?" Does this point to a lack of information in a referendum which is regarded as the ultimate decision-making instrument in a democracy? One may emphasize that knowledge about the EU seems to be rather modest in the UK according to a recent survey: just 49% of British respondents could give at least one correct answer to two very basic questions about the EU, 4 percentage points less than Polish respondents (53%)—with Poland acceding to the EU 31 years after the UK. The respective figures for Germany and Italy were 81% and 80%, respectively (Bertelsmann Foundation 2016).

From an economic perspective, the foreseeable Brexit effects are clearly negative as many studies show, including a study by the UK's own Treasury which puts the long-run output decline at an expected 3–10% (HM Government 2016b). These and other economic findings were not communicated to private households and voters. This is a major problem and in fact represents an information blunder so fundamental that it needs to be analyzed in more detail.

As regards the rather unexpected referendum result, many politicians and European experts were rather surprised about the Brexit majority of June 23. However, in a March 30, 2016, contribution for AICGS/The Johns Hopkins University, this author wrote (Welfens 2016a):

> On 23 June 2016, should a majority of British voters decide to leave the EU—nearly forty-five years after joining the Community—the EU would lose 17 percent of its GDP and 12 percent of its population. This referendum result would reveal Prime Minister David Cameron's poor political calculations and he would now find that his pro-EU membership campaign has failed miserably. The great winner of the British election of 2015 will step down as prime minister after the failed referendum, while UKIP anti-EU activists cheer on the developments as do other anti-EU

forces. As regards Cameron's potential defeat, there has been a moral failure on the part of the prime minister: he had assigned a special taskforce of scientists to write a critical EU Report in 2014 and the result had been that in no field was the EU a serious impediment to British interest and British policy; the division of competences between Brussels and London could be improved in some fields but there were no serious inconsistencies—a message that was not clearly communicated to the British public. The final chapters of the report were published in 2015.

The main reason that so many British citizens are rather skeptical about EU membership and immigration, respectively, is the fact that after the Transatlantic Banking Crisis national government funding of local communities has been strongly reduced—sometimes not only reflecting adjustment pressure from high government deficit–GDP ratios, but conservative ideology as well; in communities facing reduced government services and excess demand problems in the health care system, sustained immigration pressure from the EU partner countries (and other countries) has created a general impression of overcrowding problems. It is unclear whether the pro-EU supporters can convey the message that EU membership for the UK is a rational choice, since leaving the UK will raise the question about the future relationship between the UK and the EU—if the UK would follow the Swiss or Norwegian model, the price tag for full access to the EU single market will be not only to accept most EU rules, but to contribute to the EU budget as well.

It is true that Cameron is not the only element to blame for the negative British referendum result. Angela Merkel's chaotic refugee policy of 2015 has certainly reinforced those British voters who are afraid of immigration and the EU's immigration policy—which has exposed just how poor the EU's ability to defend its own southern external borders really is. As Margaret Thatcher once said in the context of Britain potentially joining the EU Schengen treaty, which allows the free circulation of people in continental EU countries: we are not going to rely on Greek civil servants to effectively control the access of foreigners to the UK. All the pictures of the EU refugee crisis of 2015 and early 2016 have simply illustrated the chaotic refugee policy of Germany and the EU, respectively: with Greece being totally overwhelmed with the task of controlling its external borders and providing sufficient humanitarian aid to the refugees.

Gideon Rachman's article in the Financial Times of March 21, 2016 describes the post-transatlantic banking crisis world where many voters are fed up with the old political elites. There exists the problem that "the political establishments in Washington and London find it hard to believe that the public will ultimately make a choice that the establishment regards as self-evidently stupid. However, in Britain, as in the US, politics has taken a populist and unpredictable turn. The financial crisis and its aftermath have undermined faith in the judgement of elites. High levels of immigration and fear of terrorism have increased the temptation to try and pull up the drawbridge and retreat behind national frontiers."

The Brussels terror attack of March 22, 2016, has reinforced the fear of terrorism and many British citizens think—reinforced by Leave activists—that living outside the EU, and thus being somehow protected from terrorist attack, is an argument in favor of Brexit. Anti-terror specialists would not agree with this, but simple answers are always popular.

The anti-EU supporters think that the UK alone will be better off than being a member country of the EU. The economic logic contradicts this view completely: the short-term economic gain is that the UK could save only about 0.4% of GDP in net contributions to the EU, but the rather poor future UK position at the international negotiating table will certainly cost the UK far more than this relatively small amount, while the UK will also experience a decrease in attractiveness for foreign investors who instead will want to invest more in continental EU countries in the future. A real depreciation of the British pound along with Brexit means that British exports will increase in real terms, but in the end the key message is that, for a given amount of imports of goods, the average British citizen will have to export more domestically produced goods so that there is a welfare loss.

Moreover, a real depreciation means that foreign investors will obtain British assets at a discount, but this is only an advantage to investors from the US, Euro countries, Russia, and Arab countries. In order to get access to the EU single market in the future, the UK would have to follow most EU regulations and would also have to make some payments toward the EU's budget so that even on the budget side there would not be a net gain for the UK. The devaluation of the British pound in the run-up to June 23 could become very significant and force the Bank of England to massively intervene in the market as liquidity could dry out and asset prices could fall dramatically as international investors anticipate the UK leaving the EU. One cannot rule out that such financial turmoil will be a last minute signal to tilt the balance at the Brexit referendum in favor of pro-EU votes. Undecided voters will be influenced by financial market signals.

The UK will lose its position in all EU-funded research projects and British innovation dynamics will suffer from this, as well as from the fact that UK tuition fees for students from the EU will strongly increase so that less skilled talent from the European continent will be attracted to study there. The UK will be a weaker actor in Europe and in the world economy—as will the EU itself without the UK. The European Union would look like a fragile union after Brexit and this means that its political weight would decline internationally. The true winners in a global perspective would thus be Russia, the US, and China. From a European perspective, the winners will also be anti-EU parties, particularly those in the Euro area, and this could also bring new problems for the Euro area. Since March 2016, Germany has faced political destabilization when the populist Alternative for Germany (AfD), a right-wing party expressing xenophobic sentiments, obtained double-digit voting shares in three German states, including the economic powerhouse of Baden-Württemberg, which has 13% of the population of Germany.

The AfD is the mirror party of UKIP to some extent and it was created in 2013 as an anti-Euro party mainly by a group of concerned German economists (Bernd Lucke, Joachim Starbatty, Olaf Henkel), none of them an expert on monetary integration. By late 2015 they already had left the AfD over internal conflicts and had created a new party "Alpha," which does not play a role in Germany. The AfD benefited from a widespread uneasy feeling among many citizens who have become nervous—not least from the very many alarmistic Ifo Institute reports on the Eurozone. In a biased approach to the issues, only worst-case scenarios were published that naturally were picked up by the popular press according to the old saying "bad news is good news." Hans Werner Sinn, the president of the partly government-financed Ifo Institute in Munich, argued in his worst-case scenarios in 2012/2013 that German taxpayers could lose up to 30% of GDP in the Euro Crisis; the true costs are less than 1% of GDP so far. Beatrix von Storch, a leading AfD figure, was so nervous at some point that she took AfD funds from the bank to keep it in cash at home since she was afraid that the Euro could go out of business.

With more regional elections coming—and the national election in 2017—the AfD will no doubt expand further and this undermines political stability in Germany and a fortiori in the EU. Less political stability implies that there will be a risk premium expected from the perspective of foreign investors and hence Germany will have lower foreign direct investment (disregarding a temporary higher inflow stemming from disappointed foreign investors after Brexit shifting investment from the UK to Germany) and hence lower innovation dynamics and weaker economic growth. All this will be reinforced by the xenophobic AfD, which also sends a negative signal to foreign investors. For Germany, there will be some temptation to really become the dominant EU country of this smaller Community, but that this would be a useful development for the EU as a whole may be doubted.

A weaker EU is less attractive as a political and economic partner for the US and China, the two economic superpowers of the twenty-first century. There is nothing that the UK could gain from less political stability and lower economic growth in continental Europe. Instead, the UK would most likely come under increased pressure from the US to more often support US foreign policy maneuvers and military actions—and this is certainly not a free lunch either.

It is absolutely clear, therefore, that the long-run result of Brexit will be quite negative for the UK. The British economy will be directly weakened, continental Europe will become weaker as well, and the negative economic spillovers from the diminished EU to the weakened UK will be strong. If the EU output should drop (disregarding the pure output reduction related to the UK's leaving of the EU) by 2% in the long run through the immediate Brexit effect, British output should decline by 1–1.5%. This will come on top of the direct output reduction effect of Brexit, which could reach 3–5% in the long run. British output decline during the Great Depression of the 1930s was 6% over two consecutive years of recession. The main difference now will be that the British output decline will be spread over about a decade or so.

A shrinking and unstable EU will cause further instability in the world economy, as other regional integration schemes—e.g., ASEAN in Asia and Mercosur in Latin America—will also be destabilized. With the EU no longer being a stable integration club, there will be doubts about the stability of other integration clubs as well and this will contribute to more regional conflicts and reduced global growth as well as more political nationalism and economic protectionism. Reduced international economic integration typically also means more conflicts so that military expenditures will increase in Europe and indeed worldwide. The Brexit equation has no winners, but will have many losers. Whether Brexit will, in the end, also lead to a new Scottish independence referendum also remains to be seen. At the bottom line, Brexit stands for political brinkmanship in the UK.

Many economists and historians have expressed their views on the Brexit referendum and the overwhelming majority have warned of the negative economic consequences of the UK leaving the EU28. Harold James (2016b) gave an interesting interview to the *Neue Zürcher Zeitung* on July 2, 2016, in which he pointed out that the Remain campaign had overemphasized the potential negative effects of Brexit and had not sufficiently underlined the strong joint benefits of EU integration. Thus, the establishment created the impression that a Remain vote would reflect the fact that the UK had no alternative and such a blocking of political thinking was apparently not accepted by the majority of voters. Moreover, the relevant key scenarios of an actual Brexit had not been developed by the Leave campaign, so that British voters did not really understand the alternative paths the referendum had really offered. At the bottom line, Harold James considered the Brexit referendum outcome to be a historical watershed moment and he suggested that Brexit will bring about a broader perception about the interdependency of major economies in the world in the early twenty-first century.

Brexit is a new decisive political step in the EU, although one might point out that Algeria effectively left the EU in 1962 when the country became independent from France (until then Algeria had been considered an integral part of France) and Greenland has also left the EU, namely when the island decided that it wanted to become independent from Denmark. Brexit is a serious weakening of the EU as it will lose almost 1/5th of its economic weight and also be without the UK's military power and the global British diplomatic network, including the British vote on the UN Security Council. So far, British political decisions have very often been made in such a way as to partly also consider

EU policy action. Looking at Brexit with this in mind, it should be clear that in negotiations with the UK, the EU should offer more generous conditions to the powerful former member than were realized in treaties with Norway or Switzerland. As regards transatlantic trade and investment, one may also point out that the UK is the most important EU partner within the EU28. With Brexit implemented, Germany may assume this role.

It is true that the UK will have to face some negative short-term economic consequences of Brexit, but the short-term effects should naturally be smaller than the long-term effects. Declining order inflows in the UK during the summer of 2016 and massively worsening economic climate indicators in July–September 2016 were the first flashing warning lights on the economic consequences of Brexit.

British Anti-EU Sentiments Partially to be Anticipated in Spring 2016

The wish of the Britons to withdraw from the EU was even in the spring of 2016 only somewhat apparent—for example in the research of Curtice (2015). However, the EU's own Eurobarometer survey showed that even in May, 31% of British respondents had a positive view of the EU; a share not much different to those found in Austria or Germany (see Table 2.2). The figures from the UK were clearly higher than in Cyprus and Greece, where there are so few clear EU supporters that one could imagine an EU exit by those countries as probable. The share of Total 'Negative' is a better indicator of a critical mass against EU membership amongst the Britons surveyed, which was 36% in the May 2016 Eurobarometer poll (the EU average was 27%). Was the European Commission not also warned by Cameron and his predecessor Tony Blair? After Blair's last appearance in Brussels in June 2007, the then President of the European Commission Manuel Barroso said, "The point I have to say is that in Britain, honestly, the debate for Europe is not yet won" (translated from Kielinger 2009, p. 250).

Table 2.2 Attitude towards the EU (%), fieldwork carried out in spring 2016 (Ranked in order of "Total Positive")

	Total positive	Sp. '16– Aut. '15	Neutral	Sp. '16– Aut. '15	Total nega-tive	Sp. '16– Aut. '15	Don't know
Ireland	58	+4	27	−3	14	0	1
Bulgaria	51	+3	30	−4	17	0	2
Poland	47	−8	37	+2	15	+8	1
Luxembourg	45	0	32	−3	22	+2	1
Lithuania	43	−10	47	+7	9	+3	1
Romania	42	−15	43	+11	14	+5	1
Malta	41	−2	43	−3	13	+3	3
Portugal	41	−1	39	−2	18	+3	2
Croatia	37	−14	43	+6	19	+7	1
Sweden	36	−6	38	+2	26	+1	0
France	36	+1	33	−5	29	+4	2
Belgium	35	−4	33	−5	31	+8	1
Denmark	34	−2	42	−3	23	+5	1
EU28	34	−3	38	0	27	+4	1
Estonia	33	−3	47	−3	17	+5	3
Finland	33	+1	44	−4	22	+2	1
Hungary	33	−6	41	+1	25	+5	1
Netherlands	33	−1	38	−3	29	+4	0
Slovenia	32	−1	46	+1	20	−1	2
Italy	32	−6	38	+1	27	+4	3
Austria	32	+9	30	−5	37	−4	1
Latvia	31	−1	49	=	18	+1	2
U.K.	**31**	**+1**	**31**	**−5**	**36**	**+5**	**2**
Spain	30	−3	44	−2	23	+5	3
Slovakia	30	−5	43	+3	26	+2	1
Germany	29	−5	41	+3	29	+2	1
Cyprus	27	+5	32	−4	41	0	0
Czech Rep.	26	−1	40	−2	34	+3	0
Greece	16	−6	33	−7	51	+13	0

Source European Commission, Standard barometer 85—Spring 2016 (fieldwork carried out May), "Public opinion in the European Union , first results, QA9, p. 16, Brussels

Almost a decade was obviously not enough time for the Commission to form a sustainable bond between the UK and the EU—and in truth, the Commission did not really attempt much in that regard. There were no great speeches in London by EU Commissioners, not even by the President of the Commission, prior to the Brexit vote, nor can one speak of the relocation of important EU institutions to the UK apart from the banking supervision body the European Banking Authority (EBA) in London. On the other hand, one can acknowledge that German Finance Minister Schäuble delivered a speech in London in which he argued for the UK to remain part of the EU. Clearly, one might argue that Cameron had signaled to Brussels that a Juncker speech in London would not have been welcome and such a warning, combined with the natural restraint in Brussels when it comes to direct involvement in major national policy decisions, might be a plausible reason for the Commission President having remained in Brussels—but in the end such a strategy is not convincing and indeed a signal of the weakness of EU institutions.

In the Eurobarometer Survey from May 2016, the negative responses are also interesting for EU integration. Very negative attitudes towards the EU were found in the crisis countries of Cyprus and Greece with 41% and 51% 'Total Negative,' respectively. The Czech Republic, with 34% 'Total Negative,' also showed a relatively high level of anti-EU feeling. The negative image of the EU has also clearly risen in Poland, Romania, Croatia, Belgium, Hungary, Spain, and Greece (by 13%), whereby the nationalist courses being taken by the governments of Poland and Hungary are clearly reinforcing anti-EU attitudes. On the other hand, in some Eastern European accession countries, there is definitely political support for the EU. EU transfers to these countries may play a large role here; also, perhaps, the feeling of citizens of these countries that, in the long term, economic prosperity, reliable 'catching-up' processes and the rule of law can best be expected as an EU member country.

Low levels of support for the EU in Cyprus and Greece are obviously related to the Euro Crisis and the necessary austerity and reform policies—partly imposed by the Troika (composed of the International Monetary Fund (IMF), the European Central Bank (ECB), and the European Union)—which were required by these states.

These countries could not simply leave the Eurozone, even if they wished to do so. Rather they would have to leave the EU as well, which is a sensible provision. No country should be able to carelessly join the Eurozone and think that it can simply withdraw from the monetary union again without much ado. Without clearly fulfilling the conditions for membership and a solid political will to continue that membership, joining the Euro area is not a sensible policy option. A monetary union is, in its nature, a long-term objective. It cannot be ruled out that countries such as Cyprus and Greece leave the EU in the medium term. Geopolitically, however, that would be problematic for both the EU and indeed the North Atlantic Treaty Organization (NATO).

That the, as yet, unresolved economic crisis in Greece led to an enormous anti-EU sentiment amongst the Greek populace is not something which should be recognized by the European Commission alone. Here, it would sensible for certain leading EU member states to react. As long as Germany prevents a sensible compromise being agreed with the Tsipras government in Athens, this will not only prevent a solution from being found—at least in relation to a possible partial debt relief—for ideological reasons, but will in fact also feed into the emergence of an anti-EU majority in Greece. That is not in Germany's interest.

In the event of Brexit being completed, the EU would be confronted with new problems vis-à-vis the possible future courses of action open to the European Investment Bank (EIB). The EIB is backing large-scale projects, currently also in the crisis countries, and Brexit would mean a reduction in equity capital of circa 10%. The opponents of sensible rules in the Eurozone would certainly be given a huge boost, should growth-promoting infrastructure projects be cut back by the EIB. The summit of southern EU member states, which Prime Minister Tsipras organized in Athens in September 2016, indicates a possible fault line running through the Eurozone: Portugal, Malta, Italy, Greece, Cyprus, those countries who question the need for a fiscal rulebook in the Eurozone on one side—as if a meaningful event like a football match or an Olympic Games could be held in the absence of any rules. It would be sensible to keep the Eurobarometer figures in mind (Table 2.2):

In Germany, France, and the Netherlands, the dissatisfaction rate, at 29%, was above the EU average; in Belgium the figure was 31%, meaning that a broad level of Euroskepticism was perceptible in four of the EU founding member countries. The attention of the European Commission should have been grabbed by the numbers in the Eurobarometer from May 2016, particularly considering the developments when comparing the figures to the results from the poll carried out the previous autumn: the negative attitudes in the EU28 had risen by 4%, in the UK the increase was 5%. On the other hand, there was only a 1% increase in positive attitudes in the UK, while in Austria there was a 9% rise in positive attitudes.

The Risk of an Endogenous EU Destabilization

As 51.9% of the voters in the British referendum voted in favor of a UK withdrawal from the EU, the Eurobarometer survey figures from spring 2016 are clearly broadly misleading in terms of the measurement of EU attitudes. Furthermore, if one had assumed that the "neutrals," meaning the undecided voters, could in an actual referendum vote in the same proportionate ratio as the Positive and Negative groups, then the European Commission would have had to assume a Brexit majority of 36:31. One can also reinterpret the figures on negative EU attitudes based on the result of the British referendum on June 23, namely a 52% rejection of the EU in the UK, using the following methodology: by increasing the negative attitudes by a factor of 1.44 to get a truer negative than what is shown in the above Eurobarometer table (it can be ruled out that in a matter of only a few weeks the number of EU opponents rose from 36% to 52%). Assuming, on the basis of the UK's negative attitude distortion, that the distortion factor for other EU countries is equally high—admittedly an over-simplification—then the EU28 Negative Attitude towards the EU would not be 27% (the Eurobarometer figure), but actually 39%.

The result of this simple, illustrative adjustment of the figures, would be a negative attitude towards the EU in Germany and France not of 29%, but actually of 42%, in Italy not 27% but rather 39%; in the Czech Republic of 39% and in Austria of 53%. On the basis of these 'revised' figures, it would be immediately apparent that with an EU disintegration dynamic, which would reduce the real economic benefits of integration and growth, respectively, the EU would rapidly enter an existential crisis: once the UK has left the EU, there could be prospects for further disintegration and since disintegration means that the growth dynamics of the EU will decline there would be an endogenous anti-EU momentum in part of the EU27—in periods of lower economic growth the popular support for EU integration always has been lower than in periods of high growth.

The national politics of some EU countries could, within only a few years, lead to an X-EXIT and it would then be only a matter of less than a decade until the EU, as a European integration area, fractured completely. As a period of intensified nationalism would follow years of EU integration, economic crisis symptoms would be linked with political radicalization and soon also with massive conflicts in continental Europe. The non-binding British referendum does not mean the UK's immediate withdrawal from the EU, but it is presumed that Brexit will finally be implemented in 2019 and thus from 2019 there will be an increased risk of EU27 disintegration dynamics should the EU27 and the European Commission prove unable to prevent a disintegration dynamic and take decisive pro-EU integration measures. This will also require that pro-EU actors and representatives publicly engage themselves in a highly visible manner for sustainable EU integration and that the complicated EU system would be simplified, made more citizen-friendly and better understandable. One should also not overlook the growing right-wing populist movement that has emerged in Germany, France, and indeed other countries—with Germany facing the most dangerous dynamics, namely in the course of the refugee wave and Mrs. Merkel's refugee policy. The right-wing Alternative for Germany (known in Germany as the AfD) achieved about 4% in opinion polls in spring 2015 only to jump to two-digit numbers in regional elections in 2016 as a result of the uncontrolled massive refugee inflows for which Mrs. Merkel's refugee policy of early September 2015 was largely responsible—with no EU summit organized to tackle the issue (which would have been possible if Mrs. Merkel had urged the holding of an emergency summit; as had been so often been the case during the Greek crisis).

It is strange that the European Commission did not decide in early 2016—prior to the Brexit referendum—to organize a pro-EU information campaign on an EU-wide basis. While an EU campaign in the UK alone would have been strange, there was no reason for the

Commission not to launch a more general pan-EU information campaign (e.g., under the heading: Taking Stock of EU Benefits and Challenges—60 years after the Treaty of Rome).

The decisive letter from Prime Minister Cameron to the European Commission on November 15, 2015, in which he asked for special negotiations on the status of the UK within the EU was a signal that the referendum was soon to take place in the UK. On February 19, 2016, the EU's negotiations with the UK ended and Cameron clearly assumed that the results would be impressive enough for the British public to secure a pro-EU referendum result. Had the British Prime Minister also considered what the costs of leaving the EU and the benefits of remaining in the community actually are? He had certainly considered this question and the experts in the Treasury were eager to deliver a report on this—with some very clear findings and arguments in favor of remaining in the EU. The point is, however, that these findings were never adequately communicated to British households as will be shown. Mr. Cameron's negotiation results with the EU—obsolete in the case of a real Brexit—were as follows (HM Govt 2016a):

- The UK would not face the obligation to cooperate in the EU under its traditional mantra of "an ever closer union"—a wording found in the Treaty of Rome in 1956. To some extent, this revisionist position of Mr. Cameron is strange, since joining the EU in 1973 meant, of course, subscribing in some way to this historical motto regarding EU integration, while prospects for the twenty-first century—with ongoing US dominance, soon shared with China—will make closer European cooperation in many fields really useful. The stronger EU countries in the EU integration club are in economic terms, the easier it will be to maintain European national and regional identities. European diversity without EU cooperation will be quite difficult to defend, not least against the ever growing influence of China and Asia, respectively.
- The EU assured that the decisions of the Eurozone would not amount to a discrimination of interests of non-Eurozone EU member countries (here, the UK certainly felt some political support from Denmark—which also has an opt-out clause from monetary

union—as well as from Sweden and some Eastern European countries). The Eurozone has experienced serious problems in the Euro Crisis, a crisis that should have been anticipated by the European Commission, national governments, and economic experts (if it had been, it would indeed have largely been avoided—this author wrote about an upcoming crisis in Portugal, Spain, Greece, and Italy in the book manuscript *Transatlantische Bankenkrise*/Transatlantic Banking Crisis in October of 2008 as it seemed fairly obvious that the Banking Crisis was such a fundamental shock to investors' confidence that it would reinforce the flight into quality investments meaning that countries with high deficit–GDP ratios and high debt–GDP ratios (possibly in combination with high current account deficits and thus high foreign indebtedness) were bound to be in financial trouble soon unless they would drastically and credibly adopt a new fiscal policy stance).

- The EU agreed that improving international competitiveness is an important task and that the EU regulatory burden should be reduced; it is, however, not clear what the EU could really do—beyond leaner regulations in some fields—to improve international competitiveness, since the power to set national framework conditions for the business community and to finance innovation support schemes lies primarily with EU member countries themselves—not with the EU.
- The UK would get the right to exclude EU immigrants into the UK from full access to the British social welfare system for several years.

The latter condition is especially confusing since the UK has a strong economic net benefit from EU immigration as the Organisation for Economic Co-operation and Development (OECD) has pointed out in various publications. It is, however, an interesting clause in the negotiation package for all EU countries since it points to potential future changes that other EU countries may seek in order to restrict immigration pressures in a way that is compatible with the EU single market. It also points to a potential clause in a future EU–UK negotiation package with a focus on British conditions for EU access.

From a game theory perspective, Cameron's strategy to go for an EU referendum was founded upon two main motivations, namely to get a stronger bargaining position vis-à-vis the EU on one hand, and to obtain the ultimate voter signal that would help to defeat the Tory backbenchers with anti-EU sentiments who were becoming restless, and even defecting from the party, on the other. After the referendum results became clear on the morning of June 24, it was obvious that Cameron's strategy had totally failed.

Betting Odds and Contradictions Between Capital Markets and Democracy

It is clear that opinion polls prior to the referendum suggested a narrow outcome. At the same time, the implied voting probabilities of British betting companies pointed towards a clear Remain majority (Fig. 2.1). Capital markets also suggested during the two weeks prior to the referendum that the outcome expected by well-informed institutional investors was a majority vote for Remain. This is all a serious paradox and represents somewhat of a problem for democracy: had the British Pound strongly depreciated and stock market prices plunged, a majority of undecided voters would have voted in favor of Remain for fear of the negative consequences indicated by such capital market reactions. However, the overly optimistic view of capital markets, that there would be a majority for Remain and thus the conclusion not to take positions expecting a declining exchange rate of the Pound and declining stock market prices, encouraged a (large) majority of undecided voters to take the risk and follow the emotional anti-EU allure of Vote Leave/ the Brexiteers. Capital markets and major investors thus contributed in bringing about a self-destructing outcome.

Democratic results in a referendum are clearly influenced and biased by capital market dynamics in certain cases, and the UK referendum of 2016 is one such case. The best way to get a neutral capital market impact would be to ban capital market transactions for at least two weeks prior to the referendum date. Can capitalism and the British

Implied Probability of a "Remain" vote in the BREXIT Referendum

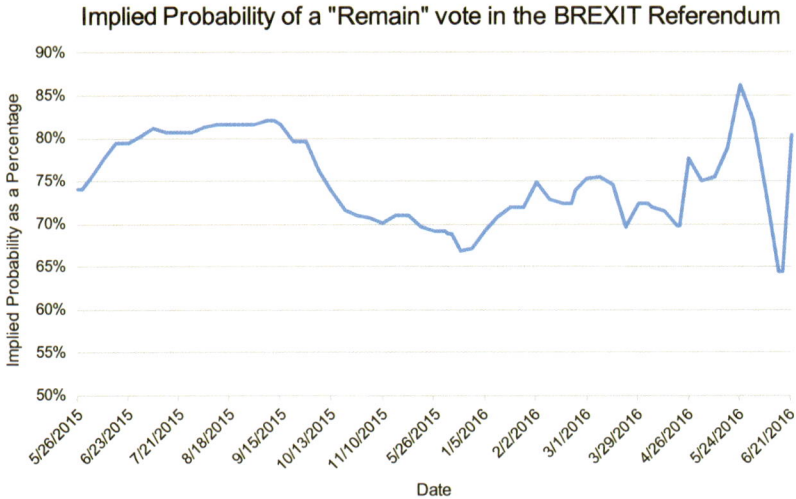

Fig. 2.1   British betting odds and implied probability of a vote to remain in the EU. *Source* Own calculations using data available at www.oddschecker.com

democracy—and the West as a whole—afford itself such a rational solution? There will be many in the business community who will say that this means lost business, and yes, it does. However, the effective capital market bias against a Brexit vote—remember: capital market signals discouraged the undecided voters to take Leave risks into consideration and thus caused an abnormally low share of undecided voters to vote for Remain—contributed to Brexit. The expected output loss, according to British government analysis (a Treasury study, published on April 18, 2016), is 3–10% and these costs are much higher than would be caused by closing down capital markets for two weeks. The alternative would possibly be for the UK not to rely on referendum decisions in future, but to expect Parliament—the traditionally strong actor in the British political system (as has been confirmed in the Supreme Court ruling of January 24, 2017)—to take up its responsibility and decide on politically critical decisions.

One may note that in the case that the capital markets had brought about a sufficiently strong devaluation of the Pound, there would likely have been a victory for the Remain side (a case of a self-fulfilling prophecy). At the bottom line, this is an interesting theoretical point, but as regards the British referendum outcome, some other points, mainly related to the Cameron government's communication strategy, were even more important and indeed baffling as will be shown subsequently. It should be noted that the majority of 51.9% for Leave was not really strong, a swing of just 700,000 Leave voters to the Remain camp would have been sufficient for a pro-EU referendum outcome. This also points to the crucial role that swing voters have in all elections and it is clear that a good campaign has two key elements: firstly, the mobilization of traditional supporters, and secondly the influencing of undecided voters in a decisive way.

As regards the signals from betting firms, it seems obvious that major investors in the UK were also making bets and many investors in capital markets probably took the resulting betting odds as a signal to speculate in capital markets and the foreign exchange market in expectation of the Remain majority the betting odds, and markets, suggested. Exactly what a mess this interaction of capital markets and voters had actually produced in the UK could only be fully understood in the days after the referendum results had become clear—when capital market actors had to correct themselves. The wisdom of capital markets is not as strong as is usually emphasized in textbook models and the rare case of confusing interactions between capital market signals and voters' behavior in a referendum have not been researched in-depth so far. The critical question of linkages between democracy and capital markets is a broader one since national elections and capital market dynamics are also interrelated.

Some Perspectives

Good governance can only occur when the sentiments of the population over the course of time are fairly accurately assessed by government. The European Commission obviously had, on the basis of its less than sound Eurobarometer surveys which are carried out twice a year, no usable information basis and it would be well advised to clearly improve the methodological basis of its important Eurobarometer polls.

The Commission's polling results are, as a result of the weak methodology employed, capable of misleading political actors and the public. As long as the Commission bases its own communication and economic policies on Eurobarometer findings, communication and policy will not be particularly effective.

It raises the question of whether in the long term there should not be an attempt to create more positive support for the EU, by improving the construction of the EU itself: it must be more beneficial for both citizens and member states. Thus, the EU must increasingly focus on relevant policy areas, which should, based on the theory of fiscal federalism (Oates 1999, 2001), be transferred to the supranational layer— infrastructure, defense, and income distribution are three areas which are completely lacking in Brussels; instead of paying income transfers to relatively poor individual regions, the EU should, via the income tax system, participate directly in redistributive transfers. As long as the EU does not have its own independent tax-raising powers, it will always be dependent on member states for more than 90% of the financing side of its budget and thus lack visibility for the electorate. If one can realize efficiency gains in terms of the fields of competence and spending, respectively, in Brussels within the framework of an intelligent vertical division of powers, then one can reduce the entire tax burden—across all policy layers. A reduction of the average income tax rate by almost one percentage point should be possible in the longer term. The individual EU member states would consider above all power gains and political autonomy: a well-organized Neo-EU, which can ensure successful growth and stability, is also an advantage at the national and regional political levels.

On the contrary, governmental work at a national level during the years of the Euro Crisis (2010–2015) was certainly made more difficult as a result of instability and uncertainty at an EU level. Moreover, it should be considered that a successful, stable monetary union offers substantial economic benefits, assuming a world market share of the Euro in global reserves of 25%; this allows the possibility of annual "free" imports in the amount of 0.5% of GDP. If this is capitalized in the long term with an interest rate of 2.5%, the relevant present value is 20% of GDP. The Euro is, taking the savings in transaction costs into account, even more valuable in a functioning monetary union; however, a transfer to a supranational fiscal policy with constitutional national limits on the deficit ratio is essential. This can only be achieved in the longer term. Brexit does, however, provide a reason to reconsider the costs and benefits of EU membership from an economic perspective. What developments were behind Brexit, what comes now for Great Britain, what EU reforms are required? The question of what the Brexit majority has created remains, as yet, unanswered: is the annoyance of a net annual contribution to the EU of £110/$135 per capita in the UK so great and the 150,000 immigrants per year from EU members such a burden in a land of 65 million inhabitants? Hardly. It is clear that some EU regulations are an irritation to the economy and that the EU did not give the best impression of itself during the Euro Crisis, even less so during the refugee crisis. But in truth, Brexit was only partly about EU issues. Above all, the population in the UK wanted to show the political establishment in London the proverbial red card and clearly demonstrate the massive smoldering loss of confidence which has existed since the Banking Crisis to the ruling political circles. The man on the street in the UK will hardly follow the advice of government any longer. Too great is the disappointment over the terrible Banking Crisis of 2007–2009 with huge job and wealth losses, the subsequent increase in the state's budget deficit ratio plus the rise in debt ratio of almost 40%, and the doubling of tuition fees as a result of a revenue crisis in the state university sector. At the same time, the public was becoming aware of the often extravagant incomes of certain poorly performing top managers of some of the large banks; one top banker was even found to have been fare dodging for years while commuting by rail to work every day in London. The reputation of the British political elites, which created the wrong conditions for the financial markets and banks, respectively, has been massively impaired.

Where Did British EU Skepticism Come From?

If one considers that the votes in favor of leaving the EU came primarily from the elderly strata of society and those with a rather modest educational background, then one can draw the following conclusions from the Brexit vote in conjunction with the analysis of Curtice (2016):

- EU integration is endangered by the aging of societies, which seems at worst to encourage the emergence of neo-nationalism—or at best a nostalgic concept of national political autonomy, which in reality no longer exists in western European countries in the twenty-first century. With the rise of China and the ASEAN-countries, the European states are confronted with huge challenges, where China will emerge as a leading global power alongside the US. That a European country acting alone has good chances to represent its interests on the world stage in the twenty-first century is doubtful.
- EU integration is also endangered by a lack of education, which also makes one susceptible to cultural nationalism and a fear of immigration. One can also assume that in the context of the refugee crisis of 2015, a stronger interest on the part of the electorate in controlled immigration will emerge.
- Above all, a majority of those people who view EU integration as undermining British identity are Euroskeptic. A British study (Curtice 2016, Table 8, p. 14f.) before the Brexit referendum showed that amongst those who feel that the EU undermines Britain's distinctive identity, 93% of those who 'strongly agree' with that hypothesis are Euroskeptic, while 82% of those who 'agree' with the hypothesis are Euroskeptic. For those who 'strongly disagree,' the share of Europhiles was 68% (results reproduced here in Table 2.3). Thus, one can, with regard to the UK, see that before the Brexit vote the EU should have appealed more with the message to British voters to ensure them that the UK would still be welcome in the EU, even if did not participate in every EU integration initiative. Such a message was sorely lacking, and one could draw the conclusion that the aforementioned study from Curtice (2016) was unknown to both the European Council and the European Commission.

Table 2.4 presents some findings from a study by Curtice (2015, Table 2; see also Cleary/Simpson 2016) showing different attitudes to Brexit depending on highest level of education: those with no qualifications were the only group who expected that after Brexit the economy of the UK would be better outside of the EU: 33% was the respective share for this group, while 44% foresaw not much difference between

Table 2.3   Attitude towards the EU by level of cultural concern

	EU is undermining Britain's distinctive identity				
	% Strongly agree	% Agree	% Neither	% Disagree	% Strongly disagree
(a) *Withdraw v Continue*					
Withdraw	80	42	9	4	3
Continue	17	46	75	92	95
Unweighted sample size	*198*	*350*	*216*	*242*	*65*
(b) *Eurosceptic v Europhile*					
Eurosceptic	93	82	47	55	27
Europhile	6	17	43	42	68
Unweighted sample size	*198*	*350*	*216*	*242*	*65*

Source Curtice (2016, Table 8, p. 14)

the UK remaining in the EU and the UK leaving the EU; just 16% foresaw a worsening of the economy after Brexit.

In the group with basic educational qualification (i.e., O-Level or equivalent), 27% felt that one could expect an improvement in the UK economy after Brexit, with 36% expecting no difference. Even amongst those with the second highest educational attainment (A-Level or equivalent), there was a majority opinion that the Brexit would not damage the UK economically, with only 44% expecting a worsened situation. That is obviously a fundamental misjudgment, and this study from 2015 should have been a double incentive for the Cameron government to include in the information for households prior to the referendum the findings of the Treasury study of April 18, 2016, about a sharp drop in income. Here, one can see that insufficient economic information from the side of government in the event of a referendum would lead to a 'veil of ignorance' for many sections of the population. For those with higher educational attainment (Bachelor Degree), the share who foresaw an economic worsening as a result of Brexit was 65%, while 19% assumed that there would be no change; only 15% in this group expected that the British economic situation would improve. What is also interesting is the relative differences in relation to the question of whether the UK would have a greater influence on the world stage after leaving the EU: for those with no qualification, the share with a

Table 2.4 Attitudes on the referendum outcome based on level of qualification

	Degree (%)	A level/Higher education below degree (%)	O Level or equivalent (%)	No qualifications (%)	All (%)
If Britain were to leave the EU, Britain's economy would be …					
Better off	15	21	27	33	24
Not much different	19	30	36	44	31
Worse off	65	44	31	16	40
If Britain were to leave the EU, immigration into Britain would be …					
Higher	6	9	8	13	9
Not much different	34	27	35	31	31
Lower	60	61	52	53	57
If Britain were to leave the EU, Britain's influence in the world would be …					
More	11	15	15	26	17
Not much different	33	45	51	49	44
Less	56	37	30	19	36
If Britain were to leave the EU, unemployment in Britain would be …					
Higher	36	19	20	26	25
Not much different	39	50	48	47	46
Lower	22	25	26	21	24
Unweighted base	260	293	280	248	1105

Source Curtice (2015, Table 2, p. 7)

positive view was 26%; for those with a degree it was 11%, and for this grouping, the share of those who saw the UK having less of an influence after Brexit was 56%. For those with no qualification, only 19% foresaw the UK having less influence globally. Put bluntly, one can say that nostalgic retirees and lower educated voters with a less than accurate world view dumped the UK, after almost 45 years of membership, out of the EU. That UKIP with their sloganeering played into the illusory viewpoint of the less educated and mobilized them as voters for Brexit is obvious. Finally, it is noteworthy that the subjective estimation of the share of immigrants in the UK amongst the British population was about three times as high as the actual share really is.

Critical questions are raised here about the benefits of referenda in the case of rather complicated issues. On the one hand, one can naturally regard referenda as the highest expression of democracy. On the other hand, considering the 'state of ignorance' in a Rawlsian sense—where one does not know his own actual future position in society—one could ask what kind of questions should be decided by referendum or whether, in a referendum, a minimum standard (e.g., a 60% majority or other qualified majority) which must be met for there to be a change in the status quo could be required, or whether there could be two-stage process with a popular consultation on an issue to begin and then, one year later, the actual decisive referendum could be held.

The Brexit decision does not cast British democracy in a particularly good light—the referendum was carried out in a formally correct manner; however, there was an absence of solid and timely information from government. As the issue of the referendum on EU membership was put on the agenda by Cameron as early as 2013, the poor preparations for the actual vote are all the more incomprehensible. As can be seen from the above, educational policy is obviously also integration policy, and a society with a high share of people with no educational qualifications in the electorate will lack the ability to engage in sustainable international integration. From this perspective, Germany, with its relatively low share of unskilled, is structurally-speaking a relatively integration-friendly EU member state.

The lessons for the UK which can be drawn from the results of the British surveys, but also for other EU countries in particular, are that the European Union would be well advised not to undermine the sense of identity of citizens of EU member states through certain political actions and/or to create a broader feeling of insecurity and uncertainty. Uncontrolled and, for the purposes of integration, badly organized immigration thus belongs to the problematic issues to be considered here, along with the possible accession of Turkey to the EU.

It cannot be overlooked that part of the anti-EU sentiment in the UK can be explained on the basis of the bad impression which EU integration—including the Euro monetary union—created between the years 2010 and 2015. A sensible and credible rulebook for deficit policies is important; to date the European Commission has seemed reluctant to fully impose the rules of the Stability and Growth Pact; at the same time, the national constitutional deficit limits, or debt brakes, in the Eurozone countries are rather weak, although a relevant regulation would actually act to relieve pressure on the economic policies and raise the stability of the Euro. A deficit limit which is too restrictive, as is the case in Germany's Basic Law, is also questionable: a 0% cyclical deficit ratio for the individual states in Germany from 2019, and 0.35% for the Federal Republic itself since 2016 is too low, as a trend growth rate of 1.5% will result in a long-term debt ratio 23.3%. The insufficient implementation of EU rules on the limit of the deficit and debt ratios of EU member states creates a dangerous credibility problem in the Euro club: both within and to the outside world, where crucial principles of liability are also undermined. Reforms, particularly after Brexit, must give better incentives in the Eurozone for sound economic policy, while in the future the deficit ratio for countries with a B rating should be set at a lower limit than countries with an A rating: countries with at least an AA rating with regard to sovereign debt could automatically receive a grace period of three years to get the deficit ratio back under 3%. Countries with a rating of at least investment grade would have two years, and C-rated countries only one. That should incentivize countries to position themselves in the top credit rating classes and furthermore it is sensible that countries with a good debtor grading or top rating (AA or AAA) would receive the largest room to maneuver in terms of deficit policies which they have earned. President of the Bundesbank Jens Weidmann (Weidmann 2016) on the topic of Brexit said in a speech in Munich on the June 1, 2016: "I completely agree with the President of the European Parliament, who wishes for a "closer and more unified European Union"."

Wishful Thinking, Interests and Nationalism

When it comes to questions of EU integration, it is worth remembering that the EU has experienced a range of crises (Knipping 2004)—and it is often argued that successful solutions are found during those crises. This EU formula for success has initially been called into question by Brexit. Neither the European Commission nor the heads of state and government of the EU27, from whom Cameron negotiated concessions for his country just four months prior to the referendum, nor indeed the British government itself, recognized the seriousness of the situation in the UK and ultimately in the EU28. Since Brexit, every group and body which seeks less European integration or wants to leave the EU altogether feels reinvigorated and given a new purpose. Brexit has the effect of an amplifier for all nationalist groups, no matter how illusory their policy platform or manifesto may seem—they obviously have a level of appeal to many voters in crucial countries and it is possible that since the end of the Soviet Union a new historic tendency towards nationalism has emerged in the west and east of Europe; beginning with the reunification of Germany and a new Polish and Hungarian nationalism, as well as the rise of Marine Le Pen and her party the Front National in France and other populist movements in Finland, Denmark, the Netherlands, and Belgium, plus Italy and Spain (Catalonia in particular).

The economist Harry G. Johnson once alluded to the fact that nationalism gives people a form of quasi value-added, which can have the effect of a rise in income (Johnson 1967). Many people clearly have a psychological disposition towards obtaining some sort of personal value-added through a nationalistic attribution of identity; this usually also involves a differentiation from other nations and therefore nationalism is seldom capable of sustainable international cooperation, rather it leads to the emergence of conflict driven by rivalries. Nationalism naturally brings a different type of value-added to that which, from an economic perspective, one can imagine as an EU member state, that is a politico-economic club benefit (according to Buchanan/Tullock 1962): together, each one can achieve his own goals better, whether in a cooperative or in a club. There is a membership contribution, which could be determined based on the self-interest of each of the members, which in turn can be affected by structural factors—such as the sectoral structure of the economy—or the size of a land or even the level of per capita income.

Club benefits, from the point of view of the member countries, rise to a certain level as a result of a rising number of member countries, as then one can more easily enforce interests globally. With the growing number of member countries, however, also grows the cost of consensus and organization. Thus, there is surely an optimal number of members, which one should not flippantly exceed. Otherwise, incentives would emerge for countries to withdraw from the club at some point. As a general rule, the first such withdrawal stimulates impulses in other countries to imitate the move. That alone already weakens the integration dynamic, and calls for an analysis of the net benefits of membership, where the benefits will be compared with the costs of membership (e.g., contribution payments). The EU functions on the basis of the assumption that a common external trade policy, a common agricultural policy—key term: a guarantee of supply—and a framework of competition and regulatory policies, deliver benefits for member states. In the case of the Eurozone, there is also the idea that a common central bank and common monetary policy, respectively, can bring economic benefits.

The consensus costs in a club such as the EU are a positive function of the difference in per capita income. This implies that economic convergence, here a harmonization of per capita incomes over the course of time, also has a political benefit—namely easier consensus building: countries with similar per capita incomes tend to have more similar interests than a group of countries with members which have highly varied per capita incomes. Economic convergence will thus always be an important goal for a sensible and rational integration area.

Of course there are also long-term differences in income between member countries; however, some sort of minimum convergence should be sustainably reached. Thus, the Banking Crisis and the Euro Crisis did not have a conducive effect on EU integration, as they caused the differences in per capita income to actually grow for some time. For all the criticism of lacking fiscal policy coordination and inadequate national deficit ratio rules for the member states of the Eurozone, it should not be overlooked that the policies implemented did indeed achieve some institutional innovations—recently, the stabilization fund for the Eurozone—and some improvements in the rules; and also in the stabilization of the crisis countries. While there are a number of grounds why Greece can be regarded as an outlying special case, it cannot be ignored that reform policies were effective in most crisis countries and brought some success, so that after four years of crisis in the Eurozone, one can be optimistic once again. Naturally, that is not to say that the reforms required by the Eurozone and the EU have all already been dealt with.

References

Baldwin, R., et al. (2016). *Brexit Beckons: Thinking ahead by leading economists.* A VoxEU.org Book. CEPR Press. Available for download at http://voxeu.org/system/files/epublication/Brexit_Beckons_VoxEU.pdf.

Bertelsmann Foundation. (2016). "Bleibt Doch. Die Kontinentaleuropäer, das Britische Referendum und ein möglicher Brexit", de Vries, C. und Hoffmann, I., eupinions #2016/2.

Buchanan, J., & Tullock, G. (1962). The calculus of consent: logical foundations of constitutional democracy, Ann Arbor.

Cleary, E., & Simpson, I. (2016). BREXIT: What will it mean for Britain? Findings from British Social Attitudes 2015. NatCen/The UK in a Changing Europe/ESRC, London.

Curtice, J. (2015). BREXIT: What will it mean for Britain? Findings from British Social Attitudes 2015. NatCen/The UK in a Changing Europe/ESRC, London.

Curtice, J. (2016). *How deeply does Britain's Euroscepticism Run?* NatCen/The UK in a Changing Europe, London. Available at http://www.bsa.natcen.ac.uk/media/39024/euroscepticism.pdf.

Francois, J., et al. (2013). *Reducing transatlantic barriers to trade and investment.* London: CEPR (for the European Commission).

The Guardian. (2016, March 20). *Britons and Europe: The survey results.* Available at https://www.theguardian.com/politics/2016/mar/20/britons-on-europe-survey-results-opinium-poll-referendum.

HM Government. (2014a). *"Our place in the world"—Scotland Office, Scottish referendum information.* https://www.gov.uk/government/publications/scottish-independence-referendum-our-place-in-the-world/scottish-independence-referendum-our-place-in-the-world.

HM Government. (2014b). *"Make sure you have all the facts when you decide Scotland's future"—Scottish referendum information.* https://www.gov.uk/government/uploads/system/uploads/attachment_data/file/340078/Make_sure_you_have_the_facts_when_you_decide_Scotland_s_future.pdf.

HM Government. (2016a, February). *The best of both worlds: The United Kingdom's special status in a reformed European Union, London.* Available at https://www.gov.uk/government/uploads/system/uploads/attachment_data/file/502291/54284_EU_Series_No1_Web_Accessible.pdf.

HM Government. (2016b, April). *HM treasury analysis: The long-term economic impact of EU membership and the alternatives, London.* Available online https://www.gov.uk/government/publications/hm-treasury-analysis-the-long-term-economic-impact-of-eu-membership-and-the-alternatives.

HM Government. (2017). Prime Minister May's speech on Brexit, Lancaster House speech delivered January 17, 2017. Available online https://www.gov.uk/government/speeches/the-governments-negotiating-objectives-for-exiting-the-eu-pm-speech.

James, H. (2016a). Britain and Europe: What ways forward? *International Economics and Economic Policy, 13,* 523–530.

James, H. (2016b). Churchill hätte sich zur EU bekannt. Warum der Brexit eine tiefe Zäsur für das moderne Großbritannien bedeutet: Gespräch mit dem britischen Historiker Harold James. *Neue Zürcher Zeitung.* International Edition, Zürich, July 2016. pp. 21–22.

Jaumotte, F., Lall, S., & Papageorgiou, C. (2008). *Rising income inequality: Technology, or trade and financial globalization.* IMF (Working Paper WP/08/185). Washington DC.

Johnson, H. G. (1967). *Economic nationalism in old and new states.* Chicago: University of Chicago Press.

Jungmittag, A., & Welfens, P. J. J. (2016). *Beyond EU-US trade dynamics: TTIP effects related to foreign direct investment and innovation.* EIIW paper No. 214—presented at the IMF, Washington DC, June 28, 2016. Forthcoming in Journal www.eiiw.eu.

Kielinger, T. (2009). *Großbritannien*. Munich: Beck.

Knipping, F. (2004). *Rom 25. März 1957. Die Einigung Europas*. Munich: Beck.

Mason, R., et al. (2016, February 20). EU referendum to take place on June 23. David Cameron confirms. *The Guardian*, Online Edition.

Mix, D. (2016). *The United Kingdom and the European Union: Stay or go*. Washington DC: Congressional Research Service.

Oates, W. E. (1999). An essay on fiscal federalism. *Journal of Economic Literature, 37*, 1120–1149.

Oates, W. E. (2001). Fiscal competition and European Union: Contrasting perspectives. *Regional Science and Urban Economics, 31*, 133–145.

Ryan, C. (2016). Where does one start to make sense of Brexit. *International Economics and Economic Policy, 13*, 531–537.

Weidmann, J. (2016). Acceptance speech having received the Hans Möller medal. Annual Event of the Alumni Club of Munich Economists, Deutsche Bundesbank Eurosystem, 1.7.2016.

Welfens, P. J. J. (2016a). British referendum pains and the EU implications of Brexit, AICGS Contribution on Brexit http://www.aicgs.org/issue/british-referendum-pains-and-the-eu-implications-of-Brexit/.

Welfens, P. J. J. (2016b). Cameron's information disaster in the referendum of 2016: An exit from Brexit? *International Economics and Economic Policy, 13*, 539–548.

Welfens, P. J. J. (2016c). *Brexit aus Versehen*. Wiesbaden: Springer.

3

A Sequencing of the Economic Effects of Brexit

The first impact is the devaluation of the Pound—about 15% in 2016. A decline of relative real estate price dynamics was also observed. Output growth was still considerable in 2016, partly reflecting the ongoing high immigration figures and real consumption growth, while the investment–Gross Domestic Product (GDP) ratio started to decline in late 2016—very strongly so in the automotive sector, where a lack of reinvestment and lower net investment have coincided. It is also clear that the Pound's real devaluation, associated with the referendum of 2016, will be beneficial for the UK's trade balance and net exports, respectively, so that GDP is raised. The real devaluation also implies that profits from foreign subsidiaries—expressed in domestic (UK) goods units—are increased, so that real income is raised. At the same time, there is a long-run implication, namely that international mergers and acquisitions will increase, that is more foreign firms will acquire British companies—which has a negative impact on long-run national income and the maximum long-run per capita consumption, respectively (a point that could be explained in the context of a modified neoclassical growth model with—cumulated—foreign direct investment flows; see Welfens 2017a). The model of Froot and Stein (1991)

© The Author(s) 2017
P.J.J. Welfens, *An Accidental Brexit*,
DOI 10.1007/978-3-319-58271-9_3

explains why a real devaluation will raise foreign direct investment inflows in a world of imperfect capital markets. One may note that Gross National Income (GNI) is equal to GDP plus net income (here mainly dividend income) from abroad and while often overlooked, even in Economics textbooks, exports, imports, and consumption are proportionate to GNI—not to GDP; this has to be emphasized for long-run analysis in open economies with foreign direct investment (Welfens 2011). One may wonder whether or not the high stock market relative price indices in the UK, triggered by the US, will be sustainable. As a short-term phenomenon, such increases in asset price will raise investment (reflecting a Tobin's Q effect). The strong devaluation rate of 2016 raises, along with higher oil and gas prices, the medium-term inflation rate. As foreign and domestic firms fear a worsening EU single market effect in the future, the investment–GDP ratio started to fall in late 2016 and a rise of the real interest rate in late 2017 could reinforce this effect (there is a dampening counter-effect from rising stock market prices which reflect US economic expansion under Trump). The real wage growth of 2016/17 is lower than anticipated and, therefore, employment growth should be positive and output can further increase in 2017, however, at a reduced rate (see Fig. 3.1).

In 2017/18, British trade unions will push for higher nominal wages so that real wage growth will dampen employment expansion and output growth. In 2019 comes the full Brexit, accompanied by a US–UK Transatlantic Trade and Investment Partnership free trade agreement (i.e., a US–UK mini-TTIP); more free trade with Japan is also possible. The budget deficit will rise since there is declining employment, but output growth can still be above 1% due to the trade expansion effects of the US–UK free trade agreement which, of course, makes the UK more dependent on the US. The inflation rate will rise and enhanced financial market volatility will become a critical challenge. UK–EU trade diversion effects will dampen growth and British foreign direct investment (FDI) inflows will temporarily be reduced, despite the real depreciation. A US-driven international wave of mergers and acquisitions could even raise foreign direct investment inflows in the medium term for specific reasons.

Post-Referendum Economic Development in UK

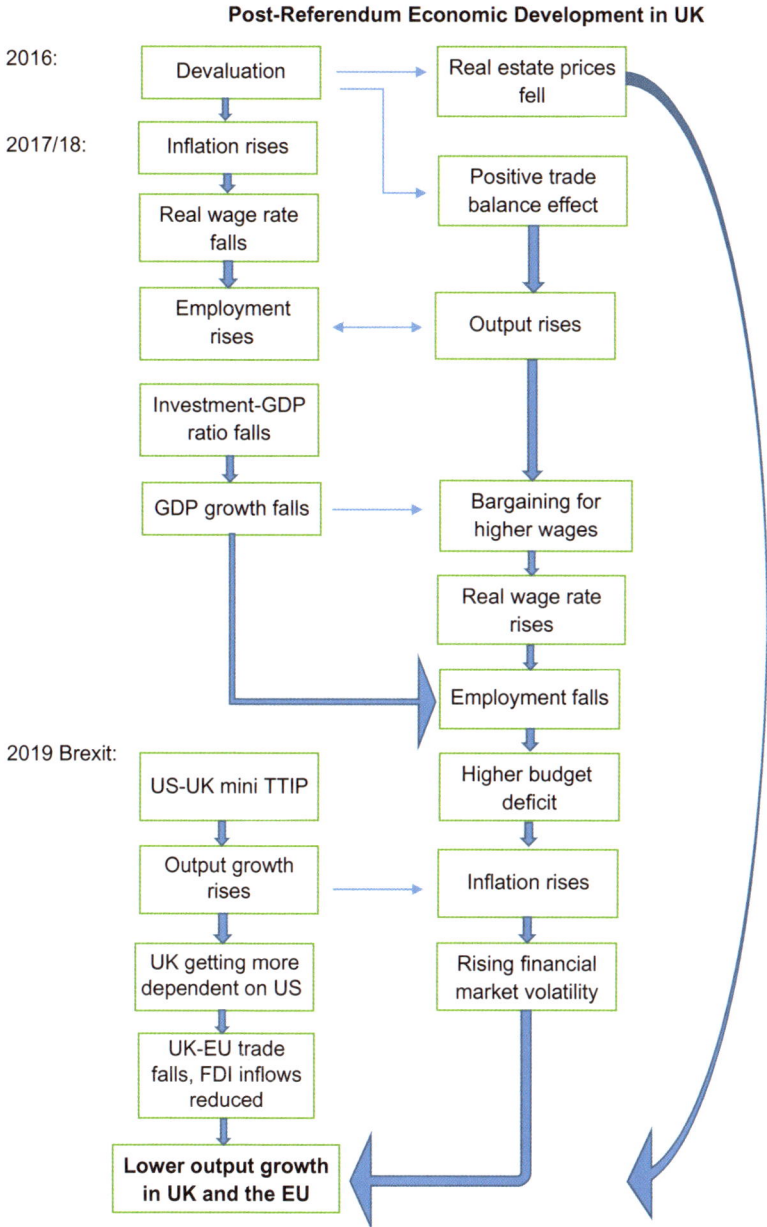

Fig. 3.1   Post-referendum Brexit economic effects in the UK

UK's Foreign Direct Investment Inflows and Brexit

The United Kingdom as an EU member country has been an important destination country for foreign investors from North America, the EU27 and Asia. The stock of foreign direct investment in 2015 was slightly above £1,000 billion ($1,220 billion) which is about 40% of the UK's GDP. After Brexit—and assuming limited access to the EU27 single market—the optimal capital stock in the UK will be lower than before Brexit so that both domestic capital formation and foreign direct investment inflows will reduce over several years. Government's ability to counter this adjustment pressure via a reduction of the corporate tax rate will not be particularly successful since foreign investors will not anticipate that significant reductions of the corporate tax rate would receive the backing of both major political parties in the UK. As regards the main recipient sectors of foreign direct investment in the UK, the leading sectors have been banking/financial services (accounting for about 45% of capital inflows), part of the manufacturing sector (e.g., automotive), and real estate.

A useful method to get an idea of how Brexit affects the UK's inward foreign direct investment is to consider the results of gravity modeling: foreign direct investment is considered to be a function of domestic GDP or the market size of GNI, the GDP of the source countries of foreign investment (1, 2…j), distance between the UK and the respective source country, plus a dummy variable which captures the impact of EU membership of the respective source country. Bruno et al. (2016) have developed such a model and Dhingra et al. (2016) discuss the key findings and further implications on UK income dynamics. McGrattan and Waddle (2017) have also developed a model, namely based on simulations of a multi-country, neoclassical growth model that includes multinational firms investing in research and development. The authors make the assumption that the British government will impose unilateral restrictions on foreign direct inflows from EU27 countries, which leads British firms to invest more in research and development; however, this assumption is not very convincing since post-Brexit, the

UK's government will have an interest in attracting more foreign direct investment from all countries. The authors come up with the finding that a British reduction of non-EU countries' foreign direct investment—the US and Japan—will lead to higher foreign direct investment in the UK and positive welfare effects. According to Bruno et al. (2016), the UK's leaving of the EU should reduce inward foreign direct investment to the UK by 14–38%. Assuming a 22% decline in foreign direct investment inflows, Dhingra et al. (2016) calculate that income losses related to reduced inflows to the UK will range from 1.3 to 2.6%. The estimated impact on the British car industry is that UK output will fall by 181,000 cars—an equivalent of 12%—and automotive prices will increase by 2.5%. If one assumes a broad sectoral EU–UK free trade deal, production would still reduce by 36,000 cars. As regards the British financial services sector, a restriction on "single passport" privileges after the UK's leaving of the EU would cause a high reduction of activities in the City.

The studies mentioned have not explicitly considered that sectoral free trade arrangements between the EU and the UK would go along with rules of origin that will typically require that 60% of value-added is from the EU and the UK, respectively; goods that are below this limit will (probably) not enjoy free trade benefits on a bilateral basis. Moreover, one also has to consider that there will be higher British foreign direct investment outflows which, in turn, imply that the mirror to the capital balance position, the current account, will become even more negative. This implies a considerable real devaluation. However, taking into account that with a high real devaluation of the British Pound, the UK becomes more attractive for foreign investors—in line with the argumentation from Froot/Stein (1991) with their focus on international mergers and acquisitions in a world of imperfect capital markets—then the medium-term impact will be that foreign direct investment inflows of the UK will be raised: in the long run, a higher share of the British capital stock will be in the hands of foreign investors and the gap between British gross national income and gross domestic product will increase. It should be emphasized that consumption is not proportionate to GDP but to GNI—a point that is mostly overlooked in the literature (however, see Welfens 2011).

If a wave of inward foreign direct investment via more international mergers and acquisitions should reinforce a concentration of suppliers, higher prices for British consumers and negative additional welfare effects can be expected. If the City should face a considerably lower inflow of foreign investment plus considerable outflows via the relocation of foreign banks' subsidiaries to EU27 countries, there will be considerable job losses—primarily jobs that are rather well paid—and possibly also the loss of significant support for British research which has been funded by banks in the UK. As the UK's financial market will be fragmented from that of the EU27, the competition intensity in financial services sectors both in the UK and in the EU single financial market could reduce—with negative welfare effects for customers. At the global regulatory policy level, the Trump administration's push for a new deregulation of the banking industry could effectively bring reduced regulation for both the US and the UK, and in the long run, also for the EU27. This, in turn, is likely to imply less financial stability as well as more fragmented markets. The attractiveness of the UK for foreign investors finally depends on the relative progress of reforms in the EU27: if the EU could organize a more efficient integration scheme as a consequence of Brexit, the UK would suffer higher foreign direct investment diversion than indicated by recent empirical models. If, however, the EU fails to come up with needed reforms, the interest of foreign investors in the UK in producing goods in and providing services from the UK for global markets will be higher than these modeling approaches suggest.

There is one small caveat for the long run: the digitization of the economy is growing worldwide, making the provision of services more easily traded—this could be a disadvantage to several OECD countries, particularly those which lack skilled workers and have insufficient broadband density infrastructure investment. The UK has some weak points in the field of skilled workers; however, the UK also has a strong history of rather efficient regulation of the telecommunications sector which implies that infrastructure modernization often comes at a lower cost than in some of the key EU27 countries. Thus, to understand the full picture, further research into certain critical topics and issues will be needed in the future.

The latter, following Froot and Stein (1991), implies higher FDI inflows as foreign investors have a better chance now in terms of international mergers and acquisitions since the Pound devaluation means that the equity of foreign investors, expressed in Sterling, will increase. The output growth of the United Kingdom will reduce in 2019—this will partly also reflect reduced EU27 output growth linked to European trade diversion in the following years, and the UK repercussion effect indeed is negative. The best the European Commission could do to reinforce EU27 growth dynamics is to make sure that there are strong, credible institutional reforms in the Eurozone and that new free trade agreements with Japan and other Asian countries are in place in 2019. In the six years following the EU–Korea free trade agreement, EU exports to South Korea have increased by 50%, which largely reflects the impact of reduced tariffs and non-tariff barriers in Korea.

This broader view of the UK Brexit effects does not imply that the UK will be in a particularly difficult situation, although there are additional risks in the world economy. For instance, the strong real appreciation of the US Dollar implies that the debt burden of many countries and firms outside the US will increase and the currency mismatch problems of these firms would then undermine investment growth and might even contribute—in a setting with rising real interest rates worldwide—to a recession in several countries. It is rather unclear whether or not the Eurozone's growth rate will be higher than that of the United Kingdom.

The verdict of the British Supreme Court in January 2017 requires the government to get approval from Parliament for writing the "EU separation letter" to the Commission under Article 50 of the EU Treaty. In a swift response, the May government has presented the relevant law to the British Parliament.

The Economic View of Uncertainty

The Brexit decision was largely unexpected and—with all due respect to the electorate—it can be viewed as being not particularly rational; the assumptions upon which the more socio-economically disadvantaged sections of society and the less educated based their vote for Leave can, from an academic viewpoint, be classed as counterfactual. What had been considered impossible, occurred on the politico-economic stage: in a period of economic upturn, it appears a majority of the population of a prosperous EU member state, contrary to all warnings from government and experts, decided on an exit from the EU. That is the third major instance of uncertainty following the Euro Crisis of 2010–2015 and the bankruptcy of the US investment bank Lehman Brothers on September 15, 2008—this event, the insolvency of a leading investment bank, was actually not really foreseen; as it is said in the textbooks "Too Big To Fail", meaning that the state will rescue the banks. However, the administration of US President George W. Bush wanted to set an example after their rescue of the investment bank Bear Stearns in spring 2008 was viewed as an unwanted ideological state intervention by Republicans. One would not have thought possible that the countries of the Eurozone for their part would construct a shaky, vulnerable monetary union: 10 years following the launch of the European Central Bank and the Eurozone, no sooner had the commemorative publications to mark the anniversary been printed than multiple countries experienced a crash in the, since the Lehman Brothers collapse, turbulent international capital markets—predominantly due to their own political shortcomings, where the Greek government, with its 15% deficit ratio in 2009, claimed its spot at the pinnacle of irresponsibility and acknowledged an extensive deficit- and politically-motivated fraud. To date, the EU has hardly drawn any meaningful conclusions and, in regard to the Banking Crisis, only some important lessons have been learned. The fact that the so-called CoCo bonds (Contingent Convertible bonds are bonds which are issued by banks and which are converted into equity in the event of a critical fall in the ratio of equity capital) can also be held by banks is evidence of a mechanical failure: if the CoCo bonds are supposed to contribute to the stabilization of the banking world—insofar as in the case of a crisis in the banking system, more equity is provided to the banks to cushion them from the effects—this will not function should there be a systematic banking crisis. If many banks, of all people, have significant CoCo bond holdings, then it would be impossible for those banks, in the situation of a hypothetical banking system failure, to be in a position to provide equity capital to other banks (more equity capital could come from profits, but during a crisis, one can expect the profits to be at a minimum).

A fourth uncertainty factor is the refugee crisis; who would have thought that a German federal government, without consultation with EU partners, would decide on the opening of the EU's borders and then after the fact want to distribute the refugees among all EU partner countries based on a quota system. The historical error by Chancellor Merkel, who in August 2015 ignored fundamental EU relationships on an emotionally and ethically driven political whim and due to her own quest for power, is itself another cause of uncertainty: at the same time, such disorganization in the admission of refugees developed that even further uncertainty emerged in the form of security issues—perhaps for many years to come; the processing of incoming refugees, in otherwise well-organized Germany, was clearly done in a chaotic fashion, a year on from the summer of 2015 and almost 400,000 refugees still have not been properly recorded by the authorities.

The great and seemingly decisive victory of the West in the Cold War after 1980 has been frittered away—that victory had provided much more of a basis for halfway reasonable future prospects than the decade after 2008, during which the destructive effects of Islamic terrorism impacted parts of Europe. This terrorism is also a new uncertainty aspect, but is one for which countries in Europe are themselves partly to blame: decades of mass youth unemployment in France is part of the problem, for which the government must accept a large degree of responsibility. The dangerous confusion of religious faith and scientific knowledge is a standard problem in many Arab countries; the 1934 book by philosopher of science Karl Popper, which is an extremely informative and differentiated work on this issue, "The Logic of Scientific Discovery" still in 2014, i.e., 80 years after it was first published, had yet to be published in Arabic. For military actions, the West mobilized billions, however a sum of £34,000/$41,500 or so for a good translation of the book into the Arabic language, which could bring enlightenment to the Arab world, could meanwhile not be found. Islamic terrorism and a form of Arab civil and religious war are, in fact, not new: the attack on the sacred sites in Saudi Arabia in 1979 marked a first dangerous climax of this phenomenon, which was only resolved with the help of French military specialists.

More uncertainty means two things from an economic viewpoint: first, the bigger income uncertainty due to a decline in the demand for goods and second, because of higher investment risks, higher costs of production which can lead to a decline of the equilibrium quantity/ production volumes on the goods markets and ultimately lead to less employment, if labor markets are not flexible. Whether the price level of goods will rise or fall, is initially unclear, for a more definite statement, one would need to estimate a variety of behavior parameters. Whether the path of growth rises or falls is equally unclear, although there are some arguments which suggest that the level will rise, but at the same time the trend growth rate of real income then falls, namely due to reduced innovation dynamics. One can, with some certainty, infer the latter as a result of the new insecurities in Europe. That does not imply, however, that the high economic dynamics in Asia, that is in China, India and the countries in the Association of Southeast Asian Nations (ASEAN), cannot continue. In that sense, one consequence of the insta- bility and uncertainty in Europe is a long-term global shift in power towards Asia and the US. If one does not learn a comprehensive les- son from Brexit and draw the right conclusions/undertake the necessary reforms, Europe could be the biggest loser of the twenty-first century, perhaps along with Latin America, where the poison of uncertainty has been spreading for some time. The issues with regard to Brexit must be analyzed urgently and accurately. Even as early as 2015 and the begin- ning of 2016, there were already analyses appearing on the costs and benefits of a withdrawal from the EU from numerous institutions and academics which almost unanimously showed negative income effects (for an overview, see Busch and Matthes 2016).

The Cost of Brexit: A Very Late Government Study and a Fatal Information Gap for Voters

The Cameron government was sensible enough to commission an in- depth study—from HM Treasury—on the long-run British benefits of EU membership; this crucial study had a clear message and was based on alternative scenarios regarding future UK access to the EU single market (which accounted for about 45% of UK exports in 2015). In a sectoral perspective, the UK records a high surplus vis-à-vis its trading partners in financial services. As regards trade in goods, the UK traditionally runs high deficits in trade with Germany and the Netherlands. If the UK would leave the EU, it could face import tariffs of about 6% in EU27 markets and as the UK would impose import tariffs on goods and intermediate products from EU27 partner countries, import prices would increase in the UK. Lower British exports to the EU will bring a loss of specialization gains, possibly also reduced opportunities for exploiting economies of scale and also reductions in R&D plus science funding from Brussels (some EU27 support for joint research and development projects should not be excluded in the case of Brexit). It is clear that both textbook models and modern economic analyses—computer simulations—suggest that there are considerable benefits for the UK to continue EU integration, i.e., with an economic area that is roughly four times that of the UK and to which the British economy has already adjusted in many ways: by importing specialized intermediate products or differentiated high-quality goods and services. Moreover, many foreign firms—from the US, China, Japan and Korea, as well as EU27 countries—had built factories in the UK to serve the whole EU single market from a British base. That London is home to thousands of banks, insurance companies, and legal firms that use the powerful creative network of skilled labor to offer sophisticated services to the whole EU is also clear and several thousand migrants from EU27 countries are employed at top and middle management level in banks, financial service firms, and industrial companies throughout the UK. In turn, 1.6 million British people live and work in the EU27.

It was only on April 18, 2016, that the Treasury (HM Govt 2016b) presented its report on the long-run British benefits of EU membership—and in a mirror perspective, this also stands for the cost of Brexit. The timing of the publication was extremely late when one considers that this was only eight weeks before the referendum and a full week too late to easily include the main economic results in the Cameron government's referendum brochure, which ran to sixteen pages and was sent out to English households in the period from April 11 to 13 (HM Govt 2016a). Households in other parts of the UK received the brochure several weeks later, in the week following May 9. In the government brochure, there was not a single word on the key economic findings of the Treasury study if one disregards the rather simple information that 3 million jobs in the UK depend on exports to the EU. This was a major failure in terms of government coordination, since all the findings from the Treasury report on the economic effects of Brexit were known within government circles when the brochure was being mailed to households in England. The key figures from the Treasury study, which any reasonable Prime Minister would have included in the brochure, were that a roughly 10% output loss was to be expected in the case of the UK leaving the EU, plus a considerable increase of income tax rates, namely at least 3 percentage points. If one takes the 6% real income loss to be expected as a direct Brexit effect in the long run, plus a 4% non-realized output increase (surrendered economic benefits) from envisaged EU single market deepening, the further implication would have been that the referendum result would have been just the opposite to the actual outcome. An estimated 52.1% would have voted in favor of Remain—if households had received the minimum economic information on the potential Brexit effect in the government's 16-page information brochure for the referendum. Either the government only commissioned the analysis of the costs of an EU exit late in the day— much too late—which would have been extremely unprofessional (consider again that Cameron first mentioned the prospect of a referendum in 2013!) or (the only other possible explanation) EU critics within the administration caused a delay in the presentation of the report to parliament and that would really be a scandal.

The question of access to the single market following a withdrawal from the EU was considered to be crucial for the investigation into the economic effects of Brexit in the government's report. As long as the UK is an EU member, firms from the country have custom-free access to all markets of the EU member states and, vice versa, firms from the EU27 countries have tariff-free access to the British market. From a duty rate of 0% on traded goods with a sales destination in the EU27, the average import duty rate on British products will rise to about 8%, if the UK leaves the EU and is treated like any other third-party country within the framework of the World Trade Organization (WTO).

The EU's customs revenue could increase by about £3.4/$4.1 billion. On the other hand, one should consider that Germany's exports to the UK amount to about £76/$93 billion; and in the future these goods—until now custom-free—will be subjected to British import duties. In leaving the EU, the worst possible position for the UK would be that no agreement with the EU27 would be reached and thus access to the EU27 would be possible only under the rules of the WTO. Of course, the EU27 then also need to negotiate access to the UK. Here, the British government analysis considered the following scenarios:

A. After leaving the EU, the United Kingdom becomes a member of the European Economic Area (EEA)—similar to Liechtenstein, Iceland, and Norway. However, Norway pays considerable contributions into the EU budget (about half of what it would pay as a full EU member country), while at the same time Norway is a shadow member of the EU single market. The EU single market means free trade in goods and services and free capital mobility plus free labor mobility. On this EEA basis, the trade effects, income effects, and budget effects for the UK are analyzed. There is full access to the EU single market but there also is free labor mobility.

B. It is assumed that the UK will obtain access to the single market within the framework of a bilateral free trade treaty, with some limitations.

C. There will be no comprehensive EU–UK treaty on single market access and hence the UK would fall back to the minimum access position that it would get as a member country of the World Trade Organization.

The estimated real income effects for the cases (A), (B), and (C) are—expressed as relative 2015 income levels—that output will decline by −3.8, −6.2, and −7.5%, respectively. It seems rather realistic to assume that case (B) will be the core outcome of EU–UK negotiations, which can be expected to start in 2017 and which should be concluded by 2018 to avoid the strange situation of Brexit UK having to take part in the European Parliament elections in 2019. Such a situation would be extremely odd in political terms and would not be acceptable for the EU27 countries since the election results in 2019 could face legal challenges if the UK is included.

Case (B) has −6.2 % output decline as a long-run effect, but it should be mentioned—see Table 3.1—that this is the mid-point of the estimated range from −4.6 to −7.8%. One may note that an 8% real income decline is equivalent to losing one's December income.

The income loss per household in the worst scenario (C), is £3,700 to £6,600 ($4,500 to $8,000) where the medium estimate figure is about £5,200 ($6,350); the medium estimation for the income loss per capita is £2,100 ($2,560). The bilateral negotiation case (B) means an income loss of between £1,800 and £4,300 per household (i.e., between $2,200 and $5,250 per capita). The estimated income reduction goes along with a decline in tax revenues of about £30/$37 billion annually which means that the basic income tax rate would have to be raised from 20 to 28%, in case (C) possibly even to 30%. Note that a rise in the average tax rate by 2 points implies in the case of a simple Solow growth model that the level of per capita income in the long run will fall by 1%. The tax-induced income decline comes on top of the output reduction due to efficiency losses in the context of reduced UK access to the EU market. The study of the Treasury shows that the UK will have an additional loss of 4% of GDP when leaving the EU, namely from non-participation in the envisaged welfare-enhancing deepening of the EU single market, including liberalization of services, digital single market deepening, energy single market deepening and the implementation of major free trade treaties (including TTIP and the EU–Canada free trade agreement called the Comprehensive Economic and Trade Agreement, (also known as 'CETA') and treaties with Japan, Mercosur, and ASEAN). These points were part of the Cameron government's negotiation results with the EU in mid-February 2016.

The Treasury simulations have not taken into account dynamic negative foreign direct investment (FDI) effects for the UK, namely that FDI inflows will reduce and that British FDI to the EU could increase as a way of "tariff-jumping" so that the growth rate of capital accumulation and knowledge accumulation would be further impaired in the UK—and as a consequence output growth would decline. Moreover,

Table 3.1 Key findings on the long-term costs of Brexit according to various government scenarios (GDP = Gross Domestic Product)

	European Economic Area	Bilaterally negotiated access to single market	WTO-member access to single market
GDP (%) central est.	−3.8	−6.2	−7.5
GDP (%) (Estimated range)	−3.8 to −4.3	−4.6 to −7.8	−5.4 to −9.5
Per capita GDP Central est.	£1,100 ($1,342)	£1,800 ($2,196)	£2,100 ($2,562)
Per capita GDP (Estimated range)	£1,000–£1,200 ($1,342–$1,464)	£1,300–£2,200 ($1,586–$2,684)	£1,500–£2,700 ($1,830–$3,294)
GDP per household central est.	£2,600 ($3,172)	£4,300 ($5,246)	£5,200 ($6,344)
GDP per household (Estimated range)	£2,400–£2,900 ($2,928–$3,538)	£3,200–£5,400 ($3,904–$6,588)	£3,700–£6,600 ($4,514–$8,052)

*central refers to the mid-point of the estimated range **expressed in 2015 Pound Sterling. *Source* HM Government (2016b), HM Treasury Analysis: the long-term economic impact of EU membership and the alternatives, London, April 2016, p. 138

with the partial relocation of the industrial plants of foreign subsidiaries to the continent—after Brexit—the UK would also lose part of its research base; indeed many researchers would leave the UK. Jungmittag and Welfens (2016) has shown, in a knowledge production function analysis for EU countries, that the number of researchers, the ratio of foreign direct investment to GDP, and per capita income explain—within an empirical panel data analysis—the creation of new knowledge, with the UK and Germany having above average effects in the 20 countries considered for the period 2000–2012. The study by the Treasury also has not considered that a long-run output decline of 6% for the UK will cause, in a macroeconomic perspective, a decline of EU27 output of about 1% and from this there will be a further negative repercussion effect of at least another 1% for the UK. Real income effects are just one dimension to consider when calculating negative welfare effects, the associated decline in consumption per capita is often more significant from an individual perspective.

It is clear that the study did not mention other negative effects for the UK, for example, a potentially necessary increase in military expenditures relative to GDP which might be required if tensions around the Ukraine question or in the Mediterranean would intensify. However, overall the Treasury study is a solid approach to cover the key British EU membership and Brexit effects, respectively.

The government's information brochure sent to private households "Why the Government believes that voting to remain in the European Union is the best decision for the UK" (HM Govt 2016b) had 16 pages but did not contain any data on the expected negative income effects as calculated by the Treasury. The timeline shown in Fig. 3.2 shows again that the Treasury study was published one week after the government's distribution of the 16-page information brochure to English households. Hence, with the exception of people in the British business community and a small minority of households, British voters were generally not informed about the crucial negative real income effects—no sentence was included in the leaflet saying that leaving the EU could bring considerable real income losses, roughly equivalent to a worker losing one month's income.

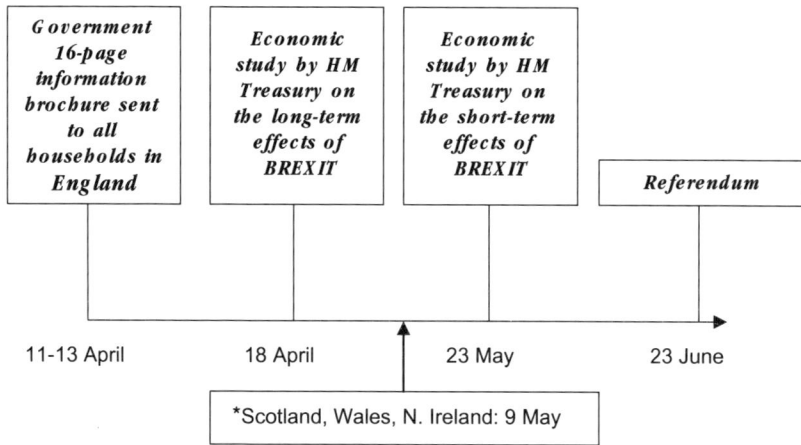

Fig. 3.2 Government referendum information: A timeline

What Would the Referendum Result Have Been with Standard Economic Information for British Households?

How would British households and voters, respectively, have reacted to such important economic information? There is no doubt about the fact that they would have reacted, and the available econometric research on popularity functions in the UK clearly suggests that conveying the information regarding a 10% real income loss plus a rise of income tax rates by at least 3 percentage points, would have resulted in a totally different referendum outcome: the alternate result would have been roughly 52% for Remain and 48% for Leave, if one considers the classical study of Bruno S. Frey and Friedrich Schneider in the Economic Journal (Frey and Schneider 1978). This study looked, within an empirical politico-economic model, at the impact of inflation, unemployment, and the growth rate of disposable income on the popularity of government—to be exact, the lead of the government party over the opposition party in terms of popularity. A 1 percentage point increase in the growth of disposable income raised the government's popularity lead by 0.8 percentage points. From this one can calculate, in an analogy, the hypothetical impact of government information saying that the long-run output loss would be 6%—the Brexit popularity index would reduce by 6 × 0.8%, which is equal to a 4.8 percentage point decline in the Brexit referendum result; the full information regarding a 10% expected output decline in the case of Brexit plus a 3% tax increase could be translated into "correct(ed) referendum results." The summary in Table 3.2 gives the actual referendum results and the adjusted results. There is absolutely no excuse which can explain why a Western government in Europe would suppress the key economic information on the impact of leaving the EU in a referendum on EU membership. Whether the Cameron government was incapable of conveying the basic economic information to households in the United Kingdom or whether intra-government sabotage purposely delayed the timely publication of the Treasury study findings: it is absolutely clear that the referendum result of June 23 leaves uncertain what the will of the majority of British voters in a normal and fair referendum would have been had this information been publicized. It is up to Parliament to create a referendum committee of inquiry and deliver a report to the public which explains the strange findings emphasized here. Whether or not there will be a second referendum has to be seen as a next step, but it is obvious that there are very sound arguments why, without a second referendum, the question of EU membership is unresolved in the UK. The referendum of 2016, organized miserably by the Cameron government, was unfair to both British voters and EU partner countries; and it fell far short of the established information standards in relation to a referendum in the UK—as implemented by Cameron's government only two years previously when the Scottish independence referendum was held. In 2014, the government sent two brochures of three pages each to households, which presented the key information that leaving the UK would mean an income loss of over £1,400/$1,700 per capita in Scotland.

There are some more recent studies with slightly different results for popularity functions in the UK; however, the basic message is always clear, namely that real income changes will affect the popularity of political parties significantly. Naturally, there is also the caveat of whether or not the results found for popularity and general election results, respectively, can easily be applied to the rare case of a

Table 3.2 Actual Result in Brexit Referendum and Adjusted Results Based on an Adequate Information Policy by Cameron's Government (*Calculated on the basis of popularity elasticities in Frey/Schneider "A Politico-Economic Model of the United Kingdom")

	Actual Result	Simulation I Corrected Result	Simulation II Corrected Result
		Basis Info: -6% realincome with Brexit = minimum information from Cameron government which one should expect to receive as a voter from the HM Treasury analysis.	Key info from the Treasury study: −10% growth effect (−6% plus −4% as a result of non-participation in EU Single Market deepening due to Brexit) plus effect of 3 percentage point increase in income tax.
UK remains in the EU(%)	48.1	50.4*	52.1*
UK leaves the EU(%)	51.9	49.6*	47.9*

referendum. However, again, there is no doubt at all that the message of a 6% income decline or even 10% output loss would have had a strong impact on the outcome of the referendum. One may note that the Treasury study, published on April 18, considers the long-run effects of British EU membership (and Brexit) and nobody should confuse these effects with the short-term effects from Brexit. The more short-term results were actually covered in a separate study prepared by the Cameron government but they are obviously less important than the long-run effects.

Why was the Cameron government able to convey basic economic information to Scottish households prior to the Scottish referendum in 2014—when the question was about Scotland's membership of the United Kingdom—while totally failing on this count in the referendum of 2016 when the question was on the UK's EU membership? One answer to this simple question is that the governance structures in the Western world have become too complicated. The complicated over-lap of the Group of Twenty (G20), supranational, national, regional, and local government has become impossible to manage efficiently and effectively by the various layers of government, and certainly the Cameron government in particular. Indeed, one conclusion which can be drawn from the referendum disaster could be to standardize certain procedures and for the United Kingdom to adopt a written constitution. The standardization of referenda in EU countries could mean, for example, that government has to provide all key information to private households at least four months in advance of a referendum. Moreover, one might consider following the Irish example and have an independent referendum commission where all citizens—and journalists—can raise questions on key aspects of the referendum campaign. With such a commission it would, for example, have become clear within a day or so that the claim on Mr. Boris Johnson's Leave campaign bus that the UK was paying £350/$427 million a week to the EU was nonsense, the relevant British net contribution to the EU budget is roughly half this figure (why did the EU not undertake an EU-wide advertising campaign on exactly how big the net contributions (or receipts) of EU member countries are? Silence means not explaining and that means leaving room for rumors and nonsense conjectures).

An older analysis by Pain and Young (2004) finds a reduction of UK gross domestic product by 2.25% in the case of a hypothetical Brexit—much lower than the British government's analysis. The authors assume that Brexit would imply that the EU would levy an effective import barrier of 8.7% on imports of British industrial goods (a 6.7% duty plus 2% in additional administrative costs). Due to the market power of EU27 firms, it is assumed that British firms will face declining profits and the net market price—the net price without effective tariff burdens—will have to be reduced. There will be a negative effect on Britain's terms of trade: more British goods will have to be exported to the EU27 per unit of goods imported than before. The authors also assume that the Bank of England will hold the inflation rate steady at 2.5% which is, of course, not a realistic assumption for the post-referendum setting in 2016; the inflation rate in the UK is barely 1% and the Bank of England has adopted a record low interest rate—the lowest in more than 200 years—to fend off recessionary forces. The newly expansionary British monetary policy is reducing interest rates in nominal and real terms in both the UK and the EU27 countries. Brexit brings a prolonged situation of an abnormally low nominal and real interest rate which, in turn, might destabilize banking systems as many banks will find that profit rates are sharply declining in this new zero interest rate world; slow equity accumulation by banks means more potential instability once further adverse shocks hit economic systems in Europe.

One particularly interesting aspect of the analysis of Pain and Young is related to the links between foreign direct investment and exports: in a modified NiDEM model, a 10% rise in the stock of foreign direct investment in the UK leads to a rise in British exports of 0.75%, which is explained by the authors in a simple way:

- The subsidiaries of foreign multinational companies raise the level of quality for many goods.
- Moreover, subsidiaries will bring a greater variety of tradable goods.
- By implication, one may conclude that to the extent that Brexit reduces the stock of foreign direct investment relative to GDP, the British current account position will further worsen and the Bank of England will face pressure to raise the stock of reserves considerably.

- There is one counterargument related to the expected strong real depreciation of the British Pound after Brexit: following the argument of Froot and Stein (1991), it is clear that higher foreign direct investment flows will come to the UK since in an imperfect capital market framework the ability of foreign investors to successfully bid to take over British firms—on the basis of a leveraged acquisition—is reinforced.

The latter effect means that more Chinese, Korean, US, German, Dutch, French, or Indian firms could take over companies in the UK. It is not fully clear what the overall effect on growth and economic stability in the UK, in the long run, will be. However, neither the official British government study on Brexit nor the study by Pain and Young considers such current account aspects. Moreover, the latter work only considers nominal import duties not the effective import duties, which one would have to include for a thorough and valid analysis and which require the consideration of imported input goods. In a model developed by the Centre for European Reform (2016), the negative trade and growth effects of Brexit are substantial. Their results are entirely comparable with those of the British Treasury, while a study by the London School of Economics also finds considerable negative effects.

The per capita income loss as a result of Brexit in the simple version of the British government's analysis amounts to about £1,800/$2,200 (Scenario B). However, that figure does not take into account the fact that in the event of a negotiated access to the single market, the UK will certainly have to pay financial contributions into the EU budget, meaning that the rise in tax rates would, in fact, be higher than the calculations of the British government suggest. With higher tax rates, per capita income will be even lower.

As far as the question of Brexit-related welfare losses goes, calculating the real income effects is only a partial approach. In a further step, the effect on per capita consumption must also be calculated. This would drop by more than 9%, as with the UK's exit from the EU, areas of European conflict—including Ukraine/Crimea—will intensify and as a result the military spending of the UK and other countries will rise: the propensity to consume and the per capita consumption will, in turn, fall.

It can be described as shocking that a credible government-sponsored expert study, which finds an income loss of over £2,000/$2,400 per person—not to mention the tax rises on top of that—did not result in a pro-Remain majority in the Brexit referendum. One can note that the EU opponents had already achieved some level of success before the referendum, as soon as the media did not refer to 'EU membership' but rather used the catchy term used by leavers: 'Brexit.' The existing financial limits on the government recognized official Leave campaign were easy to circumvent, as a number of extremely wealthy Britons paid employees at their own expense and made them available to the pro-Brexit group as a form of benefit-in-kind. It is simply baffling that this scheme, which was carried out on a large-scale, supposedly conformed to the rules.

The analysis of Aichele and Felbermayr (2015) on the effects of Brexit on the UK found a decline in the degree of openness of between -3% and -13%, and this in turn brings a long-run output decline of -6% to -26%. Using more recent approaches from the literature gives a narrowing of the output decline, namely -2% to -14% in the UK. The impact on Germany—including dynamic effects—is -0.3% to -2% in terms of real income. As regards the decline of per capita income, the authors point out that there would be an additional decline of between -2.7% and -6.2% in the case that the number of EU citizens in the UK would fall by half. If the decline in the number of EU citizens in the UK would be just 10%, the real income loss would still be in the range of -0.5% to -1.1%. As is argued here, the United Kingdom's Brexit decision has broad and serious negative effects.

The study by the Centre for Economic Performance (Ottaviano et al. 2014) showsthat Brexit could bring a real income loss of -1.1% to -10% in the long run, while Open Europe (Persson et al. 2015) suggests a worst-case scenario figure of -2.2% and a best case scenario of $+1.6\%$. In the latter case, the authors have assumed that there will be further extensive deregulation and additional unilateral British reductions of import tariffs. Such an analysis does not, however, show the separate costs of Brexit per se, but rather presents the results of a mixture of Brexit-related effects and government interventions designed to counter these effects.

In reality, it should be clear that part of the negative Brexit effects will already be manifest during the transition phase prior to actually leaving the EU, namely to the extent that investors' anticipation effects can bring major reactionary measures—typically reduced investment, a decline in both the hiring of labor and on housing markets should also indicate falling prices. As the UK is a rather big country, the reduced ability of British households to rely on high real estate collateral—partly determined by the price ratio of the housing price index to the general price level—will not only impair construction activities in the UK, but in Spain and Portugal as well: both countries stand for regions that are favored destinations for British retirees. Rising British budget deficits will raise the debt–GDP ratio in an interim period and further undermine the strategic ability of government to fight future recessions. With regard to the debt–GDP ratio, the expected long-run output fall of 10% in the UK will raise the debt–GDP ratio by roughly 10 percentage points. This effect will be attenuated by the Bank of England's

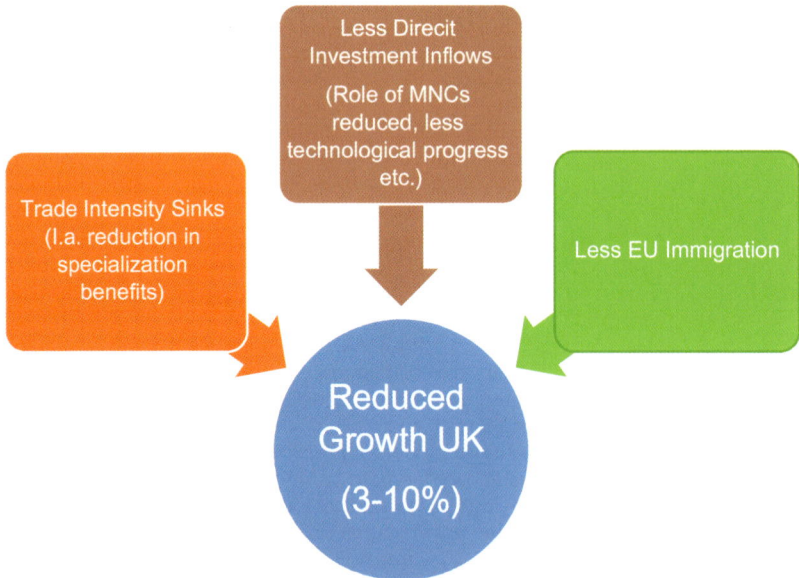

Fig. 3.3 Brexit effect channels reducing real income in the UK

low interest rate policy which reduces the interest payments of government—and of companies. However, a very low nominal and real interest rate also creates distortions and inefficiencies in the economy. Certainly, there is an additional potential for an asset market bubble. Figure 3.3 presents an overview of some of channels of Brexit-related effects in the UK.

The International Monetary Fund's (IMF) first revision of forecasts for industrialized countries which was published in July 2016, shortly after the Brexit referendum, already suggests that there will be recessionary pressure in the UK in the medium term plus a reduced growth rate of output in EU27 countries. Many firms in EU27 countries will face some adjustment pressure, but managers may often simply use the Brexit problem as an impulse to consider adjustment measures aimed at making firms more profitable. To some extent, the Brexit effects will, of course, depend not only on British economic policy measures taken by the May government, but also on the EU27 countries' policy initiatives and EU policy reforms. The stimulus of net exports of goods via the Pound devaluation and lower interest rates have helped stabilize British GDP in 2016. With the traditional liberal quartet of UK–Germany–Denmark–the Netherlands no longer active in the EU, the community could become more protectionist und face further reductions of growth. There is also a danger that growth in the Eurozone could be weakened by inadequate policy reforms in certain countries, including Portugal, Greece, and Italy. It is obvious that Italy has certain constitutional problems, and the failed attempt by the Renzi government to secure majority support for constitutional reforms in a referendum in December 2016 shows how difficult such reforms might be; one may, however, also point out that Mr. Renzi, as the leader of a party with little more than 30% support among the electorate, was always poorly placed to win the referendum: without the support of other parties, it was virtually impossible to obtain a majority in the referendum. The Greek governments under Mr. Tsipras have not even tried to start a reform of the constitution; this political deficit is more decisive for Greece than most economic policy reforms—for example, within a new constitution it should clearly be stated that the National Statistical Office has to be politically independent (and thus it would be ruled out that the former head of the Greek National Statistical Office would be taken to court simply for having done his job). The two key tasks of every constitution are to define a system of consistent institutions and responsibilities on the one hand and to define the core values for which there is broad agreement within society on the other.

The Government's Official Analysis of the Costs of Brexit not Communicated to Voters

Upon closer inspection, the findings of the British government vis-à-vis the cost of Brexit had a double disadvantage: for one thing, the publication of the results of the study, which occurred barely eight weeks prior to the date of the referendum, came far too late in order for them to have a meaningful impact on the awareness of large swathes of the electorate. That was a failure on the part of Cameron's government. It was already clear in November 2015 that official negotiations would take place between the UK and the EU. A second problem was that six ministers in Cameron's cabinet rebelled against the Prime Minister's position of pro-EU membership—and not only did he allow this to happen unchallenged but he also let each of the renegades remain in government: thus the Cameron government appeared to take a position on the fence, meaning it was impossible for government to appear as a credible messenger of its own analyses—which would require it to adopt a clearly pro-EU position. The pro-Brexit ministers in the cabinet included Michael Gove, the Secretary of State for Justice, who, according to the Financial Times, "refused to name any economists who back Britain's exit from the European Union, saying that 'people in this country have had enough of experts'" in response to a June 3, 2016, question on whether he knew of any economists who supported Brexit (Mance 2016).

This is a rather typical populist approach, namely to adopt an emotionally charged position, which not even a handful of economic experts from renowned universities can be found to support. With the exception of the former Thatcher advisor Patrick Minford, virtually no well-respected economist in the UK supports Brexit. Jeremy Adler, Senior Research Fellow at King's College London, has referred, in the German *Frankfurter Allgemeinen Zeitung* (FAZ) newspaper on August 8, 2016, to Brexit supporter Gove's dismissing of expert opinion as being reminiscent of the behavior of a stubborn and petulant child (Adler 2016).

What does this rejection of expertise in relation to crucial economic matters by the British public—at least by those who really share this attitude—tell us? It symbolizes a new anti-rationalist mindset taking hold in the UK and perhaps in the West as a whole: it could come to pass, that the West—including the US under President Trump—threatens to destroy the foundations of its own global rise, namely the relationship between politics and rationality and the application by actors in the political system of scientific knowledge.

These kinds of anti-scientific undercurrents do not only exist in relation to Brexit. They are also visible in part in Germany, for example, in the anti-TTIP movements of the environmental organizations, who have little expertise in matters of trade and direct investment, but who have created a broad movement to challenge the transatlantic EU–US trade liberalization project TTIP (here it is important to note that the environmental group BUND had more members than any of the major political parties in Germany and the internet presence of BUND is also extremely visible). This is particularly strange if one considers that the largest demonstration against TTIP in Berlin in 2015 was primarily organized by environmental interest groups, including BUND, through which the European Commission itself actually ended up contributing to the funding for the demo. BUND, as an NGO, is a part of Friends of the Earth Europe umbrella organization, more than half of whose budget is financed through project grants from the European Commission.

Of course, one can also argue that the influence of economists in Europe has been undermined as a result of the poor prognostic performance in relation to the Transatlantic Banking Crisis. However, above all, it appears that there is a new wave of political populism, which is characterized by an anti-scientific attitude. In Germany, the Alternative for Germany is perhaps best representative of this emerging populist movement; that the party itself was originally co-founded by economists is clearly a paradox. Many of these economists subsequently left the party following internal disagreements and instead joined a new party, which, however, is of little significance politically speaking.

Prime Minister Cameron saw himself confronted in parliament by about 40 Euroskeptic MPs from his own Conservative Party and obviously wanted to politically suppress these, and indeed other Euroskeptic critics. To this end, Cameron started down the road towards an EU referendum, a referendum which he and his party badly organized and which was clearly intended to serve domestic rather than foreign political objectives. With the Brexit majority, the referendum in the end served totally different interests than what it was intended to do. According to the *Frankfurter Allgemeinen Zeitung* (Kafsack and Stabenow (2016), English translation: "Juncker's Vow and Farage's Invective"), on the 29 June, 2016, the Lithuanian President Dalia Grybauskaite was sharply critical, and stressed that with "the referendum result, Brexit has been psychologically completed." Alluding to the role of Cameron, President Grybauskaite criticized Brexit as the result of "tactical political party considerations." Those who employed such means had "taken an entire country hostage." The insinuation could not have been made any clearer and one can now only regret that a British Conservative Prime Minister, for party political reasons, has condemned the whole of Europe to years of unrest along with economic and political upheavals. One cannot regard it as a responsible policy, and one will be hard pressed to find many academics who regard Brexit as a positive development for the UK and Europe.

Can Brexit even be explained from an economic perspective? It would be possible if, as a result of Brexit, the long-term income and consumptions levels would rise; or if the UK's EU membership caused relatively high fluctuations in consumption which would be more stable after a withdrawal. In answering the question, the reflections of Robert Lucas (Lucas 1987) must be considered. Lucas posed the question of how much a risk-averse individual would be prepared to pay in order to stabilize consumption, that is to have a smooth rather than volatile consumption path. In further discussions on this issue, a figure of circa 2% of the level of consumption is obtained, which a reasonable person would forgo to eliminate volatility and achieve a stable with time, smooth consumption path (Dolmas 1998). It is not to be expected, however, that consumption will be smoother after the UK leaves the EU; on the contrary: Brexit destabilizes income and consumption trends—in the UK and the EU27, and from the EU27 there is even further negative feedback effects for the UK. Thus, there is no theory which can explain the UK's EU exit, with the expected long-term decline in real income of 3–10% caused by Brexit, from an economic perspective. The explanations for Brexit, therefore, are as follows: (a) that non-economic motives dominated the decision and/or (b) that voters did not understand what economic consequences Brexit would actually have—particularly because they were not supplied with the relevant information in a timely manner.

A Defective British Referendum Campaign and the Solution: Another Referendum

When a referendum is being held, one may expect the careful adherence to certain standards regarding information—a closer analysis of the Brexit vote is appropriate from this point of view. Before the Scottish independence referendum in 2014, the British government could provide everyone with the relevant information in a timely manner. The EU referendum on June 23, 2016, on the other hand, did not conform to this benchmark with regard to the minimum requirements for voter information from government: no information was provided directly to households regarding the substantial negative income effects (−6.2% in the most likely scenario according to the government's own study) as a result of Brexit, although the Cameron government had received this information from HM Treasury's study on the long-term costs and benefits of EU membership when it was presented at the beginning of April. This stands in contrast to the actions of government before the Scottish referendum on September 18, 2014, when households were given brochures well in advance featuring comprehensive information on the economic effects of Scotland leaving the union with England, Wales, and Northern Ireland. When it came to maintaining the integrity of the British union, the Cameron government engaged in a professional information campaign, however when it came to keeping the UK part of the European Union in 2016, it did not.

That real (i.e., adjusted for inflation) income is an important parameter concerning elections in western democracies could already be shown in relation to the US in scientific studies at the beginning of the 1970s; for the United Kingdom, one early study was that of Frey and Schneider (1978) which tackled the subject of income, inflation, and the unemployment rate as influencing variables on national election outcomes. Hibbs (2005) has developed some newer theories on the role of macroeconomic influences on voting behavior in democracies. A yes/no referendum on the question of a British exit from the EU is not primarily a question on current economic developments, although these could certainly have an influence on the outcome (in the case of Brexit, see the study by Colantone and Stanig (2016) from the Bocconi University, who argue that in regions which have a relatively high share of Chinese imports, the share of Brexit supporters was particularly high—a fear of increased globalization can clearly promote economic nationalism). With regard to the British EU referendum, one question which was surely in the focus of private households was whether in the case of remaining in the European Union, economic benefits would accrue—and, in the case of leaving the EU, how high the expected long-term loss of income would be. Here, individual voters are unable to draw on their own estimates of experiences; thus academic studies from universities, research institutes, and official sources are required. Her Majesty's Treasury did indeed produce such a study, in which the expected loss in income as a result of leaving the EU was estimated at 6.2%, only this, and other, figures were first released by the Treasury/government in April 2016 and as they were not included in the official government information leaflets, they may have remained unknown to the majority of households.

It can only be described as a bizarre failure in coordination that the Treasury report on the long-term effects of Brexit (HM Government 2016b) was first published on April 18, while the distribution of the government information to households in England had begun the previous week. Mysteriously, one figure which was contained in the Treasury study—that there are 3.3 million UK jobs which depend on EU exports—also appeared in the government brochure. However, not a single word on the threatened loss of income of 3–10% in the case of Brexit, depending on the various analyses of the Treasury, was contained in the 16-page brochure, although they were crucial to the referendum on June 23.

While the British government certainly influenced the outcome in the case of the September 18, 2014, Scottish referendum by supplying households in good time with info booklets which included relevant economic data (released on March 26 and June 2, 2014, with a mailing of an eight-page summary info booklet on June 23 and further three-page leaflet on August 2), continued UK membership of the EU was apparently not worth the same type of professional information campaign. With its publication on April 18, 2016, the study of the Treasury clearly came too late in the day to have an impact on the referendum on June 23, 2016. The Cameron government had obviously judged the EU referendum to be of much less importance than the Scottish referendum. That is simply unacceptable.

For many observers, the decision for Brexit in the British referendum came as a surprise. A surprise which showed that Prime Minister Cameron's strategy had misfired: he had announced in 2013 that if he were to be re-elected, he would hold a referendum on EU membership. Following electoral success and upon becoming Prime Minister once again in 2015, Cameron was forced into living up to his word and announced, on February 20, 2016, that a referendum would be held the following June. That was straight after the UK's successful negotiations with the European Commission on improvements to their conditions of membership. The government advised a vote to remain a member of the EU. The actual result was a 51.9% majority for Leave, which was swiftly followed by Cameron's resignation. With regard to the referendum, there was—so far unnoticed—clear information deficits from the side of government. Due to the procedural failures in the run-up to the referendum, there is considerable doubt about the vote and the result—as an analysis of the facts shows.

It is worth looking at the details which show how the British information campaign for the EU referendum was defective. The government of an industrialized country, which prepares for a referendum on a possible EU withdrawal, would, from a rational perspective, present prior to the referendum an analysis on the economic benefits of EU membership (or, inversely, on the costs of an exit) and communicate the most important findings directly to the voters: by sending information to households, a referendum requires that the national electorate be properly informed. Cameron's government however, incredible as it seems, did not do so. For no apparent reason, Chancellor of the Exchequer Osborne did not present the Treasury's report before the sending of the government's 16-page brochure, and although all the facts and figures from Osborne's report were known within government circles, not a single figure on income from this crucial economic study on Brexit appeared in the aforementioned 16-page government brochure: "Why the Government Believes that voting to remain in the European Union is the best decision for the UK" (see link in Appendix): the brochure was sent to all households in England between the 11 and 13 of April, 2016; however, it could easily have been sent a week later—*after* the publication of the government study on the long-term economic benefits of British membership of the EU, that is after it was presented to parliament. Not a single word on the core of that momentous study, which put a figure on the long-term benefits for Britain of EU membership at 3–10% of GDP, plus a further 4% as a result of foreseeable future benefits, is to be found in the information supplied to households.

If, however, government unintentionally forgot, or indeed intentionally suppressed, the most important economic information—according to an April 18 press release on the Treasury website, Brexit threatens to cost UK households £4,300 ($5,250) annually, stemming from a reduction in GDP of 6.2% after 15 years—then the government information policy was clearly either extremely unprofessional or irresponsible. That the government glossed over this reduction in income with only a single line, while highlighting in the 16-page brochure another figure from the Treasury study, namely that 3.3 million British jobs depended on EU exports (the 3.3 million jobs were referred to in the press release from

Chancellor Osborne on April 18), shows that the rest of the information from that study could, and indeed should as an imperative, also have been included in the brochure for households. If the specter of an income loss of 6.2%—almost a month's income—is, from the government's perspective, not important enough to be communicated to households, then the Cameron government did not have the ability to appropriately and responsibly judge the importance of the information available for the EU referendum: economically speaking, this figure is the single most important piece of information for households regarding the UK's membership of the EU.

The 16-page information brochure from government, which according to the title on the cover was aimed at explaining why the government saw continued EU membership as the best option in the fast approaching June referendum, was first sent to households in Wales, Scotland, and Northern Ireland in the week from May 9 (so as not to cause confusion surrounding local elections which were being held); yet it still did not contain the income information from the Treasury study, which essentially implied that Brexit would bring a loss of income of between one and two month's salary for every household. No mention was made of the expected reduction in income per household of almost £3,400/$4,150—the middle estimate based on the three examined scenarios. The failure to include these data represents a de facto manipulation of the information and resulted in, from an information standpoint, a distorted and skewed referendum which can hardly be described as proper and fair.

The shocking figures were known by government already in the first week of April, meaning selected findings and the relevant figures, respectively, could indeed have been included in the brochures in a distribution to English households from April 11 to 13. Either the British government under Cameron's leadership was strangely disorganized with regard to the referendum, or there was possibly a deliberate and intentional delaying effort by EU critics within HM Treasury, which contributed to the end result that the sending of government booklets to private households would proceed without the crucial findings on income.

The whole affair is indicative of a broadly flawed referendum, and one can assume that the diffusion of information to households via press releases, which must be sought out online, had only a small fraction of the impact that an explanation of the economic costs of Brexit in a brochure delivered to the doors of households would have had. The British public may vote in a referendum however they wish, but without the timely dissemination of the main economic points in government information literature aimed at households, then the referendum will be biased, and unfair to both the population itself and indeed the EU. One can assume that in election analysis looking at the UK or other OECD member countries, the economic aspects are always regarded as important factors with regard to voting behavior.

If the government felt that it was sufficient for households in Scotland, Wales, and Northern Ireland to receive the brochure only at the start of May, then it could easily have undertaken to distribute the brochures—including the relevant Treasury study figures—to all households nationwide at that point in time. Britons and EU27 citizens are left with the impression that these figures, which clearly undermined the case for Brexit, were intentionally withheld. That is deeply inadequate, misleading, and unfair and it creates doubt about whether the result of the June 23 referendum can be taken seriously. Thus, there are valid arguments to support calls for a second referendum, in which case crucial information must be supplied by the government well in advance of the vote, that is at least four months prior to the vote. It is preposterous to think that Chancellor Osborne and Prime Minister Cameron were incapable of simply coordinating the timing of the release of the most important government study on the British costs of an exit from the EU with the sending of the official government information to UK households: a scandalous situation in London, with consequences for Europe and the entire world. It is impossible to say, without a second referendum, what British voters—on the basis of being well informed—really want in relation to the question of Brexit.

If it is the case that the Cameron government had overseen a completely disorganized referendum, one can ask why the EU should negotiate with the UK over access to the EU single market at all. The EU Commission and the citizens of Europe must be able to expect at least a minimum level of gravitas and resolve from the government in London. It is difficult to imagine that the Queen of England would be impressed by the disarray which marked the government's approach to information.

On April 11, the Minister for Europe David Lidington confirmed in a House of Commons debate that this 16-page government info brochure relating to the coming referendum was available online and would be sent by post to all households, firstly to those in England and later to those in the other constituent parts of the UK—having been delayed due to local elections taking place: "…every household in the country will receive a leaflet from the Government. The leaflet sets out the facts, explains why the Government believe that a vote to remain in the European Union is in the best interests of the British people and shows some of the choices that the country would face if the British people were to vote to leave." (House of Commons 2016).

Going by the statement of Mr. Lidington, one cannot fail to notice that without the Treasury's study on the long-term economic benefits of British EU membership, it would be completely unclear to the electorate what the relevant economic facts on a UK withdrawal from the EU actually are; meaning what the important arguments of government for a Remain vote are. The government did not even make the effort to update the digital version of the information brochure, which was available online, with the estimated income-related effects of Brexit contained in the Treasury's report.

How Would a Proper Information Policy Have Affected the Result of the Referendum?

According to the study from Frey and Schneider (1978) in the Economic Journal, three things have a special influence on the government popularity margin (i.e., the popularity of government relative to the popularity of the opposition): the unemployment rate, the rate of inflation, and the rate of growth of disposable real income. Taking the analysis of Frey and Schneider (1978) which looked at national elections and the measured popularity of government as evidenced by opinion polls in Great Britain as an example, this classic study finds that a 1% rise in the growth of disposable real income leads to an improvement in the relative popularity of government of 0.8%. Thus, in the hypothetical scenario that the information from the Treasury's April 18 EU report—that Brexit would case an income loss of circa 6%—was indeed sent to all households, one could project the how the result of the referendum would have been: the difference between the two sides on the day of the actual referendum, at the expense of the government's pro-Remain position, was $51.9\% - 48.1\% = 3.8\%$; if the population had understood that Brexit threatens a decline in real income of 6%, the pro-EU vote would have actually been higher by a factor of 1.048 ($6 \times 0.8\%$): the vote for Remain in the referendum would have been 50.4%. Thus with a proper information policy from government, the pro-Brexit Leave vote share would have been 49.6%. Going one step further, if one had considered not only the 6% fall in real income but also the additional 4% which the UK could expect as a result of EU single market deepening and a 3 percentage point increase in the income tax rate (the study suggested a 2–10% rise), then the correction factor is 1.0824 ($10.3 \times 0.8\%$) and thus the referendum result 52.1% for the UK to remain in the EU. Naturally, there are more recent examples of election research which would provide slightly different results to those suggested here (for example Sanders 2000; Lebo and Norpoth 2006; Paldam 2008; Stegmaier and Williams 2016); moreover, one can take confidence intervals and develop a differentiated view—that is a task for a future scientific publication. To summarize, the fundamental finding remains, that without providing basic economic information, a rational decision by voters in an EU referendum is impossible. Thus, the result of the 2016 Brexit referendum was, as a result of fault on the part of the Cameron government, grossly distorted.

Had this not been the case, Prime Minister Cameron would still be in office, there would not have been a depreciation of the Pound and there would have been no Brexit. There can be no real doubt that a sound and reasonable information policy could and should have been implemented ahead of the referendum (even in the case of a slight majority for Remain, there would certainly have been a debate about further required EU reforms). The assertion that a professional information policy would have been necessary in the UK also applies to the hypothetical case that one had determined less of an elasticity with regard to the effect of economic growth on the relative popularity of government, in this EU referendum case, if 'government info: −6% growth' had less of an effect on voter preferences. If, for example, the growth elasticity with regard to the referendum was only half as large as suggested by Frey/Schneider, then the pro-EU (Remain) camp would have received 49.3%, while the pro-Brexit (Leave) camp would still have won with 50.7% of the vote.

The key point here is that the non-communication of very important, and of interest to all voters, economic information on the benefits of EU membership/costs of an exit had certainly and considerably influenced the result of the referendum. There was no valid reason for withholding the findings of the Treasury study from the electorate, whose tax pounds had funded it in the first place—apart from sabotage on the part of pro-Brexit hardliners within the government of the UK itself. On a side note, the Treasury study also contained other important findings, such as that Brexit would make significant tax rises—or cuts to public services—necessary. Tax hikes have the effect of reducing the variable of the growth of real disposable income (i.e., income after tax but including transfers received) which is central to popularity and election results according to Frey/Schneider (1978). Thus, there are good arguments which imply the formulation of the following hypothesis: had there been a proper government policy vis-à-vis information which included the government's own findings with regard to the expected economic effects of Brexit, then there would have been a majority of circa 52%:48% in favor of the UK remaining within the European Union. Why, then, the seriously impaired and biased referendum result of June 23 should be taken as a policy foundation for the United Kingdom, the EU, the G20, etc., is completely unclear. Never has a large western country experienced such a serious voting distortion.

The economic influencing factors from the government's study would, had they been of general knowledge among households (i.e., had they been included in the 16-page information brochure received by households), have had quite a substantial impact on the result of the referendum on June 23; even if the elasticity with regard to disposable income was less than that in Frey/Schneider. The British government must surely be held to account by Parliament, and indeed the British and European public, for its procedural weaknesses and shortcomings in coordination and its obvious indifference to the rather poor information policy/the unprecedented information failure. Certainly, had there been a narrow victory, there would still have been cause to carefully consider a European reform agenda. However, the lessons learned from the referendum result, which have clearly not taken the government's information failures into consideration, need to be qualified. Moreover, it is astonishing how little the EU and national governments in Berlin, Paris, and other European capitals, monitored and observed both the run-up to and indeed the referendum itself. If they had, the information deficit and procedural irregularities highlighted here would certainly have been identified sooner. The citizens of Europe cannot but voice concerns about the incredible superficiality of their governments' work in this regard. A much higher level of professionalism from the government must be expected and demanded. Great emphasis must be placed on political accountability in the future—and, when necessary, the partial shallowness of the internet must also be opposed.

The level of knowledge among the British electorate in all things EU-related was incredibly poor; and that not long before a historical EU referendum—on the day of the referendum itself, according to CNN, the second most common EU-related Google search in the UK was "What is the EU?". If one considers the decisive key points of the Brexit campaign, then it can easily be shown how inadequate the government's campaign was, and how contradictory the Leave campaign was. With just the second EU referendum in UK history being so badly organized by government, one can call the procedural failures an unprecedented occurrence—as the vote on June 23 was not a relatively unexpected and rushed referendum, but traced its origins back to 2013.

For a successful referendum campaign, it was important that crucial information regarding the key points involved was made available in a timely manner, that clear arguments on the advantages for the UK of remaining a member of the EU were presented and that the government as a whole was mobilized to form a united front behind Cameron's position, which was that the UK should stay in the EU.

The two most important dimensions for electoral success are the turnout (mobilizing voters) and of course the ability of government actors to win over undecided or even pro-Brexit voters to the other side (winning voters). The primary mistake made during Cameron's campaign can be summarized as follows: the Treasury report on the costs of Brexit from April 18 was available to government far too late, as a consequence, one can expect that it had no role at all in terms of voter mobilization and only a very slight role in winning voters over to the government position—gross political negligence or sabotage within Her Majesty's Treasury are possible explanations for the fact that no figure from the study on the long-term economic costs of Brexit was included in the 16-page government information brochure. Strangely, from the Cameron government itself, very few arguments on the advantages of the EU were forthcoming, which meant worse voter participation and a weakened position from which to attract the undecided. The Exchequer's Brexit cost study calculated primarily the costs of a UK withdrawal from the EU, the report however was quite long and did not contain a summary which was understandable for ordinary citizens; it is also noteworthy that the study also focused on the income effects and not on the important, from a welfare economics perspective, consumption effects. The higher British military spending alone, which is to be expected after Brexit, implies that the consumption rate will fall.

The consistency of the Cameron campaign suffered from the belief that the Prime Minister could drastically reduce the numbers immigrating to the UK from EU member countries—under the promised 100,000 annually—while between 2014 and 2015, the number of migrants from the EU had quickly risen to 150,000. That was certainly viewed by many voters as a serious contradiction. Cameron also had to accept that six members of his cabinet joined the pro-Brexit camp. That he chose not to immediately replace these ministers is incomprehensible. Cameron, the big winner in terms of the 2015 national elections, certainly had the power and political capital to take the step of appointing six loyal MPs to his cabinet in their stead and in doing so to guarantee a clear, unanimous government position on the question of EU

Table 3.3 Weak aspects of the referendum campaign

	Voter mobilization	Voter winning
Timing of the Treasury study on the costs of Brexit—Totally Inadequate	0	very low
Pro-EU argumentation	weak	weak
Consistency	low	medium
Mobilization of government	low	medium

membership. Such a comprehensive rallying around of government did not occur, which, as with the aforementioned weak consistency, contributed to low voter mobilization and medium-intensity vote winning.

One could add that Cameron was not fully convincing in the TV debates, so that neither the government nor the Prime Minister could contribute much to efforts intended to mobilize and win over voters (see Table 3.3). That Cameron, perhaps in overestimating his own support, asked President of the Commission Juncker not to appear publicly in London is remarkable and also indicative of a lack of European convictions: in the end, Cameron did not really stand by the EU and his public protestations about how often he himself had criticized the EU is very revealing. Furthermore, the entire axis of conservative parties, spanning Spain, the UK, Germany, and indeed Juncker as Commission President did not really function well. What in the US in certain fields would be perceived as inner party conflict and a process of consensus building within the two large parties, the Republicans and Democrats, was portrayed in the EU28 as foreign policy grandstanding and games—the difference between the EU and the Eurozone, respectively, and the US is and will remain very large.

Strangely, in the UK, the government's 16-page referendum information brochure was distributed to all households in England from April 11 to 13 without any of the economic information from the Treasury's study: for example, the estimated loss of income per household of between £2,000 and £5,200 (range of estimates—between $2,400 and $6,350). Although the shocking figures from the study were known within government circles by the first week of April, none of these were included in the 16-page booklet. In Scotland, Wales, and Northern

Ireland, the sending of this information to households was delayed until after May 9, and yet still no information from the Treasury study was incorporated. If, from the government's perspective, it was enough for households in Scotland, Wales, and Northern Ireland to receive the information only at the start of May, then the distribution of the brochure—inclusive of the figures from the Treasury report—could have been carried out nationwide at the beginning of May. Britons and EU27 citizens could be forgiven for getting the impression that these figures, which argue against Brexit, were deliberately concealed.

To reiterate: the EU-related knowledge of the British electorate was incredibly poor; even shortly before a historic EU referendum. Prime Minister Cameron had seen that in the run-up to Brexit six ministers had taken an anti-EU stance and nevertheless he had allowed these ministers to remain in his cabinet. How can one want to face into a historic referendum with a completely divided government knowing that according to opinion pills the result would be extremely close? The credibility and strength of leadership needed to relieve these ministers of their duties were clearly lacking.

From these considerations, it follows that a head of government with a solid convictions, a clear communication strategy vis-à-vis the entire population—and that is exactly what is needed in the case of a referendum—and good timing with regard to a cost/benefit report on EU membership would have a good chance to secure a pro-EU majority in a second referendum; especially as the British people have experienced the first tangible economic drawbacks just a few months after the UK announced an intention to leave the EU, and they will continue to do so for many years to come. The European Union thus has no incentive to guarantee the UK easy access to the EU single market, after all, then Home Secretary and ostensible pro-Remainer, Theresa May, was a key player in supporting the shoddy, unreliable, and unfair referendum policies of Prime Minister Cameron.

A certain contradiction awaits a May government which would want to try to hold such a second referendum, in that they would have to explain to voters why they believe that the EU–UK negotiated settlement is not good enough, in order to recommend to pro-Brexit voters to accept a second popular vote. Prime Minister May also has the problem in that, with Exit Minister David Davis and Foreign Secretary Boris Johnson, she has two prominent pro-Brexit representatives in her cabinet. Should May recommend a pro-EU position in a second referendum, then Davis and Johnson would not remain in her cabinet for long—the same could apply to other ministers. This set of circumstances could be so daunting that May could recoil from the prospect of another referendum. Of course, another weak campaign would reduce such a referendum to absurdity.

Nevertheless, May has one advantage, namely that she, as a moderate pro-Europe supporter in the Cameron government, is not seen within her own party as an extremist. One could suspect that a longer process of negotiations between the EU and the UK would take the option of a referendum away from the May government. It also cannot be entirely ruled out that May will stand by her comments that 'Brexit means Brexit' in the strongest sense of the words. Naturally, from a democratic perspective, it would be sensible to give the last word to the electorate—for example, in 2018. There could also be another general election that year; possibly with the effect that Brexit can be avoided.

How Big Will the Cost of Brexit Really Be?

The Treasury report of 2016 suggested that the long-run cost of Brexit will be a 6% output decline in the UK. Is this a solid analysis? Ebell et al. (2016) used the NiGEM approach that stands for the National Institute's large-scale structural global econometric model. In their analysis and modeling simulation, the authors assume a scenario where the UK has to rely on its membership of the World Trade Organization—that is, no free trade deal with the EU is achieved. The authors focus on four shock elements that are therefore linked to Brexit:

- a permanent decline of the UK's export market share in EU27;
- an increase in tariffs;
- a permanent reduction of foreign direct investment inflows to the UK; and

- the repatriation of the UK's net contribution to the European Union's budget.

The result is a 2.7% real output decline where about 80% of this effect arises from the reduced UK market share in the EU single market. In the simulation analysis, the decline in output relative to the baseline scenario (a case in which there is no Brexit) is a strong decrease of investment in 2017—by −15%—followed by declines of −12.8%, −8.1%, and −4.6% in 2018, 2019, and 2020, respectively. Exports reduce in 2017 by 6.1%, in 2018 the effect is −17.5% and in 2019 it is −23.1%. There is an effective real exchange rate depreciation of 16% in 2017 and it stays like this until the end of the simulation horizon in 2030. After 2019, the current account balance relative to GDP is worsening, in the long run by about 1%. In 2017 (year 2 of the simulation), the inflation rate is higher by 2.2 percentage points than in the baseline scenario, after 2019 the inflation rate effect is below 1%. The terms of trade will worsen by 4% by 2030 so that the UK will trade less and what it does import has a higher relative price than would be the case without a Brexit. The authors assume no productivity effect from Brexit—however, this is not very convincing since having lower foreign direct investment flows and a reduced trade intensity should dampen productivity growth. Indeed the authors consider the case of an exogenous decline of productivity growth by 5% and the result then is roughly the same as that of the Treasury study, namely a 6% reduction of real gross domestic product. With less foreign direct investment inflows than in the baseline scenario, there will indeed be negative productivity effects from Brexit; however, the real depreciation of the currency will stimulate foreign direct investment inflows to some extent (in line with the arguments—related to the real exchange rate and the FDI inflow intensity—of Froot and Stein 1991).

One may add that a bilateral free trade treaty between the UK and the EU is not necessarily much better than the WTO case considered by the modern Keynesian macro model as used by Ebell et al. (2016). While their modeling approach is quite useful, one may argue that the approach chosen ignores some additional crucial aspects of Brexit which tilt the balance much more towards negative output and consumption effects in the long run.

- Their considerations do not include budget or tax effects of potential extra Brexit-related payments of about €40–60 ($49–73) billion (about 2% of the UK's annual national income) which the UK will have to make for covering the cost of British civil servants in the Commission, e.g., pension payment obligations, and previously agreed upon programs involving the UK and which will continue running until 2020.
- As some form of EU–UK free trade treaty will force the UK to extend the associated tariff reduction to other countries—think of a sectoral automotive EU–UK free trade agreement that would give, via WTO membership, free imports to automotive producers in third countries so that their market share in the UK will rise via higher British imports—the negative current account effect for the UK will be larger than assumed in the authors' modeling.
- Moreover, steel demand in the UK reduces as more cars are imported from the EU and the rest of the world after 2019 (the Brexit implementation year) and hence the British government might start to spend ever larger amounts in the form of subsidies intended to save ailing British steel mills and this, in turn, will lead to higher tax rates since subsidization will have to be financed in the end through rising tax revenues: the latter have a negative real income effect.
- Moreover, if there are EU immigrants who should decide to leave the UK, there will be additional negative real income effects for the UK.
- With a lower ratio of inward foreign direct investment to GDP and a lower number of researchers than in the baseline scenario—the latter reflecting the reduced scientific cooperation of UK researchers with EU27 researchers after Brexit—there could be a considerable dampening effect on UK innovation dynamics (for more on this mechanism, see the empirical analysis of Jungmittag and Welfens 2016).
- If the Froot–Stein effect of a depreciation-induced FDI flow is strong enough to raise the share of foreign ownership in the British capital stock, then the so-called golden age per capita consumption—this is the long-run per capita consumption in a growth model—will

be reduced (if this share of foreign ownership is denoted by α^* and the share of capital income in gross domestic income is ß, while the population is assumed to be constant, the semi-elasticity of per capita consumption C/(AL) with respect to α^* is $-ß^2/(a + \delta)$, where a is the exogenous growth rate of knowledge and δ is the depreciation rate in an economy with a Cobb–Douglas production function $Y = K^ß(AL)^{1-ß}$, where AL is labor in efficiency units, Y is the gross domestic product, A is the stock of knowledge, L the number of workers, and 0 < ß<1). The implication of such a strong Froot–Stein effect (after the real depreciation of the Pound, foreign investors can more easily obtain UK assets whose price has reduced relative to the equity capital of potential foreign investors expressed in Pounds Sterling) is that Brexit will cause a relative decline of the gross national income compared to gross national product in the United Kingdom. The latter is production in country 1(here the UK), while gross national income is equal to GDP plus net income from abroad; if, for simplicity, country 1 is not a source country and country 2 is the only source country of foreign direct investment, then the effects mentioned are straightforward. With a higher share of foreign ownership in the British capital stock, a higher share of gross domestic product will accrue in the form of dividend payments to companies with headquarters abroad. Assuming that international dividend payments are not taxed—or at least taxed at a lower effective rate than the profits of domestic companies—this internalization effect in the British capital stock will bring about new budget deficit problems (if dividends accruing to foreign capital owners are not taxed, the tax revenue is simply T = average income tax times $Y(1-\alpha^*ß)$ and, assuming $\alpha^*ß$ to be close to zero, the semi-elasticity of the tax revenue with respect to the foreign ownership share α^* is $-ß$: if the foreign ownership share increases by 1 percentage point, the income tax revenue will reduce by about one-third of a percentage point—if the standard assumption ß = 0.33 is assumed; it is worth noting, that this result—as an approximation—holds even if one takes into account the role of value-added taxation for the overall tax revenue).

Certainly, the British economy shows considerable resilience and should be able to absorb the long-term, self-inflicted shock of Brexit. One may expect that Brexit will have a long-run negative output effect which is more than 6%, the figure in the Treasury study, and the effect on the UK per capita consumption could even be more negative, as is argued subsequently; this might not be a serious consideration for wealthy households but for the rather poor strata, facing a decline in per capita consumption of more than 6%—relative to the baseline scenario—is a considerable economic shock. If corporate tax rates are reduced, the key effect could be that the labor income/capital income ratio will further decline in a net of taxation perspective, namely both in the UK and possibly in EU27 countries as well to the extent that the British tax policy puts considerable downward tax pressure on continental EU countries and Ireland. That the UK's government can credibly threaten vis-à-vis the EU27 to create a low corporate-tax economy in the long run is doubtful—such a threat has been voiced by the May government for the case that the UK would not obtain broad access to the EU single market. A low corporate tax rate strategy could be realized for some time in the UK; however, the increasing difference between labor income taxation and capital income taxation would lead to political conflicts in the United Kingdom.

If the overall output decline in the UK would be 6–8%, the EU GDP will decline by about 1% as will be the US decline; the combined repercussion effect for the UK could be about −0.5% of gross domestic product. To the extent that Brexit encourages the US populist and anti-multilateralist campaign of the Trump administration, there will be an indirect additional effect from more uncertain international rules for trade, international investment and intellectual property rights protection which could in the long run actually cost the UK more than Brexit itself. Undermining the multilateral international order, shaped by international organizations that represent joint international institutional capital, means higher risk for trade and international investment and that certainly is not in the interests of the UK (nor of the EU27, nor of most other countries in the world). One should not underestimate the willingness of the Trump administration to weaken multilateralism and to push for bilateralism both in many policy fields and in the key regions of the world economy. Informal talks in Washington DC, including in the German embassy, suggest that the Trump administration does not have much of an interest in holding negotiations with the EU, rather it prefers bilateral deals with each EU country individually. Due to Brexit, the UK is taking a strange lead role for such new transatlantic bilateralism.

Would Mr. Trump dare to suggest a bilateral negotiation approach to Brussels if the UK was still an integral part of an EU28? Probably not. If there is a dampening of EU27 output growth, it will have negative real income effects in the UK—and in the US—via trade and foreign direct investment channels. One should, of course, not underestimate the resilience of the British economy, at the same time it is clear that 2017–2020 will be years of low political stability in the UK, since Brexit will lead to the raising of the question of Scottish independence once again and also that of the peace process and security on the border between Northern Ireland and the Irish Republic. It would be surprising if the volatility of financial markets would not be rather high in the medium term. The quite high British stock market price index—which to a large extent is raised by the upward movement on Wall Street—will serve to again stimulate the bonus payment culture in many firms and companies, and this will be partly doubtful since strong UK and Eurozone stock market dynamics largely reflect positive spillover effects from the US. An adequate capital gains tax in the US and Europe could be useful here, both to finance some income redistribution and to help avoid new extreme boom–bust cycles. Looking at the political programs of the respective governments, we are, however, quite unlikely to witness new taxation in the UK or the US.

Some Reflections on the Economist's Role in the Brexit Debate

An economist's analysis of Brexit is not convincing if the key mechanisms which led to the referendum outcome are not understood or if the main consequences of the Brexit vote are over- or underestimated. The Bank of England and indeed some other skeptical forecasters—who

emphasized a quick deterioration of the British economy in 2016—
have lost credibility because there was an overestimation of the short-
term effects of the Brexit vote. However, it was the Bank of England
itself that cut the interest rate within a few weeks of the referendum
and this has helped to stabilize the economy as did the US Trump stock
market rally which has raised stock price indices everywhere in the
EU. The negative effects of Brexit will become noticeable in the British
economy only gradually and the strong Pound depreciation of 2016/17
could even raise employment through higher non-anticipated inflation
in the medium term—the decline of real wage rates will stimulate hiring on the side of firms. Eventually, the rise of the inflation rate will
undermine the real income of workers unless trade unions could get off-
setting nominal wage increases which, however, is not very likely. Hence
the growth of consumer demand will decline in the medium term in
the UK, but given the expansionary impulses from the US, there
will not be an immediate recession that would possibly shock many
people—and the later a possible recession comes, the less voters will
associate this with the referendum's outcome. As long as there are at
least modest growth rates in the UK, few Brexiteers would have doubts
about the historical vote to leave the European Union—and most of
them would probably deny that their vote would have been any different if credible economists or a well-organized government had informed
them prior to June 23, 2016, that the long-term economic costs of
Brexit will be about 10% of income. The strange "coincidence" that
the 16-page information brochure of the Cameron government, mailed
to all households in England between April 11 and 13, 2016, had not
picked up any of the key insights from the Treasury study—the latter
published on April 18—calls for a committee of inquiry or for investi-
gative journalists to explain this apparent historical disorganization of
an experienced Cameron government that had shown a very different
and much better and more effective information policy in the run-up to
the Scottish referendum in 2014.

    As the Brexit decision has been made, the probability that the British
political system wants to reconsider the historical issue of EU membership seems to be low; unless the British growth rate would be below
that of the Eurozone or the EU27 for several years. Germany's output

growth has outpaced the British growth rate in 2016 and it is likely to continue to do so in the medium term as well. However, the question is whether or not the 19 Eurozone countries will experience considerably higher growth than the UK—here, Italy is a critical country as is France—both countries need reforms and better economic policy in order to achieve higher growth. Moreover, in the EU there would also have to be sufficient leadership in the form of a new initiative by Eurozone countries that should be able to finally solve the problem of Greece through a combination of Greek constitutional reforms, partial debt forgiveness, and a regional Marshall Plan for Greece plus Bulgaria and Romania. So, the final Brexit equation will not only be written in London, but in Ireland and in the continental EU countries as well.

In London, the May government seems to be determined to move out of the EU and to redefine the United Kingdom's international role—a serious challenge in itself and a double problem in the context of the sweeping US and global changes brought about by the anti-establishment political winner in Washington DC: Mr. Trump, the new President of the United States, who has a very special view of multilateral US policy traditions and international institutions, respectively.

The May government's plan for a "Global Britain" namely a broad international free trade approach that would rely on a series of new free trade arrangements after 2018—that would actually have to go beyond the more than 40 EU free trade agreements already existing—could partly work if the World Trade Organization continues to function as a powerful international organization: as part of the international rule of law and reason which is represented by the 70-year-old modern network of international economic organizations plus the older Bank for International Settlements (BIS). This, however, is doubtful since the Trump administration signaled in early March 2017 that it is unwilling to accept WTO dispute settlement verdicts in the future, having already indicated a month earlier that the US would no longer be active in negotiating future international regulation of financial markets at the BIS. If this really stands for a new anti-multilateral US policy strategy, other countries are likely to ignore the WTO rules and principles as well and the world economy will move towards a situation of both hidden and open trade wars so that a Global Britain approach simply cannot work. Moreover, as the Trump administration is blocking the Basel III rule implementation of the Bank for International Settlements, which deals with the prudential supervision of big banks with international operations, the world is witnessing the dangerous demise of multilateralism and the role of international organizations which have played a key role for the US, the Western world, Asia, and other regions of the global system since 1944.

The Trump administration's partial renouncing of the application of the rule of international law and the explicit focus on bilateralism, plus the "America first" rhetoric of Mr. Trump himself, is likely to destroy the existing international system to which the US and the leading western countries—including the UK—had effectively invited China and Russia in the 1990s: with China joining the WTO in 2001 and Russia coming on board in 2012. It is clear that the losers of de-multilateralization will above all be small countries with almost no political leverage at the international negotiating table, as well as leading global trading countries such as Germany, the UK, France, Italy, Spain, Netherlands, Switzerland, Sweden, and many more in Europe. The US is also preparing some form of import taxation—possibly linked to a new tax regime plus a border adjustment for exports that would effectively subsidize exports—which itself could lead to a negative verdict from the World Trade Organization. The more strange measures Mr. Trump and his administration are taking, the louder one may expect the populist defense of the US President to be since this will help him to rally his political supporters behind him. That most of the Trump arguments and measures are counter to 200 years of economic research will in the end lead to major contradictions in terms of policy promises and results, and will also, of course, raise the issue of to what extent a rational British government and political system will want to associate itself with the Trump administration.

For the EU28, Brexit means losing almost one-fifth of its economic weight, at the same time 60 million British citizens lose the right to easily study, work or retire in the 27 EU partner countries. Giving up these options through Brexit is a serious loss for many British families—beyond the long-run negative economic effects. The City of London will lose part of its global financial center quality since for major US banks the future lack of access to the EU27 single market from the UK implies some relocation to EU27 countries on the one hand, and on the other hand, the relocation of certain activities to New York will also will be an attractive option as exploitation of financial economies of scale in the US financial center often is the second-best alternative after Brexit. A strong real depreciation of the Pound is to be expected as the British financial sector stood for a large bilateral current account surplus within the EU28. In the end, British workers will have to export more UK goods for a given amount of imported goods—this means a decline of living standards—and the fact that foreign investors will more easily take over part of British industry after a Pound devaluation implies that the British national income will have lower growth rates than the UK gross domestic product: a larger part of gross domestic product will flow to US, Asian and EU27 investors than before Brexit and this is also a negative welfare effect. For the poorer strata, this is all the more negative since these profits of foreign multinationals are typically subject to low corporate tax rates (and possibly even lower ones in the future).

Critics of Prime Minister May's Brexit strategy, as well as critics of President Trump, are likely to face the sentence "you are remoaners and you just want to talk the country down." However, in the end, scientific analysis and reality will be of the utmost importance. Is it conceivable that the UK, as an enlightened country, has both a government and a Parliament that will want to implement a largely contradictory Brexit project that has the support of four British popular newspapers while facing serious doubts on the side of most university economists in the country? As regards the US—and ignoring possible parallels between President Andrew Jackson (the first populist president in US political history, who served as president No. 7 and was re-elected) and President Donald Trump—should one really assume that the Trump administration will work against several hundred experts organized in the US Society of Government Economists, not to mention the voices from the leading US universities' Departments of Economics and of the managers of leading multinational companies from the tradable goods sector of the US?

The international economy is likely to face a period of partial turmoil in the context of Brexit and the election of Mr. Trump, both of which are historical events—with Mr. Trump receiving a legitimate outright majority of the Electoral College, while the Brexit majority is subject to very serious doubts linked to a disorderly British referendum under the Cameron government. The Trump election and the associated temporary stock market rally in the US, which also drives up stock market indices in the UK, the Eurozone, Switzerland, and many newly industrialized countries, creates a temporary upswing in many countries but hardly higher sustained and stable growth in the OECD. Thus, the economic adjustment pain from Brexit remains invisible for some time, but after 2017 lower investment–GDP ratios and a higher share of foreign investment in the UK capital stock—reflecting rising international mergers and acquisitions after the strong real devaluation of the Pound—will be part of the price to be paid for Brexit. If the share of foreign investors in the UK's capital stock is raised, a higher share of UK profits will be transferred abroad so that the gross national income will decline; and one really has to emphasize that consumer demand and import demand is not proportionate to GDP (as is explained in almost every textbook) but to gross national income. Better research is needed in modern economic analysis and whether it is Brexit or TTIP, one does not have a complete analysis if one is not combining trade aspects, foreign direct investment dynamics, and innovation aspects plus the related implications for growth, employment, and tax revenues.

EU Integration and Euro-Reforms with Modernization Impulses Pressing Issues Due to Brexit

With Brexit in 2019, the European Union would lose almost 1/5th of its economic weight and 13% of its population—on the basis of the negative referendum result of 2016 which was organized by the Cameron government in a broadly inadequate manner; under standard conditions, a pro-Remain majority would have resulted. Moreover, since the beginning of 2017, the EU is also coming under pressure due to a Trump administration which has broken with over six decades of

US tradition by appearing to be unsupportive of European integration, and which apparently wishes to replace 70 years of US multilateralism with a new bilateral approach. From 2019 on, the Eurozone will come under increasing critical observation from an economic perspective, as the electorates, particularly in Euroskeptic countries, will pay ever more attention to different economic developments vis-à-vis the EU and/or Eurozone and the United Kingdom. Due to Brexit, the UK could be dealing with a fall in terms of gross domestic product of circa 6% in the long term, which spread over a decade entails a reduction of the annual growth rate of about 0.5% compared to a benchmark scenario without a UK withdrawal from the European Union. This slowing of economic growth means new budgetary problems for the UK, which could possibly be further exacerbated by the emigration of EU27 citizens who had lived and worked in the UK and who, according to OECD research, were net contributors to the British state coffers.

This suggests that in the medium term, the EU27, at least for the first decade after Brexit, should be in a better position with regard to economic growth than the UK, even though Brexit will also have a dampening effect on EU growth—with an annual effect of about 0.1% for a decade. Performance comparisons between the UK and EU/Eurozone must—even beyond the decade following 2019—result in a sustained relative success for the EU, if the situation is to be avoided that more EU countries replicate the Brexit model in the long term and seek more national policy autonomy and more growth and employment outside of the European Union. The risk exists that Eurozone members, in the case of initially slower UK growth after 2019—at which point the restricted access to the EU single market will be very apparent—will ease up on or neglect reform efforts altogether—a situation which in a few years would result in the scenario which should be avoided: the UK would gradually normalize its growth rate, while the EU countries, having not undertaken the necessary reforms, would enter a period of weak economic growth and rising budget deficits. With the 2017 EU White Paper, the EU Commission of President Juncker submitted five possible directions for future EU integration, in which the foreseeable Brexit effects play a curiously small role (European Commission 2017a). A sound and sustainable integration policy must, however, consider economic and political logic. Without the necessary pro-growth reforms on the part of the EU and sensible structural reforms in the Eurozone, the EU27 will not achieve a long-term growth advantage compared to the UK. In this regard, the governments of the EU member states should urgently pursue expedient steps towards deregulation and reasonable elements of a political union are just as important for sustainable achievements in terms of EU integration as an optimal promotion of digital innovation dynamics in the EU single market. Each successful reform will reinforce regional integration clubs in other parts of the world and the concept of multilateralism, which has been seriously weakened by the Trump administration. Here, Europe has a great historical responsibility to live up to. However, it still cannot be completely ruled out that the United Kingdom will in fact reconsider Brexit.

References

Adler, J. (2016). Ist dies schon Tollheit, hat es doch Methode, *Frankfurter Allgemeine Zeitung*, Guest Contribution on August 8, 2016. http://www.faz.net/aktuell/feuilleton/BREXIT-offenbart-das-britische-verfassungsdefizit-14376231.html.

Aichele, R., & Felbermayr, G. (2015). *Costs and benefits of a United Kingdom exit from the European Union*. Gütersloh: Ifo Study for the Bertelsmann Foundation.

Bruno, R. et al. (2016). Gravitating towards Europe: An Econometric Analysis of the FDI Effects of EU Membership, Technical Appendix to Dhingra et al. (2016), Center for Economic Performance, London School of Economics, London.

Busch, B., & Matthes, J. (2016). *Brexit—The Economic Impact*. A Meta-Analysis. Köln: Institut der deutschen Wirtschaft.

Centre for European Reform. (2016). The economic consequences of leaving the EU. The final report of the CER commission on Brexit 2016, April 2016, London.

Colantone, I., & Stanig, P. (2016). Global Competition and Brexit. (September 28, 2016). BAFFI CAREFIN Centre Research Paper No. 2016–2044. Available at SSRN: https://ssrn.com/abstract=2870313 or http://dx.doi.org/10.2139/ssrn.2870313.

Dhingra, S., Ottaviano, G., Sampson, T., & van Reenen, J. (2016). *The impact of Brexit on foreign investment in the UK*, PAPERBREXIT03. London School of Economics, London: Center for Economic Performance.

Dolmas, J. (1998). Risk Preferences and the Welfare Cost of Business Cycles. *Review of Economic Dynamics*, 646–676.

Ebell, M., Hurst, I., & Warren, J. (2016). Modelling the Long-Run Economic Impact of Leaving the European Union. *Economic Modelling, 59*, 196–208.

European Commission. (2017a). European Economic Forecast, Winter 2017, DG ECFIN, Institutional Paper 048, February 2017, Brussels.

European Commission. (2017b). *White paper on the future of Europe, reflections and scenarios for the EU27 by 2025*, March 2017, Brussels.

Frey, B., & Schneider, F. (1978). A Politico-Economic Model of the United Kingdom. *Economic Journal, 88*, 243–253.

Froot, K., & Stein, J. (1991). Exchange rates and foreign direct investments. *Quarterly Journal of Economics, 106*(4), 1191–1217.

Hibbs, D. A. Jnr. (2005). Voting and the Macroeconomy, University of Göteborg (for the Oxford Handbook of Political Economy).

HM Government. (2015). Prime Minister's speech on Europe, PM Cameron's Chatham House speech delivered 10 November 2015. Available at: https://www.gov.uk/government/speeches/prime-ministers-speech-on-europe.

HM Government. (2016a). *Why the Government believes that voting to remain in the European Union is the best decision for the UK, London.* Available at: https://www.gov.uk/government/uploads/system/uploads/attachment_data/file/515068/why-the-government-believes-that-voting-to-remain-in-the-european-union-is-the-best-decision-for-the-uk.pdf.

HM Government. (2016b). *HM Treasury analysis: The long-term economic impact of EU membership and the alternatives, London, April 2016.* Available at: https://www.gov.uk/government/publications/hm-treasury-analysis-the-long-term-economic-impact-of-eu-membership-and-the-alternatives.

House of Commons. (2016). *Commons Chamber debate transcript.* April 11, 2016, Vol. 608, Minister for Europe, Mr. David Lidington. Available at: https://hansard.parliament.uk/commons/2016-04-11/debates/16041110000001/GovernmentReferendumLeaflet.

Jungmittag, A. & Welfens, P. J. J. (2016). *Beyond EU-US trade dynamics: TTIP effects related to foreign direct investment and innovation.* EIIW Paper No. 212—Presented at the IMF, Washington DC, June 28, 2016; forthcoming in Journal www.eiiw.eu.

Kafsack, H. & Stabenow, M. (2016). Junckers Gelübde und Farages Schmähkritik, *Frankfurter Allgemeine Zeitung*, No. 149, Politics Section, 29 June 2016, p. 3.

Lebo, M., & Norpoth, H. (2006). The PM and the pendulum: Dynamic forecasting of British elections. *British Journal of Political Science, 37*, 71–87.

Lucas, R. (1987). *Models of business cycles*. Oxford: Blackwell.

Mance, H. (2016). Britain has had enough of experts, says Gove. *Financial Times*, Online Edition, 3 June.

McGrattan, E. R., & Waddle, A. (2017). *The impact of Brexit on foreign investment and production* (NBER Working Paper No. 23217). Cambridge, MA.

Ottaviano, G., et al. (2014). *The costs and benefits of leaving the EU*. London: Centre for Economic Performance.

Pain, N., & Young, G. (2004). The macroeconomic impact of UK withdrawal from the EU. *Economic Modelling, 21*, 387–408.

Paldam, M. (2008). Vote and Popularity Functions. In C. K. Rowley and F. G. Schneider (Eds.), *Readings in public choice and constitutional political economy* (pp. 533–550). Springer.

Persson, M., et al. (2015). *What if...? The Consequences, challenges & opportunities facing Britain outside EU, Open Europe Report 3/2015*. London: Brussels, Berlin.

Sanders, D. (2000). The real economy and the perceived economy in popularity functions: How much do voters need to know?: A study of British data, 1974–1997. *Electoral Studies, 19*, 275–294.

Stegmaier, M., & Williams, L. (2016). Forecasting the 2015 British election through party popularity functions. *Electoral Studies, 41*, 260–263.

Welfens, P. J. J. (2011). *Innovations in Macroeconomics, 3rd revised/enlarged printing*. Heidelberg: Springer.

Welfens, P. J. J. (2017a). *Negative welfare effects from enhanced international M&As in the Post-Brexit-Referendum UK*, EIIW Paper No. 232, forthcoming www.eiiw.eu.

Part II
UK, US and EU Perspectives

4

Aspects of British History and Policy

British history, in itself, was seldom particularly peaceful, but it always represented a continuous step-by-step journey towards the development of civil rights, a social contract, and a balance of powers. The 1707 union between the traditional older kingdoms of Scotland and England under a single monarch resulted in Great Britain (which later expanded further to include the Kingdom of Ireland, and henceforth became known as the United Kingdom of Great Britain and Ireland—today only Northern Ireland remains part of the union, which is now referred to as the United Kingdom of Great Britain and Northern Ireland), which was a large step towards the establishment of peace and an era of prosperity through unimpeded trade on the island. However, it was soon followed by a period of historic political ineptitude, as during the 1770s, the American colonies were increasingly snubbed by politicians in London, which resulted in the American Declaration of Independence with its focus on the objectives of 'Life, Liberty and the Pursuit of Happiness,' while in England the ideals which were striven for were 'Life, Liberty and Property.'

1872 saw the beginning of the end of the aristocracy as a powerful political force in Britain. That year the secret ballot was introduced—in

© The Author(s) 2017
P.J.J. Welfens, *An Accidental Brexit*,
DOI 10.1007/978-3-319-58271-9_4

total, however, only about 60% of men had the right to vote. An altera-
tion of the constituencies in 1884 gave more power to London and the
financial interests which were centralized there: the number of delegates
from London rose from 22 to 68 (Schröder 2010). 1906 saw the last
modern election in the history of England which was partly influenced
by a question relating to religion—the issue at hand being the financing
of church-run schools with public money, a position which was, contrary to their own principles, supported by the Conservative Party, but
which was rejected by the majority of the electorate. The Liberal Party
won the election to the lower house, the House of Commons, that
year. In 1911, a new piece of legislation, the Parliament Act, deprived
the upper house, that is the House of Lords—which is populated by
many aristocrats—of some of its power. By 1918, all men had received
the right to vote, along with women over the age of 30, and only in
1928 could women under the age of 30 first vote. In the meantime,
the First World War had shown that the old British strategy intended
to secure peace in continental Europe, that of using a carrot-and-stick
approach comprised of diplomacy and the threat of military might,
through a balance of powers, was no longer effective. After the Great
War, the British Empire reached its peak in terms of territorial extent
and the United Kingdom sought a leading political role on the international stage. This could not really be achieved, however, due to the
UK's lack of real economic power. Since 1890 or so, the United States
of America had secured its position as a leading economic power globally. The US did not want to adopt a corresponding leading role politically; however, the young anti-colonial nation confronted the more
established European powers in China and Japan and also claimed
Latin America to be in its sphere of influence. The Second World War
ended with the United Kingdom on the victorious allied side; however,
the British Empire quickly began to collapse and from then on the UK
presided over an international network of countries referred to as the
Commonwealth of Nations. The Commonwealth was suggested by the
Leave campaign, that is those who supported a Brexit, as an alternative
opportunity to the European Union for the UK to expand its economic
power—because, amongst other reasons, the British export share to the

Commonwealth nations is growing (a development which can above all else be ascribed to India's economic boom).

Apart from the British parliamentary elections, there were also—albeit limited in number—referenda: including a referendum in 1975 relating to the European Union in which two-thirds of the electorate voted for EU membership, confirming support for the 1973 accession to the EU, which occurred under a Conservative government. A year later, the United Kingdom experienced massive problems with the balance of payments and needed to take a loan from the International Monetary Fund of over $3.9 billion. The oil price shocks of the 1970s were a problem; however, they did lead to the exploitation of the North Sea oil fields on the British seabed and the expansion of a new industry, which, however, did not overcome the dominance of the services sector. In 1986, under the government of Prime Minister Margaret Thatcher, a liberalization of the financial markets took place, which contributed to the further expansion of the traditionally strong sectors of banking and insurance via pressures to innovate and internationalization (for more British political history, see also Pearce and Stewart 2001).

Following the EU-skeptic Margaret Thatcher, as Conservative Prime Minister, came the EU-friendly John Major (1990–1997), who, however, could not keep the British Pound Sterling within the European Monetary System—even then it was clear from a British perspective that a strong linkage between Sterling and other currencies could present problems for the United Kingdom. Then came the Labour Party governments of Tony Blair and Gordon Brown, which were succeeded by the Conservative government with David Cameron as Prime Minister, who, in effect, led the country out of the EU. On June 23, 2016, the historic Brexit vote occurred during his second term in office, with a majority of voters backing an exit from the EU; a majority primarily made up of men in England, blue-collar workers and retirees; their number clearly included nostalgic dreamers, who wish for a British return to great power status as head of the Commonwealth. The EU, with its mechanisms and advantages, was rejected. In the end, one should not blame voters: the critical point is rather the minimum required information policy of the government for a historical referendum.

Central Government vs. Local Authorities in the UK and Immigration

The relationship between the centralized state and local municipalities changed drastically in the UK under Prime Minister Thatcher and in the run-up to the Brexit referendum there were important developments in this regard. England has a long history which, until the late nineteenth century, was shaped to a large extent by the balancing of centralized political authority and local power holders. The former, central government, was heavily reliant upon the latter, localized authorities, to be able to implement its decisions.

The counterweights to centralized power became less important as Industrialization progressed and the historian Hans-Christoph Schröder (2010, p. 97f) writes, in relation to the Thatcher government and the decreasing significance of alternative centers of influence and local power: "They have been further weakened by the deliberate disenfranchisement of local authorities by the Thatcher government. Since the attacks on the Elizabethan poor laws and the enforcement of the New Poor Law of 1834 in Great Britain, there has been a policy of social dismantling which has traditionally gone along with a serious mistrust of the allegedly too generous local authorities the associated tendency towards centralization. Nobody, however, has taken up this cause so ruthlessly and radically as Margaret Thatcher... England was de facto the most centralized state in Europe." Even individual rights appeared to be threatened by the Thatcher government, towards the end of her tenure; the United Kingdom was the country against which most legal actions had been filed at the European Court of Human Rights (Schröder, p. 98).

Cameron, as a Conservative Prime Minister, showed the full extent of the power of the centralized state following the Banking Crisis, when it came to the containment of the enormous government deficit which had resulted from the British banking bailouts and the stimulus packages between 2008 and 2010: Cameron's government sharply cut the financial allocations to local authorities over a number of years; in the cities and towns of the UK, there was increasingly an impression of insufficient local services, which was, in fact, being caused by the cuts in London. The extent of these cuts is shown in Fig. 4.1a–c. Figure 4.1a shows the percentage change—based on the previous year—in central government transfers to local authorities. From Fig. 4.1b, it is immediately clear that from 2010 onwards transfers from central government to local authorities were cut sharply, falling from almost 10% of real Gross Domestic Product (GDP) in 2009/10, to about 7% in 2014/15, while Fig. 4.1c shows the drop in monetary terms. No matter how it is measured, the change from 2010 is obvious, and this change was implemented by the Conservative government of David Cameron, who became Prime Minister for the first time in May 2010. His government instituted the cuts in an attempt to manage the budget deficit.

Many people, however, saw the responsibility for these cuts elsewhere: they felt that too much immigration was the root cause of the inadequate provision of public services, and Cameron, in a perfidious and unwise way, had created this scapegoat of immigrants among the electorate. The immigration issue was probably decisive for the Brexit decision, which seems quite absurd.

Immigration to the UK from other EU countries is, according to Organisation for Economic Co-operation and Development (OECD) analyses, economically advantageous, while the magnitude of the annual inflow during the decade from 2005 to 2015 was, at only about 0.2% of the population, not particularly high. Furthermore, the UK itself had decided—like Ireland and Sweden—, in light of the first EU eastern enlargement, not to have a transition period limiting immigration from these countries. Germany, on the other hand, had imposed a 7-year transition period, which from an economic point of view was able to help reduce part of the difference in incomes between Eastern Europe and Germany through rapidly growing trade and moreover allowed time for positive growth expectations in Eastern European EU accession countries to materialize. Both elements mitigated the migratory pressures and the fact that many EU countries chose to implement similar transition periods ensured a substantial geographic distribution of the emigration flows.

With the UK expecting economic benefits from an early liberalization of the immigration regime and the associated inflow of labor, it

Change in UK Central Govt. Transfers to Local Authorities
(a)   (Percentage Change year on year)*

(b)   UK Central Govt. Transfers to Local Authorities (% Real GDP)

(c)   UK Central Govt. Transfers to Local Authorities (Millions of
Pounds Sterling)

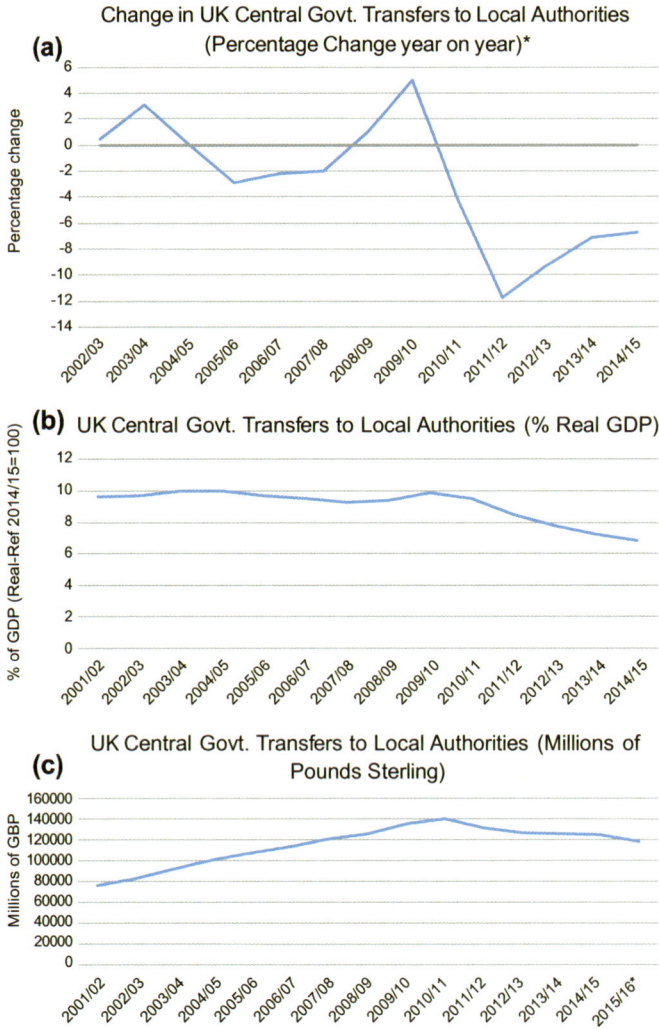

Fig. 4.1   a–c UK central government transfers to local authorities. *Source* Own calculations based on the Public Expenditure Statistical Analyses (PESA 2004, 2008, 2011 and 2015) and UK Government's Budget 2016 GDP deflator. Due to revisions of prior data in later releases, the 'newest' available data for each year was included. Transfers refer to Total Central Government Support in DEL (Departmental Expenditure Limits) and AME (Annually Managed Expenditure).*Change in percentage y-*on*-y related to change in transfers as a percentage of real GDP

would only have been fair for the country to have instituted a reasonable integration of newcomers. The free movement of labor, according to the reports on migration in the British review on the EU balances of competences, belongs not only to the four freedoms of the single market, but is also a complementary freedom to the other elements which are highly valued by the UK, namely the free movement of goods, services, and capital. In the United States, there has been no such debate on this issue, and one would never hear vocal complaints about internal US migratory flows (albeit a different issue to the conflicts over the issue of immigration from Mexico). The level of political debate in the United Kingdom, and partly in Germany also, in relation to internal EU migration is far removed from that in the US—which also applies in terms of the expert discussion on the issue, where, for example, the Ifo Institute has often stressed the high fiscal costs of immigration as a negative aspect, while Sinn (2016) claims that the wave of refugees who have come to Germany is a causal factor of Brexit. On the other hand, in the United States there is awareness that 40% of the Fortune 500 companies were founded by either immigrants or the children of immigrants, so that immigrants are seen not only as migrant workers, but also as hard-working entrepreneurs who have the ability to create new jobs. In Great Britain, the debate under the Cameron government party reflected that in Germany, despite the fact that in the UK there also exists a large immigrant start-up culture.

Cameron's Review on the Balance of Competences: Does the EU Wield Too Much Power?

During the first Cameron ministry, it was decided that a broad and comprehensive expert review into the division of competences between the member states and the EU would be launched. On December 18, 2014, the last seven reports of the thirty-two which were prepared, in total comprising "The Review of the Balance of Competences between the UK and the EU", were released. In the press release which accompanied the publication of this final batch of reports, a compact and concise outline of the scope of the review was presented (HM Govt 2014c):

> The 32 reports draw on nearly 2300 pieces of written evidence which together demonstrate why the EU needs ambitious reform to make it more open, competitive, flexible and democratically accountable, for the benefit of everyone in Europe.

In welcoming the conclusions of the review, Foreign Secretary Phillip Hammond wrote:

> This two-year review to examine the impact of EU membership on the UK is unprecedented in its size and scale...There are many areas where action can and should be taken in Member States rather than at the EU level. The final reports pick up on a number of themes which recur across the review:

- Subsidiarity and proportionality underpins the application of EU competence in all areas.
- Respondents (Note from the author PJJW: the respondents in this case were experts in their respective fields) highlighted the need for greater democratic accountability of EU institutions with some arguing that the ECJ had too wide a scope for the interpretation of competences. They thought accountability could be improved by giving national parliaments a greater role.
- Contributors also commented that the UK has often been successful in shaping the EU agenda. Respondents to the (PJJW: EU-) Enlargement report emphasised the UK's influence in directing reforms of the enlargement process. Other reports highlighted how EU programs benefit the UK—the Russell Group (PJJW: a group of leading UK universities) noted the importance of wider funding opportunities offered by the EU for UK universities in light of the importance of education as an export industry to the UK.
- But respondents also called for further progress in many areas. The need for less and better EU regulation was a common theme in all reports.
- Finally, many stated the importance of the EU focusing on the areas where it adds genuine value.

In not one single chapter does the Review, which was compiled based on the opinions and statements of many experts and institutes, give the impression that a large majority in Great Britain were skeptical of British involvement in the EU. However, it is clear that the Conservative–Liberal Democrat coalition government of David Cameron, which commissioned the review, wished for less power for the European Commission and that more policy areas would be reserved for the national level. The report on immigration indicates that there were indeed fears that the British social system could be exploited by EU immigrants. The result was that the issue of the payment of child benefits to immigrant families became somewhat of a prominent theme in the agitated British tabloid press, and indeed that the same amount of child benefits was paid for children living outside of the UK as those residing within the UK was not a convincing solution. As the majority of immigrants were coming from relatively poor countries, it would have been equitable to pay adjusted child benefits for children living abroad on the basis of the price level or purchasing power parity, respectively, in the country where the children were actually resident—i.e., usually involving a lower amount than in the UK (Welfens 2014b). In this regard, Prime Minister Cameron had negotiated with the EU changes to the system which would benefit the United Kingdom immediately prior to the Brexit referendum.

Moreover, the EU competences review certainly appreciated that the UK itself had been significantly involved in the designing of many areas of the policy agenda, as indeed did Foreign Secretary Hammond himself. Nevertheless, it is possible that the Review contributed to an anti-EU sentiment, namely as it was difficult for the electorate to understand where the UK, as an EU member, had enjoyed important advantages as a result of that membership.

Finally, it is of course clear from recent UK history that many British governments have maintained a certain distance from the EU. This includes not only the UK's non-participation in the Eurozone project, a decision in which significant weighting was presumably given to the importance of the British banking and financial sectors, with which shocks could be relatively well cushioned as a result of flexible exchange rates on a broad front (that is, not just against the US Dollar). In the

end, there lacked in the UK—with the exception of Prime Minister
John Major and his two social democratic successors—a willingness and
preparedness to be actively involved in the shaping of fundamental EU
social policy. Considering the theory of fiscal federalism, one can hardly
imagine that the EU policy level, responsible for an expenditure ratio
of just 1%, is optimally positioned for an EU single market with the
free movement of labor. The US, with a federal government consumption rate of 9% in 2013, is not known for being an excessive super-
state; Washington DC is also responsible for a social expenditure ratio
of 11%. The principle of subsidiarity, so often stressed in the Review of
Competences—which implies that the EU should not have any involvement in areas which can be better dealt with at a national level by member states themselves—was used by London (and often also by Berlin)
as strategic leverage in order to keep the Brussels policy layer as small
as possible. Certainly, the basic idea of subsidiarity is indeed a sound
one. However, that does not mean that there are no important fields
of competence which could be transferred to Brussels delivering large
efficiency gains. Naturally, one must also consider the weakness of the
EU to date in the overspending of EU monies, for example, in the case
of structural funds where only about half of the money invested is done
so in a sensible and useful manner (Becker/Egger/Von Ehrlich 2010),
with the result that, at least initially, there are few arguments for raising
the EU expenditure ratio. However, this viewpoint can be countered,
in that one could argue that institutional reforms aimed at improving
the efficiency of expenditure areas, based on previous poor experiences,
must be implemented prior to a consolidation of powers and a shift of
spending power to Brussels.

Measured in terms of the sound economic arguments of the theory
of fiscal federalism, the EU level is clearly insufficient. It is easy to recognize that large infrastructure projects and defense expenditures could
be managed at an EU policy layer; and perhaps even a part of the redistribution policy—if labor mobility is high, redistribution policy is
inefficient if organized solely at the national level (Oates 1999).

It may be noted that there is an interest in the United Kingdom
for firms to have a high degree of flexibility in determining the working conditions of low-skilled workers, both domestic and foreign. It

appears, however, that the high share of immigrants from non-EU countries brings even more pressure to move towards so-called "super flexibility." These immigrants, as the Review shows, have more language difficulties than immigrants from EU countries and generate their income in simple jobs. It cannot be ruled out that the British minimum wage—which is set at a uniform level nationally—leads to this business and policy pressure. Low-skilled workers from both non-EU and EU countries may have better chances of employment if they are flexible in terms of wages and if they can be engaged for longer working hours. With regard to EU citizens, this approach, however, does not correspond to the current guidelines for employers in place in most EU countries. There are good reasons to doubt, however, whether it makes sense to work more than 48 hours a week, even where one can.

The fact remains that the Competence Review gave little to suggest that the UK was fundamentally dissatisfied with the EU. However, the EU's good points, as found by the Review, were not communicated to the electorate in a prudent and competent manner, while the Euro Crisis 2010–2015 provided the background for the continuous cultivation of a negative sentiment, vis-à-vis EU integration, in the British press. That the United Kingdom took part in almost none of the stabilization measures during the Euro Crisis is remarkable and, with regard to Spain for example, not fair. There, according to the OECD, British banks had a similarly high exposure to risk as German and French banks. However, the British government left it entirely up to Eurozone countries to organize the stabilization of banks in Spain (Welfens 2014a). Finally, if one considers the opinion polls of the European Commission on EU integration, then it becomes clear that even as late as the spring of 2015, no extremely negative feedback was forthcoming from the UK based on the results of the surveys.

Thus, from a British perspective, where did Brexit actually come from? How surprising is the British majority decision in the referendum of June 23, 2016? The pro-Brexit majority obviously came as a surprise to the Federal Government of Germany, the governments of France and Italy, and many other governments across Europe—not to mention the European Commission. Firstly, one can point out that, in about four decades, only one British politician had been appointed as President of the European Commission, a fact which can be viewed critically when one considers the number of previous Commission presidents from Germany and France. Both EU member countries and the European Commission itself had invested little energy in establishing important institutions in the UK. With the introduction of the Euro in 1999 as an 'on paper' accounting currency—without the United Kingdom—a certain division in the EU was created, although the UK, in choosing an opt-out, found Denmark on its side. It was up to the other Eurozone countries to convince the hesitant and reluctant United Kingdom and Denmark (and others) through a successful monetary integration.

That the decisive test of this monetary integration was not to be found during a phase of fair weather conditions, but in the context of international economic shocks, was clear. The Eurozone, however, did not pass the test of the shock of the Transatlantic Banking Crisis. In the wake of the disquieting bankruptcy of the fourth largest US investment bank, Lehman Brothers, on September 15, 2008, it was immediately clear that the appetite for risk of international investors had dramatically reduced and the governments of all Eurozone countries should have come together during that autumn in 2008 to agree coordinated actions in terms of financial adjustments and limits to deficit ratios; nothing of the sort happened. On the contrary, each government acted in isolation doing what they thought was right for themselves. In Greece, the EU allowed itself be defrauded by the conservative *Nea Dimocratia* government whose successor government notified the Commission of a politically motivated deficit ratio of 15%; 11 percentage points higher than Athens had reported to Brussels at the beginning of the election year 2009. During the Euro Crisis, institutional innovations were implemented in the EU which were designed to overcome the Crisis, which was eventually achieved by 2015, with the exception of the permanent crisis case of Greece.

By way of comparison, the United States, when faced with the irritating case of the national bankruptcy of Puerto Rico—a quasi-state of the US—in the summer of 2016, quickly tackled the issue with decisions of Congress, while the countries of the Eurozone in 2016 still had not solved the relatively manageable issue of Greece, partly due to the inflexibility and intransigence of Germany. In 2013, Prime Minister Cameron had pointed out the unsolved problems of the Eurozone and other EU-related challenges, including the obvious democratic deficits regarding the EU and the European Commission. The latter had shown little awareness of the issue of a democratic deficit and the EU does indeed have a flaw in its construction, in that it functions without EU-wide political parties, with a European Parliament in the almost permanent state of a grand coalition and with a Commission which has both governmental and parliamentary functions. Most draft legislation in the EU has, for decades, come from the European Commission.

The speech by Prime Minister Cameron at Chatham House (The Royal Institute of International Affairs) in London on November 10, 2015, on the relationship between the United Kingdom and the European Union (The Future of Britain's Relationship with the EU) explains in great detail some of the key points in relation to the EU problem from the perspective of the British government. Cameron drew heavily for inspiration on his Bloomberg speech from three years previously in which he had identified three major problems with regard to the EU—these issues were still relevant in 2015, and there was an additional fourth point:

- The problems of the Eurozone, which should be solved by the countries in the monetary union in the interests of all EU member states.
- The problem of the EU's competitiveness internationally in light of the dynamic rise of new, large suppliers, meaning countries, in the world economy.
- A lack of democratic accountability in politics in Brussels and a divide between the respective national electorates and the politicians at EU level, which is felt especially strongly by the British electorate.
- As a fourth point, Cameron added: "The issue is one of scale and speed, and the pressures on communities that brings, at a time when public finances are already under severe strain as a consequence of the financial crisis. This was a matter of enormous concern in our recent general election campaign and it remains so today… Unlike some other member states, Britain's population is already expanding. Our population is set to reach over 70 million in the next decades

and we are forecast to become the most populous country in the EU by 2050. At the same time, our net migrating is running at over 300,000 a year. That is not sustainable."

The EU tendency to engage in increasing integration (i.e., the goal of an "ever closer union") is not a goal shared by the United Kingdom. In the UK, there is far more interest in international trade liberalization and joint security policies. However, even when a country is willing to engage in EU cooperation in the area of defense/security, national security must remain a competence of national governments. Cameron's government also disliked part of the legal framework in a European context: it wishes to replace the European Convention of Human Rights, which had been approved by a previous Labour government, with a new British Bill of Rights.

One can certainly regard the estimation of Prime Minister Cameron, that the United Kingdom, with a population growth of 0.4%, is overburdened by the levels of immigration referred to, as questionable. The cutbacks in terms of fiscal transfers to local authorities, carried out by his own government—as a result of the pressure to reduce the deficit—caused the impression of excessive demand in many British cities: this took the form of an insufficient provision of communal services and the failing performance of the National Health Service (NHS)— the standard offerings of which are free for patients. Cameron, strangely, interpreted these developments as resulting from an overburden on British systems as a result of immigration. In his speech, Cameron called on new EU member countries to in future accept limited access to social benefits for their citizens after accession. Here, however, one must critically consider that it was the United Kingdom of all countries, together with only Sweden and Ireland, which chose not to impose any transitional period on migration from the Eastern European accession countries in 2004, unlike Germany which settled on a seven-year timeframe for a transition period. This fact was not mentioned by Cameron in his speech. Cameron stressed though, that he had achieved a compromise meaning that EU immigrants who had not found a job within six months would have to return to their home country; however, he still

(a) UK employment rates by country of birth
As a percentage of population aged 16-64, 2015 Q4[1]

PAK & BGD, Rest of world, Africa (excl. ZAF), IND, USA, United Kingdom, EU14, ZAF, EU27, EU2, EU8, AUS & NZL

(b) Migrants from the EU by educational attainment
Percentage, 2014[2]

■ Less than primary, primary and lower secondary education (levels 0-2)
□ Upper secondary and post-secondary non-tertiary education (levels 3 and 4)
■ Tertiary education (levels 5-8)

ITA, GRC, FIN, DEU, PRT, FRA, NLD, ESP, HUN, BEL, AUT, CZE, SVN, IRL, United Kingdom, SWE, DNK, LUX

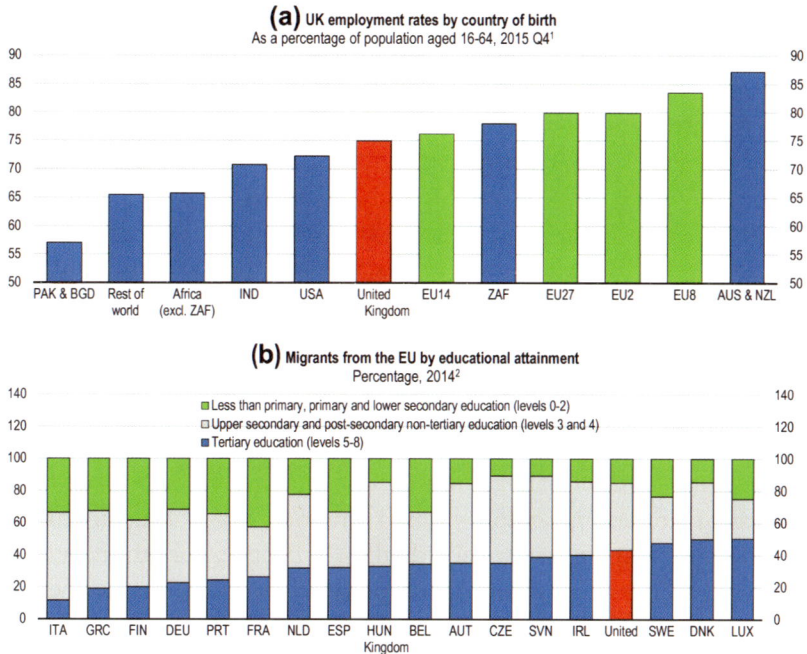

Fig. 4.2 UK employment rates of immigrants by country of birth (A; Numbers for 4th Quarter 2015; EU8 = Eastern European EU members from 2004 Enlargement, EU2=Bulgaria and Romania) and Educational Attainment by Nationality (B; *green* = low-level qualification, *gray* = medium, *blue/red* = high-level qualification). *Source* OECD (2016a), The Economic Consequences of Brexit: A Taxing Decision, OECD Economic Policy Paper, No. 16, Paris, p.26. Statlink http://dx.doi.org/10.1787/888933351113

wished that future EU migrants would have to work for a minimum of four years before they could avail of work-related transfers from the state or other advantages such as social housing. Cameron indicated that the relevant transfers amounted to £6,000 ($7,300) annually for many immigrants and that 10,000 newly arrived families were receiving over £10,000 ($12,200) per year in transfers from the state.

Statistics for the United Kingdom (Fig. 4.2) clearly show that the rate of employment for migrants from Eastern European EU member countries (EU8 relates to the 2004 accession countries, while EU2 relates to the 2007 accession states of Romania and Bulgaria) are, on average, actually higher than for British citizens of working age. However, the share of immigrants with a third-level educational qualification is in many migrant groups below the British average; in the case of Sweden, Denmark, and Luxembourg, the qualification structure is better. In the 10 years following 2004, immigrants from Eastern European EU countries certainly played a large contributory role in the growth of British real income and there is also evidence of a high level of entrepreneurship in terms of the founding of firms. Why Cameron chose to present EU immigration in such a bad light is difficult to understand.

In the thinking of the conservative Cameron government, and presumably also in that of many of their voters, the high numbers of immigrants played an important role in putting a strain on the British public finances; for English workers, the fear of downward wage pressures in the context of migrants coming from relatively poor EU member states was an important aspect. In negotiations with the EU in early 2015, Cameron did in fact reach a compromise that immigrants should only receive certain transfer payments (i.e., particular state benefits) after four years. Obviously, the concessions by the EU were insufficient to prevent a pro-Brexit majority in the referendum on June 23, 2016.

A study from PWC (2015), "The World in 2050," clearly contributed to forming the opinion of Prime Minister Cameron. That study predicted an annual population growth between 2014 and 2050 of + 0.4% for the United Kingdom, + 0.6% for the United States, and − 0.4% for Germany. Additionally, the PwC analysis estimated, for the same time period, 2.2% growth in real per capita income in the UK, 2% in the US, 1.9% in the Netherlands and Germany, 1.8% in the case of Japan, and 1.6% for both France and Italy. It is evidently implausible for the annual population growth in the UK to reach 0.4%, particularly as the May government clearly would like to introduce considerable restrictions on immigration from EU countries. Exactly why the per capita income growth should be higher in the United Kingdom than in the United States is unclear. It seems to be the case that the Cameron government put a lot of trust in the study from PwC, and Cameron referred to the figures contained in that analysis, and in the UN population projections, in this speech at Chatham House. In any event, it must be noted that prognoses covering a time period of almost forty years into the future are subject to great uncertainty and should be treated accordingly, i.e., interpreted with caution. As regards downward wage pressure from immigrants, this is only a modestly significant problem for unskilled workers (see Nickell and Saleheen 2015) and UK government support for immigrant entrepreneurship plus a special EU fund to encourage such activities could help make immigration a general win–win situation; to effectively say no to immigration from EU countries—unless it involves high-skilled workers— is very strange for a leading OECD country. Mrs. May's emphasis on more justice in society can be understood to mean only the British society but the UK is part of a wider European society, and for a Prime Minister who wants her country to be a globally open economy, a purely inward-looking view is inadequate.

Some months prior to the referendum, Oliver (2016) noted in relation to the anti-EU United Kingdom Independence Party (UKIP) and the common Euroskepticism in the United Kingdom (which had increased as a result of difficult EU–Russia relations over the Ukraine question): "The surge in support for UKIP is not simply about the EU. Its support is also about anti-politics, anti-immigration and anti-London. As a result of the UK's majoritarian electoral system, UKIP has struggled to turn votes into MPs, but it has succeeded in taking votes from all the other UK parties." This implies, however, that the referendum result was not simply an expression of broad anti-EU sentiment, although the "European question" had definitely played a role in discussions in the UK for many years. The attempt, over four decades, to create a sustainable pro-EU majority of the people in the United Kingdom was ultimately unsuccessful.

The Government White Paper on the United Kingdom's Exit

In the government White Paper, "The United Kingdom's exit from and new partnership with the European Union" (HM Govt 2017b), the May government argues that regaining control over immigration is a key motive for the UK's leaving of the European Union. However, not only was immigration from both the EU15 (Western Europe) and EU12 (Eastern European EU countries) economically useful for the United Kingdom, it even brought a net fiscal bonus for the United Kingdom as Organisation for Economic Co-operation and Development (OECD) studies have shown (Fig. 4.3); the chart on net migration to the UK shown in the government's White Paper indeed indicates that immigration from Eastern Europe was relatively small and the main dynamics of overall net immigration in the decade before 2016 resulted primarily from immigration from non-EU countries. In a political economy perspective, one may argue with respect to the facts on immigration: the May government clearly misleads the public under the heading 'Controlling Immigration' in the White Paper: "…in the last decade or so, we have seen record levels of long-term net migration in the UK…and that sheer volume has given rise to public concern about pressure on public services, like schools and our infrastructure, especially housing, as well as placing downward pressure on wages for people on the lowest incomes. The public must have confidence in our ability to control immigration. It is simply not possible to control immigration overall when there is unlimited free movement of people to the UK from the EU…We will design our immigration system to ensure that we are able to control the numbers of people who come here from the EU. In future, therefore, the Free Movement Directive will no longer apply and the migration of EU nationals will be subject to UK law" (HM Govt 2017b).

Is leaving 27 EU partner countries really a natural and rational solution for a strong and rising immigration pressure from non-EU countries? Chart 5.1 from the British government's White Paper of Brexit—see Fig. 4.4—simply shows how inconsistent the rhetoric of both the Cameron governments and the current May government on EU immigration policy has been. Is the UK really overwhelmed by EU immigrants so that government is facing problems in providing sufficient public investment for more schools, more defense, more

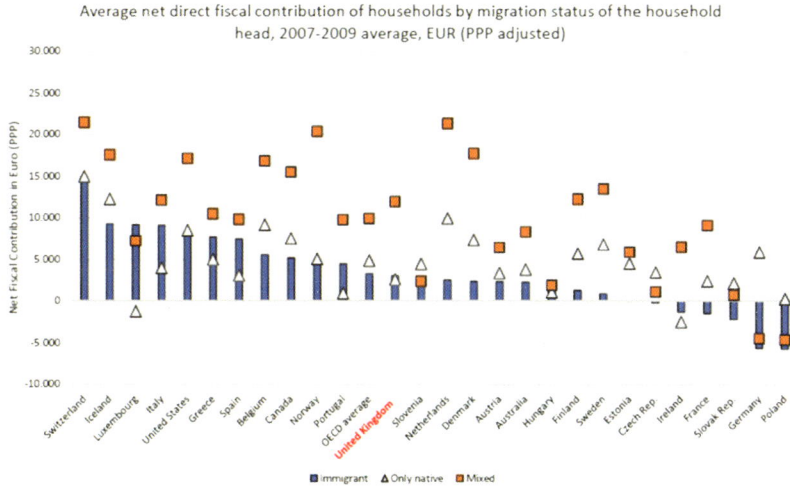

Average net direct fiscal contribution of households by migration status of the household head, 2007-2009 average, EUR (PPP adjusted)

Fig. 4.3 Average net direct fiscal contribution of households by migration status. *Source* Own calculations based on data contained in OECD International Migration Outlook 2013

police, et cetera? OECD studies show that EU immigrants actually bring a net contribution to the UK government budget so that immigrants from EU countries actually help finance public expenditures for British citizens. If the UK has a functioning housing market—as one may assume—then increasing demand for housing should bring about more construction activities, and if a large number of immigrants are initially working in the construction sector, these immigrants would actually build the houses and apartments they need. If, however, local or regional government is blocking additional housing construction by way of an administrative wait-and-see policy, then the resulting housing problems in the UK should not be blamed on EU net immigration.

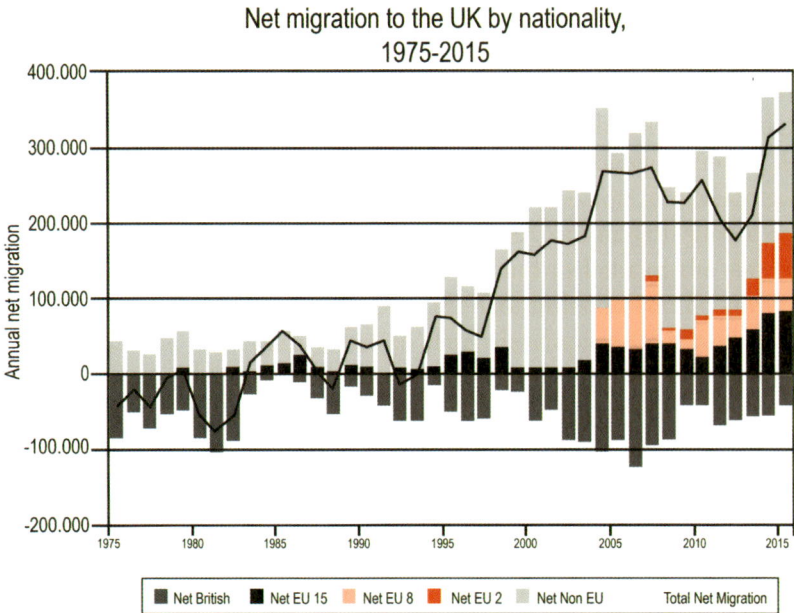

Fig. 4.4 Net immigration to the UK by nationality (1975–2015). *Source* HM Govt. White Paper: The United Kingdom's exit from and new partnership with the European Union, February 2017 (Color added for clarity: PJJW)

Institutional Weaknesses and European Disintegration

With Brexit, the danger has emerged of a rift between the United Kingdom and the EU27. Furthermore, one can assume that a more intense conflict in Ukraine, or Crimea, will break out. The government in Kiev could try to strengthen their position in eastern Ukraine and, in doing so, provoke a Russia counteraction; Russia could also consider taking advantage of Brexit, and the resulting uncertainty in the West, to improve their own position in the Ukraine conflict.

The European Union will, as a result of the withdrawal of the United Kingdom, in the longer term see itself confronted with a considerable EU disintegration dynamic. The starting point is the consideration that the EU withdrawal will burden the UK with considerable adjustment costs and that this could initially reinforce EU solidarity and cohesion. However, after a number of years of reduced growth in the United Kingdom, the effect of the currently just planned—and by then possibly ratified—free trade agreements with the US, Canada, Australia, and other Asian countries, as well as countries in Africa and Latin America, will have an expansive impact on the economy in the UK, as will deregulation measures. The EU27, on the other hand, coming under the pressure of unresolved Eurozone problems, could experience persistent weak growth leading to more and more countries asking the question of if they should not also follow the UK's lead and move towards an exit from the EU: more national control over the borders, over immigration, and over regulation. Economically speaking, that may be a disadvantage for a vast majority of EU member countries in the sense of a loss of EU's trade creation effects and innovation dynamics. However, firstly, economic aspects aside, there are other benefits—for example relating to internal security—and secondly, it is very possible that a comparison of the economic growth rates of the Eurozone or EU27 with non-EU countries, and with the UK in particular, will show the EU falling behind in the long run.

With the withdrawal from the EU, the conservative May government will have a number of years to put the UK on a growth-friendly track. In this respect, Prime Minister May has announced that the government will promote and support an economy which will be of benefit to all citizens. Secretary of State for International Trade Liam Fox and Secretary of State for Exiting the European Union (also known as the Exit Minister) David Davis have stated that they want to strengthen the growth dynamics of the UK through the concluding of international trade agreements with countries outside of Europe. That will first only be possible in the medium term; however, the government has a large incentive to prove to its own citizens, and indeed the other 27 EU member states, that one can achieve stable, permanent economic development outside the EU. The European Commission and the European Council, on the other hand, have a quasi-'parallel but opposite' incentive, to show that European integration is a model for economic success. However, conceptually, there are hardly any approaches towards growth-friendly and integration-strengthening EU reforms and the abundance of unsolved problems, from the Euro Crisis to the refugee crisis, and the related differences over the implementation of the Schengen Agreement, means that an economically and politically weakened EU27 could try to live on as is. Germany and France, as the traditional leaders, could not even agree in 2016 to complete the negotiations on the Transatlantic Trade and Investment Partnership (TTIP)—important for more growth and jobs—by the end of the year came the suggestion from both governments that, following Brexit, TTIP was a politically defunct project.

The tendency towards EU integration may decline in many EU countries in the long term, should the EU and its member countries not undertake comprehensive reforms and find solutions to important questions such as the Eurozone, the refugee wave, and the Ukraine–Russia question. One thing can be said with certainty, the EU without the United Kingdom is in a worse position with regard to Russia than before. Conversely, Russia's diplomatic position in the Ukraine conflict has been clearly improved by Brexit. This is sure to be seen as a worrisome development by the US.

One skeptical view of the EU remains after Brexit, particularly as the EU may have persistent security problems as a result of the Schengen Area—further Islamist attacks in EU countries may lead to a rising voter share for populist and right-extremist parties in European countries: the manifestos of these parties often support withdrawal from the EU and a renewed nationalism.

Should the security situation in the EU not be improved considerably, then less freedom of movement and thus the de facto abolition of the Schengen Agreement can be expected in the medium term. It is unlikely that security can be enhanced to a sustainable level, as some of the Muslim youth from immigrant families in EU countries are obviously susceptible to radical Islamist Internet-based propaganda. That may in fact help in maintaining cooperation between the UK and the EU27 in terms of security policies, but it may also lead to difficulties for France and Belgium, above all, as their youth unemployment has been high for over 30 years. The youth unemployment rates in these countries—three times that of Switzerland—are essentially caused by misguided economic policies. In particular, the far too high national minimum wages force large numbers of low-skilled youths into unemployment and sometimes, indirectly, into a move towards petty criminality. From there, and occasionally via radicalizing periods of incarceration (under the influence of extremist cellmates or prison spiritual counselors), some turn to engaging in terrorism, as numerous examples in Belgium and France have shown. This frightening potential side effect of excessive minimum wages is often overlooked in the discussion about minimum wages; for example, in Germany, the then SPD politician and later head of the *Die Linke* party, Oskar Lafontaine, was allowed to enthuse, unchallenged, for a decade on German TV talkshows about the allegedly unproblematic minimum wage in France. This fundamental error in judgment was eventually made clear to everyone under President Hollande—as the French government introduced a state subvention of firms with minimum wage staff—first, the country introduced, by law, a minimum wage higher than necessary and at a uniform level nationally (i.e., undifferentiated by region), and then in order to avoid an even higher youth unemployment rate—and long-term unemployment—the state needs to pay firms a subvention to help cover the cost of offering minimum wage jobs: this subvention amounts to circa 1% of Gross Domestic Product, which, assuming a real trend growth rate of economic output of 1.5%, leads to a long-term general government debt ratio of 67% according to the Domar formula. The failed French minimum wage policy alone breaks the Maastricht Treaty target of a debt ratio ceiling of 60% contained in the Stability and Growth Pact of the Eurozone.

Conversely, Germany's fiscal policy is also not well advised. If one sets an upper limit for the cyclically adjusted state deficit ratio in the constitution of 0.35%, then that would imply, with a 1.5% trend growth rate of real income, a debt ratio of 23.3%. That is peculiarly low, even lower than in Switzerland. Clearly, the setting of this extremely low upper limit for the deficit quote of the Federal Republic—and the setting the structural deficit rate of the federal states at zero from 2020—during the Euro Crisis was intended by Berlin as a signal of the highest levels of debt policy virtue, in order to enable Germany to exert pressure more easily on Eurozone countries in breach of the deficit and debt limits contained in the Maastricht Treaty. However, with a long-term German debt ratio of 23.3%, the average rating classification of government bonds (i.e., the important grading of the trustworthiness of the state in terms of bonds) in the Eurozone would, in general, deteriorate, and the result would be higher real interest rates for practically the entire Eurozone—and that is not at all in Germany's interest. The wrong objectives in terms of economic policy from Berlin, Paris, Rome, and other capital cities are in no way helpful in overcoming the problems in Europe. After Brexit, there is a need for all EU member states to critically reassess their own national economic and political situation and to develop a broader international perspective in this analysis. Smart and effective policy consultation could play an important role; however, this seems to be available in only a small number of EU countries. Here, with regard to Germany, one can take as an example the role of the Council of Economic Experts, under then Chairman Bernd Rürup, which with one annual expert report clearly shaped the program of the second Schröder government and significantly contributed to successful reforms in Germany and the return to full employment. A pragmatic dialogue between science and politics (i.e., between experts and politicians) was helpful. In the strained atmosphere surrounding Brexit, it is extremely important that such a dialogue occurs once again.

A survey by the Bertelsmann Foundation from spring 2016 resulted in a number of interesting findings, which showed, in particular, that EU supporters in many EU countries wished for the UK to remain in the EU (Bertelsmann Foundation 2016). This finding makes clear that from the perspective of the citizens of the EU27, there is, on the one hand, support for British membership of the EU, while on the other hand an awareness of the economic benefits of UK membership is also present. Thus, there is certainly a reasonable basis, from a political point of view, upon which to try to continue the process of EU integration, as it has occurred for over four decades now, with the active participation and cooperation of the United Kingdom.

References

Becker, S. O., Egger, P., & Von Ehrlich, M. (2010). Going NUTS: The Effects of EU structural funds on regional performance. *Journal of Public Economics, 94,* 578–590.

Bertelsmann Foundation. (2016). "Bleibt Doch. Die Kontinentaleuropäer, das Britische Referendum und ein möglicher Brexit", de Vries, C. und Hoffmann, I., eupinions #2016/2.

HM Government. (2014c). "The government published the last 7 reports in UK's review of EU Balance of Competences today". https://www.gov.uk/government/news/final-reports-in-review-of-eu-balance-of-competences-published.

HM Government. (2017b). *The United Kingdom's exit from and new partnership with the European Union.* London: Government White Paper.

Nickell, S., & Saleheen, J. (2015). The impact of immigration on occupational wages: evidence from Britain, Bank of England, Staff Working Paper N. 574, December 2015.

Oates, W. E. (1999). An Essay on Fiscal Federalism. *Journal of Economic Literature, 37,* 1120–1149.

OECD. (2016a). The Economic Consequences of Brexit: A Taxing Decision, OECD Economic Policy Paper, No. 16, Paris: OECD Publishing.

Oliver, T. (2016). A European Union without the United Kingdom: The Geopolitics of a British Exit from the EU, LSE Ideas, Strategic Update 16.1, February 2016, London.

Pearce, M., & Stewart, G. (2001). *British Political History 1867–2001: Democracy and Decline (3rd ed.).* London: Routledge.

PWC (2015). *The World in 2050: Will the shift in global economic power continue?* February 2015. London.

Schröder, H. -C. (2010). *Geschichte Englands* (6th ed.). Munich: Beck.

Sinn, H. W. (2016). *Der Schwarze Juni: Brexit, Flüchtlingswelle, Euro-Desaster – Wie die Neugründung Europas gelingt.* Freiburg: Herder.

Welfens, P. J. J. (2014a). Overcoming the EU Crisis and Prospects for a Political Union, Paper presented at the bdvb research institute/EIIW conference 'Overcoming the Euro Crisis', March 2014. *International Economics and Economic Policy, 13*(1), 2016.

Welfens, P. J. J. (2014b). Nationale und grenzübergreifende Kindergeldzahlungen Deutschlands: ein Reformvorschlag auf Kaufkraftparitätenbasis, EIIW Press Release, 14. May 2014. www.eiiw.eu.

5

Key Issues for the New British Government

The first political victim of the Brexit referendum was British Prime Minister David Cameron, who announced in the immediate wake of the vote that he would resign by October 2016. The Conservative Party leadership decided that two candidates should quickly be proposed, such that at the party's conference which was due to take place at the end of September—and which was soon brought forward to the beginning of September—a new party leader could be elected; the new leader of the party would also automatically assume the role of Prime Minister. Just one week after the referendum, the ex-Mayor of London, Boris Johnson, declared that he would not be putting his name forward as a candidate for party leader. Evidently, his "partner in crime" during the Brexit campaign, Secretary of State for Justice Michael Gove, had cast doubt on the leadership qualities of Johnson—and the latter threw in the towel. In any case, it was a particularly strange occurrence that quite soon after the British cabinet had reached a majority decision on an EU referendum, six ministers had posed for a photograph before the head-quarters of the Leave.EU movement. The internal cleavages regarding European policy which were dividing the Conservative Party were clear

© The Author(s) 2017
P.J.J. Welfens, *An Accidental Brexit*,
DOI 10.1007/978-3-319-58271-9_5

for all to see. On July 13, the new government, led by Theresa May, emerged.

The new minister with responsibility for EU exit negotiations in Theresa May's cabinet, David Davis, delivered a Brexit-themed lecture as a Member of Parliament on February 4, 2016, at the Institute of Chartered Engineers (Davis 2016) in which he formulated the most important aspects of an EU withdrawal from his point of view. One can assume that these perspectives are also core considerations in terms of Davis' realpolitik and will also be key to the negotiations with the EU. It is evident that part of the British criticism of the EU is entirely justified and that the European Commission, under Presidents Barroso and Juncker, did not have a reasonable strategy to appropriately accommodate the interests of the second-largest EU member state in Gross Domestic Product (GDP) terms; while Germany and France, in particular, with their common critical position vis-à-vis the Transatlantic Trade and Investment Partnership (TTIP) to some extent also drove the United Kingdom towards the door. Nevertheless, without the effective anti-EU rhetoric of David Davis—one-time Europe Minister under Conservative PM John Major—and the disorganization surrounding the referendum process, there would not have been a Brexit.

In his speech, Davis criticized the fact that the European Union had negotiated free trade agreements with numerous countries; however, the only Commonwealth country with whom such an agreement was reached was South Africa. That the EU did not make much progress with the US in terms of the TTIP liberalization project and that the inclusion of the financial markets, crucial from the United Kingdom's point of view, was not necessarily secured within the framework of TTIP, appeared to be severe shortcomings; indirectly responsible for these failings are unresolved conflicts between the American and French film industries.

One can note, that during 2015/16 there was an apparent tendency for representatives of both the French and German governments not to really support TTIP. That hesitance was not only problematic from the perspective of French and German economic and labor market interests, but also contributed indirectly to the Brexit sentiment in the United Kingdom. The transatlantic free trade project TTIP, particularly important to the UK, was not adequately promoted by the governments in Paris and Berlin due to unsubstantive and invalid reservations (with the exception of the issues regarding the courts of arbitration). Germany did not show itself to be an effective go-between bringing large EU member states together and if the largest EU country should only follow a course of egocentric self-interest, then that is not conducive to community interests and EU stability, respectively.

After all, in surveys conducted in the aftermath of Brexit, 70% of Germans declared that the involvement of the United Kingdom in the EU is important to them. Did the government of the Federal Republic of Germany pay sufficient heed to this aspect?

Davis also referred to possible negotiation approaches with respect to access to the EU single market and indicated that neither the Norway–EU nor the Switzerland–EU model would be sensible solutions, as these would entail retaining the freedom of movement, in the end a majority of the British people did indeed vote in the referendum to reject the dynamic of high immigration. Thus the Norwegian and Swiss models are out of the question. A customs union between the UK and the EU, similar to the arrangement between Turkey and the EU, is also out of the question as that would mean that the UK could not pursue truly independent trade policies.

As a model worthy of consideration with respect to the design of the future UK–EU relationship, Davis refers to the recently concluded Canada–EU Comprehensive and Economic Trade Agreement (CETA). Considering the anti-liberalization sentiment within the political circles of certain continental European countries—strengthened by the Brexit referendum—it is not a certainty that a full European ratification of the CETA Treaty will actually take place (not only does the European Parliament have to consent, but also the national parliaments in all member states and even the regional parliaments in Belgium—the parliament of Wallonia initially refused to endorse the deal, however this was subsequently reversed). This problem remains even though in 2015 Canada, under pressure from the EU, agreed to the establishment of a form of commercial tribunal rather than the originally foreseen court of arbitration for the resolution of conflicts between states and foreign investors; the opening of Canadian public invitations to tender to firms from Europe and vice versa was agreed; and the wide-ranging abolition of tariffs. The UK will certainly seek to emulate this liberalization approach with regard to the EU.

Thus, in contrast to both the Norway–EU Agreement and the Switzerland–EU Agreement, there would be neither contributory payments to the EU budget—which for the UK amounted to almost £7.6/$9.3 billion in contibution payments to the EU in 2015—nor would there be free migration from EU countries towards the United Kingdom. In the document with the pro-Brexit arguments for the presentation on February 4, it is indicated that this money could be used by the UK for its own goals and interests.

The United Kingdom can also expect rising levels of immigration from Eastern European EU members. The relationship between the British minimum wage and the average wage in Poland was still relatively high in 2015/16—almost 2:1—and this should increase further until 2020. Thus, the incentive to move to the United Kingdom will increase and this is structurally reflective of the problem of high uncontrolled migration from EU countries. The advantages of the EU single market for the United Kingdom are deemed by David Davis to be marginal, in terms of migration he clearly assumed negative effects; however, the economic analysis shows that migration from EU countries is, in fact, a positive for the UK. The immigration analyses, examining migrants from EU member states show positive effects in almost all aspects; even the employment rate of EU migrants in the UK is higher than that for Britons themselves.

Furthermore, claimed Davis, the United Kingdom, when compared to seven other non-EU, Organisation for Economic Co-operation and Development (OECD) member states, had, since the foundation of the EU single market, shown lower growth rates in terms of exports—which he claimed indicated that the United Kingdom had a good chance to record a stronger growth in exports (PJJW: in real income) as non-EU member. (PJJW: from an economic perspective, that is not the case—as the solid analysis of Aichele and Felbermayr (2015) shows). Moreover, the European Commission had continued its excessive regulatory activities despite British objections. The share of British exports which went to the EU fell over time which shows that there are good opportunities to grow export rates outside the EU (PJJW: that is, however, a trivial argument, as economic growth in Asia was higher than in Europe with its high per capita income and will likely remain so for decades to come). The Euro monetary integraton area, with its own quite evident problems with regard to stability, threatens to be a growing risk for the EU in the long term. This interjection can be understood as meaning that the countries of the Eurozone and the European Commission are obviously incapable of solving the problems of the Eurozone with regard to compliance with, and adherence to, the Stability.

Moreoever, argued Davis, as a result of the tendency favoured by most of the other EU countries, the United Kingdom over time would be increasingly sidelined in an evolving EU (the so-called "ever closer union"). The political interest and will to engage in this kind of integration deepening is not present in the UK; the political arguments in favor of withdrawing from the EU outweigh the economic reasons for remaining.

There are certainly aspects of Davis' analysis which one can agree with. It can be acknowledged as an objective fact, that the European Commission has engaged in regulatory activities in a growing range of areas, which often represent little more than a hindrance to innovative competition and with that to the international competitiveness of firms—and also to employment—in the EU, i.e., in EU member states; and moreover, represents a paternalistic approach to consumers in Europe. Can one imagine that the US Congress would concern itself in its legislative capacity, in the spirit of Barroso, with different types of light bulb and the strength of vacuum cleaners as the European Commission and Parliament have done in the EU?

References by economically experienced critics to certain institutional weaknesses of the Eurozone are certainly worthy of serious consideration. Only in July 2016, did the European Economic and Financial Affairs Council (ECOFIN, made up of EU Finance Ministers) essentially decide in the course of excessive deficit procedures against member states that a penalty would be imposed on Spain and Portugal due to their failure to abide by previous commitments to reduce their respective deficits; however, no fines were imposed (sums which would be deposited by the countries in question into a form of escrow account, in the event of further transgressions, deposited amounts would be forfeited as a financial penalty). Without a political union, the Eurozone is destined to collapse, in comparison with other OECD countries it will experience below average economic growth and due to continuing political differences will become a less attractive partner to the United States, China, and other countries.

One considerable and possibly even drastic misjudgement by the United Kingdom, and Minister Davis in particular, is to believe that the EU27 could to some extent simply be cut adrift by Brexit and that the UK could simply seek out and assume undisturbed a new independent position in the world economy, in the process of globalization; and that on that basis the UK would then reach an agreement on trade with its former EU partners in order to secure British interests. The influence which the United Kingdom can exert from outside of the European Union on the remaining EU27, or indeed the entire continent, can be expected to be significantly less than was the case while they, as a full member of the EU, sat at the decision-making table in Brussels. Should the EU27 experience a negative economic development in the longer term and a process of disintegration ensue, in which some countries could effectively become pariahs within the Union and others follow the UK's example by actually leaving, then this disintegration trend would result in a bitter end: Europe would return to a situation reminiscent of the late nineteenth century, apart from the fact that many countries are also members of the North Atlantic Treaty Organization (NATO). However, NATO itself could also be destabilized and threatened by EU disintegration.

As was made clear in announcements by the then US presidential candidate Donald Trump in 2016, there are influential voices in the US which could also support an American withdrawal from NATO. Thus it is quite probable that Brexit does not, in fact, serve the economic and security interests of the United Kingdom. Worse still, as the potential of a process of EU disintegation also threatens, there is a risk of contagion with disintegration forces sooner or later also spreading to other integration areas of the world—in such a scenario, the chances for the UK (outside the EU after Brexit) to enjoy high rates of growth in terms of exports to a dynamic world economy are rather slim. The perspective of such an international, indeed global, integration analysis is not to be found in the comments of David Davis, although he did argue that the UK has a good chance to benefit from globalization. Stressing that point in relation to Brexit is almost paradoxical, as being a former colonial power the UK is accustomed to drawing attention to its international connections and relationships.

From Davis' point of view, in relation to trade liberalization, the United Kingdom is first and foremost interested in a free trade agreement with "High Priority" countries: the United States of America, along with Canada and China+Hong Kong. The "Medium Priority" category refers to Australia, Brazil, India, and South Korea. While in the third group are Japan, Indonesia, Mexico, Saudi Arabia, Singapore, Turkey, and South Africa (Fig. 5.1). With the exception of agreements with South Africa, Mexico, and Singapore, plus Canada—and with a relatively low likelihood—the US, the EU has delivered very little from a British perspective. It cannot be disputed that the European Union, as an actor in the matter of the politics and policies of international trade, is extremely slow and hardly active in Asia.

Priority	Country
High	China
	USA
	Canada
	Hong Kong
Medium	Australia
	Brazil
	India
	South Korea
Low	Japan
	Indonesia
	Mexico
	Saudi Arabia
	Singapore
	Turkey
	South Africa

Fig. 5.1 David Davis' List of trade targets ranked by priority. *Source* David Davis' speech on Brexit at the Institute of Chartered Engineers; http://www.daviddavismp.com/david-davis-speech-on-Brexit-at-the-institute-of-chartered-engineers/

One cannot entirely rule out the possibility that, through sophisticated and decisive leadership by the British government in negotiations regarding important international free trade agreements, the UK could achieve good results relatively quickly, that is by 2020/21. If the Eurozone is not capable of tackling its problems by means of intelligent and sustainable reforms, then it is sure to fall behind the UK in terms of growth in the longer term. In turn, that will increase the incentive for non-Euro countries to rather align themselves with the United Kingdom than with the EU. The UK may also remain on a pragmatic course of engaged economic cooperation with China: for example, contrary to the US warnings regarding membership of the China-dominated Asian Infrastructure Investment Bank (AIIB), which was launched in 2015 with its headquarters in Beijing, the United Kingdom agreed relatively early on that it wished to participate as a founding member, on condition however, that China would establish the European headquarters of the AIIB in London. In 2015, China gave the green light on this request.

Under US pressure, Germany delayed taking any action on matters relating to AIIB membership for many months, and it was only when considerations on the matter were transferred from the Federal Ministry for Economic Cooperation and Development, under Minister Müller, to the Office of the Chancellor, was a positive decision on German participation as a founding member of the bank reached. Here, it is quite clear that British diplomacy is traditionally more internationally oriented and decisive than the politics of the Federal Government of Germany.

It remains doubtful whether the UK was well advised to leave the EU after more than 40 years of membership. The country will be facing uncertainty for years to come: during the EU–UK negotiations, which will affect British access to the single market, but also in relation to new agreements and treaties under the World Trade Organization which the UK now needs to conclude. On there other hand, following a certain phase of recession or slowdown in economic growth, the UK could also achieve sustained growth during a period of energetically liberalizing UK-international trade and of step-by-step deregulation—that is the regulations introduced under the EU. However, should the withdrawal from the EU cause, both directly and indirectly, a sinking of economic growth rates, then it is far from certain that the per capita income of the United Kingdom will be higher than it would have been if the country had remained a member state. With regard to the economic welfare aspects, the important thing to note is not the growth rates of the economy as a whole, but the growth rates of per capita income and/or real consumption. If new serious conflicts should emerge as a result of a weakening of integration dynamics in various regions of the world, which would also cause the UK to increase military spending, it is certainly doubtful that Brexit represents a sensible politico-economic development for the UK. One can criticize the entire Brexit referendum manouvre by Conservative PM Cameron, but it was also incumbent upon EU partner countries to demonstrate the benefits of EU membership and argue against Brexit. The European Commission did not, for example, invest money in buying time on British television prior to the referendum to allow an information or advertising campaign—no EU 'info bus' was driven around the streets of London on which the correct weekly UK contribution payments to the EU budget appeared. The EU Representation in London did not have a website presenting basic EU-relevant knowledge in an original and effective way. The anti-EU focus of the British tabloid press hampered the European Commission's attempts to make the EU institutions and politics understandable. From 2013 at least, however, the Commission should indeed have invested more in UK information projects.

Minister David Davis was also responsible for uniquely contradictory comments surrounding Brexit. After the vote against EU integration, Davis claimed he wanted to lead the UK towards a liberalization of global trade: thus presenting more globalization of the British economy as a remedy and strategy for the UK in a post-Brexit scenario. That is a serious contradiction insofar as the industrial workforce of England, who thus far are increasingly seeing themselves as victims of further liberalization in the context of both the EU single market and liberalization rounds of the World Trade Organization, will now not get less globalization of the British economy, but rather the opposite: the Conservative Party government of Theresa May, who among other things had promised to change the UK economy such that it would benefit everybody rather than just increase the income of the upper echelons of society, will as a result of the Davis strategy and the policies of Trade Minister Fox actually move towards further economic liberalization.

That will bring more economic growth, but also lead to larger variations in income between skilled and unskilled workers. Meanwhile, as the Opinium Reseach polls prior to the referendum showed, there is a widespread concern in relation to inequality and low wages. Brexit can also bring temporary benefits, for example, if through reductions in import duties on foodstuffs and groceries the purchasing power of wages, i.e. income, rises. However, if one considers recent studies by the International Monetary Fund (Jaumotte et al. 2008), then economic globalization leads to a convergence of the per capita income of countries, but within each individual country there is a tendency for the ratio of the wages of skilled workers to those of unskilled workers to rise. The differences in income and wealth in the UK, which have risen dramatically during the three decades since 1985—as is also the case in the US—could increase even further. Sharply rising disparities in income in western OECD countries could lead to political tensions, which in turn can adversely affect medium- and long-term real economic growth. There are numerous reasons to doubt whether the world economy has really stabilized since the Transatlantic Banking Crisis began.

References

Aichele, R., & Felbermayr, G. (2015). *Costs and benefits of a United Kingdom exit from the European Union*. Gütersloh: Ifo Study for the Bertelsmann Foundation.

Davis, D. (2016). David Davis' speech on Brexit at the Institute of Chartered Engineers, delivered February 4, 2016, transcript http://www.daviddavismp.com/david-davis-speech-on-Brexit-at-the-institute-of-chartered-engineers/.

Jaumotte, F., Lall, S., & Papageorgiou, C. (2008). *Rising Income Inequality: Technology, or Trade and Financial Globalization*. IMF Working Paper WP/08/185, Washington, DC.

6

Medium-Term UK Macroeconomic Perspectives

It is easy to understand that the first economic reactions to the Brexit vote come from the financial markets, where changing expectations play a crucial role in price formation. The massive depreciation of the Pound after June 23 came as little surprise to anyone. The brakes were applied to the British economy, which had been developing well during the first six months of 2016. The International Monetary Fund (IMF 2016), in a July 19 update of the World Economic Outlook, presented the first revised prognoses: the Eurozone should actually experience marginally higher growth in 2016 compared to the IMF's spring forecast, but this would fall in 2017 by 0.2 percentage points—to 1.4% growth. This forecast has turned out to be too pessimistic. The United Kingdom's growth rate for 2016 would fall slightly, namely by 0.2 percentage points compared to the spring forecast; however, the downward revision of the projected growth rate for 2017 by 0.9 percentage points was an ominous sign—the UK could expect, according to the IMF, 1.3% economic growth in 2017. Brexit, however, has not yet formally taken place, and 2019 will be the really decisive year, when it is presumed the UK will actually leave the EU. There was no British banking collapse, no major malfunctions of British financial markets as was the

© The Author(s) 2017
P.J.J. Welfens, *An Accidental Brexit*,
DOI 10.1007/978-3-319-58271-9_6

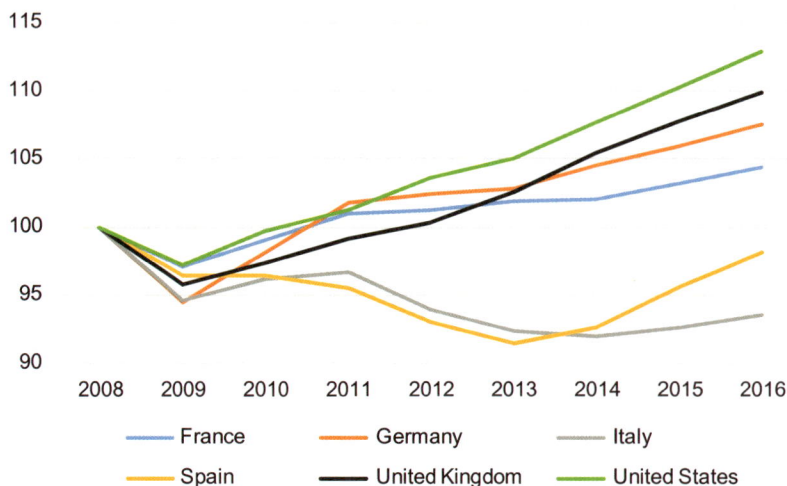

Fig. 6.1 The real gross domestic product of selected countries (Base year 2008 = 100). *Source* IMF, own calculations

case in the run-up to the 2007–2009 Banking Crisis. It was the threatened bankruptcy of Northern Rock—with long queues at the counters and indeed even outside the bank outlets—which made 2007 the first year of the Transatlantic Banking Crisis. In 2008/09, the US, UK, and the Eurozone resisted the forces of a downturn by implementing massive stimulus packages. In the US and the UK, unusual monetary policy quickly followed, which was heavily based on a highly expansive open market approach: the central banks bought huge quantities of sovereign bonds, after central bank interest rate reductions had soon resulted in rates approaching zero. The UK is not threatened with the immediate repetition of a large crisis such as occurred from 2007 to 2010, rather a gradual leveling off of economic growth. Nevertheless, a new financial crisis could still emerge from a politically mismanaged Brexit.

If one considers the real economic development in Germany, France, Spain, Italy, the United Kingdom, and the US between 2008 and 2016 (see Fig. 6.1, 2008 = 100 for all countries), then one can see that following the general economic collapse of 2008/09—the major recession after the bankruptcy of Lehman Brothers—the US, UK, France, and Germany recovered relatively quickly, while for Spain and Italy, the values of 2016 still lay below the starting point in 2008. The US led the way, followed by the UK and Germany, France has fallen behind Germany in terms of economic development. As one can see from the figures for Spain and Italy, almost a fifth of the Eurozone is in serious economic difficulties, although Spain may be able to close the gap in terms of the development of real income in the medium term—however, this is improbable given the ongoing political blocking of coalitions in Madrid, which hampers the establishment of a reliable government.

British economic development will sink to the level of Germany in the medium term and will likely fall under it temporarily. However, one should not overlook the possibility of a European downturn with a domino effect, which could be briefly and simply described as follows: in 2014 and 2015, Germany recorded about £76/$93 billion in exports to the UK, which corresponds to about 3% of Gross Domestic Product (GDP). On the basis of value-added figures it is actually close to 2% of GDP, meaning a reduction of exports to Britain by 10% would immediately reduce GDP by 0.2%. In addition, there is a negative macroeconomic multiplicator effect, which could bring the minus effect for Germany up to 0.4%. A fall of real income in the United Kingdom and Germany entails reduced French exports to the UK and Germany, which would then reduce France's real income by 0.2%. The decrease in real income in the United Kingdom, Germany, and France leads to a reduction of the exports of Italy and Spain, where the growth of real income could fall by between 0.1 and 0.2%. The fall in the growth of real income in the Eurozone, in turn, implies that British exports to the Eurozone, that is to the EU27 reduce, which ultimately reinforces the original Brexit-related weakened growth prospects due to falling consumption and investment rates.

With regard to Brexit, the primary problem for the UK is the current account deficit, as a high deficit rate must be financed by capital imports. The current account position of the United Kingdom has been negative since 2008—over 3%—and, following an improvement in 2010/11, is again reaching a critical negative magnitude (see Fig. 6.2).

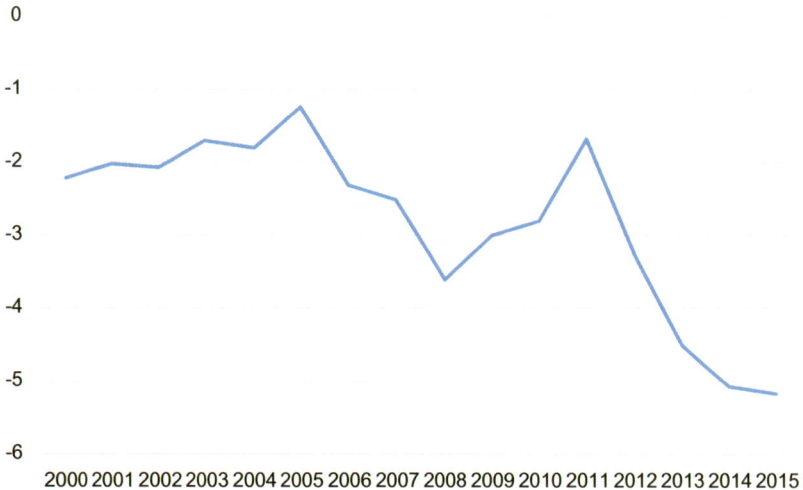

Fig. 6.2 UK current account balance relative to gross domestic product. *Source* IMF, own calculations

The UK imports far more than it exports. The prospects of a significant increase in exports are limited despite a real devaluation in 2016.

Brexit is driving the fluctuation intensity of stock markets across the whole EU, including Germany, to new heights (see Fig. 6.3, which shows a volatility measure for the DAX on the basis of daily data). As instable share prices can also negatively influence the real economy, one should follow the development of such indices closely. The exchange instability indicator is still far removed from the maximum levels reached during the crisis in 2008—with the bankruptcy of Lehman Brothers bank in September of that year—but the financial system in Germany is heading in a problematic direction. Apart from share price volatility, the state of the banking system should be considered, where two major German banks, Commerzbank and Deutsche Bank, give rise to concern. In August 2016, Deutsche Bank dropped out of the Eurozone's Top-50-Stoxx-Indicator (a share price index) and that same month the economist Martin Hellwig commented that, if necessary, Deutsche Bank should be helped in the interest of stabilizing the entire German financial system; one hopes that the fundamentals of large German banks are

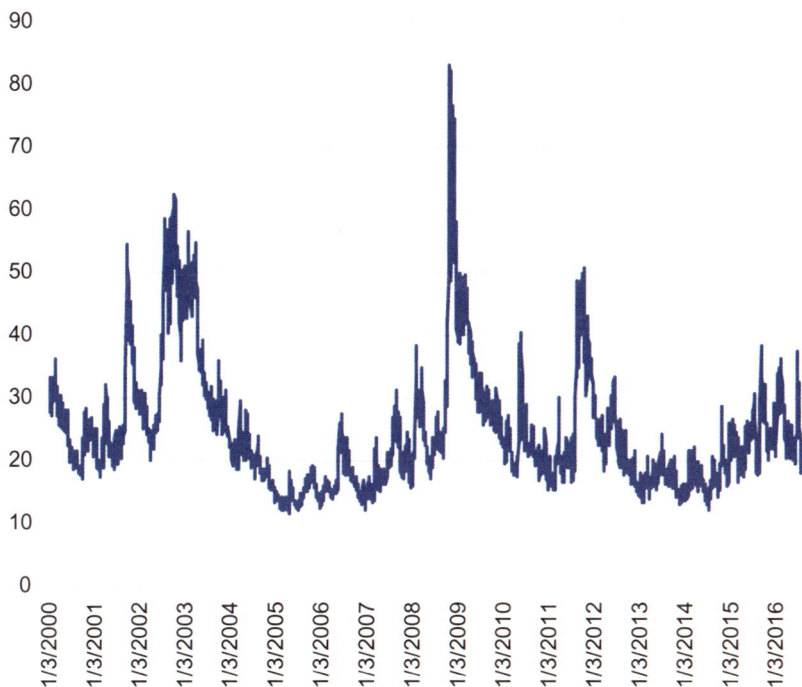

Fig. 6.3 VDAX, German stock market volatility measure (01/01/03–03/08/16, daily data). *Source* datastream, Thomson Reuters

sufficiently sound and that relevant and required restructuring will be undertaken quickly and successfully. There may indeed be banks from the US, UK, France, or China who would be interested in acquisitions in the German banking system should the share prices of major German banks fall further. For British banks, the prospects in this regard are rather limited by the devaluation of the Pound relative to the Euro.

Brexit: Lowest UK Interest Rate and Instability Risks in Europe

On August 4, 2016, the Bank of England reduced their interest rate from 0.5% to just 0.25%, its lowest rate since 1694; this was both a historic and dramatic step to take, as the UK was threatened with a politically self-inflicted downturn thanks to the electoral majority against remaining in the EU. The Governor of the Bank of England, Mark Carney, who had already warned prior to the referendum of the negative effects a decision to leave the EU would entail, expressed his fear that about 250,000 jobs could be lost in the short term due to Brexit shocks. It should be noted, however, that the Bank of England later withdrew somewhat from this pessimistic outlook, citing issues regarding the timeframe of the Brexit process. He defended the decision to lower the interest rates, for the first time in seven years, and to extend the quantitative easing program of purchasing sovereign bonds by £60/$73 billion, by referring to the feared, and expected, downturn—considering the customary leading economic indicators, the following danger exists: growth of 0.1% is expected in the third quarter of 2016 and stagnation during the two-quarters which follow. There would be an immediate depreciation of the Pound by 1.5% on the market, share prices will rise in expectation of falling interest rates—the rate on 10-year government bonds fell to 0.63% in expectation of the Bank of England's bond-buying move (which could be interpreted as a 10-year market expectation of a stable or continuously falling price level). In the medium term, the Bank of England will eventually, due to the extension of the bond-buying program, hold about a third of outstanding sovereign bonds on the balance sheet.

Assuming an average interest rate of 3%, £1,000 ($1,220) billion recorded on the balance sheet of the Bank of England will save the British state £30/$37 billion in terms of interest payments annually (about 1% of GDP), as long as it is assumed that the interest payments by the state to the Bank of England will in turn return to the state via higher central bank profits. That will reduce the UK's general government debt ratio from 90% to about 45% as long as only that part of the debt is considered which is held by the private sector. Indirectly, the long-standing policy of purchasing sovereign bonds allows the UK to keep income tax rates circa 1% lower than would otherwise be the case. The level of the growth path, under normal assumptions in a Solow growth model, will then be about half a percentage point higher than without it. In actual fact, the impact will be somewhat higher, as the central bank's bond-buying strategy also has the effect of reducing interest rates on new debt, which means that for £110/$134 billion of new debt—at an interest rate of just 0.6% rather than the previous 3%—an additional £2.5/$3.05 billion could be saved in terms of expenditure on interest payments. On August 10, 2016, the long-term interest rate on sovereign bonds fell to zero.

British voters brought the risks of a Brexit-related downturn on themselves by voting to leave the European Union, and zero interest income on bank deposits will increasingly be a feature of daily life in the UK, particularly as another reduction of interest rates by the Bank of England is conceivable in the medium term. The rate reductions and the monetary policy steps being taken by the Bank are increasing pressure on the British Pound, the depreciation of the currency increases the price of imports and the prospects of a further depreciation could raise the market interest rate—which would reduce the effectiveness of the monetary policy. The sinking of the central bank interest rate to close to zero raises fears that the effectiveness of the monetary policy is already almost exhausted, and an intensified policy with regard to bond-buying on the part of the Bank of England would, should it continue, have efficiency minimizing distortion effects and cause yet a further depreciation of the Pound, which results in appreciation effects for the US Dollar and the Euro and thus brings new deflationary pressure.

A British reduction of interest rates means further pressure on the EU27 to also reduce rates to ultra-low levels. Such a response endangers the profitability and stability of banks across Europe. The European Central Bank had completed a stress test of banks in July 2016, and the Bank of England has basically heralded the need for a new round of testing; sensible policy cooperation in Europe should look different. The challenges facing the European Union have been exacerbated, as the banks can now barely earn enough to cover the cost of capital—instable banks are certainly not an ingredient in the recipe for a long-term economic upturn. The problems in the UK may be less pronounced than in the Eurozone, as in the UK (like the US) a relatively high number of firms are financed via corporate bonds. In the Eurozone, the problem of major banking institutions in certain countries being unstable will be intensified, and the foreseeable moves of the Bank of England to reduce interest rates further will significantly heighten the threat caused by European banking instability. This development is a hindrance to the real economy, especially as share price volatility also increased substantially in Germany and other countries following the June 23 referendum vote for Brexit. As much as the Bank of England's August 4 rate reduction counteracted the first signs of a possible recession, this monetary policy step undermined the perspectives for banking system stability across Europe to the same extent. Moreover, uncertainty in the context of Brexit also adversely affected the UK's real estate sector, losses in wealth are apparent and of a long-term nature—with further insecurities also affecting the UK's relatively important private pension system.

The gradual British economic downturn, which set in after the Brexit vote, together with the real depreciation of the Pound, worsened the perspectives for German exports to the United Kingdom: affecting, above all, the high share of the UK in terms of German automobile exports—which accounted for 32% of German exports to the UK in 2015—Machinery and Equipment (13%), Pharmaceutical products (8%), and Electro-Technical products (7%) in a sectoral perspective. On the import side, parts of German industry will also come under pressure via the high real depreciation of the Pound: British automobiles account for 13% of German imports from the UK; Machinery and Equipment for 12%; Electronic products and aircraft for 8 and 7%, respectively; and Mineral Fuels, in particular, account for a further 12% of German imports from the UK. As one can see, just four branches make up about 50% of exports and imports between Germany and the UK.

Selected Macroeconomic Indicators for the UK

The following graphs show some of the key economic indicators for the UK. The Economic Policy Uncertainty Index for the UK has increased in the months since the referendum and that of the EU was also raised (with a partial artificial overlap since the EU28 contains the UK). As a side effect, one has to anticipate lower investment–GDP ratios in both the UK and in the EU in the medium term. The Policy Uncertainty Index shows greater fluctuations in the context of Brexit than in the

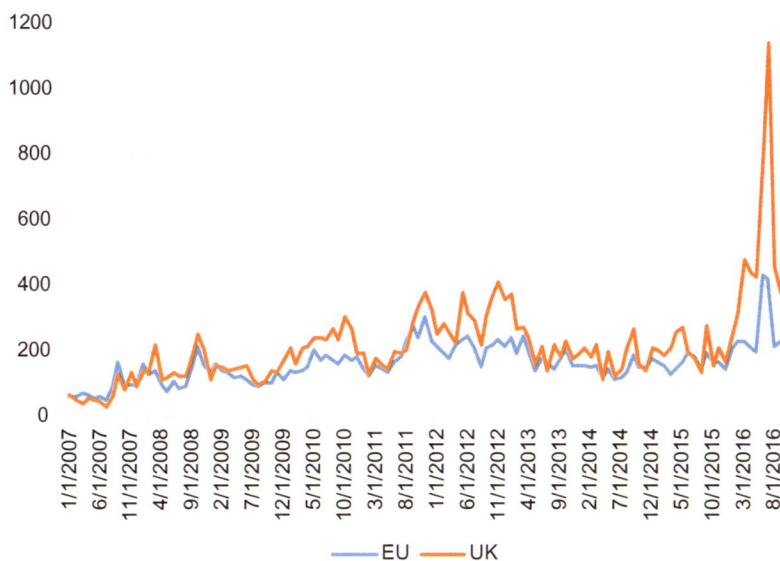

Fig. 6.4 Economic policy uncertainty indices. *Source* financial datastream

context of the Transatlantic Banking Crisis of 2007/08 and two years of Brexit negotiations could mean continued uncertainties in the UK and Europe, respectively—on top of this come the additional new uncertainties created by the Trump administration in the US (see Fig. 6.4); add to this the unclear reaction patterns from China and Japan, and one might face a critical level of heightened investor risk worldwide. As regards the Pound exchange rate (Fig. 6.5), the devaluation after the referendum has been rather strong, but there could be further devaluation pressure in the medium term. The British stock price index has faced an initial decline—immediately after the Brexit decision—and later an increase which, however, was largely driven by the US stock market dynamics: with medium-term prospects that the US stock market rally will not continue much beyond 2018 (Fig. 6.6). British output growth has been fairly stable in 2016—measured as quarterly changes of output (current quarter against previous quarter). At the end of 2016, the growth rate of the EU had been parallel to that the UK—previous quarters typically witnessed lower EU growth rates than in the UK (Fig. 6.7). The British

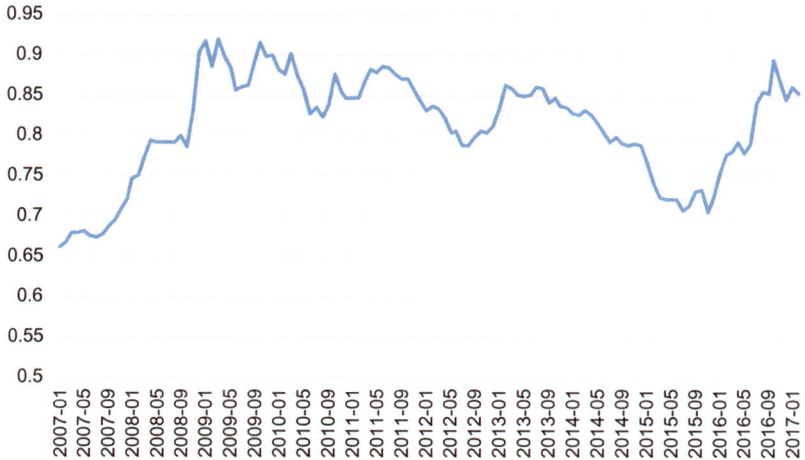

Fig. 6.5 ECB reference exchange rate, UK pound/Euro (monthly). *Source* ECB statistical data warehouse

unemployment rates have remained below those of the EU in 2016 and it is not clear that the British unemployment rates will strongly increase in the medium term (see Fig. 6.8); expansionary impulses from the US economic policy could help the UK to maintain a rather low unemployment rate, moreover, the temporary rise of the British inflation rate in the context of a rather high medium-term devaluation of the Pound implies a Phillips curve-type temporary reduction of the unemployment rate. Furthermore, one cannot rule out that a considerable number of EU citizens would leave the EU during 2017–2020, namely as a consequence of increased uncertainty about the legal and economic status of immigrants from EU countries in the UK (for example, if there are legal uncertainties, immigrant families will be unable to buy their own home since banks usually require a clear legal status if clients want to get a mortgage loan). The November 2016 forecast of the Bank of England is not pessimistic since it assumes that the growth rate of real GDP would remain roughly as it was in 2016—with a tendency to become somewhat lower over time (Bank of England 2016). If, however, the US economic policy should become increasingly inconsistent so that the economic expansion pace of the US remains moderate, or if world

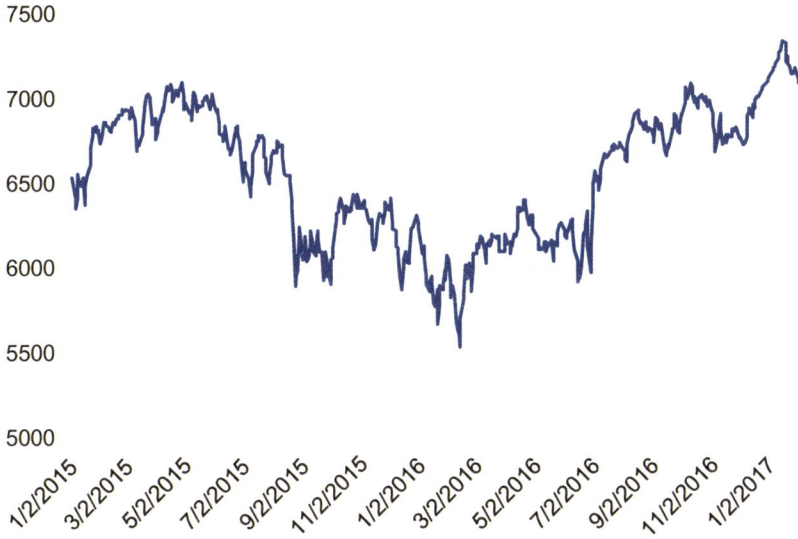

Fig. 6.6 FTSE 100 (daily). *Source* London stock exchange

output growth—facing new US policy uncertainties—should reduce considerably, the British economy would face a fall of output growth to below 1%. The critical issue will be whether or not the UK growth can remain ahead of that in the Eurozone. One should also consider the Bank of England's GDP Forecast (as of late 2016) for the coming years 2017: 1.7%; 2018: 1.5%; and 2019: 1.6%.

What is a Viable New British–EU Trade Policy?

The list of trade targets, which David Davis and other Leave activists suggested as being preferred partners in relation to new trade liberalization agreements with the UK, is not very convincing from an economic perspective, with the exceptions of the US—to date engaged with the EU in negotiating the Transatlantic Trade and Investment Partnership (TTIP)—and China. The latter will be a difficult partner. Free trade with China will be extremely difficult to negotiate, as the UK is a

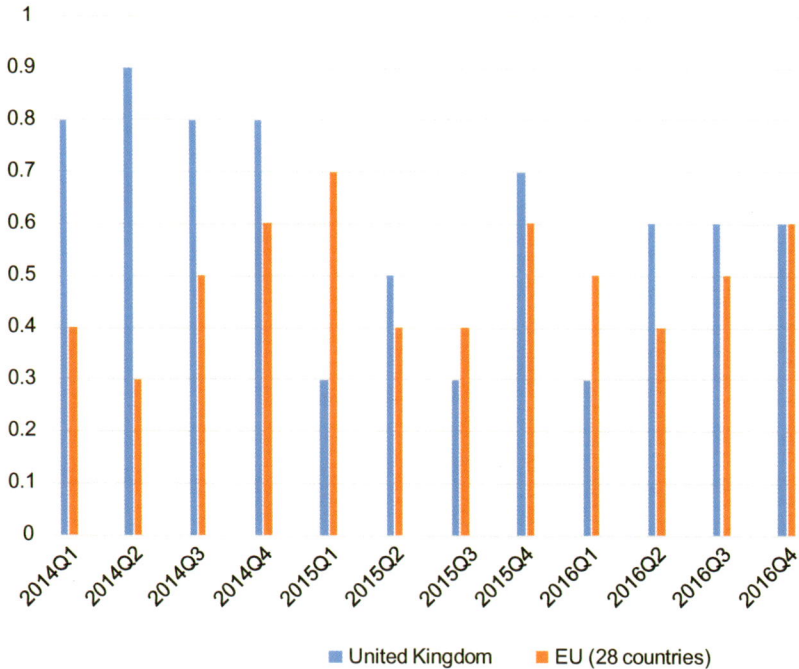

Fig. 6.7 Gross Domestic Product of the EU and United Kingdom, percentage change q/q-1 (quarterly). *Source* Eurostat

relatively small country, in any event it brings less to the table than the EU28 or EU27. Furthermore, free trade with China would sound the death knell for the British steel industry while many other sectors would be confronted with enormous pressure to consolidate. That exports of British services will rise is obvious; however, a simple process of structural transformation in favor of the production of more services will not take place. Moreover, one can also ask where the economic and strategic benefit for the UK lies, should the country become strongly dependent on China in the future. Trade policy is not simply a case of wishful thinking, but must also always reflect key political considerations. Thus, David Davis' list of targets is contradictory, an expression of a generally convincing strategy it most certainly is not.

In a contribution for Global Counsel (Irwin 2016), former Bank of England economist Gregor Irwin argued that the countries often

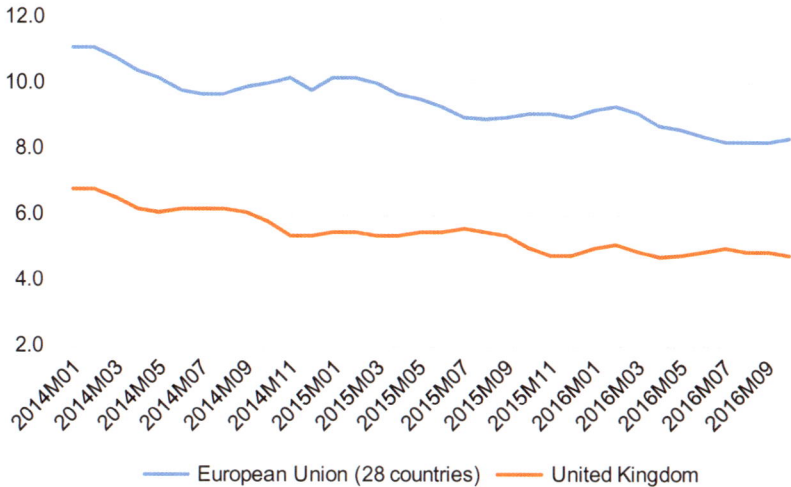

Fig. 6.8   Harmonized unemployment rates (%)—monthly data. *Source* Eurostat

favored in relation to new British trade agreements by the Leave camp during the referendum campaign did not really represent true economic potential for optimal trade creation: giving priority status to Commonwealth countries, as was suggested during the campaign by new members of May's cabinet—Exit Minister David Davis and Trade Minister Liam Fox—is a mistake. It is true that India could be an attractive trade partner; however, the political barriers to trade and liberalization are high and India will certainly require reforms easing Indian migration to the UK and a relaxing of visa requirements. Irwin's analysis shows that Canada and Australia have relatively little added trade potential. The particularly promising countries, which Irwin determined on the basis of the highest growth rates in terms of UK imports (US, China, Mexico, Hong Kong, Vietnam), existing British foreign direct investment stock abroad (the potential for British supplying of intermediate products), and a variance analysis with the EU27, are the US, China, Russia, Brazil, Switzerland, and Singapore.

In the case of Russia, there are limitations to trade for political reasons, while the EU has already signed an extensive free trade agreement with Singapore. Furthermore, Gregor Irwin overlooks the latent conflict between China and the US, in stressing their respective strengths. Nevertheless, it is clear that it would not be advisable for Trade Minister Fox to follow up on the Commonwealth-related trade expansion options emphasized by many EU-skeptics during the Brexit campaign, as they do not seem to offer the large potential for more trade, growth, and jobs suggested. This is yet further evidence that arguments relating to key elements of the Brexit campaign were questionable at best—the voters were misled.

The easiest, most profitable, and productive course of action for the UK with regard to trade liberalization may involve the US, as courts of arbitration are not seen as so sensitive an issue in the UK as they are in, for example, Germany or France. A transatlantic US–UK Trade and Investment Partnership is likely to be implemented from 2020, particularly as the US government will support strengthened cooperation. At the same time, the US will also not want to neglect trade relationships with the EU27; firstly, because US exports to the EU27 are three times as high as those to the UK and secondly, because key political issues are also defined by trade networks. The fact remains, that in regard to TTIP-related matters, there were hidden conflicts of interest between the UK and Germany plus France (as well as other countries). The true significance of the TTIP negotiations and its relevance for intra-EU relationships largely escaped the German government. EU integration means not only egocentrically pursuing one's own self-interest. The thinking within Merkel's government in Berlin is often clearly not EU-focused. From there, the path to a new nationalism is a short one.

References

Bank of England. (2016). Inflation Report, November 2016, London.
IMF. (2016). Uncertainty in the Aftermath of the U.K. Referendum. World Economic Outlook Update, July 19, 2016, Washington DC.
Irwin, G. (2016). British Trade Policy After Brexit: Ruthless Prioritisation Required, Global Counsel, August 15, 2016, London.

7

Brexit from a US Point of View

US Support for the EU or the UK or for Economic Science Fiction

With Brexit the Trump administration is facing a strange potential political alternative, namely that the US will have to decide to what extent it wants to support the UK—with roughly 60 million inhabitants—or the EU27 with about 440 million inhabitants. In the 1950s and 1960s, the US was clearly supportive of EU integration which was considered to be part of the defense against the Soviet Union. From a pragmatic (and scientific) perspective, EU integration was expected to reinforce economic development and economic growth which in turn would be good for US exports and which should also represent investment opportunities for US multinationals. As Lundestad (1998) has emphasized, the US supported EU integration for several reasons: a stronger Western Europe could help to contain the Soviet Union and also bringing the Federal Republic of Germany into federal European structures could prevent problems with that country emerging in the future. The Marshall Plan was the visible US support for early Western European integration and economic recovery in 1945–1950 (the UK

© The Author(s) 2017
P.J.J. Welfens, *An Accidental Brexit*,
DOI 10.1007/978-3-319-58271-9_7

and France were considered too weak to organize Western Europe's recovery). The US considered EU integration as an important element to keep France, under De Gaulle, in the Western defense community—but De Gaulle nevertheless took France out of the military command structure of NATO. US Presidents Kennedy and Johnson expected EU integration to be a crucial political and economic networking element in Western Europe and particular emphasis could be placed on both Germany and France. The visible reinforcement of the Franco-German cooperation was not really in the interest of the US; at least there was some US mistrust that stronger EU integration with enhanced political cooperation between Germany and France could undermine US leadership of the West. One may notice that by mid-1968 the EU had established free trade in goods and the US could avoid trade diversion effects of EU deepening by global trade liberalization rounds organized within the GATT (the predecessor of WTO). Under Nixon, relations with the EU were strained to some extent since Germany had adopted the *Ostpolitik*: an approach designed to improve political and economic relations with the Soviet Union and other socialist Eastern European countries. Moreover, there were transatlantic discussions about the exchange rate system that switched to a flexible exchange rate system in 1973. President Carter emphasized a new approach of trilateralism in which the US would seek to cooperate with both Japan—having become a big economic power—and the EU.

President Reagan was publicly supportive of EU deepening (Single European Act) but he was also afraid that reinforced EU integration would lead to 'fortress Europe', namely stronger EU protectionism. President George Bush (Snr.) was more supportive of EU integration as various economic studies had shown that the EU's enlargement of 1973 (i.e., the accession of the UK, Denmark, and Ireland) and the southern enlargement (i.e., the accession of Greece, Portugal, and Spain during the 1980s) had contributed to higher EU economic growth and transatlantic trade creation; trade diversion thus did not seem to be critical for the US. From a US perspective, and with respect to broader US security interests, it was also obvious that with NATO member countries Greece, Portugal and Spain now firmly anchored in the EU and its institutions, the political stabilization of these countries in a democratic framework was also in the interest of the US. NATO in turn had turned out to be quite useful to avoid military conflict between NATO member countries as the mid-1970s had shown when it was US pressure—and some US–German–Turkey cooperation—that helped to avoid a war between Greece and Turkey.

President Clinton followed the Bush approach and even supported Euro monetary integration. With the end of the Cold War the EU countries naturally enjoyed more policy autonomy—in relation to the US. At the same time, one may argue that the political discipline in Western Europe reduced in this new situation; many governments pursued their own policy and the EU did not offer a reinforced European leadership that would have replaced the weaker US role. German reunification and the demise of the Soviet Union brought about a stronger relationship between Germany and the US as well as between Eastern Europe's post-socialist countries and the US. However, President George W. Bush's decision to start a new war in Iraq brought a division between the US and the EU countries; while the UK sided strongly with the US, Germany and France did not. Military issues thus were crucial for transatlantic policy cooperation. President Obama again supported EU integration, but the Transatlantic Banking Crisis and later the Euro crisis brought two destabilizing elements for transatlantic relations. Neither crisis has been solved in a sustained manner. The US and the UK are pushing towards a new wave of banking deregulation and the Eurozone countries have not really solved the Euro crisis—no solution has been found to the question of Greece and Germany's policy in this field is quite doubtful. In a strange way, the Internet is also undermining Western stability; it makes all crises more visible and allows extreme political voices to get more influence as even very extreme or fringe political groups can generate thousands or sometimes millions of 'likes' in digital social networks. Thus the internet makes finding compromises—so important in a democracy—more difficult in Western countries and it makes creating "political waves" a more common phenomenon which undermines the ability of traditional parties to get majorities in elections.

The new US view—close to the Trump administration—of EU economic integration was expressed by Ted Malloch who stated in an op-ed in The Parliament on February 14, 2017: "Brexit gives the US an opportunity for pause and an appreciation that the EU is actually weak and getting weaker. It could under certain scenarios even come apart... Take note: the architecture of the world is changing, shifting to more reliance on sovereign nation states and away from integrated blocs or supranational entities. In Trump's world the future is not what it was" (Malloch 2017).

It is quite obvious that the Trump administration has expressed public support for Brexit (Mr. Trump had already used that line of argumentation during the presidential election campaign and he claimed that Brexit would be a great step forward for the UK). To the extent that Brexit will be a great economic and political success, this view may be reinforced in the Trump administration. However, if the UK should rather face serious problems in the context of Brexit—with the special circumstances of the Brexit referendum emphasized in the context of Prime Minister Cameron's information policy blunder, such problems are rather likely—this strange anti-EU integration view will lose support in the US. The long-term contradictions between the great politico-economic advantages promised by the Leave campaign and the May government for Brexit and the actual political instability and economic disadvantages that the UK may face in the future will be too large to ignore. Why should it be in the interests of the US to destabilize the EU and NATO? A contradictory US policy towards EU integration will cause considerable damage in Europe and in the West; it will undermine public support for the US in Europe.

There is not much doubt that under President Putin, Russia tries to undermine EU integration. What arguments could be invoked by the Trump administration for adopting the same policy vis-à-vis the EU as Russia whose international position would be reinforced by a weakening of the EU integration? If there were a stable and prosperous EU, there would be a basis for effective international fiscal and monetary policy coordination that would raise the efficiency of economic policies and indeed could help to reduce output volatility and inflation in the world economy, namely by economic policy cooperation between the US, the EU, Japan, and China, which jointly stand for about 60% of the world economy. A new G4 group could become the nucleus of a better international policy coordination within a small group of countries (the EU or the Eurozone considered as a quasi-country here); G4 could be much better in terms of international coordination than the much bigger and the economically more heterogeneous G20. Moreover, the strong rise of China's real per capita income—in purchasing power parity terms—means that there will not only be enhanced economic convergence after a decade but indeed a convergence of policy preferences in many fields—preferences which are largely determined by per capita income. Regional integration reduces political transaction costs in international negotiations and this benefit, beyond standard economic benefits, should not be overlooked when discussing the advantages of regional integration. Even for the Trump administration, regional disintegration in all parts of the world would be a massive disadvantage not only in regard to the associated respective output decline, but the enormous increase in international political transaction costs would also be part of the cost of disintegration; most politicians will understand these arguments, even if they come from the business community and the tradable goods sector, respectively. Any UK government should certainly be able to understand these arguments. The biggest contradiction of the May government is to promise the poorer strata of society economic benefits from Brexit which are non-existent and the Treasury Report of the Cameron government explains in-depth the losses from Brexit over 201 pages. To combine the economic science fiction of benefits from Brexit with US power, under the heading of a strong cooperation with US President Trump, does not change the problem of a largely contradictory (and as Shakespeare would probably have said: dishonest) policy of the May government. In the end the British population should decide in another referendum whatever the majority vote on EU membership is; however, to simply implement the narrow result of the disorderly 2016 EU referendum is not a signal of strength and stability—qualities so often emphasized by Prime Minister May—but is in fact a sign of confusion and instability.

Doubts over the quality of US leadership and policy consistency will also undermine stability in other regions of the world and this in turn will undermine economic globalization which is the basis of the prosperity in the US, Europe, Japan, ASEAN and China as well as in many other countries. As many critical points as there are which one might raise against inconsistent policies in the Cameron/May governments and in the Trump administration, there are just as many good arguments for Brussels to swiftly adopt EU reforms. One may argue that the key initiatives for major institutional reforms and better economic policies must come from the big EU member states. Major European reform conferences should start in 2018/19 at the latest and broader discussions in the general public will also be needed. The Pulse of Europe movements has shown in many European cities that there is a minority willing to raise its voice in a pro-EU manner.

US–British relations have been very close for more than a century and it is clear that strong economic ties, migration, and cultural links, as well as joint political interests, are a strong basis for political cooperation. After the Second World War, the UK could not gain much from its lead role in the Commonwealth as political independence movements in former colonies brought a broad unwillingness in the newly independent countries to follow the political leadership from London. Countries such as India or Pakistan wanted to pursue specific national policies. In the early 1960s, the British political system started to court the forerunner to European Union which then consisted of France, Germany, Italy, Belgium, the Netherlands, and Luxembourg. The EU had become a customs union by mid-1968 so that goods were traded internally without tariffs—this did not yet apply to services—while all countries had common external tariffs. This approach was in contrast to the European Free Trade Association (EFTA) which was under the leadership of the UK: EFTA countries had individual import tariffs which, of course, give incentives for foreign exporters to seek access to the EFTA market via the respective country with the lowest import tariff. The EU had common institutions such as a European Commission, a European Court of Justice, and a European Parliament, while the EFTA only had a secretariat. Thus the EU had economic integration and political integration—with the supranational policy layer having exclusive responsibility for trade policy.

In the run-up to the British EU referendum, the Obama administration left no doubt that the US would support the UK's membership of the European Union. This was the message of President Obama in his speech in London in 2016. Mr. Obama basically held the view that

British power had not been diminished by EU membership, on the contrary, by adhering to a big club of EU countries, the UK always had a strong influence on agenda setting in Brussels and also had a considerable influence on decision-making in Brussels whenever there was weighted majority voting, as is the case in many policy fields; and, of course, whenever unanimous voting is relevant for specific policy fields, e.g., taxation. Certainly, the UK, the Netherlands, Denmark, and Germany together were, in many cases, a quartet of countries with critical weight in decision-making in Brussels and often the coalition of these four countries prevented protectionist policies from being adopted. In this context, the UK, with its EU partners, was often indirectly supporting the strategic case of liberal free trade policies and open markets (no longer a priority under the Trump administration). One may add that from a game theory perspective—referring to the Banzhaf Index—the percentage of all coalitions in which the UK's vote would tip the balance by joining an existing minority coalition of EU countries was fairly high. The weighting of the UK would even increase under the double majority rule that was fully enacted in 2017: a majority of 55% of member states and 65% of the EU population are needed for a decision in fields where a weighted majority voting is required (with countries' individual votes having different weights).

In London, President Obama said (White House 2016):

> I think it's fair to say that maybe some point down the line, there might be a UK-US trade agreement, but it's not going to happen anytime soon, because our focus is in negotiating with a big bloc, the European Union, to get a trade agreement done, and the UK is going to be in the back of the queue – not because we don't have a special relationship, but because, given the heavy lift on any trade agreement, us having access to a big market with a lot of countries – rather than trying to do piecemeal trade agreements is hugely inefficient.

In 2016, Mr. Trump, the successor of Mr. Obama as President of the United States, expressed, during the presidential election campaign, that he endorsed Brexit which he considered as a project by which the UK would take back its full national sovereignty. During the press conference on the occasion of Prime Minister May's first visit to the US, President Trump argued that Brexit would bring benefits for the UK, including that the United Kingdom would in future be able to conclude free trade agreements without any restrictions (as long as the UK would remain an EU member country any international free trade treaties are negotiated by the European Commission on behalf of all EU countries which represent a customs union, i.e., a free trade area with common external tariffs). This US view is clearly in contrast to decades of US foreign policy. Full national sovereignty cannot be an exclusive goal in a world of globalization and international organizations—organizations such as the International Monetary Fund (IMF), the World Bank, the so-called Group of Twenty (G20), the World Trade Organization (WTO), and the Organisation for Economic Co-operation and Development (OECD), organizations of which both the US and the UK are leading member countries. Both countries have been champions of multilateral policy approaches in which cooperation among several—or many—countries is crucial. The UK has been a strong member country in the European Union since 1973, but it has given up this role in 2016. Since then, the UK has lost the political support of its EU partner countries, thus it will be all the more crucial for the United Kingdom to maintain strong relations with the US.

In late January 2017, the British Prime Minister met the new US President; Mrs. May was the first head of government to visit Mr. Trump. This was shortly after Donald Trump had politically buried the Pacific free trade pact which is a rather strange decision as the US thus gives up a project that the Obama administration had adopted with the aim of creating a strong US-led network in Asia and in the Pacific Rim, respectively, which could counterbalance China. Such a Trans-Pacific Partnership (TPP) would include Vietnam and Malaysia—two low-wage economies with fairly high-skilled workers. Was the Trump administration right by not starting TPP, namely in the sense that TPP would be to the disadvantage of the US? There are no arguments in the Economics literature against switching from a protectionist regime to a free trade agreement unless there is immiserizing growth or hyper-technology catching-up in the low per capita income country. Immiserizing growth is a special case where a big country with a strong specialization in one sector—and economic growth that will witness a further expansion of that sector in total output—opens up to free trade. This opening to free trade would lead to a strong relative price change in the dominant sector which implies a welfare loss for that big country. However, such one-sided specialization is not found in the US or any other big country (Japan) that wanted to participate in TPP. Could one argue that TPP would bring about a special problem which was first emphasized by Samuelson (2004) when he argued that free trade would bring a US welfare loss if the respective partner country—he was referring to China—would be able to achieve radical technological catching-up in one sector in which the US had been strongly specialized early on? Indeed, one might argue that the relocation of US industrial production to subsidiaries in Vietnam could allow newly developed modern manufacturing sectors to become such a problem after a decade or so; however, Vietnam and Malaysia are so far away from the continental US that transportation costs—a relevant dampening factor for international trade in the so-called gravity equation of trade—would be relatively high and would not be conducive to the easy generation of a very high growth in the exports of Vietnamese or Malaysian high-technology products.

Among the 12 countries involved in the Trans-Pacific Partnership are Japan, Australia, Vietnam, Malaysia, Mexico, and Canada. Such a treaty would clearly reinforce the economic catching-up process of Mexico and all other low-income countries in the TPP, and it would be in the interest of the US that favorable economic development reduces the outward migration pressure in Mexico. Hence, from this perspective, not ratifying TPP is a strange step for the new US administration. This holds all the more since the Australian Prime Minister, in an interview in January 2017, said that he would welcome the US returning to the TPP project—otherwise China might be willing to replace the US. This option creates strange potential dynamics in the context of TPP, namely if China would indeed come on board. Mrs. May in turn has declared in her Brexit speech in January 2017 that the UK aims at implementing more free trade treaties with other countries, including countries in Asia. Thus the UK and the US have rather different perceptions of adequate international trade policies in Asia.

Mrs. May was the first head of government to visit Trump as the new president. Given the prospects of reduced growth in the UK in the first years after Brexit, she is quite interested in enhancing cooperation with the United States and in preparing a transatlantic UK–US free trade arrangement. The strong Pound devaluation of 2016 raises the inflation rate for several years and brings an unanticipated decline of the real wage rate so that firms will hire more workers for some time—thus there is the paradox of a first stage of economic stabilization in the post-referendum period. Once wage increases catch up with the inflation rate, there will be a decline of British output growth and 2019/20 could be a rather difficult time for the UK. If, however, US growth would be rather strong, the UK would certainly benefit from its rather close economic relations with the US. At the same time, one should not underestimate that US diplomats have often been very demanding in free trade negotiations and there is no guarantee that a UK–US Transatlantic Trade and Investment Partnership (a mini-TTIP) will be a politically easy project that could be implemented quickly. The United Kingdom is likely to face a period of heightened uncertainty for several years to come and it also seems obvious that several institutions in the UK will be involved in the whole Brexit process.

During the first weeks of 2017, the Brexit path of the UK was still rather unclear. However, the speech of the Prime Minister has highlighted some critical points: Theresa May's speech of January 17, 2017, emphasized the following British government intentions, plans, and preparations (HM Govt 2017a):

1. Firstly, for the UK to leave the EU single market—this means potentially giving up free trade, free capital flows, and the free migration of workers (obviously free capital flows should be maintained, but the point was not mentioned in the speech). Secondly, for the UK to achieve strict immigration control and, finally, for the UK to be free of interference from the European Court of Justice. The Prime Minister has argued that immigration has depressed wages in the UK. While the issue of free capital flows was not explicitly mentioned as a policy challenge in the speech of Mrs. May, the other

economic freedoms of the EU single market came into focus, namely free migration and free trade.

2. To make the UK a center of global free trade. To this end, the British government has already started unofficial and informal negotiations with Australia, New Zealand, and India; the UK would like to welcome (skilled) workers from all over the world, but would like to have control over immigration dynamics.

3. To remain strongly linked with the EU27 via trade relations.

Point (1) echoes the anti-immigration rhetoric of Mrs. May's predecessor, namely that the UK is facing an excessive immigration pressure/ burden from EU partner countries. Looking at the facts and figures, this conjecture is very unconvincing as OECD studies have shown that the UK has actually benefitted from EU immigration. It is possible that short-term immigration puts downward pressure on the UK wages of unskilled workers, but the medium- and long-term effect is rather different unless there would be rising unemployment—and this was not observed in the UK in 2004–2016, if one ignores the clearly negative impulses from the Transatlantic Banking Crisis. Over time, immigrants from Eastern European countries will learn and improve their English language skills and this will facilitate many immigrants in improving skills through learning-by-doing and training and thus to find a job as a skilled worker in the long run. Thus GDP will be raised and this will, in turn, also generate labor demand so that the wages of unskilled workers should also increase (the potential decline of unskilled workers' wages in the context of biased technological change is a separate issue).

As regards point (2), the UK could unilaterally reduce import tariffs, although existing EU import tariffs are already rather low except in the field of agriculture. If the UK has already started formal free trade negotiations with other countries, then this would be in breach of EU membership rules since only the European Commission is allowed to negotiate a free trade agreement (FTA) on behalf of all EU member countries. Except for Australia and New Zealand, as well as the US, there are no bright prospects for free trade arrangements and the economic effects will be rather modest except for a transatlantic US–UK trade agreement. A free trade treaty with India will be rather complex and the Indian government is certain to bring up the question of visa regulation and better Indian access to British labor markets; this, however, is certainly not something the government in London could accept since substituting Indian workers for EU workers is a move which will hardly be welcomed by the population in the UK.

On point (3), the prospects for maintaining strong trade links with the EU27 are not clear. The EU27 countries will certainly want to impose import tariffs in many sectors except for those sectors in which a sectoral FTA is agreed upon—Mrs. May has suggested that an FTA for the automotive sector should be considered. Since the EU will impose import tariffs on British exports and the UK will impose import tariffs on EU27 countries' exports, there will be a loss of economic specialization in the EU27 + UK which amounts to increases of the price levels in both the UK and the EU27 and thus there will be real income losses. One may emphasize that a 6% output reduction in the UK will bring about an output loss of about 1% in the EU27. Such a decline of real income in Ireland and on the EU continent amounts to further negative British output and real income effects, respectively.

A Global Britain Looks Across the Atlantic?

Mrs. May aims at a larger role for Britain in the twenty-first century as she has expressed in her speech in Philadelphia at the beginning of her US visit in January 2017. She argued that the US and the UK could again provide joint leadership for the international system and this seems to suggest that she thinks that the UK could find its new role as a 'Global Britain' at the side of a neo-protectionist United States under President Trump. This looks contradictory and is not likely to reinforce her position in Europe and in the EU–UK negotiations in 2017/18 (and beyond). The British government might hope to achieve a special status from such a new role that could prove helpful for the May government in any US–EU27 negotiations. Whether or not the EU will accept the UK claiming such a role remains to be seen. As the EU27 is four times as big as the UK in economic terms, there are no strong arguments against seeking bilateral EU27–US trade deals directly, and to use London only as a useful back-up channel in negotiations when needed. Even the modest role mentioned here will give the UK an improved negotiation position vis-à-vis Brussels in the medium term and thus the conditions for access to the EU single market should, at least one would expect, in the end be somewhat better than those for Switzerland and Norway; the fact that the UK is a nuclear power reinforces this point. However, there is also some risk that this presumed British government strategy could fail, namely if the US economic policy should turn out to be so contradictory that sustained high economic growth is not achieved by the Trump administration. There is a considerable likelihood that the Trump administration, having no economist from leading universities in the government team—including on the Council of Economic Advisers, will adopt a policy mix that brings new jobs from infrastructure projects while the US Dollar will face a sharp appreciation so that the current account position will further deteriorate: net exports will shrink while real government expenditures rise, at the same time private investment might increase only transitorily as a consequence of lower corporate taxation. The Trump administration will end with a huge budget deficit–GDP ratio and a high current account–GDP ratio and thus face a similar problem to the Reagan administration. As President Trump will seek to improve the current account deficit–GDP ratio, the US will adopt an even more protectionist policy that will undermine the global growth rate and also discourage innovators and investors in the US so that there could indeed be a recession in the US which would ultimately become a transatlantic recession. If such a development should become reality, the UK would sit beside the US as the main culprits behind a dangerous economic situation in the West and in such a setting few EU countries will want to rely much on the British government.

There is one potential election outcome in Europe that would change the transatlantic and European picture dramatically, namely if a populist/nationalist movement like the Front National could win the French presidential election or the parliamentary elections in France. Such a situation—which seems more likely since the populist voter majorities visible in the UK and the US in 2016—would bring an almost complete disintegration of the EU. If France would leave the EU, Germany might still want to lead a residual smaller EU in which Austria and Spain as well as Eastern European countries would cooperate; this would look more akin to the older, historical '*Mitteleuropa*' approaches of Germany and all this would bring Europe back to the nineteenth century: with several competing big rival powers; the only difference in the early twenty-first century would be that China and the US are the two globally leading powers and it is clear that these two countries, plus Russia, are likely to benefit economically and politically from such an EU disintegration process. It is not clear that the Trump administration sees the risks and disadvantages associated with EU disintegration. At the same time, one may argue that the Trump administration's new and partly strange economic and foreign policies will stimulate more EU27 integration or at least more regional integration in the Eurozone. Germany could sooner or later became a champion of Eurozone political integration, particularly if the Trump administration should start to put a harsh critical focus on Germany's structural current account surplus which has reached a staggering 9% in 2016 and indeed which also represents a bilateral current account surplus of almost $60 billion (about 2% of Germany's GDP). The largest part of Germany's current account relates to other EU countries—including the UK. However, if one takes a look at the Eurozone's current account position as whole, it stands for only a rather small surplus and Germany could continue its traditional export-oriented growth model without serious problems if the US and other third countries would consider international economic relations mainly under the heading country X-Eurozone. Germany could adopt such a strategy quickly, but this would require that the German government and other EU countries would help Greece to better cope with its very high debt–GDP ratio. Both Greece and Portugal will face very serious additional debt problems once higher interest rates in the UK and the US start having spillover effects on the Eurozone (Germany's government has no attractive alternatives to reduce the big current account surplus: higher wage rates could be encouraged as this would stimulate imports and reduce export dynamics; or government could reduce the value-added tax rate which is imposed on imports as well as domestically produced consumer goods, but this would translate into a federal deficit–GDP ratio above the 0.35% that is the permissible upper limit imposed by Germany's constitution). British interest rates will certainly rise in 2017/18 in the context of rising inflation expectations and rising US interest rates. The unanticipated inflation rate will transitorily stimulate employment in the UK, but there is no perspective for sustained high economic growth in the United Kingdom if there would be Brexit plus a rather low growth rate in the US and in the world economy. If the EU–UK negotiations should really end with a 'hard' Brexit solution, then neo-protectionist policy approaches could also spread to the EU27 and the UK, respectively.

At the beginning of 2017, there are many uncertainties—it is, however, clear that the May government wants a hard Brexit. The speech of Mrs. May in January has made clear that there will be a hard Brexit and this message will bring about further depreciation of the British Pound which, in turn, will translate into rising inflation rates in the medium term. As the price level in the UK will rise unexpectedly, real wage rates shall fall and hence—in a kind of a quasi-Phillips-curve effect—firms' demand for labor will rise temporarily so that the unemployment rate could fall in the short run. However, once inflation expectations are adjusted, wage inflation will increase and the unemployment rate will start to increase again.

As Mrs. May emphasized in her speech, the US has already given a signal to the UK that a free trade agreement could be agreed upon rather quickly. This suggests that the UK will try to reinforce economic and political relations with the US which, under a Trump administration, will adopt a rather protectionist policy stance. This, in turn, will make it difficult for the UK to pursue much of a global free trade strategy unless it is unilateral. The latter, however, is impossible since the UK would face enormous problems if it would liberalize unilaterally imports from China for example—the UK steel industry, as well as other sectors, would face enormous problems in the rather short term.

While one may argue that Mrs. May's speech is contradictory and rather unrealistic, one may also emphasize that she has backing from Labour Party leader Jeremy Corbyn in the field of anti-immigration policy: in January 2017, Mr. Corbyn explained in a speech of his own that he favors managed immigration and that he also favors future government intervention in support of ailing British industries. So far,

EU membership has made national government subsidization of ailing industries a difficult prospect since the European Commission's subsidization control puts strict limits on subsidization within the EU single market. This control has been to the advantage of taxpayers, structural change, and growth; if the UK's economic policy would be to subsidize ailing industries in the future, then there is a considerable likelihood that EU27 countries' governments will also introduce subsidies in the respective sectors, so that a subsidization race in Europe could become more likely and this will be at the cost of the taxpayer in both the UK and in EU27 countries.

If the May government seeks further cooperation with the Trump administration in the US in the future, this will result in a political odd couple with internal contradictions: Mr. Trump apparently wants to have free trade areas only with high-income countries and only on a bilateral basis, while the UK is in favor of global free trade. This also raises questions about the role of the World Trade Organization in the future: membership of the WTO and WTO rules will be of paramount importance for the UK in the future, a strategy of protectionism and bilateralism is only attractive for big countries such as the US or China. All other countries in the world—with the possible exceptions of Japan and India—require a general rule-based free trade system as enshrined in the WTO. It was Adam Smith, whose book *An Inquiry into the Nature and Causes of the Wealth of Nations*, published in 1776, the year of US independence, emphasized the benefits of free trade for all countries. It is clear from modern trade theory that through protectionism big countries can obtain national welfare gains due to reduced world market prices and hence lower import prices. However, for the world economy, a nationalistic economic policy strategy undertaken by the US (or China) will not be acceptable in the long run. The very large majority of countries have an interest in institutionalized free trade, based on international organizations and the rule of law.

The May government, with its hard Brexit strategy, is about to contribute to new international conflicts in Europe—here between the UK and the EU27—and it is fairly clear that Putin's Russia is carefully observing the disintegration and demise of the West. President Putin might remain calm in the Ukraine for two years or so (until after the mid-term elections in the US), but later he might consider the new western setting with Brexit and a US Trump administration to be the ideal moment for tightening the Russian grip on the eastern parts of Ukraine and also in exerting influence in the Balkans. Bulgaria, for example, is a country that could be rather easily destabilized by Russia and thus the EU27 might lose not only Western countries joining the UK, in a potential new European Free Trade Association (EFTA+) project, but it could also face a partial reversal of EU enlargement in the east.

Mr. Trump's emphasis on EU countries spending at least 2% of GDP on defense will put some fiscal burden on Spain, Italy, and Germany, which would each have to increase their respective military expenditure–GDP ratio by about 0.8 percentage points to come close to reaching the 2% threshold. For Italy and Spain, this could help to raise output growth slightly but this would also bring an increase of the deficit–GDP ratio. Italy, which had lost its AAA status with all major rating agencies by January 16, 2017 (DBRS then downgraded Italy to B), could face serious problems from an interplay of Brexit, the Italian banking crisis—involving two big banks—and higher interest rates plus political instability. This, in turn, could bring new issues of instability in the Eurozone. As Mr. Trump expressed in an interview with a German newspaper (BILD) and The Times in January (The Times 2017), he does not care about EU integration and potential nationalistic policies in Europe. With the EU facing Brexit and Mr. Trump's policy stance, there is considerable risk of EU disintegration unless EU27 leaders and the European Parliament adopt a rigorous strategy of reforms for the EU. Such reforms should strongly consider the usefulness of EU integration in the context of a digital single market, more free trade treaties with countries in Asia (for example, not just Singapore and Vietnam in the Association of Southeast Asian Nations (ASEAN) but the whole group of ten countries from that group), and also the nucleus of a joint unemployment insurance system—e.g., supranational coverage of benefits for the first six months of unemployment while making an exception for youth unemployment; as regards the latter, it is national policy rules and national minimum wage legislation which are responsible above all for youth unemployment and therefore it would not be wise for the supranational policy layer in Brussels to assume any responsibility here.

The UK–EU negotiations will last about two years; by late 2018, all major elements for an agreement—for political divorce—must be ready since the EU will hold European Parliament elections in spring 2019. It is inconceivable that the UK should be on a clear Brexit course while still being expected to hold elections for UK representatives to the European Parliament. It remains to be seen how Brexit dynamics will unfold. Brexit will certainly distract much political attention in Brussels and in the other capitals of the EU. This, in turn, implies a non-optimal national policy in many EU countries and this is part of the politico-economic price faced by EU countries in the context of Brexit.

While the UK will want to postpone part of the divorce settlement for later—i.e., after 2019—the EU27 will have an interest in resolving all of the main problems rather quickly. One key challenge for EU firms is that certain very sophisticated banking services can currently be obtained in London but not in other EU banking centers. This means that the EU27 faces some dependency on the UK in terms of financial market services; the best way to deal with this rather unexpected problem is for EU countries—all or just some of them—to negotiate a special project for supporting high-tech financial technology in the Eurozone and the EU27, respectively. Funding for such a financial innovation project should come from national policymakers; Germany, with its considerable budget surplus, could easily make a major contribution to such a project in which partner countries, such as France, the Netherlands, Luxembourg, Belgium, and Italy, also have a strong interest.

High Barriers for UK Clearing Houses in a Post-Brexit Setting

In early February 2017, the European Central Bank (ECB) explained that banks in the UK could maintain their role as Euro clearing houses only if these institutions would continue to be subject to verdicts of the European Court of Justice (ECJ). For derivatives markets—reflecting complex transactions based on traditional financial markets—clearing houses play a major role in the case that one market side fails; the failed actor is replaced by the clearing house which thus acts as a backstop for maintaining high liquidity in derivatives markets. The May government had explained in late 2016 and again in January 2017 that the UK does not want to accept free EU labor migration, nor the EU customs union, nor indeed the verdicts of the European Court of Justice. From this perspective, it is rather unlikely that the British clearing houses will be able to maintain their traditional positions. Hence leading British clearing houses would have to establish subsidiaries in the EU27.

It is also obvious that the proposed merger between the London Stock Exchange and the Frankfurt Stock Exchange (*Deutsche Börse*) could be reconsidered along this line of reasoning. The plan of the two partner exchanges in 2016 was based on the assumption that the seat of the merged company, or the seat of the holding company, would be in London, while the CEO would be a German national. This solution is, however, clearly biased in favor of London since the merged institution's seat will be in London forever, while the German proposal for CEO, Mr. Kengeter, could only serve as CEO for a few years; and without the UK's willingness to accept the verdict of the ECJ, the merger of the two stock exchanges will most likely now not be realized in the form initially proposed. The issue of the involvement of the ECJ, and the application of EU legislation and acceptance of the Court's verdict, is all the more crucial since the EU will have to consider the impact of the deregulation of financial markets in the US and the expected potential transatlantic spillover effects from such US deregulation will raise new fears in Europe that EU regulation could be watered down by weaker UK banking regulations.

This could endanger the financial stability of the EU, and undermine the EU as an integration project itself. Other integration clubs in the world economy—e.g., ASEAN and Mercosur (not to mention the North American Free Trade Agreement (NAFTA), which is already half-buried by Mr. Trump's political rhetoric)—are carefully watching the EU disintegration dynamics. The worse Brexit challenges are handled by the EU, the weaker the EU27's international influence in the future will be.

The UK can expect the US to quickly offer a kind of mini-TTIP, namely on the basis of a UK–US deal on transatlantic free trade: the broader EU–US TTIP, which had been negotiated under the Obama administration, could not be finalized by the end of 2016, largely because there was no broad support for it in Germany and in France—and the rather weak willingness of the US to forge a compromise. There is no doubt that the May government will seek to pick up the opportunity for a transatlantic free trade area with the US that could start as early as 2019.

The expansionary fiscal policy of the Trump administration is likely to raise US output for some time and to thereby also contribute to high real income in the UK. However, the ratio of UK exports to the US to the UK's GDP is only about 4%, so that transatlantic trade creation is not likely to have a very strong positive impact on British real income (Table 7.1). One may additionally emphasize that US subsidiaries represent 6% of the British GDP, so that a rising profitability of US firms—stimulated by US tax cuts—might also raise investment and output in US subsidiaries in the UK.

At the same time, one may point out that Trump's pressure on US firms to cut US outward foreign direct investment (FDI) could

Table 7.1 UK–US trade relations (exports/imports of goods and services in millions of USD)

	2011	2012	2013	2014	2015
US imports from UK in USD*	114,663	115,525	108,214	118,666	123,462
US exports to UK in USD[a]	99,858	103,222	102,811	108,046	111,454
GDP[b] UK in USD	2,609,000	2,646,000	2,720,000	2,999,000	2,858,000
GDP US in USD	15,518,000	16,155,000	16,692,000	17,393,000	18,037,000
Export/GDP UK to US (%)	4.39	4.37	3.98	3.96	4.32
Export/GDP US to UK (%)	0.64	0.64	0.62	0.62	0.62

Source Bureau of economic analysis, US Dept. of Commerce [a]*USD* United States Dollars [b]*GDP* Gross Domestic Product contribute to reducing US FDI flows to the United Kingdom. Of course, Brexit, in turn, is an impulse for lower British FDI inflows. This argument does not mean to overlook the effect of a high real Pound depreciation—observed in the year after the EU referendum—, namely that a depreciation will stimulate higher foreign direct investment inflows (an argument in line with Froot/Stein 1991). US exports to the UK were a modest 0.3% of US GDP in 2015, so that the economic interest of the United States in UK expansion is rather modest. However, one should not overlook that the US exports to the UK represent one-quarter of total US exports to EU28.

At the international level, the cooperation between the US and the UK is also strange to some extent. The combination of a protectionist United States with a free-trade UK stands for inconsistencies. Moreover, US President Trump is encouraging Brexit and thinks that this attitude is in line with a Brexit whose dynamics reinforce the US. If, however, Brexit leads to a decline of British output, and finally to the independence of Scotland after 2019, the position of the UK would be undermined in economic, political, and military terms. This would clearly be to the disadvantage of the United States.

Brexit, Trump's Program and Structural Change in the Banking Sector in Europe

As British banks are likely to lose the One Market Passport access to the EU single market in the future—after the implementation of Brexit and assuming that the UK–EU negotiations will not give British banks privileged access to the EU market—one may anticipate that many big banks from London will relocate part of their activities to Ireland or to continental EU financial centers such as Paris, Frankfurt, or Luxembourg. The announcement by President Trump that he will deregulate US banks and financial markets will bring pressure on the UK and the EU27 to also reintroduce light-touch regulation (this could mean for the medium term that excessive risk-taking in the banking sector will once again become attractive in the US). Ireland has a history of introducing the light regulation of banks in the decade before 2008 and this could encourage many banks from London to move to Dublin. However, the creation of an EU capital market union means that national banking authorities will have rather restricted opportunities to implement light regulation. Paris and Frankfurt thus have good opportunities to attract part of the banking business from London. More digital banking might be an alternative to physical relocation and some sophisticated digital banking services for EU corporate clients and wealthy individuals might indeed be provided from New York rather than London in the future. However, for banks, the new risk of the Trump administration is the strange unconventional foreign economic policy approach favored by Mr. Trump und his key economic advisor Peter Navarro.

As regards the discussion among British economists, one may point out that the book by Baldwin et al. (2016) has brought together many interesting contributions. Particularly intriguing is the historical perspective of O'Rourke (2016), who has argued that a fear of globalization is part of the anti-EU movement in the United Kingdom; but this conjecture implies that the European Commission's argument that the EU is a powerful actor in shaping the international rules of globalization has not been credible and that the EU's globalization fund that can help member countries to cope with negative globalization shocks leading to high unemployment is not highly regarded. As in the 1890s, there was a rather small group of individuals who were clear winners as a result of economic globalization in the UK, while several groups were on the losing side and started to voice their opposition to the government. Increasing average per capita income seems to have dominated the perception of leading politicians who did not notice the role of rising economic inequality—a rising ratio of the skilled labor wage to unskilled labor wage might be part of the anti-EU sentiments held by the British public (and the EU single market is a smaller version of economic globalization). The new political narrative of the Brexit supporters that emphasizes that the UK would enjoy more national sovereignty and more international power after leaving the EU is, however, largely illusory. At the same time, it is unclear whether or not the EU27 will be able to adopt broad reforms that help to stabilize the European Union.

There is a potential new problem in Europe, namely that both the UK and the EU would be destabilized through Brexit. At the bottom line, democracy is the rule of the majority and if there is a clear majority of British voters who want to pursue a development which has negative economic consequences for themselves and for the UK's neighbors, one will have to accept this and then search for policy options that minimize the negative economic consequences of that decision. If Brexit is realized, it will undermine confidence in other regional integration schemes since what has happened in the EU could obviously also happen in other regional integration schemes.

If the US should support disintegration in Europe, the EU countries—those that stick together—can hardly follow US leadership on the world stage any longer and thus a full political union will be the necessary consequence of Brexit. What constitution will be the basis of a neo-EU remains to be seen, but it seems obvious that joint defense and infrastructure plus elements of a joint unemployment insurance system (for the first six months of unemployment and without coverage of youth unemployment) should be key elements of such a system. One should not rule out that a political union will be possible only for a small group of countries—that it would work without Germany and France, however, is rather unlikely. A political union would be very useful within the Eurozone. However, it is rather unclear whether EU integration could find majority support. After EU eastern enlargement, there could be eastern disintegration, namely to the extent that the US would promise Eastern European countries military protection through a new North Atlantic Treaty Organization (NATO) while pushing these countries to give up EU membership. With the Trump administration ruling the US, one cannot exclude that such rather inconsistent US foreign policy would indeed be realized. The way Mr. Trump has been elected—without much support from the Republican Party—implies that the new US President will not feel much obligation to follow the standard program of that party: free trade, pro-NATO and multilateralism. It is true that the US Senate's vote is needed for certain political innovation in US foreign policy, but one cannot rule out that an enlarged Republican majority after the mid-term elections will allow the Trump administration to implement really sweeping changes of policy.

As regards the contradictions between Mrs. May's rhetoric regarding a 'Global Britain' free trade policy and the neo-protectionist approach of the Trump administration, it will only be a question of time until political conflicts between the US and the UK emerge. This holds even more, if the Trump administration should want to undermine international organizations and multilateralism on a broad scale—since the dream of the Leave campaign to anchor the UK as a leader of the Commonwealth cannot be realized without relying on existing and new pillars of multilateralism.

China's role in the post-Brexit world—and with a Trump administration in the US—will be uncomfortable and powerful at the same time. The Chinese government has a large stake in London and the UK being the natural Chinese access point to the whole EU, but this strategy will fail if Brexit is implemented. The Chinese fear that regional integration schemes in Asia—e.g., ASEAN—or the Pacific (read the Trans-Pacific Partnership which is dead under the Trump administration) would be a counterweight to China's rising economic and political power is weakening and many countries in Asia will increasingly look for a stronger partnership with China. As the world's largest economy, measured in terms of purchasing power parity, China has a strong position in the world economy and since 2015 it has also become the world's No. 2 source country in the field of foreign direct investment. Most of China's FDI outflows go, following the logic of the gravity equation, to countries in Asia, but rising FDI flows also arrive in the US and the EU27 plus the UK. Since China can be expected to grow at about 5% annually and to double its GDP in 2015–2019, the rise of China's power will continue. However, unilateralism and US bilateralism pose new risks here since China's politico-economic leadership is facing a new power paradigm that is strange. The Trump administration's anti-multilateral rhetoric also sounds like an inconsistent US policy since the US and dozens of OECD countries have pushed China to become a member country of the WTO, whose set of rules was praised by all its member countries, and so China joined the WTO in 2001 to the benefit of its own growth and global economic welfare. The UK has been a leading EU country in terms of encouraging China to anchor itself in multilateral organizations. If the Trump administration should really part from 70 years of US multilateralism, China's questions about Western credibility will not only concern the US but the UK as well. For China, and indeed many countries in Asia, it is difficult to understand the logic of British and US economic policy after 2016 and new international political conflicts can emerge from this. The US has the power to destroy the old international system and to partly replace multilateralism with bilateral deal-making. One may hope that such a disruptive era will be short-lived and that the United Kingdom will not be a co-champion of such dangerous institutional dismantling. Disintegration and "de-multilateralization" have a common denominator, namely to destroy international institutional capital, to undermine trust, to raise the variance of white noise error terms—to bring more risk for decision-makers—and to slow down economic growth in the long run. The idea of many economic macro models to treat white noise error terms with zero mean and finite variance as economically equal—for the model's solution, the size of the variance of the error term is irrelevant—is not convincing; this means that economic model building will also face new challenges in the context of Brexit and the election of the new US President Trump.

New US Protectionism and the Role of the Diminished Political Reputation of the UK

As regards the protectionism of the Trump administration, this will not leave the UK and the EU27 unaffected. If the US should become more protectionist vis-à-vis China and other countries, this will reinforce protectionist attitudes around the world—just as much as a kind of new US nationalism is likely to reinforce nationalism in many countries across the globe. In an international climate of rising protectionism, the global economic growth rate will slow down which facilitates neither UK exports nor the May government's plans to push for many new bilateral free trade treaties. Moreover, as China's bilateral export surplus vis-à-vis the US will decline, the excess supply of China's tradable sector will translate into higher Chinese net exports to Asian countries, EU28 countries, and Latin American countries as well; this, in turn, amounts to deflationary pressure in the UK, EU27, and other countries so that the profitability of many firms will decline—lower investment dynamics in the medium term in the United Kingdom and EU27 countries thus have to be expected.

With the UK leaving the EU, the country will lose much of the political reputational capital accumulated in the EU (and the EU28 in addition will suffer from a depreciation of joint institutional capital accumulated since 1973) and this will reduce the UK's ability to pursue its economic, political, and military interests in Europe; the weakening of the EU27 related to the depreciation of its institutional capital and a higher internationally perceived risk of EU27 instability, in turn, is weakening the whole of Europe and thus has negative repercussion effects on the UK. That the UK would formally gain more political sovereignty through Brexit is clear, but the more important concept is effective British sovereignty or power. The effective power (EP; in logarithmic formulation) of a country at the international level can be considered as a weighted logarithmic sum of national sovereignty N, power derived from regional club membership C', and power G" derived from membership in globally active international organizations (such as the International Monetary Fund, the World Trade Organization, the Bank for International Settlements etc.); one may write $EP = N^{ß}(C')^{ß'}(G")^{ß"}$ where ß, ß', and ß" are positive parameters. Brexit can be interpreted as a deliberate weakening of the regional club power of the EU, part of which was accruing to the UK as long as it remained an EU member; and as a weakening of G" as well. The latter is partly linked to the reinforcement of the UK–US political alliance and, as the Trump administration's political emphasis on bilateralism is weakening multilateralism and global organizations, respectively; the power derived from the membership of international organizations is also reduced. It is quite doubtful that Brexit is an operation that sufficiently reinforces national sovereignty to offset the negative effects associated with the undermining of the implicit regional club influence and the influence in global organizations. Populist political parties have a tendency to ignore the role of regional club power and global power, respectively—and this is, of course, quite inadequate for countries which derive a high share of their power from regional club power (EU) and global power (various global organizations, including the Group of Twenty). Brexit, therefore, could be a self-inflicted loss of British power in a period of economic globalization. The origins of the modern international system date back to the late 1890s when international organizations started to play an increasing role in international political power games; the system was reinforced in the 1970s and 1980s when globalization intensified (Tilly/Welfens 2000; Welfens/Knipping/Suthiphand 2006).

References

Baldwin, R., et al. (2016). *Brexit Beckons: Thinking ahead by leading economists.* A VoxEU.org Book. CEPR Press. Available for download at http://voxeu. org/system/files/epublication/Brexit_Beckons_VoxEU.pdf.

Froot, K., & Stein, J. (1991). Exchange rates and foreign direct investments. *Quarterly Journal of Economics*, 1191–1217.

HM Government. (2017a). Prime Minister May's speech on Brexit, Lancaster House speech delivered January 17, 2017. Available online https://www. gov.uk/government/speeches/the-governments-negotiating-objectives-for-exiting-the-eu-pm-speech.

Lundestad, G. (1998). *"Empire" by integration: The United States and European integration, 1945–1997.* Oxford: Oxford University Press.

Malloch, T. (2017). Ted Malloch: The US view of European integration. *The Parliament Magazine.* 14 February 2017. Available at https:// www.theparliamentmagazine.eu/articles/opinion/ted-malloch-us-view-european-integration.

O'Rourke, K. H. (2016). This backlash has been a long time coming. In Baldwin, et al. (Eds.), *Brexit Beckons: Thinking ahead by leading economists.* A VoxEU.org Book. CEPR Press.

Samuelson, P. A. (2004). Where Ricardo and Mill Rebut and confirm arguments of mainstream economists supporting globalization. *Journal of Economic Perspectives, 18,* 135–146.

Tilly, R., & Welfens, P. J. J. (Eds.). (2000). *Economic globalization, international organizations and crisis management, contemporary and historical perspectives on growth, impact and evolution of major organizations in an interdependent world.* Heidelberg: Springer.

The Times. (2017). Michael Gove and Kai Diekmann—Interview with Donald Trump, January 16, 2017. Available online at http://www.thetimes.co.uk/article/full-transcript-of-interview-with-donald-trump-5d39sr09d.

Welfens, P. J. J., Knipping, F., & Suthiphand, C. (Eds.). (2006). *Integration in Asia and Europe*. Heidelberg: Springer.

White House. (2016). Obama White House Archives, Remarks by the President Obama and Prime Minister Cameron in Joint Press Conference, April 22, 2016. Available at https://obamawhitehouse.archives.gov/the-press-office/2016/04/22/remarks-president-obama-and-prime-minister-cameron-joint-press.

8

Trump Policies Expected to Contradict 70 Years of American Principles and Rationale

Donald Trump is the new US President and countries across the globe need to come to terms with a fundamental change in US policy—in terms of both content and style. According to Trump's announcements, his administration will pursue an extremely contradictory economic policy with regard to domestic fiscal policies which, considering that capacities are already stretched, will soon result in rising inflation. Together with the appreciation of the US Dollar due to speculative capital inflows, there will be a decline in net exports in the medium term, which will overshadow perspectives for growth. It is very unlikely that Trump will realize a 3.5% growth rate without high inflation. The signaled foreign trade policy raises deflationary pressures outside of the US, since as a large economy, import protectionism on the part of the US accounts for excess supply in many other regions and countries of the world, respectively. China's growth will also be dampened, which will decrease Chinese demand for foreign exchange reserves—to the disadvantage of the US. China's central bank may soon also reduce interest rates, which will only increase the appreciation of the Dollar. In the US, this appreciation may, however, act as a constraint on inflation and could lead to the central bank adopting a more conservative position.

© The Author(s) 2017   **217**
P.J.J. Welfens, *An Accidental Brexit*,
DOI 10.1007/978-3-319-58271-9_8

Trump's xenophobic and misogynistic rhetoric, coupled with his own polarizing style, represents a negative signal for the West, his anti-scientific comments—for example, in the context of climate change—go against more than one hundred years of US policy tradition of productive cooperation and links between top universities, government, and other authorities. Trump's position against US foreign direct investment (FDI) outflows is economically contradictory, as US firms generate higher returns through investments abroad than investments within the US, which for many years has benefitted the intrinsic value of firms and insurance policies—such as life insurance—and, in doing so, helped to establish America as a global power. Higher incomes through US FDI in the destination country raises the import demand of that country, which also benefits the US and many US partners in the form of higher exports. The US has been a pioneer in terms of investing FDI abroad since about 1880, and the country's role as a global leader would be unthinkable without the international activities of US multinationals.

Trump Economics is, to a large extent, voodoo economics and finds little to no support among leading economists—with the exception of Arthur Laffer. Initially, one can expect two turbulent years in terms of US politics, the mid-term elections, that is the next US parliamentary elections which take place two years from now, could lead to the Republican Party losing its majority and, in turn, the downfall of President Trump; however, it cannot be ruled out that Trump will indeed serve out his full four-year term. The longer he stays in office, the greater the rise of populist politicians in EU and other countries.

Since his inauguration, Trump, the political late-comer, who garnered attention during the presidential campaign for various violations, will be faced with new rules and regulations which now apply to him in his first public office. As with the previous presidents, Trump took the oath of office on the US Constitution by swearing to abide by and defend it. In the medium term, this is likely to cause some serious problems for Trump when one considers his lack of political experience and his spontaneous and unpredictable nature. That the policy stance of the Trump administration will deviate much from the large body of tweets Trump himself sent announcing the main points of his program during the presidential campaign is unlikely; the power of the office of President of the United States is too high and the US has not seen many cases of officials willing to leave office, at least due to a difference of political opinion with the president of the day. The Trump administration is thus likely to follow the lead of the new president in the coming years. Trump is certain to try and seek out new allies, with the United Kingdom one of the few countries which will be by his side; the UK does not have many other options in the West, after splitting with the other 27 EU member states. The economic adventure of Brexit, which the May government—which also employs a xenophobic narrative, building upon Cameron's perfidious misleading rhetoric in relation to immigration—wishes to enforce, will not result in a global leadership role for the UK (a possibility which could be celebrated in London as some form of resurgence of the Commonwealth). In this regard, Dean Acheson, then a retired former US Secretary of State, in a 1962 speech at the US Military Academy at West Point, said the following: "Great Britain has lost an empire and has not yet found a role. The attempt to play a separate power role apart from Europe, a role based on a 'special relationship' with the US and on being the head of a "commonwealth" which has no political structure, unity, or strength—this role is about played out."[1]

Trump's exit from office will need to be left up to the US political system. However, what is threatening to the EU, and indeed Europe as a whole, is the combination of political irrationality in London and Washington DC. In the UK, a referendum on a withdrawal from the EU which lacked in legitimacy has served as the foundation for Brexit, which—if actually carried out—could lead to a disintegration of the UK itself, should Scotland decide to leave *that* union, and damage the whole of Europe economically. The 16-page official information brochure for the referendum, commissioned by the Cameron government and which was sent to all households in the UK, made no reference to a study by Her Majesty's Treasury (the UK finance ministry) which found that the long-term effect of Brexit would be a 10% loss in income. Prior to the Scottish independence referendum in 2014, however, Cameron's government provided households with the information that Scottish independence threatened to lead to a loss in per capita income for Scots of circa £1,400/$1,700. Before the Brexit vote, on the other hand, Cameron apparently did not see the threatened income loss of £4,000/$4,880 per capita worthy of mentioning—that failure amounts to either political fraud or incredible stupidity—both scenarios reprehensible. On the basis of popularity functions for the UK, it can be calculated that a correct information policy by Cameron would have resulted in a Remain, that is a pro-EU, majority of 52%. Thus, it can be argued that the referendum is lacking in real legitimacy and the glib remark by Prime Minster May that "Brexit means Brexit" could yet lead to a 'may-day, may-day' call on behalf of the British government.

It is shocking that almost nothing in terms of defending the benefits of the EU occurred to any EU politician, or indeed leading national politician from the EU27 countries, and that no sensible, vigorous reforms were discussed—even the case of a 52% majority in favor of the UK remaining in the EU could hardly have been seen as an over-whelming vote of confidence in EU integration. Here are just some of the advantages of the EU:

- raising incomes in the EU customs union, which are also realized thanks to the supranational external trade policy of the European Commission (and common institutions are part of the common institutional capital of the EU);
- market liberalization and the related impulses for innovation, for example, in the fixed-line telephony market and the electricity market;
- competition policy which benefits consumers through controls on mergers and a partially good framework for regulation policies;
- state aid supervision which prevents unnecessary subsidization from being carried out by government at the expense of taxpayers;
- the cross-border networking of people via town-twinning programs, which are culturally and socially enriching for those involved; and
- higher growth dynamics through the EU single market, including freedom of movement.

US President Trump is a vocal proponent of Brexit and thus an oppo-nent of the EU; the first US president to adopt a position of not sup-porting European integration since the Second World War. If the Trump administration should weaken the North Atlantic Treaty

Organization (NATO), new instability in Europe and worldwide is likely; a strong NATO can generate stability for everybody and reduce the burden of defense expenditures in all NATO member countries. A lack of multilateral policy orientation seems to be a new problem of the incoming Trump administration—this undermines the role of smaller countries and might encourage regional integration approaches.

The EU27 will, in the medium term, increasingly turn away from the US, and China will certainly see an increased preparedness on the side of the EU to engage in cooperation in many fields. The claim by Prime Minister May in her Brexit speech, that the UK is overburdened by immigration from other EU countries, and the emphasis that the country needs full control of migration, is odd considering that prior to the referendum, EU immigration did not account for a population growth of more than 0.2% (according to the Organisation for Economic Co-operation and Development (OECD), EU immigrants had a higher employment rate than native British on average and EU immigration actually represents a net fiscal benefit to the British state). The wage reductions due to immigration, also claimed by May in her Brexit speech on January 17, 2017, can, according to the Bank of England study by Nickell and Saleheen (2015), only really be determined among unskilled workers in the services sector. That the UK should divorce itself from the single market and the customs union after 43 years of membership, and in doing so incur a 10% loss in income in the long term, is politically strange and irrational. The May government can, however, hope for some help from the US in the form of a UK–US bilateral transatlantic trade and investment partnership—here, Germany and France blundered in 2016, as they could not finalize a possible agreement on the Transatlantic Trade and Investment Partnership (TTIP), an EU–US transatlantic free trade agreement, due to ideological delusions in sections of their respective national governments. Instead, in Germany in particular, elements from the Green political scene and some other groups torpedoed TTIP in an odd way: first and foremost, Thilo Bode, head of the non-governmental organization foodwatch, with his anti-TTIP book *"Die Freihandelslüge"* (The Free Trade Lie), which is overwhelmingly composed of economic nonsense and seems to be written without the required specialist knowledge in crucial aspects.

Trump has already declared that he will not ratify the Trans-Pacific Partnership (TPP) agreement. He only wants to conclude bilateral free trade agreements—expecting to achieve good deals for the US. That is a rejection of US policy since 1944 in terms of multilateralism in the context of international organizations and cooperation among Western, and indeed many other, countries. The motto of the World Trade Organization (WTO) is "To make the weak strong and the strong civilized"; with his philosophy of protectionism and the recurrent stressing of 'America First', billionaire Trump infringes upon the ideas of enlightenment and humanity that gave rise to this guiding principle and which served to make the leading role of the US acceptable at all to dozens of countries in the first place. European countries and indeed Asian countries will not follow an egotistical American president in terms of policies which undermine the spirit of the WTO going forward. Trump's idea to steer American trade using purely bilateral trade deals—and to agree free trade deals only with countries with a high per capita incomes—contradicts seven decades of successful multilateral US policies.

US and Anti-Multilateralism

The fact that the US under the Trump administration has, within four weeks of Mr. Trump's inauguration, stopped cooperating with the Bank for International Settlements' (BIS) Committee dealing with banking supervision rules for big banks with international operations is a first step towards destroying multilateralism in the world economy and to thereby unravel 70 years of US foreign policy. The January 31 letter of Congressman Patrick McHenry, Vice Chairman of the Financial Services Committee, to Federal Reserve Chair Janet Yellen, which is in effect an instruction to 'cease and desist' international cooperation until the new administration can take steps to ensure its aims are followed, makes clear that the new administration is indeed intent on taking the US in a new direction. Mr. Trump has already indicated that he also takes a critical view of the WTO. While one might argue that during the Obama administration, the Doha trade liberalization round

(Millennium round) did not deliver expected results due to the refusal of India and Brazil—with their emphasis on blocking certain intellectual property rights and agricultural interests, respectively—to be part of a compromise deal with OECD countries, China, Russia, and other countries, the expectation in Washington, London, Brussels, Tokyo, Canberra, and many other capitals in 2016 was still that a transatlantic US–EU trade liberalization deal and the finalized trade liberalization deal TPP (US, Mexico, Canada, Japan, Australia, etc.) would be a partial substitute for a global liberalization round. However, as the Trump administration is burying both TPP and TTIP and switching to an aggressive bilateralism in trade negotiations, the role of the WTO becomes quite important again—for all countries except possibly for the US under Trump.

The anti-multilateralism of the Trump administration suggests that the US will also destabilize EU integration and thus have a political program to push Europe back into the late nineteenth century. If the US would undermine the EU integration, it means that every other regional integration club would also be undermined and this is only because the Trump administration holds the view that a bilateral negotiation approach would yield better results for the US than a multilateral approach: such a Trumpian ideology not only overlooks the fact that regional integration contributes to peace, prosperity, and stability in the respective region—and thus helps the US and all other countries to reduce military expenditure–GDP ratios and thus to raise consumption per capita; it also stands for an egocentric approach (emphasized by the slogan 'America First') which is aimed towards generating advantages for the US while weakening the income and welfare position of every other country: for some countries, often relatively poor countries, this will mean that their per capita consumption will decline so that rising global inequalities can be anticipated; the world economy would be characterized by a non-Rawlsian situation in which (international) inequalities are not to the benefit of the poorest countries—and from this philosophical perspective, one may well ask what intellectual approach underpins the Trump administration. Trumpian ideology seems to be far away from Rawls and Kant, but close to Hobbes and many other supporters of political Darwinism and imperialism in the nineteenth century. In this perspective, the Trump administration is far removed from modern British society and continental Europe, as well as China and many other Asian countries. It is hardly conceivable that the UK government would want to support a US government that deliberately destroys the international organizations established after 1944 under the leadership of the US, the UK, and several other countries.

The idea that the US would always be better off under bilateral deal-making is nonsense since it ignores the "team-building costs" for the US if there is no system of international organizations; the Trumpian ideology ignores the international social capital of international organization. If the US has a leadership role in international organizations, the US administration will be able to obtain political support at low cost compared to a situation in which there is an open rivalry between big powers with each power putting pressure on the smaller countries in order to push them into their own respective political camp. The history of the late nineteenth century is a period which shows how unstable the world economy was without a modern system of international organizations; ongoing rivalry led to imperialism and this in turn to World War I which led to about 20 million military and civilian deaths. It would create a dangerous world if the US were to leave the international organizations and would instead push for a new global rivalry of big countries—under the heading of bilateralism. One can hardly imagine that the UK, being one of the champions of international organization building, would support the Trump administration in such a dangerous international economic policy approach. Rather the UK should consider its old role in the European Union and join EU27 countries in their effort to defend and enhance the multilateral system and to promote the rule of law.

As regards the question of respect for the rule of law, the first two months of Mr. Trump's presidency have raised doubts about the willingness of the new US President to follow the US—and British—tradition of showing general respect for the rule of law. The federal judge who had temporarily stopped the presidential executive order imposing an immigration ban on seven countries—each with a Muslim majority in terms of population—was dubbed by Mr. Trump as a "so-called judge." For certain observers in the US and Europe, such wording is strange and unacceptable; and this raised problems in the context of the swift invitation of Mrs. May to President Trump to visit the United Kingdom soon. The speaker of the British Parliament, Mr. John Bercow—with a conservative political background—declared, in a short speech on February 6, that he was "strongly opposed" to US President Donald Trump addressing the Houses of Parliament during his state visit to the UK. The House of Commons speaker declared that he considered the sexism and racism expressed by Mr. Trump as unacceptable. Mr. Bercow also emphasized that he was critical of Trump's imposition of an immigration ban in the US. He said "We value our relationship with the United States. If a state visit takes place, that is way beyond and above the pay grade of the Speaker … However, as far as this place is concerned, I feel very strongly that our opposition to racism and sexism and our support for equality before the law and an independent judiciary are hugely important considerations in the House of Commons."

The Trump administration obviously aims at tax reforms that would reduce corporate tax rates considerably and thus redistribute income in favor of capital owners and the wealthy strata of society. The new tax plans, which could include a Border Tax Adjustment as was already discussed by Republicans in Congress in 2016, are likely to create a trade-distorting regime through an emphasis on cash-flow taxation. This would effectively amount to a hidden import tariff plus a hidden export subsidy which, of course, is incompatible with the rules of the WTO. Such a tax reform could, however, be implemented for some time until there is a verdict by the WTO dispute settlement panel and this would then allow other countries to adopt countervailing measures, e.g., import tariffs on US products. One can only hope that British and EU27 politicians will be able to convince the Trump administration not to implement such doubtful measures which would undermine prosperity worldwide through trade wars.

As President Trump will unwind Obamacare, he is reinforcing the gap in life expectancy between the EU and the US—Germany, France, and the UK have a life expectancy that exceeds that of the US by about three years and infant mortality in the US is also much higher than in the EU. The new health policy of the Trump administration is not in the interest of the majority of US citizens and their children.

Some Conclusions

EU countries should, as a reaction to the egocentric and self-ish Trump policies, come together even more and move towards a new integration debate. The UK should get the chance for a second referendum on EU membership in 2018 and the EU institutions should also be vigorously reformed. Partial debt relief for Greece, linked to reasonable constitutional reforms in the country, is both necessary and sensible. The Venice Commission, a body of inde-pendent experts—including excellent legal experts—under the aus-pices of the Council of Europe, could offer good advice for Greece here. The US would do well to reconsider its electoral laws. That Hillary Clinton is the second victor of the popular vote in the last 20 years not to become President of the US—following Al Gore against George W. Bush—seems bizarre. Perhaps, the US should consider a constitutional amendment to change the antiquated and democratically questionable role of the Electoral College in the presidential elections. With Brexit and Trump, the role of the West and the Western-influenced world economic order is under threat. This should be resisted: with rational arguments and sound analy-ses. It is unfortunate that in 2017 a land as big as the US should inaugurate a president hostile to EU integration, which would weaken the concepts of integration which offer hopes of peace and economic progress, both regionally and indeed globally. That can-not be in the long-term interests of the US. That the British govern-ment should, at the same time, become entangled in its own major and odd contradictions, reflects a historical descent of the West and of the two aforementioned countries in particular. Now, it greatly depends on political astuteness in continental Europe, whether or not the West can be stabilized—and on whether, in Europe, a naïve populism can be rejected and a new voice for reason and sanity in the West emerge.

Note

1. Dean Acheson quote reproduced with thanks to the Truman Presidential Library and Museum.

Reference

Nickell, S., & Saleheen, J. (2015). *The impact of immigration on occupational wages: Evidence from Britain*, Bank of England. (Staff Working Paper No. 574).

9

Can Brexit Be an Economic Success and What Effects Can Be Expected for the EU27?

Brexit and the Pound Devaluation

Brexit will bring about a strong devaluation of the Pound Sterling—possibly by about 20%. This will raise the inflation rate which brings negative welfare effects and it will also reduce the global demand for Sterling as a reserve currency (thus "free" imports of goods and services for the UK will be reduced; the international seigniorage will fall for the UK). Moreover, the share of the British economy in world GDP falls by the same percentage as the rate of the Pound's devaluation; a lower share in the global economy means a reduction of power and political leverage in international negotiations on trade, investment treaties and so on. If one considers a 10% real income reduction due to Brexit as realistic—following the findings of the report by the UK's Treasury—the overall reduction of the UK's weight in the global economy due to Brexit could reach about 30% in the long run. Welfare losses for the UK will thus be considerable and the country may also expect to have reduced political influence. It is also obvious that foreign investors will be able to take over a larger share of the British capital stock which reduces the growth rate of real gross national income as a higher share

© The Author(s) 2017
P.J.J. Welfens, *An Accidental Brexit*,
DOI 10.1007/978-3-319-58271-9_9

of British profits will be transferred abroad (to MNC parent companies). It is not gross domestic product which matters for consumption but actually gross national income (Welfens 2011) and hence the consumption growth rate in the UK will be negatively affected.

The real depreciation of the Pound will stimulate net exports in the medium term, but in effect this amounts to worsening terms of trade: for a given amount of imported goods, more goods have to be exported—for a given output, a real devaluation thus amounts to a tax on British citizens. To the extent that the British government will adopt a new round of excessive banking deregulation (in parallel to the US)—in an attempt to raise output growth—there is a risk of a new European banking crisis; and a repetition of the high cost of the banking crisis of 2007–2009 is quite likely to be faced by all parts of the UK and indeed by the whole of Europe and the US in the long run (for further arguments on this aspect, see also the EIIW Discussion Paper No. 238 by Welfens 2017b).

The immediate impact of the referendum result has been a strong devaluation of the British Pound: about 15% by January 2017. Output growth in 2016 has not reduced much although investment dynamics have weakened. One should, however, not overlook the reaction of the Bank of England to the Brexit majority, namely by cutting the interest rate. Moreover, the government has announced a reduction in the speed of consolidation so that firms will anticipate higher government consumption in the medium term and households could expect lower tax rates for some time. 2017 will bring a higher inflation rate and since this was not anticipated there will be a quasi-Phillips-curve effect, namely reduced real wage rates which will, in turn, encourage firms to hire more workers: unemployment will fall temporarily, but one should not forget that Mrs. May's Brexit speech of January 2017—making clear that there will be a hard Brexit—is a signal to domestic and foreign firms to reduce investment. Thus, the aggregate demand will fall in 2017/18 unless the real depreciation of the trade-weighted exchange rate should bring about a strong improvement of the current account. This is not very likely since the price elasticity of British exports is not very high; only on the import side will real depreciation bring a considerable medium-term reaction, namely a decline of the import volume.

2019—the year of the UK's leaving of the EU—could see high levels of nervousness in financial markets since it is unclear whether or not the British Parliament will come up with a majority to leave the European Union. At the same time, it is clear that the Trump administration will offer a lifeline for the UK in the form a US–UK Transatlantic Trade and Investment Partnership (TTIP); the TTIP project had been started under the Obama administration but resistance from Germany and France slowed down the negotiation process and the envisaged closing of an EU–US TTIP deal become unrealistic.

Anti-US groups, anti-globalization groups, and parts of a misled green opposition in Berlin and Brussels derailed a timely agreement on TTIP which would have brought an output increase of about 2% for Germany and the EU, respectively (Jungmittag/Welfens 2016). This estimate is clearly higher than the strange 0.5% estimate of the official CEPR study for the European Commission which, however, takes into account only trade effects, while the Jungmittag/Welfens analysis also includes foreign direct investment (FDI) effects and innovation aspects. Clearly, the effects of a bilateral US–UK TTIP could exceed 2% for the UK since the US cumulated FDI in the United Kingdom is fairly high: the share of UK output in US subsidiaries is about 6%, much higher than in Germany, but there is a caveat—much of the US foreign direct investment in the UK is in banking and this has not been a very innovative sector in past years—except for strange securitization constructions whose global expansion almost derailed the world economy in 2007–2009. Part of the output of the British banking sector in 2000–2009 was obviously negative value-added in a strict economic sense. Nevertheless, the May government is likely to be able to conclude a bilateral TTIP with the US and this, in turn, would stimulate the FDI inflows to the UK from the US and elsewhere. Moreover, the trade creation effects—largely stimulated by lower non-tariff barriers in US–UK trade—would bring specialization and real income gains. With the UK having a rather limited access to the EU single market, it is, however, also clear that certain foreign investment projects which would have been realized in the context of the originally envisaged EU28–US TTIP project will now not be completed. Ultimately, a bilateral UK–US TTIP, plus prospects for a free trade agreement with Canada, Australia, and New Zealand, could help avoid a strong British output decline in the true Brexit year of 2019.

With a broader deregulation campaign, the May government might be able to mobilize some initial additional growth and to achieve sustained growth going forward. Whether or not this will be sufficient to obtain a Conservative majority in a UK general election in 2020 is doubtful. The rising inflation rate in 2018/19 will not only bring about a higher interest rate from the Bank of England, but trade unions will also be rather dissatisfied in the context of real wage reduction effects linked to the new inflation dynamics (and certainly there will be the question of whether the Labour Party is a serious challenger for the Conservative Party). The British public will have become aware by 2018 at the latest that the impending Brexit is weakening the EU and that Russian pressure on the continent signals new future problems in Europe. A renewed Euro Crisis could also play a role: higher Eurozone interest rates, stimulated by higher interest rates in the US and the UK, will put additional pressure on Portugal, Spain, France, Greece, and Italy which are all countries with rather high debt–Gross Domestic Product (GDP) ratios; the protracted inability and unwillingness of Germany and its EU partner countries to solve the Greek debt problem—and the key constitutional problems of Greece (impossible to solve without a new Greek political strategy)—would most likely reinforce pro-Brexit sentiments among the British public. 2019 is very difficult to predict. The government will not propose a new referendum, but the Labour Party opposition could try to attach some strings to the decisions of Parliament in 2019 that leave open the option of having a second EU referendum; actually, this would be the third referendum on EU membership if that of 1975, organized by the Labour Party government under Prime Minister Wilson, is included.

If the UK should really leave the EU in 2019/20, there will be a strong destabilization of the EU27, but one can, of course, not rule out that the UK itself will also be destabilized—less so by economic problems, but more so by a movement in favor of a new Scottish independence referendum and possibly also serious political and security concerns regarding the border between Northern Ireland (part of the UK) and the Republic of Ireland—which will remain a member of

the EU. While much progress has been made through the peace process and devolution of powers to Belfast, Northern Ireland voted by a
majority to Remain in the European Union. Political differences with
a Conservative government in London could lead to a renewing of old
tensions between dissident republicans and loyalist factions. Any move
to reinstate a "hard border," and thus disrupt freedom of movement and
trade between Northern Ireland and the Republic, will present a serious
political and security concern. The United Kingdom is the Republic of
Ireland's second most important trading partner (after the US and taking all EU countries individually) and the Republic will face a substantial negative economic impact of its own. The government in Dublin
has commissioned its own studies on the potential long-term macroeconomic effects of Brexit on the Irish economy (Bergin et al. 2016).
However, Ireland may also benefit from the relocation of firms from the
UK in order to secure access to the single market. The Trump administration can be expected to support the Brexit process simply because
Donald Trump will want to prove that his early support of Brexit was
realistic and wise. This will alienate Germany and other EU27 countries
from the US. It follows that the EU27 will seek stronger cooperation
with China and rising Sino—EU trade and investment, plus infrastructure links, will indeed contribute to a stronger cooperation between EU
capitals and Beijing. This mix of economic and political challenges and
opportunities is shown in Fig. 9.1.

Cooperation between Germany and France within the EU27 is
likely to intensify since Germany—facing a fragile North Atlantic
Treaty Organization (NATO)—will have to seek much stronger links
to France. Without the UK, the EU will be more protectionist than
before and this will create some conflict of interest between Germany,
having a large current account surplus, and France which faces three
decades of a negative current account position. If EU27 growth should
be below that of the UK for several years, it would be no surprise if
further exits from the EU would occur so that the UK might want to
create a new European Free Trade Association (EFTA+) regional integration club which, in turn, creates further prospects for EU destabilization. In such a setting, it is not unlikely that some Eastern European
countries might want to leave the EU and indeed seek cooperation with

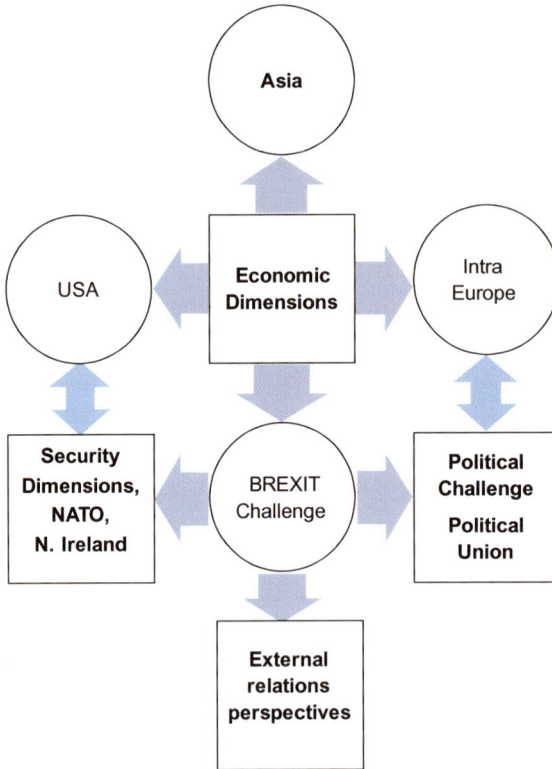

Fig. 9.1 Politico-economic challenges of Brexit

the Russia-dominated Eurasian Economic Union integration group. Bulgaria and several other Balkan countries might want to consider this option and it is clear that such a historical shift in the European balance of power would undermine the role of the US. How the US debate in 2019/20 will be is, however, rather difficult to anticipate. At the bottom line, it is rather likely that in the coming years the need for enhanced cooperation by big countries in the field of stabilization policy will not be explored. US–China conflicts and UK/US–EU27 debates will make more and better economic policy cooperation quite difficult. This, in the end, could also make an EU green light on an EU–US TTIP agreement rather unlikely since enhanced transatlantic cooperation in competition policy and in regulatory policy will be very hard to achieve.

European and Global Policy Conclusions

The roots of the story of European integration go back a long way: at least as early as the 1920s, there were some concrete proposals being made—in the middle of that decade, Aristide Briand and Gustav Stresemann tried to bring their respective countries of France and Germany closer together. In 1929, Briand gave a speech at the League of Nations, while acting as both Minister-President and Foreign Minister of France, in which he called for the development of a European Union, to which the then 27 European members of the League should belong—common decisions in certain policy fields, an advisory role on their shared interests, and a type of "federal bank" were included in the idea, which Briand also presented one year later in a memo on European integration. The re-emergence of nationalism, the global financial crisis, and the rivalry between Germany and France were not conducive to any real steps being taken towards the realization of Briand's plan. Only in 1948, after the destruction of the Second World War, were renewed efforts made in this regard, and France was once again central to this development. On May 9, 1950, Robert Schumann, French Foreign Minister, published a plan for the founding of a community, referred to as the 'Montanunion' or the European Coal and Steel Community (ECSC), which was focused on the establishment of a common supranational administration of the sectors key to armaments and military capabilities of the countries involved, coal and steel. On March 25, 1957, a decisive step towards European integration was finally made with the signing of the Treaty of Rome by Germany, France, Italy, Belgium, the Netherlands, and Luxembourg: with the idea of regional free trade and a common external customs policy (i.e., a customs union), where common and supranational institutions were intended to implement and indeed shape EU integration (Knipping 2004).

The European Commission was a form of government, and at the same time the Commission could also make legislative proposals which would be reviewed by a European Parliament—which was directly elected for the first time in 1979. Furthermore, a European Court of Justice, with a seat in Luxembourg, should ensure, and where necessary enforce, compliance with the Treaties. It took almost a decade after Schumann's proposal before free trade in goods could be achieved in 1958. That same year with the help of the International Monetary Fund (IMF)—and thus indirectly also of the US, which had already played an important role with regard to the former European Payments Union—world trade was reinvigorated through the introduction of simplified payment terms. That development certainly contributed to the success of the new integrated Europe: foreign trade, production, and employment rose markedly in the member countries. By the early years of the 1960s, the United Kingdom was also beginning to show an interest in becoming a member of the club. From an economic perspective, increased regional free trade should, through specialization advantages, result in a raising of the standards of living and income of the European countries involved. It can be shown using trade theory that with free trade and competition an economic 'catching up' process takes place: the poorer countries—even lacking flows of labor and capital—catch up to the leading countries in terms of per capita income and this leads to the process of capital accumulation and investment in the longer term. For the Federal Republic of Germany (i.e., the then West Germany), which since the mid-1950s had become an increasingly important export land and was frequently achieving foreign trade surpluses, this was an expansive environment. Fixed US Dollar exchange rates, to which the EU countries were bound by the Bretton Woods System from 1958 to 1973, facilitated the expansion of trade in the EU enormously.

US–UK–EU27–China

Brexit means that the UK will leave the European Union and that part of the City of London financial market can no longer be based in the UK. Legal and political restrictions imposed by the European Central

Bank (ECB) and the European Commission imply that possibly about one-sixth of London's financial services activities will be physically relocated to EU27 countries where British, US, Japanese, Chinese, and other international banks already active in London will set up new subsidiaries or increase the size and operations of current subsidiaries. The damage for the UK is twofold: losing income and jobs on the one hand, while on the other hand there will also be a negative impact on the British current account position that will face a further deterioration. Further relocation will be in favor of New York since the European economies of scale thus far realized in London are no longer feasible as the banks in London no longer have an EU passport, which allowed them to serve EU27 clients from London. The biggest foreign banking investor country in London is the US and thus US banks in London will relocate some activities into EU27 countries, but possibly even more activities back to New York. The traditionally high sectoral current account surpluses of the UK vis-à-vis the EU27 will therefore reduce and the UK current account deficit problem could become quite serious within a decade after 2019. This author is not aware of any macroeconomic modeling and, in particular, current account analysis of the UK in which the coming international relocation of banks has been considered as a structural shock. Further implications are a strong devaluation of the British Pound and rising FDI: if by 2020 the real devaluation of the Pound—compared to early June 2016—should be 25%, the implication is that foreign investors from the US, China, and the EU27 (just to name the leading three sources of outward FDI in 2015) could easily take over large parts of British industry. The kind of free trade agreement that the UK might be able to achieve with China in the long run will be affected by this; say, if China owns a quarter of British industry in 2030, the Chinese pressure on the UK to open up its market will be quite strong and with China's structural current account surplus vis-à-vis the UK, then the growing real devaluation of the British Pound will be an even stronger phenomenon in the long run. The UK's foreign indebtedness will grow—not just vis-à-vis China—and the degree of policy autonomy that the UK will experience in such a setting could be quite limited.

In turn, China will redirect the growing Chinese banking activities towards Germany and France (as well as some other countries), and Japanese banks, which play a large role in London, could follow China's footsteps. As China will roughly double its GDP between 2016 and 2029—with an expected growth rate of 5% per year—the EU trade relations with China will strongly increase. Germany and France are at an advantage compared to the UK in that there is a direct rail link to China whose freight capacity is growing and due to Chinese infrastructure investment in many countries along the land-based new Silk Road (under the One Belt, One Road initiative of the Chinese government), Eurozone exports to China in sectors characterized by just-in-time production—e.g., the automotive industry—will increase. Germany's automotive exports, to take just one example, has strongly increased since 2000, but increasingly those exports are intermediate exports of the German automotive industry. Chinese investors from the automotive sector, in turn, have become strong actors in the EU, for example, Dongfeng has a 14% share in the French carmaker PSA (Peugeot-Citroen); as PSA announced that it would buy Opel/Vauxhall from General Motors, the Chinese investor Dongfeng has indirectly acquired a share of 14% in Vauxhall and Opel, respectively. The economic links between the Eurozone and China will be strongly reinforced over the next decade, but it could be a more even international exchange than the case of the UK.

With many foreign investors and top expats from the US and Japan as well as other countries leaving the UK after Brexit, house prices in London and elsewhere in the UK will decrease. The Bank of England seems to be eager to focus in the future on a new price index that would place a greater emphasis on the housing market and this, in turn, would bring a more modest increase of the inflation rate.

If the Trump administration should put protectionist pressure on China, part of the traditional Chinese trade surplus vis-à-vis the US will be redirected to Asia and Europe where prices of tradables will fall—China is a big economy and one cannot assume that Chinese exports would be internationally redirected without affecting regional price levels in the newly preferred export markets. US protectionist pressure vis-à-vis China will thus indirectly undermine the profitability of firms in Asia and Europe, and China's output growth will slow down. This would particularly hold if the Trump administration makes US FDI flows to China more difficult. With lower growth in China and possibly somewhat higher growth in the US under the Trump administration, the net effect for the UK and the EU, respectively, is unclear. EU28 exports to the US will increase, particularly if the Dollar appreciates vis-à-vis European currencies, but EU28 exports to China will be dampened through lower growth in China; this triangular mechanism should be even stronger for some Association of Southeast Asian Nations (ASEAN) countries having strong trade relations with China. The US and the EU share the view that they do not want to easily recognize China as a market economy, but given the rhetoric of the Trump administration this conflict might become more of a US–China conflict than an EU27–China conflict—with the UK probably taking sides with the US since the UK is dependent to some extent on the United States: not only for trade reasons, but also because 6% of the UK's gross domestic output is in US subsidiaries and the post-Brexit UK will also not have much room to maneuver in foreign policy. One may argue that the UK has returned some power back to London from Brussels only to lose power to the US—while also giving up the power to sit at the EU negotiating table in Brussels. If this view should turn out to be adequate, most of the Brexiteers' promises to raise British policy autonomy will turn out to be political science fiction—misleading themselves and the British public. The situation could, to some degree, be manageable if the EU27 could be stabilized; however, if the EU27 should disintegrate, the destabilization fall-out on the UK would be even larger.

How Complex and Costly the UK's Trade Negotiations with the EU Will be

In the analysis of Holmes et al. (2016), it is shown how complex British trade negotiations with the EU will be if one assumes a hard Brexit—i.e., no single market membership, no customs union, and no membership of the European Economic Area; the latter would mean that the

UK would accept a passive regulatory union with the EU plus free trade plus free movement of labor (such as is the case with Norway, Iceland, or Liechtenstein), and this is not what the May government wants. If there is to be a bilateral free trade agreement—similar to Switzerland—it could take many years to negotiate and for foreign investors in the UK this means that rules of origin will apply presenting a major new problem as new costs and risks will have to be incurred by UK exporters and this will reduce British exports of goods to the EU considerably (in the case of services most problems are even more complex than in the case of goods). A standard EU requirement is that 60% of the value-added of the respective good should be generated in the post-Brexit UK. EU27 countries' customs agencies will have the right to physically inspect imports from the UK and to verify that the 60% requirement is fulfilled: this will cost both time and money. Moreover, existing EU28 value-added chains, which so far have resulted in a British final good that is then exported to an EU partner country, assume that 30% of the value-added of the British export product is intermediate inputs from EU27 countries, 20% is from the US, and 50% is from the UK.

In the future, the British firm will have to raise the share of value-added in the UK and rely less on intermediate imports from Ireland or continental EU countries; instead of relying on imports from a highly specialized firm in the EU27 countries, some British firms will have to be found to produce an equivalent intermediated input—so that in the end the share of intermediate products imported from the EU could decrease by one-third. However, this implies a cost disadvantage and British firms facing such problems, while not having any room to raise prices in the EU single market (or only to a very modest degree), will require real wage reductions in the UK which is not to the advantage of British workers. Alternatively, these firms will switch to a more capital-intensive production which, however, typically has the disadvantage that British jobs are lost and British imports of machinery and equipment—often from Germany or other EU27 countries—will rise so that the structural British trade balance deficit will worsen. The equilibrium Pound exchange rate will adjust, and there will be a depreciation of the British Pound which makes all imports more expensive, while the rise of the general price level will translate into a reduction of real income for all British families. There will be considerable negative welfare effects in the UK and the probability of losing one's job is likely to rise for unskilled workers, particularly for those groups whose jobs will be replaced by imported machinery and equipment. The very small UK manufacturing sector—which relative to gross domestic product is only about half of the size of the German manufacturing sector—implies a low probability that the additional machinery and equipment ordered will come from British firms. The May government has announced that it wants to raise the share of manufacturing output in total GDP, but to achieve this goal in a non-trivial sense (i.e., not by maintaining current output while the services sector starts shrinking as British services exports to the EU will reduce strongly) will be quite difficult. If leaving the EU is not carefully managed, and this seems almost impossible given the long delays that the May government has itself imposed on the Brexit process, British growth will decline considerably in the medium term. It is not clear that the British and EU27 export growth perspectives towards Asia will be bright in the era of the Trump administration and this could further raise the price tag of Brexit, namely if the US imposes protectionist measures on China which then will dampen income growth in China and Asia, respectively, and hence Asian imports from Europe.

The election of Mr. Trump as the 45th US president has created new international constraints and options for the UK. Obviously, it should be rather easy for the UK to conclude the UK–US transatlantic free trade arrangement (and, under certain conditions, to possibly join a revised North American Free Trade Agreement (NAFTA)). The May government might think that with respect to a future EU–UK treaty on access to the EU27 single market, there will always be the option—in case of serious problems in the negotiation process—to resume the old British position as a member of the World Trade Organization (WTO) and at the same time for the UK to undertake the rather simple task of concluding sectoral free trade agreements with the EU27. However, the WTO principle of most favored nation (third countries are entitled to the same tariff concessions of the UK as those which the UK is giving to the EU) makes bilateral free trade arrangements a global issue: as emphasized by Holmes et al. (2016) and The Economist (2017), respectively, the UK would have to give the same tariff concessions to all other WTO member countries as those given to the EU27 countries, that is if there would be the bilateral UK–EU free trade agreement for the automotive sector, the US and the Chinese car industries would also enjoy free access to the British market—and would no longer face the previous 10% EU import tariff for selling cars to the UK market. This will make the British car market more competitive and easier to access for Asian and US car exporters and at the same time would reduce the incentive for FDI in automotive industry in the UK itself.

References

Bergin, A. et al. (2016). Macroeconomic Impact of Brexit on Ireland, Economic and Social Research Institute, Working Paper No. 548, November 2016, Dublin.

Economist. (2017). The "WTO option" for Brexit is far from straightforward, from the print edition, Finance and Economics, January 7, 2017. Available at http://www.economist.com/news/finance/21713818-becoming-independent-member-wto-could-be-difficult-process.

Holmes, P., Rollo, J. and Winters, A. (2016). Negotiating the UK's post-Brexit Trade Arrangements, National Institute Economic Review, 238 (1). R22-R30. ISSN 0027-9501 http://dx.doi.org/10.1177/002795011623800112.

Jungmittag, A., Welfens, P. J. J. (2016). "Beyond EU-US Trade Dynamics: TTIP Effects Related to Foreign Direct Investment and Innovation", EIIW paper No. 212—presented at the IMF, Washington DC, June 28, 2016. www.eiiw.eu.

Knipping, F. (2004). *Rom 25. März 1957. Die Einigung Europas.* Munich: Beck.

Welfens, P. J. J. (2011). *Innovations in macroeconomics, 3rd revised/enlarged printing.* Heidelberg: Springer.

Welfens, P. J. J. (2017b). Foreign financial deregulation under flexible and fixed exchange rates, EIIW Paper No. 238.

Part III

EU Developments

10

What Is the EU? A Redistribution and Trade Engine with a Political Element

The European Union is primarily composed of the European Commission, the European Parliament, the European Court of Justice (ECJ), and some other institutions. These now include the European Council, the assembly of the heads of state and government, which actually did not become an official EU institution until the Treaty of Lisbon. With that treaty, an institution directly representing the nations themselves was created on par with the supranational Commission and its Commissioners—one from each member state. That was not a particularly clever move, as the European Union had for decades stood for cross-border cooperation and EU institutions which were supposed to transcend national interests (see Fig. 10.1 for an overview).

Thus, no member of the European Commission should receive or accept instructions directly from national governments—that is from the very bodies and people which sent them to Brussels in the first place. The Commission has circa 33,000 civil servants at its disposal, of which roughly 1/6th are involved in providing translation and interpretation services. Some of these civil servants are certainly superfluous, and seem to spend their days constantly concocting new regulations for the EU single market—which often serve to only burden the economy

© The Author(s) 2017
P.J.J. Welfens, *An Accidental Brexit*,
DOI 10.1007/978-3-319-58271-9_10

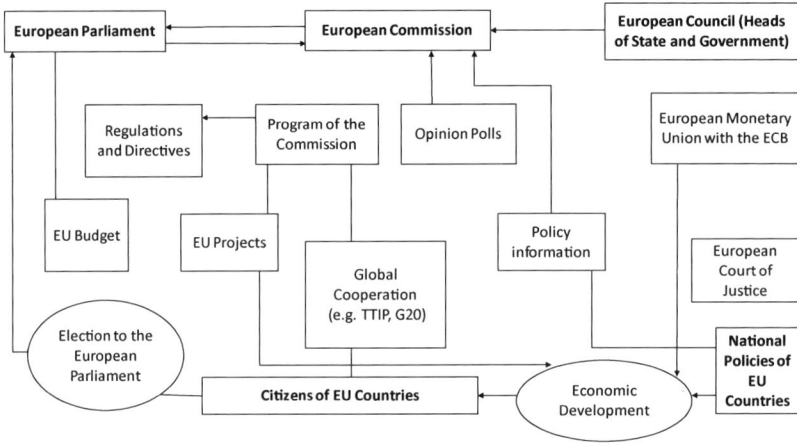

Fig. 10.1 Institutional structure of the EU and European government

with unnecessary costs and which contribute nothing to the international competitiveness of EU suppliers—quite the opposite. There are, for example, thousands of medium-sized UK and other EU firms, which need to retain representatives and lobbyists in Brussels in order to try and prevent the questionable regulations of Commission staffers from progressing. The regulations on the suction power of vacuum cleaners, popular among Commission civil servants, are just one example of the well-known but absurd pieces of legislation produced by the Commission.

Nevertheless, there are valid reasons behind the majority of the Commission's work which serves the EU single market, competition policy or the framework regulation of telecommunication networks; or it involves the negotiations regarding free trade agreements with other countries, because the EU is organized as a customs union, the Commission is always responsible for leading negotiations on behalf of all EU member states: customs policy is a supranational policy field which, for good reasons, is shaped in Brussels. The European Union currently has 35 free trade agreements and the conditions which a community with a Gross Domestic Product (GDP) of circa £12,700/$15,500 billion (2015: five times that of Germany) and

510 million inhabitants or consumers can negotiate are naturally better than the conditions on market access which individual countries could achieve, for example, in an agreement with Mexico, Canada, or the US. As a customs union, the EU is unusual in that responsibility for external trade and the task of negotiating international investor protection agreements also rests with the Commission. As a result, all EU countries have the same import duties on goods imported from third countries. Amongst all the integration zones globally, only Mercosur in Latin America is also a customs union, and Mercosur, like the Association of Southeast Asian Nations (ASEAN) in Asia and many other "regional integration clubs", is strongly modeled on the EU itself. Besides external trade activities, the EU is also active in many other areas which, however, are seldom of real importance.

The EU has an important and tight control over subventions to industry, which should prevent member states from preventing competition by means of paying subsidies: that is extremely reasonable and, in the end, protects the pockets of taxpayers, as otherwise, during every recession, there would be—as was the case in times past with the steel industry—an expensive race by the national providers of subventions of EU member countries to assist steel production. In the event that a breach in Community law has been determined to have taken place by the Commission, the respective member state must be reimbursed for the illegally paid national subventions. Part of the environmental policy is also a competence of the EU, and this also makes sense in relation to many environmental issues from an economic perspective—not, for example, in relation to local water supplies, but for climate change policy and questions relating to the overfishing of seas globally.

The EU also has a role as an actor in financial redistribution, which in particular subsidizes agricultural production—the agricultural sector is an exception to the rule, for which France has always sought financial assistance. In this sector there are also high import duties, which are intended to protect domestic farmers from competition via imports. Furthermore, within the framework of structural funds, the EU gives aid to regions with a per capita income which lies below 75% of the EU average (measured in terms of purchasing price parity (PPP); under PPP, the different prices for non-tradable goods in various EU countries are considered: a haircut in Warsaw costs a lot less than a haircut in Vienna, thus £1,000 or $1,000 in income buys a lot more in Warsaw than in Vienna). This benefits primarily regions in Eastern Europe, and also in Greece, Spain, Portugal, Italy, and even in the former East Germany.

The official supranational EU budget in Brussels in 2015 amounted to approximately 1% of the economic output of the European Union. That is a modest figure when compared to the national consumption rates of about 20% in EU member states, where the same magnitude of expenditure is incurred again by national governments for social expenditure. The European Union has various goals including growth, environmental protection, and economic convergence—the leveling of economic differences in terms of per capita income between EU countries through the successful economic catching-up process of poorer EU members.

These goals of the EU can partly be determined by looking at the EU budget. For 2016, the total budget is about £122/$149 billion. From that, about 39% goes to the area of agriculture, 36% for structural funds, i.e., help for the poorer regions of EU countries, 11% is intended to support and promote innovation, 5% for external affairs, 6% on administration, and 1% on internal affairs/security (breakdown according to the website of the BMF, 2016). Accounting for the UK rebate, then—based on the figures for 2015—12.6% of the EU budget comes from the United Kingdom.

The 2015 British net contribution to the budget (payments less services and amounts etc. received) was about half the amount of the gross figure, meaning that £6.7–£7.6 billion (approx. $8.2–$9.3 billion) will be missing from the EU budget in the event of a UK exit. In the media in August 2016, the figure of £9.75 billion ($11.9 billion) was suggested as the British net contribution; however, this includes the one-off effect of a late contribution payment of £1.8/$2.2 billion, which the Commission allowed the UK to postpone in 2014. Thus, either the relatively poor net recipient countries in Eastern Europe especially, plus Greece going forward, must accept cuts to receipts from 2020/21 (i.e., the next budget period), or Germany, France, Italy, the Netherlands, Sweden, and other net contributing countries must contribute even more.

It is also possible, that the United Kingdom could receive access to the EU single market at the cost of a financial contribution, which could possibly be in the region of 60% of net UK contributions to date—about £4.25/$5.2 billion. That would ameliorate the EU's budgetary problems after Brexit to some extent. The budget gap could be bridged by means of a 50:50 split in terms of net expenditures and net contributions. There are critical limits to how high the net contributions can be raised—in the case of the Netherlands, this ceiling has almost been reached at 0.7% of GDP. If this amount could be capitalized over a long timeframe, at an interest rate of 3%, then the sum of expected Dutch contributions amounts to 23% of annual economic output. For the UK, a net contribution ratio of even 0.3–0.4% of GDP, taking a comprehensive look at all negative arguments, was already too much for Brexit voters.

The Netherlands has always had close political and economic linkages with the United Kingdom and there is also an anti-EU party involved in Dutch politics. That party is also hoping for a referendum on Dutch membership of the EU in the near future. However, the expected serious short-term weakening of British economic development may dampen the political appetite for similar EU withdrawal projects for the foreseeable future. Nevertheless, it is important to remember that popular referenda in the Netherlands and France in relation to the EU Constitution (the Convention's draft) failed by a clear and narrow majority, respectively, in 2005.

There is a correlation (BPB 2016) between an EU country's per capita income and its status as a contributor to or recipient from the EU's budget. Countries with high per capita incomes tend to be net contributors to the EU budget, while relatively poorer member states tend to be net recipients. For 2014, the leading net contributing countries were the Netherlands (0.71% of GDP), Germany and Sweden (both contributing 0.52%), and Finland (0.4%). The leading net recipients were Hungary (5.6% of GDP), Bulgaria (4.5%), Lithuania (4.4%), and Poland (3.5%). On a per capita basis, the leading net contributors are the Netherlands, Sweden, Germany, and Denmark (contributing £221 ($270), £204 ($249), £163 ($199), and £126 ($154) per capita, respectively). On the same basis, the leading net recipients are Hungary, Lithuania, Greece, and Malta (receiving £488 ($595), £445 ($543), £401 ($489), and £358 ($437), respectively). In absolute terms, the net contributors are Germany, France, the United Kingdom, and the Netherlands (£13.15/$16 billion, £6.1/$7.44 billion, £4.16/$5.08 billion, and £4/$4.9 billion, respectively). The leading recipients were Poland, Hungary, Greece, and Romania (£11.6/$14.15 billion, £4.8/$5.9 billion, £4.4/$5.4 billion, and £3.8/$4.6 billion, respectively).

What interests motivate countries such as Germany, France, Italy, the Netherlands, Sweden, and others, as net contributors to the EU, to participate and cooperate in the EU? The answer, in part, is that through contributions, EU projects in relatively poor member countries are part-financed, which promote the goals of economic growth and the catching-up process. That has two advantages from the perspective of the net contributors with high per capita incomes:

• The import demand of the economically catching-up countries increase and thus also the exports of the contributor countries. With an increased per capita income in the catch-up member states, there will be a rise in the production of differentiated products in these countries for export. The foreign trade, that is the expected additional trade created as a result of free trade between the EU members leads to gains in real income for the EU countries involved. Moreover, when more direct investment flows into poorer EU countries, there will be positive production and income effects in the destination countries as a result of international technology transfers and a higher capital intensity; thus direct investment flows could strengthen economic convergence in the European Union—meaning per capita incomes will converge at a relatively high level. A higher per capita income in the EU means higher aggregate demand for differentiated technology-intensive products: highly innovative firms, primarily in Western Europe, can better refinance their Research & Development costs in a larger, high-income, and high-price single market, and a considerable part of profits will be realized through the export of Western European firms in the direction of Eastern Europe. Higher profits mean higher share prices and every saver who has invested in equity investments, either directly via private share-holdings or indirectly via life insurance policies which are invested in share funds, will realize a gain. Furthermore, trade theory suggests that through trade creation via intra-EU free trade, specialization and income gains result for all countries involved.

• If there is an economic catching-up process through intra-Europe financial transfers—organized by the EU—then this will facilitate the political consensus-finding process: countries with similarly high per capita incomes share similar interests as countries with more varied levels of per capita income. The EU will thus become more capable of concerted action through economic convergence and that promises a better chance of promoting the bloc's interests globally, which entails benefits for, above all, high-income member states which are strong in terms of foreign trade and high levels of direct investment abroad via multinational firms.

Economic catching-up processes are also important, because otherwise political and social unrest will ferment in the relatively poor member states at the periphery of the EU and, based on experience, that would result in security problems on the external borders of the EU, a situation which would, in the end, also be detrimental to the relatively prosperous EU members.

The expenditure side of the EU budget is beset by certain problems, particularly in relation to projects to do with Structural Funds for poorer regions. There is reason to doubt that spending in the form of supports for agriculture and fisheries is, from an economic perspective, logical and wise. In the area of the fisheries, EU subventions are used for the building of modern trawlers and other fishing vessels which, in turn, partly contribute to the overfishing of the seas—hardly a sensible, sustainable policy. Why exactly the EU's spending on agriculture and fisheries comes under the heading of 'Sustainable Resource Development' is a good question—it appears to be somewhat of a marketing scam, far removed from the concepts of transparency and economic rationale.

One can only consider raising the EU budget in the longer term under certain institutional conditions. Furthermore, the financing side of the budget cannot be far from one's mind when contemplating changes in spending. In 2015, traditional own resources (above all income from customs and duties) accounted for 14%, a share of the Value-Added Tax (VAT) receipts accounted for a further 14%, while the contributions of member states themselves, which depend on economic performance, accounted for the other 72% of the financing side of the EU budget.

A UK withdrawal from the EU will surely lead to a surge in trade liberalization measures by the British, which will act as an impulse for the EU to engage in its own trade liberalization. Thus, it will be necessary in the long term for the EU to raise its share of VAT receipts and effectively also its share of income tax receipts. The British exit will put the EU27 under pressure in terms of taxation, as the government in London seems to be planning a reduction of the corporate tax rates in order to make the United Kingdom a more attractive destination for foreign investors—a particularly pressing need after Brexit. Tax competition between European countries will also create political pressure on the continental EU members to also reduce corporate tax rates, which could lead to conflict in some countries with regard to redistribution policies. The trade unions and some other voter groups will surely find a new direct or indirect preferential treatment of capital in tax policy unacceptable. The UK is, economically speaking, large enough to exert pressure on the EU27 in this regard, as the relative economic weighting of the UK to the EU27 is 1:4.

Immediately following the Brexit referendum, Cameron's Chancellor of the Exchequer, George Osborne, announced that he intended reducing the corporate tax rate. This contradicts the goals of the new May government, which Theresa May herself announced as she took office as new Prime Minister, which is to create an economic system in the UK which works for all groups in society. This announcement will not make it any easier to reduce tax rates on firms. However, it is hard for the May government to see any real alternatives if the UK is to reach a situation of sustained economic growth. The cabinet must come to terms with the fact that British industrial firms and service providers will increase direct investment in continental EU countries in order to secure immediate access to the EU27 single market.

Thus, the UK is threatened with a structural reduction in the investment rate, which is bad for both growth and employment. Therefore, a reduction in the headline rates of corporate tax, and other advantages for firms, can soon be expected—with parliamentary elections expected by 2020, London needs to take positive steps towards more growth and employment as early as 2017/18. The British government would be well advised to have completed negotiations with the EU27 by 2019, to avoid the possibility of having to arrange European Parliament elections in the UK.

The EU27 countries will view any move by the British government to reduce corporate tax rates with displeasure and could perhaps, during the EU–UK negotiations on access to the EU single market, offer less attractive conditions to the United Kingdom. The May government will only be able to counter that by agreeing the terms and rules of access to the single market with the EU relatively quickly, to allow it to make changes in relation to corporate taxation once negotiations have been concluded without fear. What is more, the UK will no longer be subject to the rules of the European Commission on state aid, so that the government in London could also attempt to improve the attractiveness of the country as a location for investment after Brexit by offering higher subventions for firms.

European integration has for a long time, within the framework of the contractual EU developments, allowed an increasing level of flexibility with regard to integration projects, namely through the Treaty of Amsterdam and also the later Treaty of Nice. While in the Treaty of Amsterdam, an intensification of integration is defined as a possibility only if it would involve a majority of EU countries, in the Nice Treaty—which then applied to 27 countries—the possibility for more intensive integration was created for groups as small as nine member states. A more intense cooperation between smaller groups of countries cannot, however, take place in the key areas of EU policy, for example, in the field of external trade policy. Furthermore, it should be ensured that countries which do not participate in this intensified integration by a sub-group do not suffer any disadvantage; while non-participating countries also reserve the right to join the sub-group engaged in closer cooperation at a later point in time. For the UK, this meant on the one hand that there was no requirement on them to commit to joining in more recent EU integration activities in advance, on the other hand, London would still have the opportunity, if it wished, to join successful "subfields of integration" later on after having seen how it developed for those involved. However, for the UK, at least from the point of view of Downing Street, one problem remained: the UK, as a non-Eurozone member, would stay on the outside of that important field of increasing integration at least.

The British government also enjoyed one advantage—that they did not have the concern of an upper limit of a 3% deficit ratio, and that advantage was certainly exploited by the Cameron governments. Such a strategy can have a logical basis if economic growth is rising. If one wishes to reduce national debt, this can be done if a budget surplus can be achieved and/or if the growth rate of the real GDP is larger than that of the real debt burden. If in an initial state, government debt ratio would be, say, 100%—approximately the situation the UK found itself in 2015—then there will be a reduction of this debt ratio (the relationship of government debt to economic output), if the sum of the national deficit ratio and the difference between economic growth and the growth of the government debt is positive. Thus, if the deficit ratio is, say, 3.5%, but the medium-term difference between economic growth and the growth of government debt is higher than 3.5%, then the debt ratio falls. Naturally, from the perspective of stability policy, the goal is to manage the level of the debt ratio and/or to reduce it over time if it is at a critically high level to begin with.

As the May cabinet assumed office, it was announced that the quick reduction of the government debt ratio, planned under the Cameron government, would be postponed. This actually represents a wise decision, realistically assuming that the Brexit decision will weaken economic growth and indeed possibly even cause a downturn. Some of the representatives of the Leave campaign vigorously contested the claim that a UK withdrawal would have a negative economic effect on the UK. The reality of 2016/17 clearly indicates that these negative effects do, in fact, exist.

Institutional and Regional EU Perspectives

The European Union has its own institutions, such as the European Commission and European Parliament, which are important and powerful actors in their own right. The EU is, however, heavily dependent on the member states and another EU institution, the European Council, shows this clearly: the heads of state and government have become particularly influential since the Euro Crisis. The weighting of the EU budget relative to the national budget is, at only 1:20 (not including the social expenditure at the national level), extremely low. Supranational expenditure of 1% is inadequate for anti-cyclical policy from Brussels, so that each and every EU member state pursues its own policies—little coordination of the national approaches to fiscal policy takes place. Nevertheless, the EU maintains its own independent role on the international stage in terms of trade policy and also at Group of Twenty (G20) summits, the EU exercises exclusive competence only in terms of external trade policies.

In the multi-layered system of the EU, there is a certain division of labor between the supranational level (Brussels), the national layer (member states—for example, national policy-setters such as the British government in London, or the Federal Government of Germany in Berlin), and the regions. Ever since the UK joined the EU, there has in British politics always been a strong emphasis on the role of the national layer and national politics; particularly as Brussels is seen to suffer from a 'democratic deficit.'

Regions are not only important actors in federal countries such as Germany and Austria. They increasingly play an important role in other EU member states, where regions are seeking, and in some cases have received, greater autonomy, for example, in the UK and Spain. The Spanish region of Catalonia is striving for independence, which is creating conflict in Spain. In Brussels, the regions are indirectly represented in the EU Committee of the Regions, in which even some individual cities are represented.

The relationship between the EU member states and the EU itself is arranged so that the European Commission alone is responsible for international free trade agreements and—since the Lisbon Treaty—also for agreements on investor protection. Here, the EU can use its collective weight as a bargaining force in order to secure better conditions for member states with regard to market access, for example, with Mexico and Singapore, and soon also Japan and Vietnam, as long as relevant agreements can be successfully concluded. There are already 35 such EU Free Trade Agreements in existence. This course of action offers massive economic benefits.

EU member states whose per capita income lies under 90% of the EU average receive financial support from the EU, in order to facilitate an easier catching-up process via funding for infrastructure and environmental projects. Furthermore, regions with a low per capita income—less than 75% of the EU average (on the basis of purchasing power parity (PPP) figures)—also receive EU grants and subsidies; as do regions with steeply declining rates of industrial employment. However, the entire budget for EU expenditure is just 1% of the EU's economic performance and as half of this is earmarked for use in the field of agriculture, in reality only a small fraction remains from the Regional and Structural Funds.

North Rhine-Westphalia (NRW), a German federal state founded in 1946 by the British occupying forces in the aftermath of the Second World War, enjoys a strong EU orientation, not only in terms of trade and direct investment by multinational firms, but it is also ideally located in Europe from a logistical perspective. If, for example, Chinese firms wish to conquer the EU single market, then North Rhine-Westphalia is located at the heart of Europe. The state has already attracted high levels of investment from American, Asian, and indeed European multinational firms, which is crucial for production and patenting dynamics. The rail connection between Chongqing, a major city in China, and Duisburg in Germany is the result of goods distribution logistics. Part of the Ruhr region and indeed some neighboring NRW regions have also received considerable funds from EU coffers over the years (amounting between 2007 and 2015 to almost £2.5 billion).

For consumers, the competitive nature of the EU single market is not only visible in terms of lower prices and the relevant real income gains. Competition with regard to innovation in terms of goods and services has also risen, meaning that both a larger and more varied supply and indeed better quality products are available. It was the European Commission which opened the national fixed-line telephony networks in 1998 and in doing so enabled lower prices and higher product innovations. With regard to the integration of the energy markets, there remains work to be done until a similar level of integration and/or an optimal connection and networking of national energy markets can be achieved. Due to the single market, public tendering processes were opened up, which certainly brings benefits for the taxpayer since if these tendering processes generate competition on European markets, then public procurement will be less costly. Cheaper opportunities for travel in Europe—without facing border and immigration controls—are, thanks to the single market and the Schengen Agreement, of benefit to everyone.

References

BPB. (2016). Zahlen und Fakten: Europa, Bundeszentrale für politische Bildung. http://www.bpb.de/nachschlagen/zahlen-und-fakten/europa/.
BMF. (2016). EU Budget 2015. https://www.bundesfinanzministerium.de/Content/DE/Bilderstrecken/Mediathek/Infografiken/infografik-europa-haushalt.html?notFirst=true&docId=63502#photogallery.

11

The History of European Integration and the Role of Rules

During the 1960s and 1970s, the European Commission was not a particularly politicized institution which under Commission President Walter Hallstein did not show an interest in getting involved in conflicts with national governments (however, France's own European policies under President De Gaulle eventually forced Hallstein's resignation). This changed under Commission President Jacques Delors, who headed the Commission from 1985 to 1994 and who repeatedly clashed with the United Kingdom under Prime Minister Margaret Thatcher. Delors' goal was more European integration and he also considered approaches towards establishing common European foreign and security policies. These developments were exactly what Margaret Thatcher did not want. One cannot rule out that a certain dragging of the heels by Britain impeded a faster deepening of integration, while the government in London certainly helped to keep the European Union on a course of liberal trade.

Until 1973, the then community of just nine member states was quite straightforward—then the United Kingdom and Denmark joined (leaving a diminishing European Free Trade Association (EFTA) behind them) along with the Republic of Ireland. In hindsight, one can see

© The Author(s) 2017
P.J.J. Welfens, *An Accidental Brexit*,
DOI 10.1007/978-3-319-58271-9_11

that the UK's accession was, from the perspective of the EU at least, a problematic decision—despite over four decades of British cooperation with and participation in the EU, a narrow majority still voted on June 23, 2016, for a UK withdrawal; EU integration obviously did not permeate British politics. Originally, the Labour Party was against EU membership and campaigned against it before the first EU referendum in the UK in 1975, a vote which ended with a clear majority in favor of membership. Since the 1980s, under the then leadership of Margaret Thatcher, the Conservative Party in the UK has been a Euroskeptic party; which the exception of the first term of government of John Major, Thatcher's successor. It should be a cause of concern in continental EU countries that even the social democratic Labour Party did not adopt a decisive pro-EU position over the decades of UK membership. The governments of Tony Blair, during this reign as Prime Minister, could certainly be friendly towards the EU at times. From the EU's point of view, this lack of a pro-EU political consensus often made cooperation with the country difficult. However, there is also no doubt that British policy proposals for EU integration were extremely valuable over the years; particularly in relation to the development of the single market. It is all the more strange, therefore, that Brexit should have been impacted to such a degree by the question of immigration, that is the EU freedom of movement for labor, which has been part of the single market for over 20 years.

In the early years, the European Commission was active above all in the area of external trade policy and tried, in the context of the British accession, to initiate an EU negotiations project with developing countries—particularly with the former British and French colonies: the Lomé Agreement. Easier access for the relevant developing countries was a political aim. Questions of a common competition policy gradually became the focus of EU politics. However, it took until the end of the 1980s until the EU could also exercise competences in the area of large cross-border mergers and acquisitions. The Commission was rightfully given credit when it initiated a liberalization of the fixed-line telephony networks in 1998.

With the start of the Eurozone in 1999, the EU integration project began to experience difficulties which, however, were not immediately exposed due to the good economic development over the following decade or so. The trial phase of the Euro should inevitably have come during turbulent economic conditions or strong international shocks. The Eurozone's lack of a political union meant that the monetary union could become a starting point for instability and political conflict in the EU—this was eventually the case from 2010, i.e. from the Euro Crisis, on. There are Commission officials at the highest levels who are of the view that the Maastricht Treaty was not negotiated carefully enough. Generally, the history of the EU is a story of recurrent tensions between technocrats and the leading politicians in Brussels and in member states, respectively, as was shown by James (2012); he stresses that the monetary union was intended on the one hand to challenge the leading global role of the US Dollar, and on the other hand to prevent high structural current account surpluses on the part of Germany, in which it was largely unsuccessful; Eurozone-wide banking supervision, introduced in 2014, also came far too late. Presumably, the British absence from the monetary union had a negative effect here, in particular, as a common unified banking authority in an internationalized financial market would have been a priority for the UK in such a monetary union.

The United Kingdom has a long history as a global power, whose governments (Cameron aside) have, as a rule, tended to handle their international responsibilities with care. It cannot be overlooked that the world economy will continue to develop rapidly leaving the US and China as the dominant countries in the twenty-first century. The former President of the European Parliament, Martin Schulz, has argued that no EU country standing alone will be well able to represent its interests on the world stage in the coming decades (Schulz 2013). Similar statements have come from Elmar Brok, a leading voice on foreign affairs in the European Parliament, and there are not many Members of the European Parliament who can put forward valid arguments which support the view that an isolationist international strategy on the side of a European county would be successful. If the UK simply wishes to substitute the EU27 for the US, that will not lead to a gain in national autonomy. Stronger economic, military, and political links with the US also bring certain dependencies and the UK would naturally also be more exposed to shocks from the US financial markets and undesirable developments in terms of US regulatory policy; as a member state within the EU, the United Kingdom could participate significantly in shaping EU regulatory policy. Of course, it must be said that the EU is generally somewhat exposed to US financial market shocks, especially since the 1970s when international ties via capital markets and multinational banks greatly increased, particularly transatlantic links.

With the collapse of the US investment bank Lehman Brothers on September 15, 2008, the fair weather period of Euro-integration was over. Despite all Eurozone member states having enjoyed similarly good ratings on sovereign bonds (such as AAA, AA, or A, between 2005 and 2008), in the wake of the shock Lehman Brothers bankruptcy, some EU countries were faced with huge challenges: the event led to a massive drop in the risk appetite of international investors. They asked themselves the question: if the fourth largest US investment bank could go bankrupt, then why not also nation states with high debt ratios? After the Lehman Brothers collapse, the motto of the highly indebted EU countries such as Italy, Belgium, Greece, and Portugal (with a high foreign debt ratio) should have been: a limiting of the government deficit and measures to control the debt ratio, that is the ratio of government debt to total economic income. The debt ratio of Greece was already 110% in 2008; in the election year of 2009, the incumbent conservative *Nea Dimocratia*-led Greek government incurred an additional 15% in government debt, while informing Brussels that the target was 4%.

As experience shows, the deficit ratio can be reduced by 3% per year at most, thus over 5 years, a 15% deficit actually adds up to 45% (15% in year one, 12% in year two, 9%, 6%, and 3% over the remaining years). This implies that the debt ratio would actually rise from 110 to 155%. This resulted in Greece losing access to international capital markets, so that a political deficit fraud became an international shock event (Welfens 2012a, b, 2013a, 2014a). Greece's government paid absolutely no heed to the 3% upper limit contained in the Stability and Growth Pact. The European Commission, which had won recognition in Europe as the 'guardian of the treaties,' could not enforce either the upper limit on the deficit ratios, 3%, nor the overall maximum debt ratio of 60% any longer. This could be observed in many countries prior to the Greek/Euro Crisis. The European Commission, under then President Barroso, the former conservative Prime Minister of Portugal, largely disappeared during the Euro Crisis.

In the early years of the Juncker Commission, they had little success; Jean-Claude Juncker, ex-Prime Minister of Luxembourg, declared that his Commission would take a political approach, and that meant that it would interpret rules on deficits and debt with some degree of flexibility. Such an approach would indeed be worthy of consideration with reasonable grounds and sensible incentives, but Juncker was being opportunistic: France received a very generous ruling from the Commission, and Juncker's reasoning was simply because "France is France". The situation was reminiscent of a football tournament, in which the referee applies the rules of the sport less stringently to players from big footballing countries than to players from smaller countries. That is unfair and unreasonable, as the incentives for big countries are thus absurd.

It is clear that Juncker's remarks created little credibility in the Commission's rules which did not really aid the Eurozone in emerging from the crisis and find its way to a functioning rulebook. An excess of arbitrariness in policy interventions led to increased uncertainty and that, in turn, reduced the rate of investment, and thus growth and employment.

One could be forgiven for drawing the unconditional conclusion based on the Eurozone politics of Brussels that the United Kingdom, in withdrawing from the EU, has left behind a policy club with a weak regulatory framework. The fear that new rescue packages could yet become necessary for some countries in the Eurozone is a thoroughly valid reason for the UK to consider leaving the European Union. In mid-2016, the Eurozone again faced new challenges with regard to Portugal, Spain, Greece, and Italy; Italy in particular threatens to be a new problem case. Prime Minister Cameron had also stressed that the United Kingdom in no way wanted to assume responsibility for bearing the burden of debt of Eurozone countries. Thanks to its weak regulations, the Eurozone for its part could generate little confidence. The enforceability of EU rules is weak in the Eurozone and that undermines the authority, reputation, and influence of the European Commission.

There is no reason to argue against a certain amount of flexibility of clear rules; however, the regulations agreed upon should be complied with. Otherwise, rules lead to neither predictability, meaning a sense of security vis-à-vis expectations—and in doing so facilitate the activities of people and efficient coordination—nor do they allow for the accrual of trust on the basis of the regular application of the rules.

If the EU wishes to be a real community of laws, then adherence to agreed rules should be highly valued. In the end, trust between citizens and states is also fostered through compliance with the rules. It is not particularly problematic if a country wishes to invoke an exception clause, but the breaking of rules—and doing so in a very public and blatant way—damages trust and undermines the effectiveness of politics. Credible policy actors can make an impact by announcing measures, the bar is set higher for less than credible actors who must increase the mix of measures to achieve the same effect, which also increases the secondary or side effects. That, in turn, impairs the chances of successful economic policies at the cost of the economy and society. That the opportunistic bending of the rules makes life simpler in the short term for some politicians and seems to enable the easy resolution of conflicts is clear. However, that does not excuse a policy of bending the rules and non-adherence to the regulations. Here, the EU, and in particular the European Commission, is facing a substantial problem.

The origin of Western European integration, in the form of the founding of the European Coal and Steel Community (ECSC) in 1952, implied that an important role would be played by independent supranational institutions; not simply the cooperation of nation states on the basis of common interests (Tilly 2007). The balancing of national interests was even more important to the foundation of the forerunner of the EU, the European Economic Community (EEC), in 1957, where Germany's role as both the largest market for sales and the largest exporter in terms of machinery and equipment was critical in the Community. Germany was extremely vested, after the Second World War, to become accepted again in the international community via its role in the EEC, and many other countries in the EEC saw European cooperation as promoting welfare, stability, and peace in Western Europe. Moreover, French and Dutch agricultural interests lead to an

EU agricultural policy from 1967 which kept the agricultural price level relatively high with high import duties.

The agricultural sector—which initially was not present in EU policy—grew in importance, and due to the high agricultural prices, conflict arose with the United Kingdom following the latter country's accession—with Denmark and Ireland—in 1973. Firstly, during the 1980s, Thatcher's Britain wanted, and indeed received, a rebate on contribution payments, as the high share of spending on agriculture by Brussels and the relatively small British agricultural sector meant that Britain received back an amount below average. Furthermore, Britain, as a traditional free trade proponent, was always interested in reducing the EU's agricultural import duties and the expensive export subventions for agricultural products from the EU.

The UK was—like Germany and some other EU countries—interested in an EU single market, which above all would strive for the elimination of duties and quantitative restrictions on intra-community trade. After the opening of trade in goods in the EEC between 1957 and 1968, a liberalization of services and the movement of capital were still lacking, along with the opening of the public procurement markets; these came later together with the fourth liberalization pillar, freedom of movement in the EU single market, which began in 1993. This broad regional integration raised expectations as follows:

• That there would be increased intra-EU trade, i.e., a trade creation effect in the EU, connected with specialization advantages and income gains for the participating EU countries.
• That there would be trade diversion effects at the expense of third countries—including the US. Here, one could, however, ensure that trade diversion effects would be limited via the subsequent General Agreement on Tariffs and Trade (GATT)/World Trade Organization (WTO) global trade liberalization negotiations and that the net effect of trade creation in the EU and trade diversion vis-à-vis third countries would remain welfare positive for the EU countries. In fact, for decades it was possible to organize global free trade rounds, which helped to reduce global tariffs and duties—from the EU perspective, those against third countries. Thus, trade diversions effects were minimized.

- That the introduction of a common currency would replace the dominance of the German Central Bank and its monetary policy with a reasonable Euro monetary policy—and a common institution: the European Central Bank (ECB). Both the Euro and the ECB functioned very well in the opening decade from 1999 to 2008, and the broad price transparency in the Eurozone intensified competition with regard to innovation and raised trade in goods and capital flows—above all in the form of direct investment by multinational firms. The Euro could generally strengthen the effects of the single market. However, from the beginning, Denmark and the UK, with their opt-out clause under the Maastricht Treaty, refrained from participation in the Euro.
- That over time a convergence of per capita income would occur due to trade and the direct investment of multinational firms, as trade can also lead to a convergence of per capita income between EU countries without migration, where applicable it is enhanced through capital flows to relatively poor countries which have a low capital intensity (machines per worker). The poorer countries catch up; eventually also in terms of capital endowment per capita and thus in terms of labor productivity and per capita income, respectively.

The United Kingdom was always a driver of market liberalization and also tried to implement lower levels of regulation, as regulation is seen as expensive and detrimental to global competition. When it came to social policies, however, the UK almost always applied the brakes.

A Neo-EU or Disintegration?

The European Union cannot survive in its current form. In the context of an exit from the EU, there are incentives for other countries to follow the UK in leaving—possibilities which come to mind include both Denmark and Ireland, both of which acceded to the EU along with the United Kingdom in 1973. Disintegration dynamics can come from disappointing EU growth figures or a new crisis in the Eurozone. With the apparently strongly declining level of US support for EU integration under the Trump administration, there are additional impulses under-mining the EU. If the European Union should not be able to modern-ize in a broad sense and achieve some form of EU deepening for at least a group of about a dozen or so EU countries—nine countries being the minimum required for a special integration scheme within the EU—the EU is likely to disintegrate. There is pressure coming from Russia on the Eastern EU countries which adds to the centrifugal forces in the EU. In a more long-term perspective, there is also the rising economic pressure from China—which will have double the economic weight of the EU by 2040 or so. An EU that is not a political union with a decent budget and a strong diplomatic strategy will implode. That the European Parliament has confirmed a new President of the European Commission who does not undertake official visits to Washington DC and Moscow is a strange situation. This observation could be under-stood as a direct criticism of Mr. Juncker, but one could also argue that it is the EU member countries who do not want to give more power to Brussels. By 2019, the EU should have clarified which way it wants to go—and here national election results will be part of the answer. If elec-tions in key member countries should bring the victory of a populist party in national or presidential elections, the EU will quickly face a political crisis and could disintegrate over internal political conflicts. A Neo-EU which is bigger, more efficient and in line with the theory of fiscal federalism would be an adequate answer to the new challenges. Those supporting the view that one should immediately take all 28 or 27 countries on board in a project for political union are effectively working to block the survival of the EU. If the UK would have a sec-ond referendum and then not leave the EU, it is unlikely that the UK will go on to be part of a future European political union. In any case, European citizens and leaders will have to learn from the British EU ref-erendum just how weak EU integration arguments seem to be in some countries and how bad the quality of political management sometimes is: in both Brussels and at the national policy layer.

That the Eurozone—or a sub-group within this area—is a natural starting point for a political union is obvious and it could be argued that fixing the Eurozone problems is necessary and not possible at zero cost. A situation in which no solution to the Greek problem can be found is quite inadequate, if the Eurozone cannot solve problems in a country that stands for just 2% of the EU's Gross Domestic Product (GDP), it cannot solve any important problem. In the end, Greece will need both constitutional reform and conditional transfers; the German Finance Ministry's conjecture that one could not forgive part of the official Greek debt is not supported by legal experts from academia. At the same time, one will have to re-emphasize the role of political responsibility in the Eurozone.

China, the US, or Russia will not wait for the EU to move towards a stable neo-EU. If the EU should be unable to come up with convincing reforms, the 27 remaining EU countries will disintegrate into several smaller groups of countries which follow old nationalistic and geopolitical logic. Several countries will effectively join the US sphere of influence, some Eastern European countries would likely come under Russian political leadership (and possibly join the Eurasia integration group), some countries are likely to then become a strategic partner of Germany which might try to reinvent the concept of *Mitteleuropa* which in earlier times was a strategy aimed at creating a kind of German-dominated Central Europe. That this would be a stable and peaceful Europe in the longer term seems unlikely. Germany would, again, be too big and unstable relations between France and Germany could quickly lead to protectionism in Europe, economic disintegration dynamics and the collapse of the North Atlantic Treaty Organization. Before speculating much on the unpleasant scenarios that might follow from Brexit and non-reform of the EU27/EU28, one may take a closer look at some post-Brexit perspectives.

References

James, H. (2012). *Making the European Monetary Union*. Harvard University Press.
Schulz, M. (2013). *Der Gefesselte Riese. Europas letzte Chance*. Berlin: Rowohlt.

Tilly, R. (2007). The European Union 50 years on: Some comments on its early history. In R. Tilly & P. J. J. Welfens (Eds.), *50 Years of EU—Economic dynamics integration, financial markets and innovations*. Heidelberg: Springer.

Welfens, P. J. J. (2012a). *Die Zukunft des Euro*. Berlin: Nicolai.

Welfens, P. J. J. (2012b). Volkswirtschaftliche Auswirkungen der Euro-Staatsschuldenkrise und neue Instrument der Staatsfinanzierung in der EU. Expert Opinion for the Finance Committee of the German Bundestag, sitting on May 9, 2012, Berlin.

Welfens, P. J. J. (2013a). Überwindung der Eurokrise und Stabilisierungsoptionen der Wirtschaftspolitik: Perspektiven für Nordrhein-Westfalen, Deutschland und Europa. Report for the Minister of Federal Affairs, Europe and Media, North Rhine-Westphalia.

Welfens, P. J. J. (2014a). *Overcoming the EU crisis and prospects for a political union*. Paper presented at the bdvb reseach institute/EIIW conference 'Overcoming the Euro Crisis', March, 2014. In *International Economics and Economic Policy, 13*(1), 2016.

12

EU Integration Perspectives After Brexit

The British government had experts study the costs for the UK of withdrawing from the EU. The findings are as follows: a 4–10% reduction in real income in the long term, but apparently even that did not shock the majority of British voters in the referendum on membership. Assuming a 6% reduction of income in the UK, then that would entail a reduction in real income for the EU27 of 1%, which would mean a loss of £124/$151 billion in 2015 terms, plus an added loss of £119/$145 billion; for every Briton, a loss of income of circa £2,120/$2,590. When a majority vote for withdrawal from the EU despite these findings, then obviously there are other fields which offer "psychological gains" which must be extremely important to the voters: the fear of further immigration from EU countries certainly played a role in Brexit, where high immigration may exert downward pressure on wages for low-skilled workers; however, immigration from Europe is known to have resulted in a positive economic balance for the US—in the UK it had the same effect; however, the government did not utter a single word to publicize this aspect. From Brexiteer Conservatives, to the populist anti-EU United Kingdom Independence Party (UKIP), to Leave.eu activists, the value of reclaimed national sovereignty was

© The Author(s) 2017   271
P.J.J. Welfens, *An Accidental Brexit*,
DOI 10.1007/978-3-319-58271-9_12

stressed, including in relation to immigration controls. That national sovereignty is gained by exiting the EU is, in the twenty-first century, a myth. As the UK represents less than one-fifth of the EU28 in terms of income, the country is weakened in terms of sovereignty.

With the expected exit from the EU, contribution payments to the EU budget will no longer be paid: 0.4% of Gross Domestic Product (GDP) in terms of saved British net EU contributions could be expressed simply as 4% capitalized with a 10% gain in GDP; however, it is worth remembering that the growth in new knowledge is heavily dependent on the stock of direct investment of multinational firms. Here, one can expect a reduction of the stock, or at best a fall in inward foreign direct investment (FDI) flows, as a result of Brexit, which could mean a loss in GDP growth of 0.2%: an economic net loss of almost £850/$1,040 per capita is a plausible estimate of the long-term losses for each and every Briton as a result of Brexit. It is also conceivable that military expenditures will rise, should more European countries once again go their own way—possibly to the 4% GDP mark (almost double the amount spent by large EU countries in 2015), which was usual for the larger European states prior to the First World War. The means a lower per capita consumption and consequently quite a substantial loss in welfare.

The EU will have a financing problem immediately following the withdrawal of the United Kingdom, as the British net contributions will have to be met by other member states, or there will need to be cuts to Structural Funds and other categories of expenditure, which will negatively impact Eastern European EU members above all. The main net contributors, on a per capita basis, have traditionally been Sweden, the Netherlands, Denmark, and Germany—meaning a raising of the contributions of EU27 members will impact the aforementioned countries most.

Beyond the question of financing, some problem areas will remain largely unchanged, for example, the field of refugee policy, where the European Council was not able to reach a consensus in 2015/16. If a majority decision should be reached regarding the distribution of refugees amongst all member states using a quota-based system—in the face of robust opposition from Eastern European members—then that will give additional impetus to populists in those and other countries. Reforms are demanded of the European Council, and above all of the refugee strategy of the Federal Government in Berlin. This affects ten Eastern European accession countries as well as some Western Europe EU members, such as Denmark, Sweden, Finland, and the Netherlands, who have positioned themselves against accepting refugees on the basis of decisions made in Brussels. Western Europe will be threatened with disintegration for years.

Considering their high (and possibly higher) net contributions, Sweden and Denmark, as former European Free Trade Association countries, could soon follow the United Kingdom's example. It is also conceivable that the Netherlands could decide to exit the EU in the medium term. The latter country is host to strong populist parties and the topic of immigration is a burning political issue. Moreover, one cannot forget that in 2005 the Netherlands also saw a negative result in a referendum on the topic of a draft European Constitution (on the basis of proposals from the Constitutional Convention). It was clear in the Netherlands, as in France before it, that on the level of important constitutional values for the Dutch, the proposed draft could not generate majority support among the electorate. Critics in France, including the then Europe Minister Fabius, highlighted the lack of a sufficient reference to social policy, that is a social Europe, in the document; this view was shared by many in France, and in 2005 a majority also voted no in a referendum on the issue. This rejection apparently did not give the heads of government in the EU much food for thought, just a few years later a more conventional treaty, the Lisbon Treaty, was agreed as a new quasi-constitution for the EU. The Lisbon Treaty contains Article 50, the rules determining how a member state should leave the EU, a clause which first became relevant in 2016 with Brexit.

The EU27 countries will need to make an extreme effort to keep the process of EU integration on track. Firstly, too much money is squandered via Structural Funds—according to recent estimates just one in every two Euro spent has a net benefit effect on the side of the recipients. Here, some improvements can be made. However, without more political competition at the EU level, improvements are unlikely. For 20 years, a grand coalition has been active in the European Parliament, which does not correspond to the traditional model found in western democracies of a government on one side and an opposition on the other and which leads to inefficiencies and encourages low voter turn-out for European Parliament elections. A comprehensive campaign to remove red tape and bureaucracy and to promote deregulation is desir-able—nobody in the EU really needs the Commission to develop stand-ards for vacuum cleaners and light bulbs, the Commission should rather concentrate on the really important areas and in light of the shortened cycle for global digital innovations, the Commission should no longer progress at the slow pace it has to date, developing Green and White Papers—from which seven or eight years later (counting from when the Green Paper is submitted) a Directive will result, which after a further two years is finally implemented in national legislation. Firstly, Green and White Papers in time-sensitive fields should really be realized within two to three years, and effective legislation should then be forthcom-ing, such that within the period of office of a single Parliament, the EU could react to important European, international and global challenges. Secondly, if the EU could at least instigate infrastructure projects at a supranational level, which are of significance for the EU, and if the lion's share of the budget for defense spending was allocated to Brussels, then this would amount to a critical level of the government consump-tion rate of circa 4–5%—enough to allow effective fiscal policy. A higher rate of government consumption makes sense first and foremost from the point of view of increasing the visibility of the EU among vot-ers. If the voters are more interested and aware, then political competi-tion will increase. More rational policymaking and efficiency gains in many areas are possible.

An independent EU income tax is required, where the EU member states could levy a surcharge—which is within their power. That fair legislation with regard to corporate tax is needed goes without saying: with the exception of young firms, a minimum corporate tax rate of 10% seems adequate. The income tax rate, composed of a national ele-ment and a supranational element, would sink in the medium term as a result of efficiency gains. It is worth considering that on the level of the EU, there could also be a budget deficit, which could be organized as a debt policy instrument dedicated to public investment. The national structural deficit rates should be reduced to zero and made constitutionally binding in the member states, a condition which should be required of all EU members—with the exception of Denmark due to its Euro opt-out clause. It should be mandatory for countries which are not yet members of the Eurozone to anchor such a requirement in their respective constitutions in the interest of raising the credibility of the Eurozone.

The government assets of member states could be transferred to the supranational policy layer, conditional on the supranational level also assuming a corresponding share of the respective member state's national debt. Thanks to the expected refinancing benefits, which result in the long term from the swapping of official Eurobonds for expiring government bonds—with one interest rate for the Eurozone as a whole, which is lower than the average interest rate of the sum of old national Eurobonds, there should be an indirect reduction of the government debt ratios in the Eurozone.

The soft policy of Commission President Juncker vis-à-vis deficit ratios is certainly comfortable politically speaking, but from the outside it reinforces the impression that the Eurozone will not and cannot deliver in terms of the deficit ratio and debt ratio. That will pre-program the next Brexit and, in turn, that means further economic disintegration and welfare losses in both the exiting country and the rest of the EU. It is a question of just a few years during which to stabilize the monetary union—if a Brexit-like case occurs in the Eurozone, meaning a country leaving the Eurozone, then the monetary union will suddenly, or in stages, come to an end. A lot of political porcelain will be broken, the economic costs will be high and the negative signals to other integration zones will be considerable. Disintegration could spread to other integration projects, and massive amounts of capital will flow out of the rest of the Eurozone or out of other integration areas. It cannot be ruled out that more and more EU countries would then join an enlarged new EFTA+ zone. It is clear that in the interim, Europe—and the North Atlantic Treaty Organization (NATO)—would be greatly destabilized. Disintegration is dangerous and therefore the EU is challenged to undertake smart reforms as a matter of urgency. As the experience of overcoming the Euro Crisis shows, institutional innovations in conjunction with better national economic policy can contribute to surmounting major problems within only a few years (Heise 2013).

Such a concentration of the Eurozone, that is steps towards a political union, could include a one-time special assistance package which could be granted to Portugal and Greece and, it could be pointed out, that within the framework of a new EU social policy, which for example could finance the first six months of short-term unemployment—except for youth unemployment—there would be a certain amount of budgetary relief for crisis countries. It would be preferable if, for all member states, well-thought-out growth and location policies, respectively, would be developed and growth conducive impulses mobilized by the start of the Transatlantic Trade and Investment Partnership (TTIP), which could be achieved within a decade in three steps: first, a liberalization of goods markets, then of transatlantic trade in services, and finally initial steps towards the strategically important capital account liberalization.

The idea of the Enlightenment in Europe and of the philosopher Immanuel Kant, as well as the integration practitioners Jean Monnet, Walter Hallstein, and Jacques Delors, that one could realize peace and economic progress via international treaties of cooperation and the economic and political integration of European countries on the basis of states bound by the rule of law is, in the twenty-first century, still an important hypothesis. One must take care that through the falling importance of the EU in the Middle East, one does not allow yet more instability and war to destabilize the region, which would inevitably lead to new waves of refugees entering Europe. The EU27 should consider showing more solidarity with, and engage in more cooperation with, the US. Moreover, it should be noted that there are economic integration approaches between Arab countries; in other integration areas, the danger is present that the bad example of the UK's withdrawal from the EU could be imitated. Only an expeditious reform policy undertaken by the EU27 as well as limited concessions in relation to cooperation with the UK will stabilize the process of EU integration and prevent further disintegration.

It is doubtful that the EU27 is capable of, or even willing to, engage in further enlargement in the medium term. That leads to problems of its own in the Balkans, where the lack of perspectives of accession in the near future could lead to the emergence of new political conflicts. The EU27 will need to develop a sensible Balkan policy if it does not want to experience massive instability on its southern borders. It can be assumed that the EU27 will, in the medium term, be more prepared to cooperate with Russia than the old EU28 would have been; if that will result in a sustainable mutual understanding remains to be seen. A temporary new destabilization of NATO cannot be ruled out, as soon as EU disintegration dynamics appear. National reform measures, which tackle the current challenges of the stability of the banking sector, the labor market, i.e., a return to full employment, and demographic change should be developed carefully. It would be expedient to actively implement the principle of EU comparisons or benchmarking to confront the relatively weak countries above all with simulations from the Organisation for Economic Co-operation and Development (OECD), for example, showing how large the economic progress would be, if the level equivalent to the average of the top three countries in a certain policy area could be achieved.

International cooperation in global economic organizations must partly be restructured. It is completely unclear going forward, if the UK will seek to coordinate and consult closely with the EU27. As fast as the United Kingdom can adopt a low tax policy on capital after Brexit, to prevent capital outflows and mobilize direct investment inflows, it could also pursue new positions in international organizations with new partners, such as China, vigorously, quickly, and flexibly in order to counter the threat of economic decline.

After Brexit, the EU is on a difficult search for a prudent model of reform. The negative result in the British referendum on EU participation, which came as a surprise to many observers, clearly stands for a political miscalculation on the part of former Prime Minister Cameron. However, the result of the referendum was not shaped by EU aspects alone. On the topic of immigration, Brexit showed that some worrying racist tendencies exist, particularly in certain sections in England. The exit of the United Kingdom from the EU in 2019, after almost 45 years of membership, would be a historical split, which entails a self-imposed British retreat. Above all, however, it is incumbent upon the EU to reflect self-critically on the shock result of a majority rejection. An ill-advised tendency from the Commission and the European Council to simply muddle through is apparent.

One cannot assume that a sustainable approval of the EU will persist in other EU countries. The well-known and clear results which rejected the EU Convention's draft constitution in France and the Netherlands in 2005—two founding members of the EU—conveyed the message that support for the EU was failing. In France, the No vote could be traced back to the insufficient inclusion of social issues at an EU level, particularly in an especially economically liberal draft. In the Netherlands, there was concern that the larger EU countries and the European Commission could dominate European politics. That the referendum in the UK was lost by a slim margin is, from the EU's perspective, of little relevance: it is far more relevant that a clear pro-EU majority could not be mobilized.

A large-scale integration project, which cannot depend on majority support in the member states, is unstable. With Brexit, the old aura of EU stability is a thing of the past, EU opponents have been boosted, at the same time the UK is economically destabilized. The Pound, share prices—partly stabilized by the announcement of central bank intervention—and property prices are falling. After a lowering of interest rates in 2016, 2017/18 will almost certainly see a raising of rates due to a rising current account deficit. Hardly two weeks after the referendum, the sharp fall in property prices led to the closure of real estate funds; the concern of many Britons regarding pension funds is increasing and with it political unrest in the UK—many private pension funds, which in the UK are crucial for private pension schemes, are facing high losses.

The European Commission and European Parliament should massively restrict their tendency towards over-regulation. It is economically misguided and serves to only stir up opposition. A concentration on the major issues is important. Since the Banking and the Euro Crises, the balance of power in the EU has shifted to the European Council, which makes no moves to reform: where should reform plans go?

For astute reforms, it is essential to take into account that a majority of voters in many countries are obviously dissatisfied with the benefits of the EU: amongst others, with the policies of the Eurozone and the refugee policies. German Chancellor Angela Merkel must bear responsibility, above all, for the latter, and here changes are needed. Furthermore, it should be noted that according to the *Forschungsgruppe Wahlen* (Electoral Research Group), voters in European Parliament elections do not know for which policy areas the EU is even primarily responsible—this explains the tendency for voters in European Parliament elections to often vote based on emotion for small, radical parties. This problem is a consequence of the EU's minor consumption ratio of 1% and the weak European Parliament. Not even in relation to the TTIP agreement—with trade being a key competence of the EU—could politicians in Germany accept that the national parliament would not be consulted, as otherwise there would be a question mark regarding its legitimacy. This indicates a problem for the EU and the European Parliament. Steps towards a political union are obviously essential; also due to the Euro, which began prematurely with defective regulations and too little political integration. As Brexit means that Germany shall lose an important ally with regard to a liberal EU trade policy, it is detrimental to German interests.

The Eurozone needs more growth and sounder fiscal policies—but without better budgetary rules, this is unlikely to happen. A banking union without such rules is doubtful. For the Eurozone, it would be necessary for all member states to anchor a debt brake in their respective constitutions, with an initial upper limit on a cyclically neutral deficit ratio of 0.35%, while also laying down a ratio of 0.5% for the EU level. The European Parliament, assuming the creation of a political union with a real parliament and Euro area government, could in future realize deficits—for example, for EU stimulus programs. To prevent irrational fiscal policies, Brussels needs to have competence over large infrastructure projects and related spending: for example, up to 2% of GDP, and an additional 2% in terms of defense spending. With a trend growth rate of 1.5%, this would entail a long-term Eurozone debt ratio of 60%.

The national expenditure ratios will sink in the course of the transfer of powers and a shift of spending to Brussels, and because of efficiency gains, one could also realize a reduction in taxes. From the perspective of the theory of fiscal federalism, one could name two fields in relation to which all subsidiarity should be reserved at the supranational policy layer in Brussels: responsibility for the first six months of unemployment insurance—excluding youth unemployment, which is largely shaped by national minimum wage provisions—and a minimum redistribution policy; because of the mobility of labor and capital required by the EU single market, national redistribution policies alone do not function well, the US is a good example here. Moreover, the absolute number of EU parliamentarians should in the future be closely related to demographic changes—in the interest of democracy and good incentives: countries, such as Greece, which could lose one million inhabitants through emigration, should lose one seat in the European Parliament, while countries, such as Germany, which attract one million EU immigrants should gain one seat.

If the EU had a government consumption ratio of 4.5%, which would still be only half that of Washington in the US, then sensible fiscal policy could be implemented in the EU and Eurozone, respectively. More jobs and more growth are possible, however only if national governments really allow Brussels to take on responsibility for some policy areas and, above all, carry out their own growth-promoting reforms. A national government consumption rate of 15% means that the main responsibility shall continue to be borne by the EU member states themselves.

A quarter of the government assets of member states could be transferred to the supranational policy level, as long as Brussels would also assume responsibility for 25% of the government debt ratio of Euro countries. With a normal interest rate of 5%, this would result in supranational interest payments by Brussels of 1.25% of GDP. As a result of the expected refinancing gains, resulting from the issuing of sovereign Eurobonds for expiring national sovereign bonds, there would be an indirect reduction of the government debt ratios of the Eurozone, when instead of the former interest rate of 5% for the average sovereign bonds in the Eurozone, a 2.5% interest rate could be realized through credit advantages. The reduction in expenditures on interest payments would be 0.625% for the Eurozone, which when capitalized corresponds to a fall in the debt ratio of one-quarter.

Thus, the income tax rate could be reduced by approximately 1%, using a simple standard growth model; this implies that long-term per capita real income would rise by 0.5%. It can be assumed that a stable Eurozone could realize effectively free goods imports of 0.5% of GDP annually on the basis of having a reserve currency (which would be half the amount of the US). The present value of the Euro when capitalized for an interest rate of 2.5% is about 20% of the GDP of the Eurozone: anyone who cannot see the incentive here for institutional modifications is not putting the interests of the people of the EU first, squandering not only the stabilization of the Euro and prospects of EU integration, but other integration clubs worldwide could also falter and-dangerous new conflicts emerge.

Due to the 2017 presidential and parliamentary elections in France and Germany, respectively, little progress will be made in terms of EU reform this year; however, a broad debate could be started. For the UK, there remains only its own withdrawal from the EU, when the country sinks into a Brexit frenzy because of EU immigration of just 0.2% of the population annually, then it cannot be expected to make valid reform suggestions for the EU. Theresa May, then a still a candidate for the office of Prime Minister, implied that the fate of 3.5 million EU citizens in the UK would be used as a bargaining chip in the EU–UK negotiations on access to the single market. After the fall of major British banks, such remarks from the favorite candidate for the position of leader of the British Tory Party could be seen as morally reprehensible.

The EU27, however, could—as a concrete helpful suggestion— make a comprehensive offer to attract migration from the UK: not only for EU citizens without a British passport, but also for Britons. Here, Germany and France should spearhead an initiative with other EU countries. In many continental EU countries and Ireland, Eastern European and British migrants could find good employment opportunities and also the chance to found new firms. The latter will, in turn, create new jobs. This aspect is often underestimated.

NEXIT in the Sights of the PVV

The right-wing, populist *Partij voor de Vrijheid* or Party for Freedom (PVV) in the Netherlands commissioned two studies to be carried out by consulting firms in London which were intended to identify the effects of abandoning the Euro (Lombard Street Research 2012) and of leaving the EU (Capital Economics 2014). Capital Economics claimed that over 21 years, the real income of the Netherlands would rise by 10–13% in the case of the country withdrawing from the EU, as long as the Netherlands could achieve access to the single market similar to that of Switzerland by way of a treaty. However, this study is very weak from a methodological point of view, and in the case of Lombard Street Research, some of the tables listed in their study prove to be questionable and largely misleading. This raises a broader question regarding private, for-profit consulting firms providing data which suit the aims of the customer, regardless of the possible negative effects on the lives of millions of people which result if their studies are relied upon as a basis for policy decisions. To the best of this author's knowledge, no renowned research institute has calculated positive effects from a NEXIT and, from an economic perspective, it is not expected that any would. However, the PVV-commissioned studies show that obvious attempts are being made to influence the public using pre-ordered analysis findings. Thus, it would be wise for the government of every member state to allow the net benefits of EU membership for their respective land to be calculated by an independent research institute once every 10 years for example. This would take the wind out of the sails of many political charlatans.

However, just a day after Mr. Trump's inauguration in Washington DC, right-wing populist parties from several EU countries gathered in the German city of Koblenz, including Mrs. Frauke Petry, the leader of the populist Alternative for Germany, who explained in her speech that the people of Europe did not want to accept political domination—referring specifically to Napoleon and Hitler—and then went on to emphasize that the EU, as a dominating institution, would also not be accepted ("God willing"). This very strange and extreme implicit comparison is revealing in terms of European populism, but Mrs. Marine Le Pen topped it all when she explained, in a 2014 interview with DER SPIEGEL, that France should again become a leader of the bloc of Non-Aligned Countries—a group of countries that did not want to align strongly with either the USA or the Soviet Union during the Cold War. In fact, France was never even a member of this group, so how logical is it for Le Pen to call for France to once again become a leader of this Non-Aligned Country Bloc? It is obvious that many populist parties in Europe are against EU integration and have cheered the election of Mr. Trump in the US. That the US could become a country that actively wants to undermine the EU—as an alleged rival to the US—is a new perspective raised by the Trump administration.

References

Capital Economics. (2014). NExit: Assessing the economic impact of the Netherlands leaving the European Union, February 2014, London.

Heise, M. (2013). *Emerging from the Euro debt crisis*. Heidelberg: Springer.

Lombard Street Research. (2012). The Netherlands & the Euro, special report, March 2012, London.

13

Eurozone Perspectives and Reform Needs

If the Eurozone's growth rate should be below that of the UK for several years, this will generate pressure in some EU countries to also consider leaving the European Union and the Eurozone, respectively. Rising US and UK interest rates will also lead to higher interest rates in the Eurozone and this, in turn, will raise interest rate spreads within the Eurozone—with Greece, Portugal, Italy, and Spain likely to face rising real interest rates, while the interest rates for Germany and France might increase much more slowly. This will, of course, put pressure on the Eurozone to reconsider launching Eurobonds which, in turn, would be only useful if member countries would shift part of their national infrastructure budgets to the EU and the Eurozone, respectively. The European Union will continue to face populist political forces. A key option to counter such populist tendencies are careful policies that adopt adequate pro-growth reforms, reinforce international competition policy (within the EU and indeed the whole Organisation for Economic Co-operation and Development (OECD) area, as multinational companies are getting more and more powerful) and also policies against the tax evasion of multinational companies which is a major driver behind growing economic inequalities in many EU countries.

© The Author(s) 2017
P.J.J. Welfens, *An Accidental Brexit*,
DOI 10.1007/978-3-319-58271-9_13

Politicians should also be stricter when it comes to governance issues in big companies. For example, no further scandals along the lines of the Volkswagen diesel affair should be acceptable and a careful drafting of a kind of Sarbanes–Oxley piece of legislation (in the US, the Sarbanes–Oxley Act related to better rules for obtaining credible balance sheet information from big companies, mainly by making the chief financial officer and the director of the company personally liable for cheating in balance sheets): in the future, the director of the company and the chief technical officer should become personally liable for new information regarding the non-meeting of minimum requirements required by government. Strict legislation should also apply to all big banks—here the new Trump deregulation wave will make it more difficult for EU countries to stick to strict regulations.

The Eurozone should have joint legislation stating that Contingent Convertible bank bonds ("CoCo bonds") cannot be held by banks, but instead only by insurance companies and certain other institutional investors. The current regulation is inadequate: it is a good idea that big banks have CoCo bonds that become new equity once critical balance sheet indicators are no longer met, but if there is a new banking crisis, the CoCo bonds would be of no help if they are largely held within the banking sector itself since there would not be broad infusing of new equity capital from outside the banking system. This should be an urgent reform—and is now all the more urgent as the Trump administration embraces new deregulation initiatives for banks in the US.

One may raise the question of whether the US and the UK—after BREXIT—are about to embrace a new round of banking deregulation and what the effects will be on the world economy; including future negative external effects on the stability of Eurozone financial markets and the stability of (appropriate) debt-GDP ratios. The banking crisis of 2007–2009 has greatly raised the debt-GDP ratios of OECD countries as several governments had to stabilize their respective national banking systems by means of costly nationalizations or equity capital injections; and expansionary fiscal policy came with considerable deficits on top of this. Recent analysis (EIIW Paper No. 238) has, in an enhanced Mundell-Fleming model, shown that foreign deregulation (and indeed global deregulation) is more likely under flexible exchange rates than under fixed exchange rates. This has dramatic implications for the long-run instability of the international economic system—shaped by flexible exchange rates since 1973—unless the IMF, the Bank for International Settlements and national prudential supervisory actors would adopt adequate policies in the field of monitoring and implementing appropriate prudential supervision—the IMF has had recurrent problems with reports within its Financial Sector Assessment Programs (for example, in the case of Ireland in 2006 with a totally misleading FSAP; similar problems with regard to FSAP reports were experiences prior to this also in Switzerland) and as of late January 2017, the US government under President Trump has started to block the Basel III talks at the Bank for International Settlements. There is hardly any doubt that the economic problems which the UK will encounter after BREXIT will push the government to reduce corporate tax rates and to embrace a new round of financial deregulation. The Trump administration is likely to join the UK in both fields. New financial instability is likely to occur in Western countries within a decade.

Moreover, it would be wise (Welfens 2013a) to introduce a penalty tax on the variance of the rate of return on equity in banks since the Transatlantic Banking Crisis of 2007–2010 would never have emerged if big banks had faced stronger incentives to think long term and to achieve a more even long-term financial performance in the field of the rate of return on equity. One might have a slightly reduced corporate tax rate for banks, but the volatility tax rate on top would then be an adequate new tax mix for achieving more long-term stability in market economies.

The Eurozone, however, cannot prosper if every member country does not share a willingness to implement a debt brake in their respective national constitutions. It should be clear that in the future a new Greek-type government debt policy fraud (notifying 4% deficit–GDP ratio to Brussels, while actually implementing a 15% deficit–GDP ratio) could lead to a quick bankruptcy of the respective country; and the EU should be able to have full and quick digital monitoring of the budgets of all EU member countries. Moreover, the Greek debt problem has to be solved in a pragmatic but also a decisive way—with a constitutional reform that would, for example, guarantee that the national

statistical office of Greece is politically independent (the Tsipras government has put the former head of that institution before the court—
obviously for political reasons and as an intimidation signal to critics
of the government), a requirement that government has to establish an
extra-government fiscal analysis office and that serious privatization projects are launched on the basis of cooperation with the European Bank
for Reconstruction and Development. Greece might face enormous new
political pressure if the North Atlantic Treaty Organization (NATO)
should be weakened—it was NATO in the mid-1970s that prevented
a war between Greece and Turkey—or if Turkey should leave NATO.
Greece alone is unable to withstand any strong military pressure from
Turkey if that country should want to occupy some of the islands close
to the Turkish coast. Any autocratic ruler in Turkey might want to consider such an adventure and Mr. Erdogan, the Turkish President, has
expressed in 2016 that the current size of Turkey is inadequately small.

There are many arguments for a Euro political union in the long run,
but it is unclear whether key EU member countries such as Germany,
France, Italy, Spain, and others are willing to shift significantly more
budget resources to Brussels and the supranational policy layer, respectively. Fighting youth unemployment is also a very serious national
policy challenge. While the EU might become responsible in the future
for financing the first six months of unemployment insurance, youth
unemployment should definitely not be part of the budget in Brussels.
There are some good arguments which suggest benefits from having an
EU pillar in the field of unemployment insurance. However, it is the
labor market and minimum wage legislation of national governments
that is responsible for long-term unemployment and youth unemployment rates, respectively.

If the EU27 should become destabilized in the context of Brexit,
so that the long-term growth rate of the EU27 should decline, this, in
turn, will undermine the economic prosperity of the UK. One can formulate the British Gross Domestic Product (GDP) as being composed
of exports to the EU plus exports to other countries plus domestic consumption plus investment plus government real expenditures minus
imports. With EU exports accounting for about 12% of the UK GDP,
a reduction of the EU27 growth rate from 1.5 to 0.75% implies that

British output growth will reduce by about 0.1%. If, on top, British inward foreign direct investment (FDI) flows in the manufacturing industry should decline, and as a consequence of this the growth rate of patents and innovations, respectively, would reduce, the British growth rate of GDP would decline for many years by 0.2 to 0.3% and if EU workers would start to leave the UK, there would be further negative effects on the British production potential. The Treasury study, commissioned by the Cameron government, that predicted a long-term decline of British output by about 6% has presented the relevant order of magnitude; as the report also stressed, the UK, being outside the EU, could not benefit from an enhanced single market (with more competition in the electricity sector and more competition and innovation in the digital sector) and here the UK would stand to lose another 4% of GDP in the long run.

Controversial Issues and New Perspectives in Europe

Some observers have suggested that the referendum was not so much about economic aspects but that the Brexit majority reflects the fact that people have lost confidence in the political and economic elites in the United Kingdom and that a fear of economic globalization has played a major role in the outcome of the referendum.

One may emphasize that economic globalization is largely linked to digital globalization which in turn creates massive challenges for national competition policy. The fact that US anti-trust authorities and the European Commission—in charge of part of competition policy in the EU—are partly cooperating is not an adequate counterbalancing force to the rapid digital globalization. Who is controlling Google and other digital giants? Google has a market share of more than 60% in many OECD countries. Digital education has been neglected in many countries, for example, in Germany most schools still have only narrowband Internet connections. While government had enough money to stabilize big banks during the banking crisis, the money was not made available to allow for a decent digital linkage of schools to the Internet in Germany: formally, the responsibility for this in the school system is with local communities and they were mainly waiting for Deutsche Telekom to donate free internet connections to schools. This, however, is a totally inadequate approach to the digital modernization of the education sector. The situation in Germany is somewhat better in the health system, while the National Health Service(NHS) in the UK suffers from chronic underfunding. Here again, many voters have the strange impression that billions are available for bailing out big banks, but not enough funds could be mobilized by government to modernize an NHS where the aging of society has put enormous stress on the system and the people working within it for very many years. Part of voters' general frustration erupted in the referendum—with the Leave campaign, above all Mr. Boris Johnson, arguing that the EU contributions that would be freed up once the UK leaves the European Union will be invested in the NHS instead. This, however, is totally implausible: firstly, of the £350 million ($427 million) of alleged weekly contributions of the UK to the EU budget, as advertised by Mr. Johnson on his campaign bus, net contributions represent just about half that figure; secondly, if the UK should face EU imports tariff of 2–3% in the future, more than one-third of previous UK contributions to the EU budget would come under the heading of paying EU import tariffs. If there is Brexit, the Scottish people will want to get some form of compensation payment and about £2–3 billion ($2.4–$3.7 billion) might be paid to keep Scotland within the United Kingdom. The UK is also likely to come under pressure to raise its military expenditure: this could be a requirement of the US if it is to engage in a broader strategic partnership with the United Kingdom. From a budget perspective, the net fiscal gain of the UK could be close to zero and this amounts to the conclusion that the promises made by Mr. Johnson during the campaign amount to little more than wishful thinking.

With Brexit, the roles of Germany, France, Italy, Spain, and Poland will naturally increase: their share in the EU27 GDP will be higher than in the previous club of EU28. Moreover, the weight of the Eurozone will increase. It had represented 67% of the EU28 population prior to Brexit, after Brexit it will be 76%. This could mean that non-Eurozone countries will come under increasing pressure to consider a rather fast joining of the Eurozone—except for Denmark, which retains an opt-out clause. Such political pressure might, however, actually be inadequate, namely to the extent that the rules and regulations of the Eurozone continue not to be fully implemented. No message could be more dangerous for the Eurozone than a political signal from Berlin/Paris that sticking to the rules of the Eurozone is irrelevant. The Eurozone has become embroiled in a serious crisis due to several member countries ignoring basic commitments—Greece stands out with its totally irresponsible budget deficit–GDP ratio of 15% in the election year 2009. Portugal has had enormous current account deficit–GDP ratios for almost a decade and the government knew that foreign indebtedness of more than 70% of GDP would bring the risk of a sudden stop meaning no further refinancing would be possible in international capital markets. Italy has raised its debt–GDP ratio in less than a decade to more than 130% after the banking crisis and the French debt–GDP ratio has also reached more than 100%. On the one hand, one may argue that no country should lecture EU partner countries about adopting this or that policy. However, such a view is inadequate since weak EU fiscal co-management, for example by Germany, would mean that one can avoid unpleasant discussions in the European Council of Finance Ministers, say with Greece, Portugal, Italy and the UK as well as other countries. However, this is not really helpful since there must be either a common constitution that sets safety barriers on both shoulders of the fiscal policy track or national governments that implement an excessive deficit/debt policy. Alternatively, each Eurozone member country can select rules to enshrine in its own respective constitution which would avoid excessive deficits in a very clear and credible way. The alternative is largely to create a supranational government where the constitution and the EU/Eurozone Parliament controls the enlarged EU budget and the budget deficit–GDP ratio.

EU countries suffer from a lack of effective taxation—much corporate taxation exists on paper only. The effective corporate tax rates are very low in many countries in certain years. This could only be avoided in the future if there is more tax policy coordination and actually some form of a distinct EU tax which has to be decided upon in Brussels.

More cooperation in taxation in the EU is the only way to achieve less inequality in a world with economic globalization. The threat of the British government to reduce corporate tax rates to a low 15%, or even below that figure, is not really credible since no government will be able to win elections where the top income tax rates are 30 or 40% for labor income while capital income is taxed at less than half of that, or the implication is that more and more workers would create a very small limited liability company and would argue that they are self-employed—in order to benefit from the low corporate income tax rate and to avoid the higher income tax rate.

A critical question for the UK, and for other countries, is labor mobility. Had there been no Euro Crisis, the United Kingdom would have faced much lower immigration pressures since part of the outward migration of Eastern European EU countries would have gone mainly to Italy, France, Spain, and Portugal—in particular, Romanians usually have a tendency to consider these countries as interesting immigration destinations since the Romanian language is also a Romance language which facilitates the learning of the respective language in these countries. However, with the Euro Crisis greatly affecting the aforementioned countries, there was some migration diversion in favor of Germany, the UK, and other countries in the EU. For some EU countries, possibly including the UK and the Netherlands, there was a widespread perception that there was too much immigration; this perception was probably reinforced by the popular feeling in many countries that the risk of Islamic terror had increased—this fear strengthened the emphasis of many people on a need for "defending the national identity" and this in turn translated into a more critical attitude of society towards immigration, including intra-EU immigration.

With respect to the UK, and taking into account the fact that the Euro Crisis had reinforced the income gap between the UK and most other EU countries, one can draw three alternative conclusions from this finding:

• The UK should have been more active in the management of the Euro Crisis since relying passively on the Eurozone member countries to sort out their problems was a guarantee that few efficient steps towards a sustainable problem solution would be made.

- The UK can remain in the EU only if immigration restrictions can be imposed—this indeed was part of the negotiation package which Mr. Cameron brought home from Brussels; but that package will now not be implemented as the UK will leave the European Union.
- The UK and other countries should seek an adequate limitation on immigration within the EU28, for example, on the basis of a rule which states that countries with relatively low growth rates have to restrict outward migration to some extent. Such a rule would be difficult to implement as long as the Schengen Area exists for 26 countries (including most of the EU28 but without the UK and Ireland who have their own common travel area) where free labor movement is possible without border controls. There is a broader picture which is even more complex. One cannot ignore that the EU's neighboring countries in Eastern Europe and some of the Balkan countries stand for very low per capita income measured in purchasing power parity. There is a need for a broader EU stabilization approach beyond the EU and the EU Neighborhood Policy might have been partly understood in this way. For example, if the per capita income in the Ukraine is rising, this will reduce the outward migration pressure in the Ukraine and hence the number of legal and illegal immigrants from that country in Poland and other EU countries would reduce. The EU, however, does not employ such a concept and the European Commission is also not in a position to mobilize private sector capital—from private banks—for the EU Neighborhood Policy. This, by comparison, is totally different in the US. Since 1900 or so, many US governments have used New York banks to support US foreign and economic policy interests abroad.

It is absolutely clear that the current European Union, with a budget of just 1% of GDP, is absolutely unable to deliver an effective fiscal policy and any form of reasonably active neighborhood policy. Which country was the driver behind reducing the EU budget in the past years? It was the United Kingdom that pushed, after the Transatlantic Banking Crisis—mainly caused by inadequate regulation in the US and the UK (with Northern Rock in 2007 being the first British bank to suffer a run on the bank since the early 1930s), for this reduction from a previous figure of 1.3% of GDP to just 1%. The British government wanted to give voters a signal that the EU government layer could not remain undiminished in a period in which the UK government had to reduce expenditures and raise taxes in an initial situation of a deficit–GDP ratio of more than 10%. In a period of enhanced economic globalization, the supranational EU policy layer should have received a bigger role in terms of fiscal policy—for example, by raising the expenditure-GDP ratio to 3% which should, of course, mean that the national policy layer would lose about 2% of government expenditures relative to GDP, say through shifting part of infrastructure expenditures and defense expenditures to the supranational policy layer.

At the same time, it is obvious that in a period of a rising risk of terror attacks, uncontrolled travel within the EU was not a good idea. Most terror suspects in France and Belgium have radicalized themselves within their respective country and this means that two of the six EU founding countries face a domestic education and integration problem; both the aforementioned countries face high youth unemployment rates for which the respective governments are largely responsible due to excessive minimum wage rates.

Those politicians who want to further raise minimum wages (the argument being that this would be popular among people with low wages and could also help to avoid poverty among pensioners in the future—since higher wage income now will mean higher contributions to social security and this, in turn, will help to avoid too many pensioners receiving too modest pensions in the future) act in a populist and irresponsible way, since a push for higher minimum wages in very many countries/cases will translate mainly into a higher youth unemployment rate. More government expenditure on raising labor productivity through training and retraining opportunities is a preferable measure.

Broad strata of society have become critics of traditional parties that have not only helped to bail out big banks in the Transatlantic Banking Crisis but have also watched over many years how big companies have paid less and less taxes per unit of profit earned at home and abroad. The EU countries cannot sit still and watch how big US multinational companies pay almost zero taxes. In Ireland, the case of Apple became famous as the European Commission intervened in the situation of Apple paying (almost) zero tax on corporate profits—the Commission argued that the fact that Apple was allowed (by the Irish State) to take advantage of measures, which were not broadly available to all other firms, in order to not pay taxes amounted to illegal subsidization.

Reference

Welfens, P. J. J. (2013a). *Überwindung der Eurokrise und Stabilisierungsoptionen der Wirtschaftspolitik: Perspektiven für Nordrhein-Westfalen, Deutschland und Europa*. Report for the Minister of Federal Affairs, Europe and Media: North Rhine-Westphalia.

Part IV
Consequences

As was made clear in the opening chapters of this book, the information policy of the Cameron government prior to the 2016 referendum was, with regard to certain important questions, completely inadequate. The information relating to the expected substantial long-term loss of income of between 3 and 10%—according to the study by HM Treasury—never reached a large share of British households (possibly more than two-thirds of households did not receive this information). The crucial economic findings were not included in the 16-page brochure prepared by the government which was distributed to households across the UK. That such an important figure, that is the expected long-term loss of income which would result from the UK withdrawing from the European Union, was only communicated to the electorate by parts of the press means the organization of the referendum was deeply flawed. It is known from all economic and political science studies, that in national elections, economic aspects always play an important and often decisive role. It can be assumed that the inclusion of the main findings of the Treasury study—published on April 18—in the government-commissioned information leaflet would have changed the result.

Ultimately, it would be astonishing if the British people do not force the government to hold a second referendum. If it becomes common knowledge that the expected result, had households received a basic standard of economic information, would be 52% for Remain, the questioning of the legitimacy of the vote could serve to mobilize the British public. The politicians in London, should they fail to make amends for the failures of the Cameron government surrounding the referendum, may soon be unable to act on the international stage in a concerted and unified way due to domestic political disputes, not only between the various parties in Westminster but also between factions within the main parties; how the May government should oversee successful exit negotiations with the EU is a mystery. How seriously can the government be taken—and Prime Minister May in particular (who personifies the continuity between Cameron's government and her own)—should it be shown to be either unwilling or incapable of organizing a simple referendum? Can Boris Johnson remain as Foreign Secretary?

14

A Second Brexit Referendum: A Scenario for Staying in the EU

It cannot be ruled out that after the conclusion of UK–EU negotiations, the British government will again refer the matter to the electorate in the form of a non-binding, advisory referendum based on the question: should the United Kingdom leave the EU (on the basis of the result of withdrawal negotiations) or Remain in the EU (on the basis of the concessions achieved by Cameron)? The EU could also have undertaken further reforms by the time a second referendum could be held, which could have a positive effect on UK attitudes vis-à-vis the EU. A committed and enthusiastic effort by the EU Representation in London in particular could bring the level of knowledge in the UK concerning EU matters up to match that of Germany, Italy, and France. If a majority of the British electorate should back Remain in a second referendum, that decision would have the following economic effects:

- An appreciation of the Pound by 10–15%, which would make imported goods relatively more expensive and affect the sales of exported goods, at the same time the price level could fall by circa 3%, that is inflation could fall from 2% to −1%. Real income would rise, but there would also be an unexpected rise of the real wage rate;

© The Author(s) 2017
P.J.J. Welfens, *An Accidental Brexit*,
DOI 10.1007/978-3-319-58271-9_14

this can lead to a transient loss of jobs. One more important effect may be that the expected long-term Brexit-related contraction of income will not come to pass.

- Stock prices will rise, as improved long-term export activities could be anticipated in the context of the better than expected EU single market access.
- Stock prices in the EU27 will also rise, as the Brexit-related trade diversion effects will not materialize as expected—nor the expected loss of real income.
- The United Kingdom will attract increased foreign direct investment inflows from the US, Asia, and Europe.
- Property prices will rise and there will be a significant upturn in construction activity, which means more jobs.
- After a short-term rise, the interest rate could fall in the medium term in expectation of a falling rate of inflation.
- The unemployment rates of both the UK and the EU27 will fall.

Remaining in the EU would certainly not occur without major political conflict in the UK, as the Brexiteers will surely continue to do everything they could to achieve Brexit—assuming, of course, that a second referendum would result in a pro-Remain majority. Moreover, there is little to support the EU readily making even more concessions to the UK than were previously offered to Cameron by the European Commission at the beginning of 2016. The UK will need to decide if it wishes to take on the role of a single country undermining EU integration and destabilizing Europe, chasing illusory Commonwealth perspectives, or that of an engaged and active member state of the European Union. Naturally, both the EU and the British government would do well to broaden and deepen EU-related knowledge in the UK, which has been shown to be quite poor. The transfer of at least one important EU institution to a seat in the UK would also be advisable, in order to achieve a stronger, albeit symbolic, link between them. A long-term dialogue regarding EU integration is desirable, which should also consider reforms, as well as the vigorous implementation of a digital Europe for citizens. The digital presence of the European Commission is not particularly visible in many areas and the creativity and diversity of the people of Europe is under-mobilized in terms of common, cross-border networking projects—this also applies to the areas of lifelong learning, higher education, and training.

Since the Banking Crisis of 2007–2009, one of the economic problems in Europe has been that the trend growth rate of production, that is the real Gross Domestic Product (GDP), has fallen, as was clearly demonstrated by Pichelmann (2015) and others; for the Eurozone, the US and the UK. It is surprising that labor productivity growth has slowed markedly since 2009 in many Organisation for Economic Co-operation and Development area countries (OECD 2015). Without structural reforms, more public investment and better supports for innovation, as well as incentives for women and older workers to increasingly participate in the labor force in many EU countries, it is unlikely they will achieve considerably higher economic growth according to a study by the McKinsey Global Institute (McKinsey Global Institute 2015); one positive to note, however, is that EU member states can realize most of the required reforms themselves at the national policy layer. It is completely foreseeable that the EU27 together with the UK can develop a policy which promises growth—with many national elements, but possibly also with a common promotion of innovation in particular innovative fields which are of common interest. In the event that a second referendum would result in a majority for Remain, such cooperation would be relatively easy, as long as the relevant political will is present. At the very least, one can conceive that at least in the field of basic research—which is long-term oriented in nature—cooperation will continue. If there is a second British referendum, it would be reasonable for the EU27 to develop alternative plans in a timely manner and for the Commission to be able to present new considerations punctually.

Economic growth requires a high level of innovative dynamics, where state support for research can be a supportive element; even more important in the long term, though, may be the targeted provision of venture capital in a sensible and conducive environment. It is unclear how continental European countries can quickly overcome their current deficit, when compared to the US or the UK, in terms of venture capital funding for start-ups and young firms. Here, tax incentives could be more effective than they have been to date. However, functioning stock markets and exchanges are also essential—the venture capitalists who finance small but innovative young companies in the early days, need to be able to reap the benefits by 'cashing-out' after a few years via the stock market: successful start-ups will be floated on the stock exchange and the high share price of an IPO creates a lucrative situation to sell part or full holdings and to realize large returns—appropriate for the high risk related to the financing of start-ups.

The ultra-low interest rates in Europe actually facilitate the possibility for investors to achieve a high price for stock when selling firms. Very low interest rates drive the relative share price indices. In the environment of an inflated equity price level—which reflects the extreme situation of years of low interest rates—the risk is there for venture capitalists that when the time comes to float a new firm on the stock market the share prices could be considerably lower. The EU27 could learn a lot from the UK with regard to the financing of start-up firms; if the UK decides to remain a member of the EU via another referendum, institutional learning will be much simpler for EU partner countries. The financial center that is London could keep serving as an important source of financing for young firms across the EU: to fund the establishment of more new firms, and the expansion of existing ones.

One can assume that after the holding of a second referendum—regardless of the outcome—cooperation between the EU27 countries and the UK will be less strained than the relations which can now be expected as a result of the 2016 referendum. A second referendum, for which a sound and timely information campaign for voters should be undertaken in advance, would result in a clear, credible, and legitimate signal of the will of the British electorate. Of course, a second referendum would also complicate political disputes in the UK; but that is the price to pay for the substantial and critical shortcomings of the government information policy prior to the first referendum in 2016, which possibly played a decisive role in the result.

Moreover, the British political establishment will encounter significant difficulties if, despite the dominant role of Parliament, it abides by the decision for a self-inflicted isolation taken in an unnecessary referendum: confronted by the peculiar result of a pro-Brexit majority, while the majority of Members of Parliament in Westminster were clearly for the UK remaining in the EU, many British politicians are now backing

Brexit for career reasons. When the Constitutional Committee of the House of Lords informed the May government—after she made clear her intention to invoke Article 50 of the Treaty of European Union without consulting Parliament—that a decision of Parliament is required in the middle of September, questions were again raised about the competence of the current government (House of Lords 2016).

Furthermore, the planned first meeting, which was due to take place in September of 2016, between the Exit Minister Davis and representatives of British industry, had to be canceled, because the industrialists did not want to attend, arguing that they had received no indication that the Minister had developed a sound work agenda which would serve as the basis for such a meeting. This was an affront to the Conservative government—and the comments from pro-Brexit Trade Minister Liam Fox, which circulated widely, that British managers are lazy and just wanted to spend Friday afternoons playing golf, are not conducive to the functioning of the government and cooperation between the government and industry. Liam Fox and others in government give the impression of being geared towards populism and of being a form of 'Tea Party'-type movement within the Cabinet. Only the weakness of the splintered Labour Party, under party leader Corbyn, has saved the May government—for the time being. That the Labour Party did not recognize and sharply criticize the massive failure of the Cameron government's information policy (either prior to or in the wake of the 2016 referendum) is indicative of just how poorly the British opposition under Corbyn has functioned in Westminster.

References

House of Lords. (2016). *The invoking of Article 50, select committee on the constitution, 4th Report of Session 2016–17*, September 3 2016. London.
McKinsey Global Institute. (2015). *A Window of Opportunity for Europe*. Washington, DC.
OECD. (2015). *The future of productivity*. Paris: OECD Publishing.
Pichelmann, K. (2015). When "Secular Stagnation" Meets Piketty's Capitalism in the 21st Century. Growth and Inequality Trends in Europe Reconsidered, 12th Euroframe Conference, 12 June 2015, Vienna. DG ECFIN working paper.

15

Beyond Brexit: Inequality Dynamics and a European Social Market Economy

If one takes a look at the referendum results in the UK and the presidential election results in the US in 2016, one may emphasize some common elements from a 'winner's' perspective:

- Populist political groups have won a majority in the UK and the US, respectively.
- A fear of immigration (relating in the UK mainly to immigration from EU partner countries and in the US to immigration from Mexico and Latin America, respectively, housing shortages were often emphasized by British respondents in national opinion surveys— but here it was not the EU that was to blame but local, regional, or national political actors). To the extent that one would listen to Mr. Nigel Farage in the UK and to Mr. Bannon in the US, 2016 also saw a strong anti-Muslim emphasis in the political rhetoric of both countries.
- A nationalist political approach seems to have been attractive to many voters since this suggests that government will give priority to domestic residents with regard to some public service provision.

© The Author(s) 2017
P.J.J. Welfens, *An Accidental Brexit*,
DOI 10.1007/978-3-319-58271-9_15

- An 'anti-elite' rhetoric has impressed many people: including the advice that one should not listen to economic experts and the ruling political elites in the respective capitals. In addition, in the case of the US, an anti-Wall Street agenda was pushed with almost religious zeal by an influential group in the campaign (notably by Mr. Bannon in the Trump team during the campaign), while Mrs. May, as an indirect winner of the British referendum, was arguing in late 2016 that it was not only the wealthy strata of society which should benefit from the market economy but workers and ordinary people as well. There is indeed a problem in both the US and in the UK—as is shown in Chap. 1 of the 2016 Economic Report of the President: the Report presents evidence that vertical mobility in society is much lower in the US and the UK than in many other Organisation for Economic Co-operation and Development (OECD) area countries (Council of Economic Advisers 2016). It is well known that since the 1990s, the banking business and the hedge funds plus insurance industries—in the US including the business of global giant AIG—were the main winners of structural change in both countries; along with the digital sector. The information and communication technology (ICT) sector was growing in nominal terms relative to nominal Gross Domestic Product (GDP). However, what was even more important is the fact that real ICT value-added (nominal value-added of this sector divided by the sectoral price level of this sector: the remarkable point is that this sectoral price level has fallen over decades) relative to real GDP has increased all the time; as regards the US or Germany, the ongoing rise of the real ratio of ICT output to overall national output is in contrast to the decline of the nominal ICT value-added relative to the nominal GDP around 2005. This means that the ICT sector's role in the economy is growing all the time in leading OECD countries. Why is this so important? The answer is that the growth of banking and finance on the one hand—itself strongly linked to an increasing use of ICT—and the relative expansion of ICT on the other are very much associated with a strongly growing concentration of income in society. ICT expansion, actually digital globalization, and financial globalization—with its twin headquarters in New York and London, respectively—were drivers of rising economic inequality in both the US and the UK.

If one then also considers immigration to be exerting downward pressure on the nominal wages of unskilled workers, and possibly also causing rising housing prices, then one can easily understand that an anti-immigration perspective was an important element for many voters both for the Brexit side in the UK and for many voters for Trump in the US in 2016. The Leave campaign in many ways emphasized that bringing political power back from Brussels to London would allow the British government to not only control immigration but also improve the economic situation in the country—and certainly also for the relatively poor strata of society.

The points mentioned above also play a role in the political debate in EU countries such as Finland, Denmark, the Netherlands, Germany, France, Belgium as well as (Northern) Italyand Austria, and to some extent also in Hungary, the Czech Republic, and Poland in 2016/17. As regards the western continental EU countries, one may, however, emphasize that, at least in Germany and the Netherlands, high unemployment and a fear of globalization did not play a prominent role in the national debate. The latter reflecting to some extent the long-standing current account surplus in both countries which can be taken as a signal that concerns economic survival in a faster, more digital, and more innovative global economy is not very common. In France, with its high unemployment rates and the negative current account position for several decades, the situation of course is different.

In his book *The Great Escape. Health, Wealth and the Origins of Inequality*, Deaton (2013) raised some doubts about the size of productivity growth and innovativeness in the banking sector in the UK and the US after the financial deregulation in both countries in the 1980s and 1990s. Both the UK and the US are rather free market economies, while most EU27 countries stand for a Social Market Economy with more regulation and government income redistribution than either the US or the UK. In the May government, the Minister of State for Trade and Investment, Mr. Greg Hands, is known to be an ardent supporter of free markets, obviously not understanding that a lack of regulation and indeed financial markets in the UK, which were too free after 2000, brought the US, the UK, and the whole western world very close to a new Great Recession in 2007/08. One may also emphasize that the share of income of the banking sector in GDP reduced after the 1930s in the US—with a higher regulatory burden imposed—only to increase again in the 1980s. As regards the ICT sector, this new field of digital value-added also certainly brings about more economic inequality both before and after taxes. Reducing corporate tax rates, as envisaged by Mrs. May and Mr. Trump, will further increase after-tax economic inequality in the UK and the US. Thus, there is an economic polarization in both countries which goes along with a new political polarization and radicalization—facilitated by the lack of personal contacts in all internet forums—in western industrialized countries. Naturally, one must raise the question of whether or not the continental EU countries (plus Ireland) will follow the British–US economic and political developments or whether they will be able to create a sustainable Social Market Economy in the medium and, perhaps, the long term.

Clearly, the Front National of Marine Le Pen is pushing in the national elections, and in future European Parliament elections, to capitalize on a wave of French populism: an anti-immigrant, anti-Muslim, nationalistic anti-EU movement. Key elements of their political program are points such as a priority of jobs for domestic residents, imposing new import tariffs vis-à-vis low per capita income countries, and slowing down economic and political globalization. Such a program would make the people of France suffer major income losses in the long run. One cannot overlook that Mrs. Le Pen is enthusiastic about both the Brexit result in the UK and the Trump victory in the US national elections in late 2016. Is there really much doubt that Brexit in combination with, potentially, Le Pen—and the disintegration of the EU— would lead Europe back into the late nineteenth century including its dangerous rivalries between big powers that ended in the First World War? It should also be clear that the political program of Mrs. May will bring enhanced economic globalization to the UK so that the income inequalities will further increase in the medium and the long term.

It is obvious that Brexit puts pressure on the EU27 to consider creating more intensive political ties within the European Union. Moreover, the US President Trump and his campaign group has suggested at the turn of 2016/17 that the EU is likely to disintegrate. One cannot rule out that such political rhetoric and the lack of international visiting activities undertaken by President Trump in the initial months of his presidency will eventually stimulate EU countries to really seek closer economic and political integration in the EU. Such a political integration could be quite useful for dealing with both the US and the United Kingdom. This does not rule out that a tighter EU—possibly with a limited number of member countries—will be strong in international cooperation with the US, the UK, Russia, Japan, Canada and China, so that a more powerful and more efficient EU could emerge from the Brexit decision and the Trump presidency in the US. Environmental sustainability topics could well be a very useful field for cooperation on a joint modern international environmental policy that would reduce energy intensities as well as material resource intensity worldwide. Here, the EU already has several policy tools and strategies to offer.

Income inequality will increase within countries in the medium term and in the long run if one follows the view of Jaumotte/Lall/Papageorgiou (2008) whose International Monetary Fund (IMF) paper has shown that rising free trade contributes to a convergence of per capita income across countries—just as standard trade theory suggests—while financial globalization (dating back to the 1970s and financial liberalization, respectively) and ICT expansion contribute to rising inequality within countries. Financial globalization brings with it lower real interest rates for all those who can benefit from loans to buy real estate, stocks, or other assets; if one is an unskilled worker, however, one will usually have neither the adequate market income nor the private wealth to directly benefit much from financial globalization. ICT expansion brings with it—probably for several decades—a bias in technological progress, namely a rising skilled labor demand so that the skilled labor–unskilled labor ratio will increase. Thus, there are two elements that contribute to rising economic inequality within industrialized countries. However, some government redistribution policy is, in principle, possible to avoid an ever rising income inequality over time. The government could also organize the training and retraining of workers.

The view within the May government on issues surrounding globalization and productivity is in part quite strange. Leading representatives from the field of economics in the May government have argued in favor of quickly pursuing a strong cooperation with the new Trump administration; as regards perspectives for a free trade agreement, a UK–US free trade agreement makes sense. However, it is unclear what type of cooperation a global free trade UK would like to establish with a protectionist US whose president seems to be inclined to undermine multilateralism and major international organizations which contribute to efficiency gains, peaceful conflict resolution, and global welfare gains. It is rather strange that senior representatives of the May government have said in conversations with journalists that the UK's rather weak productivity growth is due to its high EU immigration numbers. One may note that the share of EU immigrants in the UK's population is not particularly high by European Union standards. It seems that the UK has a weakness in training and integrating immigrant workers, while the general lack of a modern apprenticeship program and of an active labor market policy is a problem.

The May government has started to re-emphasize the role of manufacturing industry and to thereby correct the long-standing relative growth of the finance and insurance sector with its often very high wages—where it is sometimes very unclear whether or not there exists the very high productivity in this sector to justify such high wages. The period of low-interest rates will further reinforce the benefits of financial globalization, but again those people who have neither wealth (read collateral) nor a high market income will largely be unable to benefit from this development which has been brought about by the US and British Quantitative Easing (QE) monetary policy; a similar monetary policy has been adopted by the European Central Bank (ECB) in 2015–2017. As the Branson model clearly shows for the case of a small open economy—such as the United Kingdom (or actually a country that is a bit smaller than the UK which ranks No. 9 in the world based on purchasing power parity figures)—the two key effects of a policy of QE, an expansionary open market policy under which the central bank buys government bonds, will be to (1) reduce the interest rate and (2) to bring about a nominal and real depreciation of the currency in the short term. Moreover, with some delay the real depreciation will bring about a rise of net exports of goods and services so that the current account position will improve in the medium term, and output and employment will increase. It is noticeable that both the US and the UK adopted such a monetary policy of QE in the five years after 2009 (when the central bank's interest rate was already very low) since there was fear of deflationary pressure in the US and protracted recessions in both the US and the UK. The ECB has implemented a QE policy only in 2015–2017 on a broader scale and the side effect was that the US faced a temporary worsening of its current account as the Eurozone countries benefitted from rising net exports of goods and services. For the US, this is a transatlantic mirror problem of what was faced by the Eurozone during 2009–2014 when the US pursued QE— with a depreciation of the US Dollar and an improving US current account; this perspective also makes clear that Mr. Navarro's conjecture that Germany was to blame for exchange rate manipulation and thus to contributing to a weak US current account position is contradictory. As a key economic advisor of Mr. Trump, the influential Mr. Navarro has a co-responsibility for organizing a useful transatlantic policy dialogue. The current account surplus of the Eurozone vis-à-vis the US is rather small, just one-fifth of the 9% current account surplus–GDP ratio of Germany in 2016. However, Germany faces a responsibility to cut its high surplus position since the EU has agreed upon rules that suggest that a surplus–GDP ratio of more than 6% should be corrected, and the German government has done nothing to do so. There are three options to bring about a lower current account surplus position: (1) The government could adopt higher infrastructure expenditure programs, including a modernization of the digital infrastructure. (2) Higher military expenditures that would close the gap between 1.1% of GDP in 2015 and the long established 2% goal could be useful. (3) A reduction of value-added tax rates could help stimulate consumption and imports, respectively, and dampen net exports of goods and services. This should be combined with a higher taxation of environmentally damaging emissions—it is strange that the green tax revenue–GDP ratio is 4–5% in the Netherlands and Denmark, but only about 1.5% in Germany. Raising green taxes in a setting with an envisaged reduction of value-added tax rates (which fall on consumption) would be useful to avoid a rapid rise in the government budget deficit. Higher green taxes as a means to internalize negative external effects from pollution or high resource intensity of production could be particularly useful if part of the extra revenue could be invested in higher R&D promotion. For Germany, promoting research and development with adequate tax incentives and Schumpeterian subsidies makes sense; other EU countries with a high structural current account surplus might consider similar reforms, but a country with a structural current account deficit such as France should rather raise its value-added tax rates. As regards the EU countries' coping with the challenges of economic globalization, one may argue that certain minimum corporate tax rates should be considered. Economic globalization clearly reinforces the opportunities for firms to use investment funds abroad and to internationally hunt for tax bargaining arrangements on the basis of a high digital and physical mobility of investment and elements of value-added, respectively. The natural result will be a tendency towards declining corporate tax revenue–GDP ratios in the long run. A rather easy way of governments to counterbalance such strategies is more international cooperation in taxation.

With Brexit, and the new aggressive foreign policy of the Trump administration vis-à-vis the EU, most EU countries are considering options for more political cooperation in the European Union. There should be no doubt that the EU is not really an attractive policy club if the Eurozone should not assume a bigger role for countercyclical fiscal policy which, in turn, requires a higher budget for the EU in Brussels. Additionally, the EU would have to be more active in the field of pushing for new free trade agreements with many countries in Asia (for example with the whole of the Association of Southeast Asian Nations (ASEAN), not just with Singapore and Vietnam, which are currently the only two countries in ASEAN with which the EU has such a free trade arrangement—although the EU–Vietnam agreement still has to be ratified). The EU should have free trade arrangements with ASEAN countries ready fairly quickly. Moreover, the EU should adopt a really comprehensive digital integration program and will have to make sure that schools in all countries will promptly receive broadband internet connections through some EU co-financing in digital infrastructure modernization. It remains to be seen whether or not the continental EU debate about more cooperation in defense—which for many years had been blocked by the UK—and more political cooperation will really produce sustained results and to what degree there are medium-term prospects to establish a Eurozone Social Market Economy. Higher expenditures in Brussels on the basis of shifting tasks and funds from the national level to the supranational level could be quite useful and would also be efficient if this leads to a more intensive political competition in terms of European Parliament elections. To have a joint Eurozone unemployment insurance for the first six months—but not for youth unemployment where national regulations, including those for minimum wages, are primarily responsible—would be useful as a means of establishing joint responsibility.

Dolls et al. (2014) have calculated the key budget aspects of a joint Eurozone unemployment insurance system, namely for a 12-month financing of unemployment insurance. The authors from ZEW show that about £42 billion ($51 billion) in funds/expenditures would be necessary per year (on the basis of six months about £21 billion (circa $26 billion) would be necessary, namely 0.25% of the Eurozone GDP) where Austria, Germany, and the Netherlands would be the main net contributors, namely with rather small net contributions of 0.2% to 0.4% of the respective GDP. Permanent net recipients of such a system would be Spain and Latvia with 0.53% and 0.33% of the respective GDP. One may consider such a new system and give up the cohesion benefits for low per capita income countries. Also with such a new system, one should consider that the maximum net transfer under the program cannot be more than 0.2% of GDP and no net contributor would have to pay more than 0.25% of GDP. This would stand for a system that reflects the long-run increase in the synchronization of national business cycles in the Eurozone; this statement does not mean to overlook the rather recent business cycle dynamics that have temporarily shown declining business cycle harmonization after the Eurozone crisis.

Post-Brexit: Options for a Social Market Economy in Europe

Assuming that the United Kingdom does indeed complete its break from the EU, then the EU27 member states and political leaders in Brussels must consider what the primary consequences for the EU will be: assuming that the will exists to continue with EU integration as a sustainable project at all. In the tense political situation in Europe which has resulted from Brexit, and for which the UK is responsible, the first questions to be faced are what the huge challenges of the twenty-first century are and what has the EU achieved to date? The answers to these questions, and considering the UK withdrawal, should inform how the EU27 as a group can move forward in a sensible direction. The prior and subsequent reflections contained in this book suggest that the answer is a European Social Market Economy which should be based on a clear division of responsibilities between the national and supranational policy layers. Thus can the EU become a competitor on the world stage with the US and UK, which are less welfare-oriented states and which are strongly characterized by the financial and services sectors; additional heavyweight players in the competition between systems are other large countries such as Russia, China, and India.

The EU has established a common trade policy, the European single market, framework conditions in terms of competition and regulatory policies (for example, the EU's merger controls with regard to the huge cross-border mergers of major firms in the EU; telecommunications regulation, etc.), a relatively nascent climate and environment policy, and some limited advances in terms of social policy. If one considers that the twenty-first century will above all be a period of Asian expansion, digitalization, and innovation dynamics—largely driven by globalization—then it becomes clear that the EU must tackle these issues head on:

- The promotion of free trade agreements with countries and integration clubs (such as ASEAN) should be high on the political agenda, whereas an agreement should also be concluded with the US as a power in both the Pacific and Atlantic areas; if necessary, without the investor resolution tribunal. The latter institution is in many ways a logical development, as investor–state disputes could result in EU countries having to pay compensation in certain cases; however, because of this national parliaments will want to have a vote on the Transatlantic Trade and Investment Partnership. Only in a future neo-EU with a bicameral, that is dual chamber, system of government in Brussels will the role of national parliaments begin to decline.

- Digital expansion and innovation is certainly a natural part of the EU's economic policies due to cross-border welfare effects through network and transfer channels. In the long term, a Digital Minister (or Commissioner) is required, who shall consider and shape international and global digital aspects of the economies and politics together with the US and others. From a US and EU perspective, the Internet is a global, digital market, which should be subject to international regulations. That is certainly not the approach of China, Russia, or Turkey, each of which supports national Internet market policies, each of which—strongly regulated at a national level—combines to form the global networked Internet. Moreover, it is obvious that autocratic regimes will increasingly have a tendency to further the concept of the 'national' Internet. The Internet, and its rules, is hugely important with regard to power, democracy, and internationalized discussions.

- High-wage European countries—primarily the Western European countries—must take care that in the growing geographic distribution of value-added processes, due to globalization dynamics, they remain at the end of the value-added chains where Schumpeterian rents are particularly high: high labor and knowledge productivity are crucial—as are all areas which are important to reach those high levels of productivity. Here, the higher education systems of continental European countries are not as market oriented as counterparts in Asia, Australia, the US, Canada, and the UK. That is a considerable problem, especially in the area of Master studies, which unfortunately cannot be explored in more detail here.

- Globalization and innovation dynamics should be actively and positively picked up, accompanied with a demand from policymakers that sensible and sound social insurance systems can cushion the effects of internationalization risks. Thus far, the EU has—to address one example—only played a small role in the context of globalization funds, which can be activated as a response to large falls in employment in large firms due to international economic shocks (conceivable, for example, in terms of the crisis in the steel industry in Europe). This raises more fundamental questions regarding how a Social Market Economy should be meaningfully designed with globalization in mind. Continental Europe will need to find new answers to these questions after Brexit—in fact, the EU should have been searching for these answers for a long time. It has already been discussed that in the area of an active labor market policy, the UK invests relatively little in its workers and unemployed, respectively. Here, the continental EU members have taken a different approach, which stresses the importance of not letting the losers of modernization fall behind in structural change. On the other hand, the EU countries, either as whole in terms of the EU or individually as member states, are often not very successful in facilitating appropriate mobility of labor and optimal job-matching processes. Often, employees are not employed in those positions which sufficiently emphasize their productivity (for example in Italy, where the legislation in this area is extremely complex and does not encourage job changes but actually creates hurdles to the process, as the OECD (2016) has stressed). Moreover, there is no great difference between the benefits relating to the further training of skilled and unskilled workers and other returns oneducation, as IZA studies have shown.

The globalization of economic relationships, however, continues on completely independently of Brexit. The first decades of EU integration involved primarily economic integration, that is an increase in trade initially in terms of goods, later with the single market came an increase in terms of services, liberalized capital flows, and the freedom of movement of labor. It was only in the late 1990s that social aspects became increasingly important, which can be understood in terms of an answer to the questions of income inequalities, on the one hand, and the role of state social insurances, such as unemployment insurance, pension insurance, and health insurance on the other. Now, with Brexit, there are new possibilities for the EU to create a European Social Market Economy.

Table 15.1 Life expectancy and child mortality in the UK, Germany, France and the US

	Life expectancy at birth (Average, 2014)	Child mortality (No. of deaths of children under 5 years of age per 1000, 2015)
United Kingdom	81	4
Germany	81	4
France	82	4
US	79	7

Source http://data.worldbank.org

The fact that there exists at least a basic general health insurance in EU countries explains the leading positions of Germany, France, and Scandinavian countries in terms of life expectancy and infant mortality—especially when compared to the fragmented nature of health insurance in the US (where in 2010 about 15% of the population were without health insurance). For example, while a high share of pregnant women in Germany undergo important medical check-ups—which can identify complications before the birth and thereby reduce risks to both mother and child—such screenings occur relatively rarely in the US among the poorer sections of society, which has a negative effect on infant mortality rates. The Obama administration's insurance reforms raised the share of people with health insurance in the US by a number of percentage points; however, in 2016 almost 10% of US citizens remain without insurance. See Table 15.1.

European integration has brought considerable economic advantages for the member states of the EU, which have implemented more regional trade on a step-by-step basis—above all, with the single market program in 1992—but which also transferred exclusive competence in the area of external trade and part of the competences in other crucial areas of competition policy (ban on cartels, merger control, abuse of market-dominating positions) to the EU. This has strengthened the EU market economy, but leaves open the question of just how embedded the social market is, or indeed should be, as an economic system. Nevertheless, the EU is fundamentally linked to social issues such as human rights through the Lisbon Treaty, and references to the goals of cohesion and social solidarity are certainly not lacking in

EU documents. A broad analysis of the EU's Social Market Economy is called for (the following draws on this author's contribution in Von Alemann (2015)).

At the beginning of the twenty-first century, the Social Market Economies of many EU countries were facing an acid test, many countries were still coming to terms with the consequences of both the Transatlantic Banking Crisis and the Euro Crisis in 2014/15: with obvious enormous strains particularly in the area of unemployment insurance. According to the EU's Employment and Social Developments in Europe report (European Commission 2014), the in-work at-risk-of-poverty rate decline in Ireland and Portugal between 2008 and 2012, while in Greece, Italy, Spain, Germany, and France, the risk of being poor despite employment increased—being limited to part-time jobs played a role here. On the findings of the same report for 2012, the EU remarked on its website: "In terms of their effectiveness at tackling poverty, the design of national welfare systems is as important as their size - similar levels of social spending by Member States result in very different rates of poverty reduction. The design of the revenue side of welfare state plays an equally important role. Shifting the tax burden […] from labour to other sources, such as CO2 emissions or consumption and property, boosts employment. However, distributional aspects of tax redesign call for a cautious approach when looking for alternative sources to replace the lost revenues from lower labour taxation. […] polarization between high and low income jobs has grown. A large pay gap between men and women persists (16.4% on average in the EU in 2010) and tends to increase with a person's age."

In the long term, the aging of societies and the related financing of pensions will be a major challenge for EU countries—by circa 2050, only in Japan and South Korea will the old-age dependency ratio, that is the share of over-65s, be higher than that of Spain, Germany, and Italy (Pew 2014), followed by some distance by France; the large-scale immigration to Germany in 2013–2016 may, however, improve the long-term position of Germany, as long as the situation of a net immigration of 400,000 annually (0.5% population growth through migration)—excluding refugees—remains constant in the medium term. In Japan, Germany, and Italy, the share of over-65s will raise from about

20% in 2010 to over 32% in 2050. In this regard, the US is in a relatively better position compared to the EU due to a high birth rate and persistent immigration; in 2050, China will rank between the EU and the US, which could also have an impact on the global competition between economic systems. Furthermore, there are in the construction of the EU certain starting points for a European social policy (Von Alemann/Dreyer/Hummel 2013). From an economic perspective, it would be limited and focused. Moreover, a better anti-cyclical fiscal policy for the Eurozone would also be a quasi-social policy, as the risk of poverty is strongly related to long-term unemployment.

A Social Market Economy is based on rules, which in the first instance link performance competition on orderly markets with social compensation on the basis of needs and criteria of fairness. In the European Union, the individual member states represent social market economies. At a supranational level, however, there are almost no activities reminiscent of social policy and state redistribution worth mentioning, apart from the distribution resulting from EU Structural Funds, which go to regions with less than 75% of the EU's per capita income, and Cohesion Funds, which are available to countries with less than 90% of the EU average income. In 2013, these funds amounted to barely 0.4% of EU GDP. The globalization funds, which are intended for regions with starkly decreasing rates of employment—for example, in large firms—could also be regarded as a part of the social policy of the EU. There are four fundamental concepts behind a Social Market Economy:

- In an orderly competition on the basis of a reasonable regulatory framework, a high national income should emerge. This is the material foundation from which welfare and prosperity result, but it is also the basis for state redistribution measures. These should, with reason, take negative incentive effects into account.
- On the basis of the tax system, and in particular through progressive income taxation, the absolute and relative disposable income position of the highest income groups should be reduced and a funding base for social transfers which benefit needy households and people created. This is a redistribution policy.

- Social transfers and the implicit redistribution within the framework of the social system benefit the poorer strata of society most and allow people with a low market income to achieve an appropriate standard of living and especially a sufficient personal health insurance in the welfare state. Aside from a public health insurance system, which prescribes obligatory health insurance, there is also private health insurance which can act as a complement or alternative to the public system. A system of state pensions and unemployment insurance are also part of social policy.
- Employee organizations, meaning trade unions, represent the interests of labor—on the basis of democratic principles—and negotiate wages and working conditions with employer organizations.

Thus, the social market economy is designed to provide a certain safety net with regard to major risks in life, such as illness, unemployment, and retirement (longevity in a time without employment), and relates to the minimum activities of the state.

The modern European welfare state also strives to prevent cases of absolute poverty. Besides the state's public social policy in the narrow sense, there are also measures driven by private solidarity, which are demonstrated in private interpersonal engagement vis-à-vis people in need and partly also in the form of donations to socially-oriented foundations and charities. The state, in Germany and other EU countries, allows citizens to write off donations to charitable and non-profit foundations, research organizations, and churches against taxes within certain limits. With an average tax rate of say 20%, this means that for a relevant donation of £100 or $100, the donee or recipient receives £20 or $20 from the state or taxpayers. On the EU level, this is already problematic, as donations can only be written off for tax purposes on a national level. From the point of view of European solidarity, this could already be seen as discriminatory—only with an EU (or indeed Eurozone) political union can this problem be resolved, in that at least a part of payroll and income taxes are paid to the supranational layer (i.e., Brussels). If this was the case, then one could if one wished make donations in relatively poorer southern European countries and still receive the tax benefit.

The international differences in per capita income have reduced in the two decades since 1985; however, income inequalities have actually increased within the individual industrialized countries (in the sense that the ratio of the wage of skilled labor relative to unskilled labor is increasing), for which a simple explanation from an empirical perspective has been offered (Jaumotte/Lall/Papageorgiou 2008): the rapid globalization of financial markets led to a reduction of real interest rates worldwide, from which households can profit via borrowing—but only those who can provide assets as collateral or who can show a medium or high income level (i.e., skilled labor); in addition, there is the influence of a distortion in terms of technological progress, which increases demand for skilled labor—a situation which can be seen, for example, in the expansion of the Information and Communication Technology (ICT) sectors. Thus, the income of skilled labor increases in all countries relative to that of unskilled labor.

Social policies and redistribution policies, respectively, are dependent on the income side on contributions to social insurance, that is health insurance, pension insurance, and unemployment insurance. Furthermore, some measure of income redistribution will be aspired to which should be achieved through progressive income taxes and, if applicable, also via consumption taxes or value-added taxes, and possibly also wealth or property taxes.

Thus far, social policy is overwhelmingly the domain of the EU member states themselves at a national level, which to some extent is supported by the principle of subsidiarity. From an economic perspective, however, one must consider that the financing cost of such social policies, which in EU countries stand for about 20% of the GDP, is a quite considerable share of GDP which could have significant effects. If the spending on social policies is financed by contributions and surcharges on net labor costs—as is the case in Germany—this results in a reduced demand for labor by firms. As long as unit labor costs in the foreign direct investment (FDI) destination country are rising relative to those in the source country, then the FDI flows of multinational companies from the source country will fall—which negatively impacts the investment ratio and technological progress (Barrell/Pain 1997). Technological advances via direct investment play an important role in industry.

For firms, the gross labor costs are what is relevant and economic employment calculus requires that labor, or workers, must earn their gross labor costs for the firm; this includes the incidental wage costs which are indirectly related to social insurance, namely via the pillars of health, unemployment, and pension insurance. From this perspective, the highly political division in the UK of National Insurance into the 'employee contribution' and the 'employer contribution' for example is, economically speaking, quite irrelevant—only the minor tax effects for firms which result via the different distribution rates lead to an economically important aspect; the lower the contribution rate of the firm, the higher the gross and net returns on capital and the higher the investment rate, respectively. In Denmark, an alternative model of social insurance has been implemented, which is financed primarily via high value-added taxes (VAT): the primary effect of raised value-added tax rates is a raising of the domestic prices for consumers and thus, in a mirror effect, to reduced consumption and higher exports; imports on the other hand, which are now more expensive for consumers having been subjected to the raised VAT, are reduced—the total net effect of which is an improvement of the balance of trade.

Social policies in the area of state pension insurance are financed in widely varying ways in different EU countries, where the Netherlands is well known for its "cappuccino system" which it has implemented for many years: a basic pension funded by state contributions, plus a company pension, plus incentives for privately funded pension provisions. This element is partly present in a less than systematic way in almost all EU countries: in Germany, company pensions play an important role for many workers. Since 2014, this role has, however, come under pressure from the de facto zero interest policy of the ECB, particularly as firms have to pay tax on artificially high capital yields; this problem will be exacerbated by post-Brexit British monetary policy as the British capital market is large enough to cause transfer effects in the direction of the EU27. Furthermore, there are the statutory private provision elements in Germany: the introduction of a funded, so-called "Riester Rente," for the implementation of which the State offers certain tax incentives, was only partially effective in Germany as a private personal provision, only half of those entitled to operate such a 'Riester' provision actually do so. Here, due to the progressive income tax system, the tax incentives for doing so are significantly higher for groups with a higher income than for those workers with a lower income. The various approaches to social policy in different EU member states come into conflict with each other in the EU single market, where the possibilities for competing on cost in terms of the free trade of goods and services are paramount; as long as a differentiated and well-developed social policy contributes to the social harmony and political stability of a country, then that social policy can—taking the freedom of movement of labor and capital into account—lead to higher immigration and higher inflows of direct investment. A social policy which contributes to a higher government debt, on the other hand, will contribute to outflows of capital and emigration, as a high government debt ratio—with the subsequent deterioration in the rating of the relevant sovereign bonds—is a signal for a significant future increase in tax rates. Mobile factors of production will seek to escape them.

This mobility of the factors of production can hinder the economic policy of a strengthened cross-border coordination (in actual fact, from a theoretical perspective, politicians could agree on a revenue-maximizing income tax rate t^{max} of 1 minus the production elasticity of capital in the macroeconomic production function, which is certainly not in the interest of citizens; on the basis of a Cobb–Douglas production function, this would result in an income tax rate of circa 66%, if the production elasticity of capital is one-third, in reality the actual average income tax rate can be written as x^*t^{max}, where x is a value between 0 and 1 and is heavily dependent on both political preferences and marginal costs of collecting tax (Welfens 2013). Redistribution policy can, to a certain extent, be pursued via the taxation system and this is a question which should be on the agenda in relation to the EU single market with its high mobility of factors of production, namely labor and capital.

Furthermore, the findings of Piketty (2014) show that income inequality in leading industrialized countries has been starkly influenced by developments in the income of the Top 1% of earners since the 1990s. This effect has been more pronounced in the US and the UK than in Germany and other continental EU countries. The first chapter of the report of the US Council of Economic Advisers (2016) also referred to these differences between industrialized countries. On the other hand, one can consider the possibilities for social advancement in various countries—once again Germany and the Scandinavian countries perform well in this regard, while the US and the UK perform relatively poorly. This means that not only did income inequality increase dramatically in these countries, but also the opportunity to rise from the lower levels of the income distribution to the top are very limited—for the US, the proverbial "land of opportunity", these findings are somewhat surprising.

The analysis of Piketty (2014), with regard to questions of distribution, has given rise to new questions, while the author asserts that there is a long-term tendency of a rising share of capital income in GDP. This finding is based on the key observation that interest rates in the long term are higher than economic growth rates, though the lowest interest phase in OECD countries since 2012 raises some doubts on this point. Rather, the Internet is contributing to growing economic inequality. In the modern, digital economy, the costs of founding new firms are lower than previously, so that the share of self-employed is clearly rising over time. This development can lead to problems in terms of state contributory pension schemes as a result of a falling number of employees liable to pay contributions. This effect can, however, be counteracted with relevant inheritance and estate taxes, a sensible law vis-à-vis foundations and appropriate capital gains taxes. It should also be noted that income redistribution is not only pursued via the system of taxation but also via the health system and health insurers.

In the single market, it has been widely ensured, thanks to EU jurisprudence, that EU citizens can avail of health services in other EU member states; in terms of statutory health insurance, there are no contributory surcharges for medical treatments received in other EU states. Private insurers, on the other hand, do impose surcharges for some countries; if, for example, one had studied or worked in another EU member state, without just cause, such additional costs and charges are a form of discrimination (indeed private German health insurers do demand a surcharge for study visits in France, for example). In terms of contributory pensions for mobile pensioners, certain problems are also apparent resulting from the different pension insurance schemes. While in Germany, on the basis of previous reforms, pension payments are taxable, similar pension payments in Spain are not taxable. Thus, Germans when reaching pensionable age are often domiciled in Spain, and there they can benefit from a considerable advantage compared to staying in Germany. On the other hand, Spaniards who are in receipt of a Spanish pension while living in Germany must pay tax on their pension, as long as they are domiciled in Germany. Here, there are distortion effects, which can only be overcome in the social European Union with a partly harmonized, from a tax perspective, pension insurance system.

In the Euro monetary union, there are also issues due to the, albeit necessary, joint liability of Eurozone countries, where some Eurozone partners pay implicit transfers, via rescue packages and interest waivers, to other Euro countries in difficulties with the goal of avoiding a general Euro Crisis. There are also certain other problems in other EU member states, and one example which could be mentioned here is the nationwide uniform minimum wage in France (about £8.50, or $10.40, per hour as of early 2016). For every employee being paid this minimum wage, firms receive a state subsidy. These subsidies for minimum wage workers amount to 1% of GDP or an additional 1% on the deficit rate, respectively; assuming a trend growth rate of real GDP of 1.5%, these figures infer that from the deficit-financed subsidization the minimum wage alone, a long-term debt ratio of 66.7% results—according to the Domar (1944) formula. That is already problematic from the perspective of the Stability and Growth Pact with its upper-limit debt ratio of 60%, bringing the credibility of the entire Eurozone into question with regard to stability policies; it also weakens France itself, insofar as with an assumed normal interest rate of 4% and a government debt ratio of 66.7%, additional interest rate payments of 2.7% relative to GDP will be required, and thus the average income tax rate in France must also be raised by a similar magnitude. That reduces, in turn, the equilibrium income in France and the domestic demand for labor by approximately 1.4% when one makes the usual assumption that the production elasticity of capital is 0.33 (in a linear homogenous Cobb–Douglas production function for the entire economy). At the same time, this reduces the exports of France's EU partner countries, reducing their GDP and employment levels, which in turn has a negative feedback effect of France.

In the EU single market and the Eurozone, respectively, such inter-dependencies are worth noting. A carefully constructed minimum wage policy is sustainable, an excessive approach on the other hand—with a lack of regional differentiation—is linked to considerable economic costs, weakening the national economy and international competitive-ness, which in turn makes many firms susceptible to being acquired by US companies, for example, in the long term. The subsidization of min-imum wages has less of a negative macro effect if the additional inter-est payments caused by a raised debt ratio are financed by a raising of value-added taxes, which would lead to higher exports in the well-estab-lished EU system: higher value-added taxes make domestic consump-tion relatively more expensive, which reduces consumption and, with a given level of production, increases the net export of consumer goods.

The differences in the social systems—with a tendency towards rela-tively good services, from an EU comparative perspective, in countries with higher incomes—incentivize many people in poorer EU countries to migrate to other member states with higher standards in terms of a social safety net (including adequate social help). Immigration can bring significant economic benefits for the destination country, for exam-ple in providing qualified labor to cover a skills shortage. That "poverty migration" is sometimes seen as a burden by the individual communities affected is certain; however, it is up to the relevant regions to cushion the effects especially in areas facing a particularly high burden by pro-viding additional funding for the construction of dwellings or the pro-vision of language and integration classes, for example. Naturally, some regions or communities could face a particularly high burden. A recent German study (Brücker 2013) has shown that the formal immigrants to Germany are relatively highly skilled and qualified—better than the average native German—and that on average they contribute a surplus of approximately £1,700 ($2,075) to the social security system, rather than being a drain on it as is often assumed. This net contribution results from the high number of migrants returning to their home coun-tries without having reached the position of being eligible for minimum entitlements, meaning that many migrants do not claim any benefits.

Moreover, Germany, like France and Italy, is an EU country with a relatively high per capita income. An analysis by the ECB found that the median wealth per household in Germany is the lowest when compared to other Eurozone countries (ECB 2013). Germany's position in terms of average wealth, based on the arithmetic mean, is somewhat better, but here too Germany actually lies below, for example, Spain, which may be explained by, among other things, the two World Wars and the extensive write-off of the capital stock of East Germany in the course of German reunification. The relatively high values for Spain, Italy, and certain other EU countries are clearly reflective of the high debt ratios of the respective states (according to the Ricardo Equivalence theory, in an extreme case, equivalently high future tax liabilities will face current and future generations, so that at most a part of the government bonds held by nationals of the respective country should be counted as net wealth).

From an economic perspective, there is a connection with regard to the income and wealth situation. Assets are a source of future income, however, imputed (arithmetic) rental income for owner-occupied properties are not included in the statistics of the OECD countries. Moreover, the informal or shadow economy also plays a considerable role with respect to real income in many OECD countries. If it is a question of improving the German position in the wealth league table of the Eurozone, better incentives for the founding of firms would be advisable, but also better tax incentives for saving in the long term. Another question relates to the possibilities to implement short-term impulses for overcoming the Euro Crisis. Here, not only is every Eurozone member country called upon to act, but also the EU as a whole and Eurozone partner countries. If Germany, via conditional loans from the KfW (*Kreditanstalt für Wiederaufbau*, a German government-owned development bank) to crisis countries, could pass on some of the crisis-related interest benefits to southern European crisis countries—as was recommended by the Federal Government in Berlin in 2013—this would definitely be a sensible impulse for stabilization. Any and all short-term measures cannot, however, simply serve as a replacement for an impartial and critical debate on the topic of a Euro political union, as the subsequent discussion on the perspectives of a European market economy shows.

Redistribution Policies in the EU

Some form of limit on income inequality is important as a rule for long-term social cohesion and harmony. Inequality can be measured in various ways, as can the results of state redistribution—here, concerning the difference between primary and secondary distribution. Even if EU policy was to have certain redistribution effects, with expenditures of just 1% of EU GDP or so, the redistribution effects would be minimal.

The *Institut der Deutschen Wirtschaft*/Cologne Institute for Economic Research Economic Research (Niehues 2013) examined the extent of income redistribution with regard to net transfers as a percentage of net income in 2009—with certain restrictions. Taxes and social contributions paid were examined, along with transfers received from the state. As an example, the position of the 20% of the population with the highest incomes and the 20% with the lowest incomes were considered—see Table 15.2.

Table 15.2 Income redistribution in EU countries according to the Cologne Institute for Economic Research (Net transfers in percent of net income—2009)

Ireland	61.7	−6.9	U.K.	39.5	−23.8	Cyprus	33.8	+2.7
Finland	53.9	−20.6	Bulgaria	38.9	+1.0	Malta	29.3	−13.2
Denmark	50.1	−36.4	Portugal	38.3	−10.8	Slovakia	27.4	−1.7
Sweden	45.8	−23.4	Latvia	37.8	−5.1	Luxembourg	26.5	−11.6
Germany	45.7	−17.3	Hungary	37.1	−9.3	Spain	23.0	−4.3
Belgium	45.2	−19.5	Slovenia	36.0	−19.5	Lithuania	22.9	−5.1
Cz. Rep.	42.3	−15.5	Austria	35.7	−18.4	Poland	17.3	−11.8
Estonia	42.2	−9.2	Netherlands	35.4	−38.4	Italy	13.2	−8.7
France	39.8	+2.6	Romania	34.3	−4.8	Greece	11.1	−15.3

Columns 2, 5 and 8 are denoted as 20% of the population with the lowest income; 3, 6 and 9 are denoted as 20% of the population with the highest income
Most citizens pay taxes and social contributions and receive transfers from the state. The net effect however differs. In Germany, the net transfer share of the 20% of the population with the lowest income amounts to 46% of net income. The 20% with the highest income pay out 17% of their net income
Taxes and social contributions: Income taxes and employee contributions to social insurances. Transfers: Pensions, unemployment benefits, illness and family benefits, other social benefits; Data source: Eurostat
Source Judith Niehues: Staatliche Umverteilung in der Europäischen Union, in IW Trends 1/2013

The net transfer share of the quintile with the lowest income, according to IDW data, was relatively high in Ireland, Finland, Denmark, Sweden, Germany, Belgium, the Czech Republic, Estonia, and France. It was, however, particularly low in Spain, Lithuania, Poland, Italy, and Greece. With regard to Greece, the lowest income quintile received 11.1% of their net income through transfers—this figure was 61.7% in Ireland, 45.7% in Germany, 39.8% in France, and 39.5% in the United Kingdom. The highest income quintile in the Netherlands and Denmark, on the other hand, pay 38.4% and 36.4%, respectively, of their net income in the form of taxes and social contributions, and in Germany this figure was 17.3%. The 20% share of the population with the highest incomes in France, oddly, were not net contributors—but actually received 2.6% of their net income from the state; small positive results were also observed in Cyprus and Bulgaria, where the latter employs a uniform flat tax without income exemptions.

If the EU was to play a stronger role in terms of income redistribution, it is conceivable that some common rules could be implemented, but all other individual measures could be left in the hands of national governments. Two obvious regulations which would find social consensus with regard to income redistribution measures could be the following:

- The top 20% of households in terms of income must contribute in terms of tax and social contributions (ruling out cases such as France, Cyprus, and Bulgaria).
- In every EU country, a certain level of income matching the subsistence level must be exempted from income taxes—this is a sensible rule which promotes fairness.

In the analysis of the IDW, the effects of value-added tax were ignored. For a broader more meaningful approach, however, the regressive character of such consumption taxes means that they must be included. The burden of VAT falls disproportionately on the lower income groups who show a high consumption share. Looking at value-added taxes and their effect on consumption, respectively, a comparison of the US and EU countries (undertaken by the OECD) clearly shows that effective redistribution activities in the US are not much lower than those in some EU member states. Poor households in Western Europe, which must pay high VAT rates in certain countries, involuntarily pay a substantial share of transfers received at the checkout. Moreover, it is also noteworthy that the analysis of the IDW did not take the employer share of social insurance contributions into account. From an economic perspective, this so-called employer contribution should in fact also be attributed to the employee—since at the end of the day it is the employees who must earn the entire sum (i.e., employee and employer contributions) on the market through their productivity. The incidental wage costs are part of the total employment costs from the point of view of firms.

EU Social Policy: A Starting Point and Possibilities for Reform

At the beginning of the second decade of the twenty-first century, social policy will still be a competence of the individual member states. The EU has, however, clarified that the single market does indeed have a social dimension:

- Regulations of maximum working times—namely, 48 hours per week.
- A ban on discrimination of EU citizens, that is equality of treatment for EU citizens with regard to their working lives in EU member states.
- Regulations on the equality between the sexes in the work life.
- Steps against "social dumping," which was attempted in Germany with the Posting of Workers Directive.
- The proposal of Prime Minister Cameron in 2016 and agreed with the European Commission at the start of February 2016—to impose a longer waiting time for immigrants to become entitled to claim benefits from the state—is a proposal to limit excessive demand on and large-scale migration to countries with relatively generous social systems (e.g., the UK)

- Retraining and requalification of the unemployed via the European Social Funds (circa £64/$78 billion between 2007 and 2013); certain measures funded by the EU Structural Funds are intended for regions where the per capita income is relatively low. Furthermore, there is a compensation mechanism on the basis of the EU Cohesion Funds, which provides countries with a national per capita income which is less than 90% of the EU average with money for infrastructure and environmental protection projects.
- Within the framework of a European Social Agenda, which was agreed in the year 2000 parallel to the Lisbon Strategy, a certain measure of social support was intended for the Lisbon Strategy, which was aimed at making the EU the most dynamic, knowledge-based economy in the world—against the background of partly weak politico-economic decisions, the Transatlantic Banking Crisis and, from 2009, the Euro Crisis, success was very limited.
- There is an EU globalization fund, which can be activated in the case of massive job losses in large firms.
- Regulations on workplace safety, which require safety devices and protective gear to deal with dangers in some workplaces, here there are many International Labor Organization (ILO) standards, which are, however, implemented in very different ways in individual OECD (or EU) countries. If the standards of the ILO in the course of the crisis in the Eurozone are insufficient or would be implemented worse than before, then the question could be asked whether this is a temporary phenomenon or a structural problem.

If taxpayers' money from one EU country should flow to another, which in fact happens via the EU budget, the question would be asked by the electorate whether unnecessary or unjustified transfer payments are being made. On the other hand, it should be noted that the magnitude of transfers, from Germany's perspective, is relatively manageable, as the net payments of Germany to the EU amount to about £8.5 billion ($10.4 billion) (a bit less than 0.5% of GDP) per year, which is about £105/$128 per capita per year. This is, relative to the economic advantages of European integration, a low amount, while some countries such as Sweden and the Netherlands usually pay higher per capita contributions than Germany. With a total budget of just 1% of Gross Domestic Product, the European layer is relatively modest in terms of political spending. That does not mean that this spending is efficient and related to positive economic effects. There is an analysis by Becker/Egger/Von Ehrlich (2010) which shows that about half of EU Structural Funds do not bring positive economic effects to the recipient region, and it is also conceivable that in some instances EU payments actually have negative effects as a result of rising corruption or environmentally damaging building projects.

International transfers and EU expenditures require transparency and control. The fact is that taking the relatively weak budgetary control on the side of the European Parliament and the strange agricultural domination of EU expenditures into account, it should be carefully reconsidered if an expansion of competences and spending in Brussels is advisable. The theory of subsidiarity initially supports the natural priority of national politics over the supranational layer in Brussels. However, one can warn against taking a naïve static interpretation of the principle of subsidiarity (Welfens 2014a): if more competences and expenditures are transferred to Brussels, supranational political competition will be reinforced and that would lead to a strengthened political efficiency and expenditure control. This argument is especially applicable should a Euro political union be created.

As has been discussed previously, to date the EU has only been active in selected areas. On the role of the EU with regard to social issues, insofar as it relates to social cohesion and the economic catching-up of poorer countries, the following points can be noted:

- Only if it is possible for EU policy and single market dynamics to support the economic convergence of member states—i.e., a catching-up of poorer countries in terms of per capita income—can the EU really contribute independently to the realization of a social market economy.
- The interaction of regional trade creation within the EU and strengthened direct investment by multinational firms, which can choose between various locations in the EU—with Croatia becoming the 28th member state on July 1, 2013—leads to a softening

of ILO standards. This can be assumed based on the analysis of Häberli/Jansen/Monteiro (2012). The mechanism for this can be explained, in simple terms, in that countries with relatively good location conditions benefit from not only the creation of trade but also from direct investment inflows; this forces countries with less advantageous locations or worse economic policies to relax ILO standards in order to still attract direct investment flows. In a next step, standards can also be relaxed in those countries with a good implementation of ILO standards. As the relaxing or weakening of ILO standards is, from a normative perspective, not desirable in the EU, it depends on countries with weak location conditions, in particular, to do their homework to improve their relative position—one can consider the Doing Business Indicator of the World Bank, in which Greece, for reasons it is difficult to comprehend, came in one of the last places until 2013.

• As long as the EU or individual EU member states hinder the economic catching-up processes in their own or in other EU states with policies which hamper growth and are detrimental to employment, there will be problems. Here, one could refer to certain aspects of the Euro Crisis, where the crisis management was impeded by the conditional solidarity on the part of EU partners with regard to the crisis countries. If one considers the political failures in Ireland, in terms of the non-implementation of EU regulations on banking supervision, and in Greece with regard to the deficit fraud in the election year of 2009, then one can regard the at times critical 'anti-solidarity' of Eurozone members as a specific phenomenon: Ireland had used its very low corporate tax rates to improve its position in terms of the competition for mobile capital, and then by not implementing banking supervision regulations also artificially encouraged high direct investment inflows to the banking sector—the latter, however, came to a disastrous end in 2009/10 and Ireland's deficit ratio shot up in 2010 to 31%: this was predominantly caused by the Irish government's bank rescue measures, and having lost access to international capital markets, Ireland accepted an almost £70 billion ($85.4 billion) bailout from Eurozone partner countries and the EU to save it from collapse. In spring 2009, the Greek government notified the

European Commission of a 4% deficit rate, when the actual deficit was 15.6%, which can be regarded as an attempt by a conservative government in Athens to win re-election on the basis of politically illicit and economically perilous borrowing—nevertheless, a change in government occurred. By realizing a deficit rate of 15% in one year, the government is incurring a 5-year raise in the debt ratio of 45%, assuming, on the basis of international experience, that the deficit rate can be reduced by just 3% per year. As Greece had an initial debt ratio of 110%, the actual deficit rate of circa 15% was synonymous with the short-term shutting out of the country from the international capital markets. Despite the massive political failures in Athens, Greece was provisionally saved by means of a £93 billion ($113.5 billion) loan from Eurozone countries and then a further credit of £102 billion ($124.4 billion) in 2011 plus a debt relief by private creditors of 60%—corresponding to about £90 billion ($110 billion). These two rescue operations are evidence, on one hand, of a clear expression of solidarity between Eurozone countries, on the other hand, that the gross politico-economic misconduct on the part of the Irish and Greek governments were partly rewarded and rather than a deterrent, national governments were given an implicit incentive to attempt further risky national political maneuvers at the cost of the Eurozone, EU and the IMF.

• A modern European welfare state, in a single market and a monetary union, must find an answer to the question of what competences, services, and financing possibilities should be anchored at the various policy layers. One must consider the principle of subsidiarity, but not in a static formulation. If one decides, for reasons of the efficiency of economic policy, to transfer exclusive competence with regard to cyclical economic policy in a future Euro political union to the supranational layer, then the question arises of whether the Brussels layer should not also assume part responsibility for financing unemployment insurance. The more efficient the cyclical economic policies are, the lower the expenditure on unemployment benefits would be—budget resources could then be used for political goals in the strict sense, which is a good incentive for a well-formulated cyclical policy. Thus, it is conceivable that the supranational policy layer would, at least in the short term, pay for unemployment benefits in all Eurozone countries. Here, it must be established whether the unemployment insurance can primarily be constructed and managed by collective bargaining parties, where the state must still have a right of participation. If the trade unions or collective bargaining parties, respectively, share the responsibility of the administration of the funds for unemployment insurance, then the incentive to reach wage agreements which conform to full employment is strengthened. It is worth mentioning that similar institutional structures must be realized at the national level as at the supranational level.

Looking at Brussels' government expenditure ratio, then in 2015 spending amounting to about 1% of GDP was actually carried out at the supranational policy layer. It is clear on the one hand that a lot of that money will be spent on agricultural policies—over 40% of the budget. However, relative to the government consumption rate of about 20% in EU countries, the expenditure rate is quite low. The main starting point for an anti-cyclical fiscal policy, that is the area of infrastructure expenditure in particular, is hardly present at the European level.

Justification for a Supranational Tax and Social Policy

Are there any arguments in favor of social and redistribution policies playing a role at the level of Brussels? One could first consider redistribution between member states, which could be set up as transfers which are targeted at assisting particular economic catching-up processes. Such catching-up processes are in the interests of all EU member countries, especially as increased economic cohesion reduces the political consensus costs in the EU. Countries with similarly high per capita incomes generally share common interests, unlike countries with very different per capita income levels. However, one can frame the question on the division of responsibilities more simply and in doing so form a link to the theory of fiscal federalism (Oates 1999, 2001). According to this theory, differentiated public services should be assigned or allocated to the local layer and should be financed via local taxes or charges, while defense, large infrastructure projects, and redistribution should be financed at the national layer—redistribution policies on the level of individual states in the US would be relatively inefficient, as mobile labor would lead to distortions. From the highest finance level, fiscal transfers should be made to the US states—in the Eurozone/EU, the member states—to allow the internalization of external effects (for example, transfers to Germany or the Netherlands, whose support for innovations creates substantial positive external effects on neighboring countries and stand for cross-border impulses for innovation). In this perspective, the EU or the Eurozone, or Brussels, must naturally have a much larger budget than is presently the case (just 1% of GDP). In the Eurozone, a transfer of expenditures and competences to the supranational layer could find majority support on the national level in the longer term; it would be advisable to increase the consumption ratio of Brussels to circa 6% with a focus on infrastructure, defense, energy, and the promotion and support of innovation, with a further 0.5% of GDP to finance the first 6 months of unemployment benefits (Welfens 2014a, b). It should be noted that, at the federal level, the US government has a consumption ratio of 11% and social expenditures which amount to a further 8.5% of GDP (in 2013). If one considers the government consumption ratio of 1% in Brussels, one can clearly see the complete undersizing of the expenditure ratio at the European supranational layer. If a Euro political union should achieve even one third of the expenditure of the US federal government—including social expenditures—this would represent at most the minimum government ratio for a functional Eurozone.

The argument of the principle of subsidiarity, often referenced in the debate, as a 'homeopathic' government expenditure ratio in Brussels, is completely flawed, as from a static perspective it can be determined that a 1% ratio will, in the case of ever falling voter participation in European Parliament elections, lead to ever weaker political competition in Brussels and thus to increasing inefficiency. Conversely, a substantially higher consumption ratio would naturally lead to an increase in voter participation in elections to the Parliament in Brussels; applying the theory of fiscal federalism and of a minimum efficiency of redistribution certainly leads to an optimal government expenditure ratio of at least 6%. This would only make sense in terms of a political union, which also requires the real separation of powers. The current quasi-concordance model, in which a permanent grand coalition in the European Parliament has for over a decade acted against the European Commission as law-making body (and executive), is actually unparliamentary—and not in any way comparable to Switzerland—and also plays into the hands of anti-EU political parties: voters who are not satisfied with the politics in Brussels cannot express their dissatisfaction at the ballot box by voting for a normal opposition party, instead in the longer term they are inevitably driven to the anti-EU parties on the fringes.

Moreover, one can also find arguments for supranational action by comparing the results of national redistribution and social policies: for example, in the interest of more transparency and accountability, the EU can stipulate that the national states must publish certain key figures with regard to economic policy and data on developments in terms of poverty in the member states could also be of interest to the community. Here, common policy initiatives or improved learning processes—for example, successful approaches by certain countries could be adopted by others in the medium term—could result. The EU as a community of laws could also agree on rules, which would represent an absolute imperative on member states to avoid certain undesirable developments. On the EU level, it would be wise to find a reasonable balance for increased economic freedom and safeguards for member states against international shocks. Overall, from an EU perspective, one could also stress the aspect that functioning social market economies belong to the list of political objectives and the fundamental consensus in Europe and that the EU itself wants to be successful as a Social Market Economy in the global competition of economic systems. Economic success and stability in the EU and Eurozone, respectively, are necessary conditions for success in this global competition. If the Eurozone increasingly presents itself as a sustainably integrated and stable economic area, the chances for Europe to export the model of a Social Market Economy improve. Even if the EU as whole represents a cumbersome behemoth which is politically difficult to steer, Brussels can nevertheless play an important and clear role in individual areas of social policy. In matters of redistribution policy, the supranational layer could not play much of a role beyond certain transfers within the EU. However, the question must be raised of what could justify redistribution activities. With regard to tackling high unemployment rates, the EU could require that every country with an unemployment rate of above 6% must invest at least 10% of state payments of unemployment benefits in the area of active labor market policies, the exact details could be determined by each country on an individual basis.

It cannot be ruled out that via increased regional integration, the income differentials within the member countries of the integration club could rise. From a theoretical perspective (here the Stolper–Samuelson Theorem), that depends in the tradable goods sector on how the relative prices develop. If the price of cars falls due to integration, then the remuneration of factors of production intensively employed in the automobile sector will decrease—that would primarily affect unskilled labor (excluding luxury car manufacturing). If, at the same time, the price of software for business enterprises would rise—here involving skilled labor—then the remuneration of skilled labor would rise. Structural change, integration, and wage differentials could interact. Moreover, rising incomes in the integration area could lead to increased immigration from third countries. If the migration of low-skilled workers rises and this leads to a medium-term increase in the availability of unskilled labor, then (according to the Rybczynski theorem) this will raise the production of economic activities which depend relatively heavily on low-skilled workers. Regional economic integration must not necessarily be to the detriment of low-skilled workers. Furthermore, it is up to the state, employees, and firms to influence and improve the qualifications structure, including by means of training and further education measures.

In the following compacted argument, a possible income inequality plays a role in the real world. However, in reality, one must note that poverty in old age is not the result of differences in income between households of pensioners or between average pensioner household and the workforce, respectively. There is, of course, also the dimension of assets and wealth, where the configuration of an owner-occupied property and low income can be classed differently to a pension household in rented accommodation and a low income or a low-income household without any property. In its study, "Growing Unequal?" (OECD 2008), the OECD stressed that the question of inequality is not limited to the matter of income. Public services in health and education may also be effective in reducing inequality (in relation to tuition fees, however, the state is required to consider behavior incentives and control effects: if one could, on the basis of an optimization model developed by students and universities, reduce study time by 10%, it would have the effect of one-tenth more fully staffed universities; conversely, the nationwide German elimination of tuition fees is problematic, insofar as it created 'access barriers' to the university system, but the emerging apparent prolongation of studying time does not necessarily result in equal opportunities and does not represent an optimal usage of scarce resources by the younger generation). The OECD found that income inequality has grown significantly in the US, Canada, Germany, Norway, Italy, and Finland since 2000—the average increase in inequality is about 2% in terms of the so-called GINI coefficient on income inequality, circa 1.5% in terms of the poverty rate (with the poverty line being 50% of the median income—meaning 50% of households are above this value, and 50% below). In Mexico, Australia, Greece, and the United Kingdom, the income inequality had fallen. Furthermore, income poverty in the older generation had reduced, while the poverty among young adults and families with children had increased. The poverty rate among jobless households is about six times as high as that in households with workers, which makes the labor market, and the taking-up of gainful employment, an important tool in combatting poverty.

From a philosophical perspective, one justification for the welfare state and redistribution, respectively, can be found by referring to Rawls (1971), who argued that one could imagine a hypothetical natural state, in which people are not aware of their later social position. For what policy principles could a majority be found? In such a decision-making situation, individuals could decide on desirable or preferable social policies. In the concept of justice proposed by Rawls, the characteristic is access for all people in the country to public offices and economic inequalities should be accepted, insofar as these also contribute to an improvement of the economic situation of the poorest—such an approach could, in fact, be capable of attaining majority support in the Rawlsian state of nature. The constitutional foundations of democratic voting rules mean that in reality a certain tendency exists for the relatively poor majority of the population to bring about a major redistribution at the expense of the wealthier minority. A certain level of redistribution via the taxation and social insurance systems is presumably desired by almost all people and many are prepared to pay taxes and contributions in order that poverty can be tackled by the state. The question remains, of course, of how one can find a reasonable balance in taxation and social policies, and this actually requires a triple balance:

- The tax system should generally not undermine production and performance incentives, that is tax rates significantly above 50% could be regarded as particularly problematic.
- The tax system should adequately internalize or tax negative external effects and in doing so repress the relevant production or consumption activity which is damaging to third parties—this involves Pigovian and environmental taxes (which generate circa 5% of revenues in some OECD countries, such as Denmark and the Netherlands, about 2% in Germany, and 1% in the US)—and simultaneously positive external effects, for example entrepreneurial innovation activities should be internalized via subventions. A simple optimal tax system could work in such a way that the revenues from Pigovian taxes aimed at internalizing negative external effects could be just enough to also finance innovation subsidies.
- From an efficiency perspective, the tax system should be so designed that the relation between marginal tax revenues and marginal tax collection costs for all types of taxes is the same. As a rule, Pigovian taxes will not be sufficient to finance state expenditures, thus further taxes will be required.
- One can also note a further starting point for optimal taxation which comes from neoclassical growth theory. According to this, the tax rate should be chosen so that in the long-term equilibrium, real growth equals the sum of the rate of population growth and technological

progress; as then the equilibrium capital intensity (machine use per capita) will be realized, which maximizes long-term per capita consumption. While the state adjusts the income tax rate or the value-added tax rate accordingly, optimum utility will be achieved—in the assumption that only per capita consumption enters the utility function.

Provided that integration leads to increased income inequality and particularly to a reduction of the real income of the lower strata, it must be considered—at least following Rawls—that the EU could also be active here in terms of income redistribution. Insofar as the EU levies a surcharge on national income tax, this could also take place on a differentiated basis in each case. That incentives for investment, education, and work should not be weakened by redistribution policy is self-evident. As the state is very active in the education sector of most EU countries and because education is key to gainful employment and social advancement, the state could tie redistribution to conditions regarding education and training. With regard to children from low-income families, particular attention should be paid to early and high-quality schooling which lays the intellectual foundations for advancement and the equality of opportunity.

The factor of capital can certainly increase its share of income in the early twenty-first century, as the expansion of Information and Communication Technologies facilitates an increased international spatial splitting-up of value-added and production activities, which increases capital mobility, which in turn entails a higher pressure on policymakers to reduce the tax rates on corporate profits. The real tax burden on labor then increases.

Fair Taxation

To date, many capital gains which accrue abroad are often inadequately taxed, which is a problem from the point of view of fairness or justice; moreover, this treatment can be divided analytically between EU countries and non-EU countries. Within the EU, problems of irregular taxation caused by political treaties between countries have been avoided or eliminated through reporting regulations and practical advances in data acquisition. Here, steps were agreed by the EU countries in 2013, such that one can expect a more uniform raising of taxes, primarily with regard to capital income; this still does not mean a general harmonization of tax rates in the EU. The minute taxation of Apple in Ireland—with an effective tax rate of less than 0.1%—was investigated by the European Commission in 2016 and the artificially low tax levied by the Irish state was deemed to be a form of illegal subsidy or state aid. According to the Commission, Apple should make a back payment of £11 billion ($13.4 billion).

What cannot be overlooked, however, is that there is also inconsistent taxation in, for example, Germany related to the fiscal equalization mechanism between federal states. Basically, one can assume that federal states that are net contributors to this mechanism have less of an interest in the normal raising of taxes, as they would fear that additional revenues raised through improved taxation practices will primarily go to benefit recipient states. Paradoxically, in the net recipient federal states, there is also a latent interest in less than thorough tax collection—as it is easier and cheaper to receive transfers from the net contributor federal states, than to collect higher taxes oneself. One example of this kind of negative solidarity in terms of the fiscal equalization mechanism is the federal state of Bremen, which despite supplementary federal grants has undertaken hardly any active measures to reduce its own high structural deficit ratio. From this German experience, it follows that a European fiscal equalization measure, should such a mechanism be implemented, would be connected with induced tax-raising inefficiencies and negative incentives, respectively. This consideration is not necessarily an argument against a fiscal equalization mechanism within the European Monetary Union, for example, but one should organize such a mechanism with sound judgment and a critical view of the incentive effects.

On the question of whether the globalization of economic relations leads to a reduction of the corporate income tax rates or of income tax relative to GDP or of value-added/consumption tax rates, Becker/Elsayyad/Fuest (2012) arrived at some curious findings: according to their study, globalization did not contribute significantly to reductions in tax rates nor of the share of value-added tax, corporate income tax, and personal income tax revenues, respectively. While the study is an empirical analysis, it is in fact an example of a questionable "measurement without theory," that is regression calculations without a theoretical foundation. As the authors do not seem to have a theoretical basis, it escapes them entirely that the tax revenue rates of both personal income and corporate income tax are not independent of the relationship between value-added taxes and GDP, and thus it is not a valid econometric approach if separate estimations for personal income tax, consumption tax, and corporate income tax relative to GDP are presented. Here, there are basic interdependencies which should be taken into account (Welfens 2013):

> The share of corporate income tax, over the period from 1970 to 2007, has in the case of large OECD countries remained relatively stable at 2.5%, in the case of small counties it has risen until 2007 to about 4%. If one assumes that corporations account for 60% of firm profits, where the latter amounts to on average 33% relative to gross domestic product of OECD countries, then on the basis of a corporate income tax rate of 20%, this would result in revenue relative to gross domestic product of 0.6 x 0.33 x 0.20 = 0.0396 or 4%, and with a tax rate of 25% a relation of revenue from corporate income tax to gross domestic product of 4.95%. It should be noted that capital is also subjected to trade taxes and, furthermore, that a certain amount of tax competition in the EU is important in order to have an efficient tax structure and for the state to have such an extent that it bring coherence to public wishes and efficiency.

High rates of social security contributions raise—almost independently of what percentage division one takes for "employee contributions" and "employer contributions"—incidental wage costs and reduce the demand for labor of firms (the actual division of employee and employer contributions is only relevant insofar as tax effects result on the side of the workforce or firms; if employees can deduct contributions to social security from gross income, then with rising contributions to social insurance there is a fiscally beneficial effect in terms of personal income tax). That raises the unemployment rate, which in turn weakens the aggregate demand in the economy.

If, as in the Scandinavian countries, one realizes a relatively high value-added tax rate, in order to finance social security with part of the revenue from consumption, then the main effect is a rise in the prices of consumption goods, which reduces consumer demand. With a given production quantity (i.e., a given amount of goods produced), net exports of goods will rise, which in a small open economy appears as simply the difference between production and domestic demand (the sum of consumption of private households, government demand, and investment demand). However, a higher value-added tax rate also fuels the growth of the shadow economy, or black market, which is problematic.

A very high expansion of social policy, relative to EU partner countries, can clearly not be sustainably realized. In any case, rising social security rates resulting from a higher social expenditure in an aging society should be a reason to reduce the pressure caused by such a rise through increased immigration, a rise in the retirement age or higher tax subsidies. Moreover, the most important protection against poverty in old age is a good education and full employment. The expected security of future state pensions depends on the rating of government debt. AAA indicates a high level of security vis-à-vis pensions; from experience, one can say that in times of financial crisis, a reduction of pension payments is a standard tactic in bitter reforms. The logic of political economy is such that politicians know that the power of pensioners is limited (except for during election years). Pensioners, unlike workers, cannot strike.

The EU single market allows considerable leeway in terms of government expenditure rates and national social expenditure rates or the extent of services, respectively. If a Euro political union should be introduced, the vertical division of policy competences must be reconsidered. Thus, not only must the rule of subsidiarity be taken into consideration in a meaningful way and incentive effects also be kept in mind, but, naturally, different political preferences too. Furthermore, political legitimacy and the (marginal) tax collection costs must also figure in deliberations. However, it is also obvious that a government expenditure ratio of over 50%—as is the case in France—is very problematic.

Social Dimension of a Euro Political Union

If one establishes a political union, then on the one hand cyclical economic policy and growth policy must be firmly embedded in the supranational level, on the other hand, social and redistribution policies too, as well as deposit protection for large banks—with complementary national policy fields. With the banking union, in 2014 the EU transferred responsibility for microprudential banking supervision with regard to individual large banks to the ECB, at the same time setting up a liability fund consisting of contributions from the banks themselves amounting to £47 billion ($57.3 billion) in the long term, and defined a liability cascade for a threatened case of bankruptcy, which should spare taxpayers as much as possible.

Every member state in the Eurozone must establish a settlement mechanism for banks near to bankruptcy, where the supervision of major banks (on a "microprudential" basis, i.e., tailored to individual banks) is a competence of the ECB. The ECB also engages in macroprudential supervision with respect to systemic risks, which a division of the ECB—the European Systemic Risk Board—oversees. This macroprudential supervision is difficult, as the ECB analysis must tie together the interactions of banking developments, economic policy, and international shocks—had this existed and worked effectively in 2006/07, the collapse of the US investment bank Lehman Brothers would have been obvious early enough so that OECD countries could have implemented countermeasures in terms of economic policy. That the leading bank and credit rating agencies were still giving Lehman Brothers the top AAA rating just one week before its bankruptcy shows that banking supervision had not truly functioned. Major banks in the US and Europe hoped until autumn 2008 that they would be 'too big to fail' and therefore would always be rescued by the state. That the bankruptcy of a large bank like Lehman Brothers affects small investors, i.e. those who possessed Lehman Brothers bonds, is clear. Sound banking supervision is in part also an element of social policy in a monetary economy. Bank customers, and in the end also depositors and clients in the banking system as whole, should be able to trust in the stability of the system itself. Here, one could mention additional tax-related rational-ity incentives for more long-term investment strategies on the part of banks (Welfens 2012): alongside a reduction in the taxation of profits, the fluctuation or variation intensities of returns on equity should also be taxed; that would lead to more long-term and sound expansion strat-egies by the banks and a more stable economy overall.

Risks from banks in southern Europe and Ireland could still have a substantial effect of Eurozone countries such as Germany and France in the medium term—how old risks have been dealt with is not yet entirely clear, so that there could be hidden distribution effects within the banking union. On the other hand, the journey towards a bank-ing union is a necessary one, whereas an independent banking super-vision—outside the ECB—would be desirable. It is clear that a banking crisis could have large-scale distribution effects. In Italy, the state attempted in 2016 to participate in the rescue of a major bank from Siena which was facing the threat of bankruptcy—despite criticism from the EU—because it was assumed that many small and medium enterprises, as well as private individuals, held bonds of the bank in question. In the event of urgent restructuring involving share-holders, depositors, and the bondholders, significant hardships for individual investors would come to pass. The view of the European Commission, which, having learned a lesson from the Banking Crisis, wanted to avoid a situation that a massive amount of public funds would flow into ailing banks, fell on deaf ears.

In terms of redistribution policies, at the supranational level, a deter-mination of the fundamentals of a sound redistribution should be estab-lished; without EU treaty changes, however, only recommendations can be made by Brussels—a general recommendation that redistribution should not be to the benefit of the top 20% on the income pyramid should find consensus (cases such as France, Bulgaria, and Cyprus in 2009 would not recur). Moreover, a certain amount of intergovernmen-tal transfer policy with careful success monitoring could be carried out via the Structural Funds. The aim of social policy is the establishment of social standards (at least a minimum standard) such as the payment of unemployment benefit from Brussels for the first six months—EU countries then retain the necessary incentive to enact and implement smart policies aimed at avoiding longer spells of unemployment—in particular longer than a year. Furthermore, this is also the location of a temporary activation of globalization funds and a special fund against youth unemployment. The responsibility of every EU or Eurozone country with regard to developments in terms of unemployment in the respective countries cannot be undermined; however, a stark rise of youth unemployment in EU countries is a problem which could be considered as important and directly relevant to the interests of the entire community, as long as an excessive national minimum wage policy has not artificially raised the youth unemployment rate.

Finally, the openness of national social security systems is absolutely to be guaranteed, otherwise efficiency losses will occur and the freedom of movement undermined; here there are quite substantial barriers in EU member states. It is quite complicated to register for social insurance in a neighboring EU country. Thanks to modern computer systems and compatible software—which is currently lacking in terms of the social security providers of EU countries—this should not be a problem in European countries. It should also be clarified how long it makes sense for EU citizens to have to wait to receive minimum entitlements after commencing work in another EU country: such rules mean that only after first working and making social security contributions in a state for a minimum number of years (for example, seven years or so) would one be entitled to receive a pension or some other services from the state's social security system. In an extreme case, someone who has worked and contributed social security contributions over 25 years in 25 different EU member states, working one year in each, may retire with no pension entitlement from any of the countries whatsoever. That would be unfair, and indeed absurd. It would be appropriate that EU citizens should receive a single EU social security number, under which all contributions in various countries would be recorded. One could easily develop a system which would cumulate the standard entitlements received in various countries in a sensible way. To this end, the necessary regulations and laws must be passed in all EU countries.

All of the measures suggested here could be implemented without the need for changing the EU treaties; but rather via better cooperation between the member states themselves. A European Social Market

Economy (see Fig. 15.1 for a suggested structure), which must naturally define logical policy fields for the national and regional policy layers, is therefore possible. A limited but justified strengthening of the centralized layer in Brussels with a clear government expenditure ratio and defined responsibilities can make the EU and the Eurozone, respectively, fully functional. If there were to be a supranational minimum income tax rate, then more fiscal justice, meaning fair taxation, would be provided for, as one could less easily escape being taxed on the supranational layer than on the national level. At the same time, in a political union—as on the national level—a broad income concept could be used as a basis for taxation, which would allow relatively low tax rates, therefore causing lower negative effects on the production side.

In a Euro political union, the government consumption rate would rise in Brussels, while at the national level of member states—each

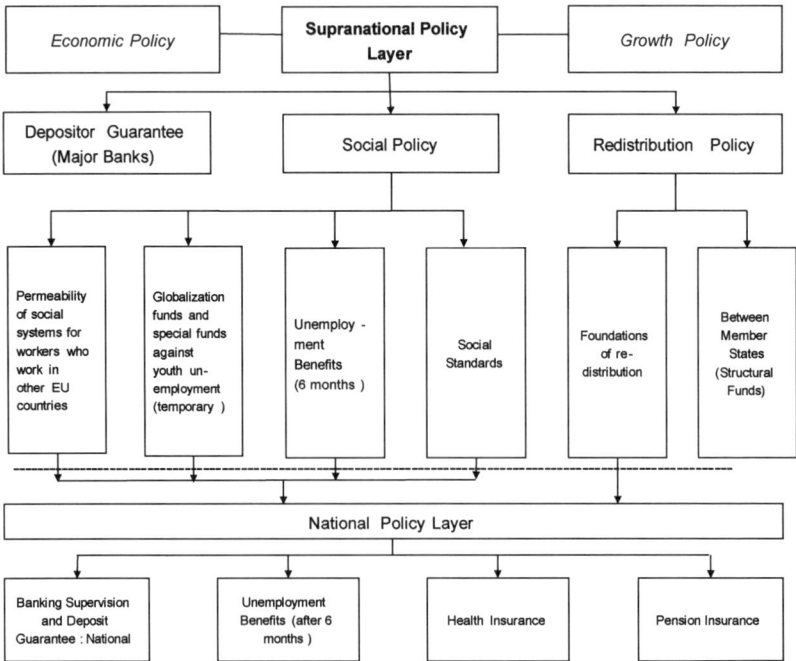

Fig. 15.1 The social dimension in a political union

relative to GDP—consumption rates could be reduced. The expenditure ratio across all vertical policy layers could be lower in a political union as in the old EU. At the supranational level, there are opportunities to realize efficiency gains, for example in common procurement programs in the area of defense. One could, however, be skeptical that details of the budget in Brussels would be sufficiently transparent. With transparency and intelligent incentive mechanisms, it should, however, be possible to limit the squandering of tax money at the supranational level.

If it should come to a redistribution to the benefit of poor households in the Eurozone within the framework of a progressive income tax system in Brussels, the southern European countries would profit, because in those countries a high share—relative to the Eurozone as a whole—of poor households are located. However, because of the low per capita income relative to France or Germany, a North–South transfer on reasonable terms—within a common framework tax system—could result in redistribution within the Eurozone. If there should be a common tax revenue, then it is also worth considering that with a generally progressive income tax system in the EU, the faster growing catching-up countries would contribute disproportionately more to marginal income tax growth. An EU or Eurozone, which cannot realize a reasonably dimensioned budget in Brussels, will not be capable of asserting itself as an independent actor in the globalization of the twenty-first century—an EU which is incapable of acting and with a miniscule budget will be left in the wake of the US, Russia, and China. With a larger budget, the political competition in Brussels will be invigorated.

References

Barrell, R., & Pain, N. (1997). Foreign direct investment, technological change, and economic growth within Europe. *The Economic Journal, 107,* 1770–1786.
Becker, S. O., Egger, P., & Von Ehrlich, M. (2010). Going NUTS: The effects of EU structural funds on regional performance. *Journal of Public Economics, 94,* 578–590.

350   P.J.J. Welfens

Becker, J., Elsayyad, M., & Fuest, C. (2012). Auswirkungen der Globalisierung auf die Struktur der Besteuerung, *Perspektiven der Wirtschaftspolitik, Bd. 13*, 4–18.

Brücker, H. (2013). *Auswirkungen der Einwanderung auf Arbeitsmarkt und Sozialstaat: Neue Erkenntnisse und Schlussfolgerungen für die Einwanderungspolitik*. Gütersloh: Bertelsmann Foundation.

Deaton, A. (2013). *The Great Escape: Health, Wealth and the Origins of Inequality* Princeton: Princeton University Press.

Dolls, M. et al. (2014). *An unemployment insurance scheme for the Euro area? A comparison of different alternatives using micro data, ZEW* (Discussion Paper No. 14-095). Mannheim.

Domar, E. D. (1944). The burden of debt and national income. *American Economic Review, 34*, 798–827.

European Central Bank. (2013). The Eurosystem Household Finance and Consumption Survey, Results from the First Wave, Statistics Paper Series 2, April.

European Commission. (2014). *Employment and social developments in Europe 2013*. Brussels: European Union.

European Commission. (2016). Standard-Eurobarometer 85 – Spring 2016 (May) "Public Opinion in the European Union, First Results", Brussels.

Häberli, C., Jansen, M., & Monteiro, J.-A. (2012). *Regional trade agreements and domestic labour market regulation*, Employment Working Paper No. 120, ILO, 11 May 2012.

Jaumotte, F., Lall, S., & Papageorgiou, C. (2008). *Rising income inequality: Technology, or trade and financial globalization*, IMF (Working Paper WP/08/185). Washington DC.

Niehues, J. (2013). Staatliche Umverteilung in der Europäischen Union, in: IW-Trends 1/2013.

Oates, W. E. (1999). An essay on fiscal federalism. *Journal of Economic Literature, 37*, 1120–1149.

Oates, W. E. (2001). Fiscal competition and european union: Contrasting perspectives. *Regional Science and Urban Economics, 31*, 133–145.

OECD. (2008). *Growing unequal?. Income distribution and poverty in OECD countries* Paris: OECD Publishing.

OECD. (2016). *The economic consequences of Brexit: A taxing decision, OECD economic policy paper, No. 16*. Paris: OECD Publishing.

PEW. (2014). *Attitudes about aging: A global perspective*. Washington DC.

Piketty, T. (2014). *Capital in the twenty-first Century*. Cambridge, MA: Harvard University Press.

Rawls, J. (1971). *A theory of justice.* Cambridge: Harvard University Press/ Belknap.

US Council of Economic Advisers. (2016). *Economic report of the President (2016).* Washington DC.

von Alemann, U., Dreyer, D., & Hummel, H. (2013). *Demokratische Mitgestaltung und soziale Sicherheit. FINE-Gutachten zur Politischen Union* [Expert Report for the Minister of Federal Affairs, Europe and Media]. North Rhine-Westphalia, Düsseldorf.

Von Alemann, U. et al. (Ed.). (2015). *Ein Soziales Europa ist möglich.* Wiesbaden: Springer VS.

Welfens, P. J. J. (2012). *Die Zukunft des Euro.* Berlin: Nicolai.

Welfens, P. J. J. (2013). *Social security and economic globalization.* Heidelberg: Springer.

Welfens, P. J. J. (2014a). *Overcoming the EU crisis and prospects for a political union.* Paper presented at the bdvb reseach institute/EIIW conference 'Overcoming the Euro Crisis', March, 2014, in *International Economics and Economic Policy, Vol. 13, Issue 1, 2016.*

Welfens, P. J. J. (2014b). Nationale und grenzübergreifende Kindergeldzahlungen Deutschlands: ein Reformvorschlag auf Kaufkraftparitätenbasis, EIIW Press Release, May 14, 2014. www.eiiw.eu.

16

Conclusions

The point I have to say is that in Britain, honestly,
the debate for Europe is not yet won.
President of the European Commission Manuel Barroso, following Tony Blair's
last visit to Brussels as British Prime Minister, June 2007

A sense that politics shouldn't be so different from the rest of life, where rational
people do somehow find a way of overcoming their disagreements.
Prime Minister David Cameron in his keynote address at the 2010
Conservative Party Conference, Birmingham.

The United Kingdom's EU referendum of 2016 was not an orderly
political event, but was in fact deeply mismanaged from an information perspective by the Cameron government. This mismanagement is
what is largely to blame for the ultimate artificial Brexit majority. The
correct result would have been a Remain majority and one must wonder why the United Kingdom should build its strategic policy for the
twenty-first century upon the wrong political outcome. To avoid disorderly referenda in the EU in the future, the European Commission
should make proposals regarding minimum quality requirements in
EU-related referenda being held in EU member countries: historical

© The Author(s) 2017
P.J.J. Welfens, *An Accidental Brexit*,
DOI 10.1007/978-3-319-58271-9_16

decisions will obviously require a minimum lead time in the field of household information provided by government and other institutions active in the referendum. There should be a Ministry nominated where the Minister of the day is personally responsible for the swift organization of the referendum and meeting the minimum requirements. An effective, independent 'Referendum Commission'—following the Irish model—would also be a useful element to be considered.

It is not surprising that the large devaluation of the Pound in 2016/17 goes along with considerable growth, since a real devaluation will stimulate net exports of goods and services—with a certain delay—and because the nominal devaluation will bring about an unanticipated rise of the inflation rate and therefore will help to raise employment temporarily through a reduction of the real wage rate. Considerable problems will emerge in 2019, however, when the United Kingdom could actually leave the European Union and face much more restricted access to the EU single market. Output growth in the UK is expected to be lower than in the European Union and the Eurozone, respectively—at least if several key EU countries adopt timely economic reforms:

- Greece needs a new and better constitution: one that, for example, makes it impossible for politicians to simply put the head of the national statistical office before a court for work-related matters; and many other improvements seem to be necessary in Greece.
- Germany should focus on reducing its very high current account–Gross Domestic Product (GDP) ratio, which for several years has exceeded the critical 6% ratio fixed in the new stability benchmarks of the European Union. Higher private investment in combination with tax incentives for workers to buy stock index papers could be useful since a rise of the investment ratio and higher consumption in the medium term (partly linked to low-taxed capital gains) could help to reduce the net export–GDP ratio.
- Italy faces major problems with regard to raising productivity and growth, and this is partly due to insufficient inflows of multinational companies' foreign direct investment (FDI). The fact that almost

60% of students in Italy do not finish their studies points to serious problems in human capital formation and higher education, respectively. Italy also suffers from an insufficient creation of domestic multinational companies that would contribute to higher growth rates of real gross national product, namely via higher profits accruing to foreign subsidiaries. Labor market reforms also seem to be quite important—the Renzi government had made some progress in this field.

- France is also facing problems in the education system and a lack of vocational training dynamics as well as an excessive—nationally uniform—minimum wage rate. A sustained high youth unemployment rate in France, and in any other EU member country, is a dangerous and potentially destabilizing, element.
- Considerable corruption in several EU countries should be addressed.
- There is a broad lack of understanding of what digital globalization really means: here the EU should create new venture capital market sources and the European Union should also consider adopting an increasingly truly global digital expansion and regulation approach. There is not much to be gained if the EU would develop specific EU regulations on the Internet, while the US or China employ and enforce totally different rules. Moreover, much more digital benchmarking is needed in the EU. Compared to the leading economy in the Organisation for Economic Co-operation and Development (OECD), Canada, EU countries are way behind (OECD 2014) in the field of finding new jobs through digital matching technologies—and at the very bottom of the table one finds countries like Italy, Spain, and Greece. A comparative digital table should recall these critical findings (with updated technology) every few weeks. The national governments of EU countries should consider adopting detailed plans to improve labor market matching via "trusted" digital projects.
- The EU27 countries should give the UK a second opportunity, namely for a new referendum on EU membership. If the UK would not consider to organize a new referendum, the United Kingdom itself might well break apart. Scotland could leave in the context of a hard Brexit. This, in turn, would lead to a break-up of the Conservative Party in the UK. If Scotland would subsequently rejoin

the EU as an independent country, this would bring the number of EU countries to 29, namely if independence dynamics would also bring about an independent Catalonia. This might destabilize Spain and the EU, respectively. The EU has enough problems with the challenge of reforming the institutions and developing reforms for the Eurozone in particular.

- A hard Brexit might, in combination with Trump's political victory in the US, reinforce the new bilateralism of the United States—and beyond. An expansion of bilateralism is rather dangerous for EU integration and the European Union, respectively. The very idea of the EU is to create a joint policy club and to rely on international institutions. Trump's bilateralism is not supportive of the EU or the World Trade Organization (WTO).

The key slogan of the latter organization should not be forgotten: 'To make the small big and the big civilized.' If, however, there would be an expansion of bilateralism, regional integration schemes would disintegrate and new trade wars might unfold—leading to lower trade dynamics and economic welfare losses. A destabilization of the EU will be to the disadvantage of the UK—the country would likely have to raise the military expenditure–GDP ratio which implies a reduction of the consumption–income ratio. Moreover, a less stable EU implies lower output growth and hence a higher long-term immigration pressure on the UK. Europe might end up in a modified late nineteenth-century setting, except for the new element of China which will, together with the US, be a co-leader of the world economy.

The European Union might be too timid in its reform which would imply that primarily the US and China would shape the twenty-first century—including the shaping of global and regional economic and political rules. The only option for the EU to avoid disintegration and a long-term decline is to become more active in the fields of EU reforms and enhanced cooperation with other regional integration schemes, for example, with Mercosur in Latin America or with the Association of Southeast Asian Nations (ASEAN) countries. Given the sustained emigration pressure from Africa, the EU might also want to consider more trade liberalization with the continent. Stabilizing Africa without a multilateral approach and international organizations, respectively, is impossible. The EU27 should thus put pressure on both the UK and the US to remain fully engaged in multilateralism. It will remain a challenge for the EU27/EU28 to avoid growing income disparities. An active labor market policy can be a useful element since this instrument can effectively help to compensate losers from regional integration and globalization, respectively. Vocational training in Germany is excellent in many regions and what will be important for the future is to forge links between top researchers, high-skilled workers, and entrepreneurs. To nurture broad human capital formation and education, respectively, will be a decisive challenge in the European Union. It seems doubtful that the EU could survive if the community would not become more active as a regional trade facilitation agency and network operator that links various integration clubs with each other. In the end, the European Commission should be replaced with an EU government, which is given strong responsibilities, and the European Parliament should get a much bigger role compared to what it has at present. The willingness of EU citizens to consider stronger integration might be reinforced by the Trump administration's policy style and policy content. It does not seem to be realistic to get Turkey on board as a reliable partner in the EU; however, the European Union should try to establish good relations with Turkey in a broader and rather modest integration framework.

Regional integration of the US–Mexican style—in the North American Free Trade Agreement (NAFTA)—is not a good example for the EU. It is remarkable that despite large-scale Mexican emigration to the US and trade creation between Mexico and the US/Canada, plus high Mexican FDI inflows from the US, the Mexican–US wage gap has hardly reduced over time. This is not what economic theory would let economists expect (Bazillier et al. 2017). Normally, Mexican wages should clearly increase rather quickly over time and the Mexican–US wage gap would be reduced in the medium term and in the long run, respectively. If US multinationals' FDI in Mexico mean that firms can replace well-paid US automotive workers through low-paid Mexican workers in the US subsidiaries in Mexico, there would be a problem in the sense that this is not only a strange situation for Mexico but also that the main effect of the relocation of plants from the US to Mexico is to reduce wages in the US while raising the profit rates of US investors in Mexico. In such a strange setup, it is fairly obvious that a key side effect of more US FDI outflows to Mexico is simply to reduce US goods prices—equivalent to a modest US real income gain—and to strongly increase profits of US firms and capital income in the US, respectively: "regional globalization" is raising US inequality in a crucial way and the enormous profits of US firms abroad—whether obtained in Mexico or Ireland—are rarely taxed. Why is there no closing of the Mexican–US wage gap? Part of the answer is that the economic success of Mexico in attracting high FDI inflows amounts to a message to even poorer people in Latin America to migrate to Mexico: for every Mexican emigrant to the US, there are new Latin American emigrants who want to go to Mexico; and possibly move further North towards the US at some point in the future. The role of China should also be included.

Whether US firms have an adequate strategy to involve workers in ways that help with the training or retraining of US employees seems not to be fully clear. From an EU perspective, it is important to encourage the gradual catching-up processes of Eastern European countries. Trade, FDI dynamics, and more innovation in these countries are crucial for catching-up and effective institutions as well. There must be an institutional framework to achieve some cohesion in the EU in an efficient way, and the training and retraining of workers must be a key element of economic policy. Encouraging unskilled labor to engage in training and retraining could be a useful element for micro-integration dynamics in the EU and hence a rise of human capital in the respective country. There is no need to be pessimistic, but it is useful to carefully study important international key effects from integration and globalization dynamics.

With the enormous economic rise of China in the early twenty-first century, it is clear that a rational policy approach in matters of international stabilization is the increasing cooperation among the big countries USA, EU27/UK, Japan, China and Russia. With Brexit, the Group of Eight (G8) cooperation in terms of economic stabilization policy becomes more complex or less complete if one would exclude the UK. EU27 is 18% smaller in GDP terms without the UK and indeed Brexit also means that the EU's population will decline by about 13%. It is very important to carefully reconsider the Brexit issue; one should, of course, not rule out that a new referendum would simply confirm the results of the referendum of 2016. If, however, the decision made in a new referendum results in a majority for Remain, a neo-EU will have to be constructed anyway.

After Brexit: Perspectives on EU–UK and EU27–US Relations

What will happen after Brexit in terms of the politico-economic relations between the EU27 and the UK? The EU27 would consider the UK to be part of its neighborhood policy and could try to organize various fields of economic, political, and military cooperation. It is as yet unclear what position the UK will take after 2019 if Brexit is indeed fully implemented. To some extent it is in the British interest to have a stable EU27 group; however, the ratio of UK GDP to EU27 GDP will be 1:4 and this means that the bargaining position of the United Kingdom is not very advantageous. As regards British influence in the EU, the British situation would be much better if the UK would be a member country of the European Union. However, this is not what Brexit means. Hence, the UK's interest is to forge a strong political alliance with those countries that share a rather liberal economic approach; in this context, Denmark, the Netherlands, Luxembourg, and Germany are the key options. This, however, leaves out the question of what institutional setting could be developed for post-Brexit UK–EU relations?

The UK could rejoin the European Free Trade Area (EFTA)—with the other member states being Norway, Iceland, Liechtenstein, and Switzerland—and then join the European Economic Area which has no supranational policy dimension and where disputes are resolved by the EFTA Court of Justice for EFTA countries and by the European Court of Justice for EU countries (the two courts try to develop a mutual consistency in their verdicts). The European Economic Area option does, however, not allow the UK to avoid accepting free labor migration and the UK would also have to implement EU single market rules without having a seat at the Commission table in Brussels. The UK could consider the Swiss–EU cooperation framework as a preferred model for shaping UK–EU relations. However, one may argue that this framework contains some haphazard elements which emerged in the shadow of the negative Swiss referendum on joining the European Economic Area in 1992; in particular, there is the problem of a lack of any rule about which Court is supposed to settle legal disputes in the field of services (Müller-Graff 2016). This suggests that the UK and the EU would have to work out a special legal framework for court decisions and this would take quite some time.

It is not possible for the UK to leave the EU after more than four decades without lengthy negotiations and certain interim agreements, and this implies considerable uncertainty for investors in the UK; particularly for foreign investors interested in knowing the UK's future access to the EU. The UK is likely to suffer from a long-term reduction of foreign direct investment inflows and it has already become apparent in early 2017 that many Japanese investors with activities in the UK are screening Germany, France, and the Netherlands as future preferred investor locations for getting full access to the EU single market. Besides the economic aspects and infrastructure questions—including the availability of international schools and universities with English Bachelor and Master Degree programs—most foreign investors are interested in tax issues and in the topic of security. The latter aspect potentially makes Belgium and France less attractive as new locations for Asian and US investors interested in full access to the EU single market. Some London banking activities, dominated by foreign subsidiaries in the UK with a focus on the EU single market, will go to Ireland, Germany, and France. As US firms and banks with activities in the UK are some of the international companies considering the relocation of production and services provision to the EU27, it will be interesting to see to what extent US firms will raise their voices in Washington DC in order to discourage the Trump administration from destabilizing the EU. If the EU27 should largely disintegrate, the bargaining advantage which some representatives of the Trump administration seems to expect from bilateralism in Europe will often be clearly outweighed by the negative economic regional dynamics linked to EU disintegration.

One can only warn the UK and the US that a destabilization of the EU27 will have global spillover effects, including disintegration dynamics in ASEAN and Mercosur and some other regional integration clubs as well.

With the UK's wish to leave the European Union, one will witness difficult negotiations about the legacy costs of British civil servants working in EU institutions and the costs of programs in which the UK is formally involved until 2020. The UK might face considerable exit costs—payments of £25.5–£42.5 billion (i.e., $31–$51 billion)—equivalent to about 1–2% of GDP alone and on top of this there will be the long-term real income losses of about 6% and the non-realization of the benefits of a deepening of the EU28 single market. In the end, several EU–UK agreements could be reached which would, however, ultimately be costly for both the UK and the EU27. The new EU could become more protectionist and, with a protectionist Trump administration in the US, one may indeed find more protectionist policies in almost all Western countries. As Ryan (2016) has noted, there are no new economic theories that would support the Leave position. One may add that in many Western OECD countries, there is an increasing desire to get quick and simple answers for established, as well as more recent, problems. Western democracies are weakened by the radicalism apparent on the Internet and indeed the Internet allows small, radical groups to muster some level of visible support via digital social networks much more easily and quickly than was previously possible. With a stronger ideological antagonism—and a revival of quasi-religious fervor in political debates—achieving compromise becomes much more difficult than in the pre-Internet age. Since democracies need political compromises in many fields, the Internet seems to undermine modern democracy.

At the bottom line, this could contribute to a new wave of autocratic policies in Western nations, while the expansion of radical Islamist groups in parts of the Muslim world also raises concerns about cultural identity in many Western countries. This, in turn, undermines economic and political globalization; moreover, new protectionism in the West will undermine the growth of trade and international investment networks and this could further weaken the prospects for the peaceful cooperation of nations. It cannot be taken as a given that the international network of scientists, business people, and artists will remain as broad as it has been in the early twenty-first century. It is still an unsolved challenge to translate Karl Popper's The Logic of Scientific Discovery (originally published as *Logik der Forschung*, Popper 1934) into the Arabic language and it is actually strange to find that no governments or foundations have been interested in or willing to make the important investment needed to translate such a crucial book, which explains the difference between scientific truth—that is the hypothesis with considerable empirical support from statistics about the facts of the real world—and religion.

One may argue that there are general lessons to be learned from Karl Popper which can be applied to Brexit issues: first, that piecemeal engineering is often a useful policy approach, but this assumes that at least a serious reform agenda is available—this is currently not the case with the EU. The second point is a critical focus on the nostalgia that seems to have inspired many Brexiteers with regard to their vote in the British EU referendum: it is obvious that the EU has long failed to provide a largely attractive integration policy for many British voters, but one should also be careful not to try deriving an artificial logic from British history that, for example, says (as emphasized by the Leave campaign) that the modern UK is a natural leader of the Commonwealth and that from that position Britain's global influence will grow and prosperity emerge. Many of the countries of the Commonwealth are rather unwilling it seems, to accept British political leadership in most fields. Finally, with the rising economic and political power of China—and, with a certain delay, also of India—all EU28 countries should avoid the illusion that any single EU country will be big enough on its own to really play a decisive role in the world economy in the twenty-first century. Many strategic policy challenges—ranging from international migration to developing competition rules for the digital world economy and fighting global warming—can be addressed successfully only from a policy club perspective. Thus, the European Union, if properly reformed, is still a valuable institution. Whether or not the EU will survive Brexit depends heavily on the willingness of EU27 member countries to rapidly develop adequate reforms in terms of both institutions and policies.

After 2019, the Western world will be very different than before—even if the UK would decide in a second EU referendum on Brexit that it would like to remain in the European Union. In the end, the cost of the disorderly EU referendum in 2016 will be enormous regardless of whether the UK should actually leave the European Union or not. A critical analysis with an economic perspective and elements from Political Economy can hopefully shed some light on some of the key issues in the UK and the OECD countries—and indeed beyond.

If the EU should show continued disintegration dynamics, it would not be surprising if Eastern European EU countries would be the first to come under new political pressure from Russia. The credibility of the North Atlantic Treaty Organization (NATO) as a security club will diminish should the EU, as a Western policy club, reveal ongoing disintegration dynamics. It would not be surprising if a disintegration of NATO would quickly follow EU disintegration and such a double regional instability cannot be without serious long-run consequences. The US and the UK, as well as most EU27 countries, would be the main losers in such a historical development. ASEAN, which started as an international military grouping in the shadow of the Vietnam War, has become a regional economic cooperation scheme. If Western Europe should face continued disintegration dynamics, strong pressure would come on ASEAN to reconsider the institutional arrangements it has developed—particularly in the wake of its recent moves towards an ASEAN single market.

Political nationalism in Asia is stronger (and younger) than in the EU, so that new internal conflicts as well as new external disintegration pressure, for example from the US Trump administration, could easily undermine the regional stability of ASEAN. The natural winner of such a development would be China. That this, in turn, is in the interests of the United States is very difficult to see. By giving up the Trans-Pacific Partnership, the US already has destroyed a political asset that could have generated long-term economic and political benefits and which could have reinforced US power in the modern world.

If the UK proceeds with Brexit and the US with a protectionist policy strategy, the Western world will disintegrate. Disintegration could become the new catchword of the early twenty-first century and to study the disadvantages of disintegration one must not wait for many years—the interim war years of the 1920s and early 1930s saw many unpleasant and dangerous dynamics which are largely known to the Economics profession. From this perspective, it is rather surprising to see the ongoing rise of populism in many Western countries. Much will depend on a potential second British referendum and the outcome thereof; it should not be overlooked that Brexiteers received a lot of funding from US sources and it would not be surprising to see representatives from the US business community becoming active in the political campaign in the United Kingdom once again. The Trump administration considers the UK a welcome role model for tax reform and populist policy. If the EU27 would survive as a group with a political union, it should be able to withstand the destabilization pressure from the Trump administration.

If there is indeed a completed Brexit, the EU27 has an opportunity to really create a more integrated European Union, including a defense partnership which for decades neither the UK nor the US has been eager to witness. One should not rule out that adequate EU reforms could reinvigorate economic and political integration in the EU, but reforms will certainly be necessary. Without new initiatives supported by Germany and France, as well as other EU countries, a stabilization of the EU's integration process cannot be expected. Since the legitimacy of the British EU referendum and of Brexit, respectively, is in fact weak and since there has been a continuous message from senior representatives of the May government (Mrs. May herself, Mr. Liam Fox, and others) that EU immigrants are a burden for the UK budget - totally wrong if one takes into account the key findings of OECD research which are known in British government circles - one may conclude that the contradictions of the May government make both it and her hard Brexit announcement weak political projects. While empirical analysis has a strong basis in the UK, it seems that both the Cameron governments and the May government have had problems in dealing with facts and in adequately informing the populace. Political conjectures that are "useful fake news" might be in line with party ideology, but government should not assume that, particularly in the Internet age, counterfactual rhetoric could not be exposed by journalists, economists, political scientists, and indeed by ordinary people.

The conjecture of the Leave campaign that Brexit will come at zero economic costs and indeed could generate strong benefits for the UK is advanced economic fiction; those interested in enjoying fiction could read a book or look at a film of this genre. It is worrying to some extent that a broad share of the population in the UK has obviously lost confidence in economic experts – at the same time, one may argue that the field of Economics has had problems in understanding the real world; as so few economists warned of the poorly managed risk of financial globalization and excessive financial deregulation in the UK and the US, the reputation of Economics as a whole has been weakened (so Brexit should also be a wake-up call for economists). One should not overlook that a UK that faces reduced output growth in the context of Brexit will push for lower corporate tax rates and a new wave of financial deregulation in the UK after March 2019 which could trigger – in combination with US deregulation already adopted in early 2017 under the Trump administration – a new banking crisis in Europe and in Western OECD countries. The IMF's Financial Sector Assessment Program and Basel III regulations, organized by the Bank for International Settlements as a project to support the enhanced prudential supervision of large banks which are active internationally, should be reinforced; however, the Trump administration has started to undermine Basel III and hence excessive deregulation should indeed be expected. The next Transatlantic Banking Crisis might have even bigger costs than the banking crisis of 2007/09. In a nutshell: the Transatlantic Banking Crisis of 2007/09 raised debt-GDP ratios by 30-40 percentage points in the US and the UK, the need to reduce such deficit-GDP ratios seems to have strongly pushed Mr. Cameron towards his anti-immigration rhetoric in order to find a scapegoat for the massive cuts in budget transfers to local communities and the anti-EU immigration story of Mr. Cameron became such a powerful obsession on the side of the Leave campaign, and other anti-EU groups, that in the end voters did not follow Mr. Cameron in the referendum 2016: a Brexit majority prevailed at the ballot box and the result will bring lower growth which in turn will encourage UK governments to push again for banking deregulation – as a means to keep international banks in the City and to raise output growth, respectively; the result could be the next banking crisis that would thus become part of long run instability cycles in Western market economies.

From an EU perspective, EU-UK negotiations should emphasize the establishment of joint EU-UK regulation of banks and financial markets; not least taking due account of the weakening of Basel III and the BIS by the Trump administration. The EU should also develop recommendations for minimum information requirements in EU referenda in EU countries. Supporting the creation of city partnerships and joint "European actitivies" – events/meetings for young people plus representatives from industry and NGOs – could be one of the integration pillars to be reinforced in the future. The reforms in the EU should emphasize an integration club that is more useful and easier to understand for voters. The EU will not survive with a budget below a critical minimum size. Reinforcing democracy in the EU should mean the creation of a Eurozone Parliament which is accountable to voters. The current core of EU power, namely the European Council, faces very weak control by voters which is a strange contradiction (at times, the European Council resembles something of a political cartel): to accumulate increased power in a framework poorly controlled by voters is counter to the ideas of EU integration. Brexit and the election of Mr. Trump as President of the US stand for part of the broader new populist forces in the West. As has been emphasized in this book, European Parliament elections paradoxically and indirectly nurture radical populist forces in EU member countries and this certainly requires adequate reforms in the EU. In the end, Brexit is not just a historical event in Europe, it is a historical step by the UK on a global scale and one that will affect the world economy. In Europe there is no reason to be overly pessimistic, but any simple wait-and-see attitude would be irresponsible. What makes some of the challenges particularly difficult is that the fear of terrorism has become part and parcel of policy debates in many Western OECD countries. The fight against youth unemployment thus should rank very high on the agenda in many EU countries. With the Eurozone's economic upswing continuing, one may hope that more reforms at the supranational level become feasible in the near future. Building new and stable UK-EU relations is important, but it might not be an easy task for many years to come. The UK might ultimately face both political and economic instability and the contradictions of the EU referendum in 2016 could point to one possible exit: a new EU referendum; voters in the United Kingdom might have to decide once again and all EU countries will have to accept the result whatever it may be. However, pushing in Europe for a better quality of referendum should be of common interest to all people in the EU. The idea of a customs union and regional integration is still alive and well in the western continental EU countries; the Eastern European accession countries, on the other hand, might need more time to better understand the benefits of EU integration and supranational policy which is naturally not a priority in countries that have only relatively recently regained sovereignty after decades of Soviet dominance. In a world economy, and facing the giants of the US and China, the EU project makes more sense now than ever before provided that the EU club adopts the necessary reforms – and the debate on this has just begun.

Final Perspectives

With Brexit, the EU is facing considerable challenges with regard to the need for adjustment and adaptation especially as it is still unclear whether or not the EU–UK negotiations over Britain's so-called "exit bill" and on future UK access to the EU single market will be concluded, and whether the resulting treaties or agreements can achieve majority approval by the relevant parliaments (European Parliament, British Parliament and the parliaments of the remaining EU member states) by March 2019. If, for example, the treaties would not be passed by the British Parliament, the UK's future access to the single market would be governed by the UK's status as a member of the World Trade Organization (a "WTO-Brexit"); this alone could lead to a tumultuous reaction on financial markets and it cannot be ruled out that it could lead to restrictions in terms of the supply of financial services to customers in the EU27. In the UK itself, the Bank of England, as the national supervisory body, will likely adopt certain provisions vis-à-vis banking supervision in early 2019. In the countries of the EU27 and Eurozone, respectively, the months following a completed Brexit—expected to be the time period after March 29, 2019—will also require careful prudential supervision (including by the European Systemic Risk Board, which will regard Brexit as an important shock impulse). If one is to assume that an uncontrolled WTO-Brexit can lead to large capital outflows from the UK—parallel to a significant depreciation of the Pound—this could inversely result in a considerable appreciation of the US Dollar, Swiss Franc, Euro and of those currencies of remaining EU countries which are, however, not part of the Eurozone.

The flow of liquidity out of the UK, and possibly also out of countries which have extensive economic ties to the UK—such as Ireland, Denmark, the Netherlands, Malta or Cyprus—could give rise to instability in the EU27. It would be sensible to undertake analyses of the degree of interconnectedness in terms of banking prior to 2019, in order to limit and control systemic externalities in the context of Brexit in the interest of financial market stability. If Brexit should be accompanied by a period of falling stock prices, the desirable raising of the equity ratios of banks could prove difficult. The European Central Bank (ECB) could still have an effect here with timely stress tests scheduled for 2018. In the run-up to 2019, preventative and strengthened cooperation activities between the relevant prudential supervisory bodies of the EU28 countries, the US, Switzerland and Norway would be expedient. An adequate international interlinking of actors in the field of prudential supervision, such as the national central banks, the ECB, the Bank for International Settlements and the IMF/G20, may prove to be a useful and crucial development. The EU countries should cover their state financing requirements for 2019 by moving forward their issuance schedule, so that comprehensive and complicated (re-)financing activities are not necessary during a possible uncertain and turbulent financial situation in 2019.

Overall, there is a significant need for further research in the area of Brexit. One aspect which could be subjected to further study is the pending geographical transfer of banks from London to other countries in the EU27. Here, the impression was created in June 2017 that as a result of the unclear parliamentary majority, which emerged in the wake of the premature general election, large foreign banks are pushing ahead with relocation activities with renewed vigor—citing political uncertainty. Certain smaller EU member states, such as Luxembourg or Ireland, are possibly not overly interested in the prospect of an extensive influx of banks and banking services to their jurisdictions, namely as a future banking crisis could cause a stark collapse in the economic performance of such countries—for which the experience of numerous OECD countries during the banking crisis of 2007–2009 provides ample evidence. Thus there could be a tendency for UK-based banks to relocate their activities rather to Germany and France, as these countries are large enough to cope with a significant transfer of London banks.

For the EU member states, Switzerland and other OECD countries, a WTO-Brexit could lead to serious turbulence on the financial markets—with negative transfer effects on the real economy. From this perspective, precautionary measures should be adopted in a sensible way in the run-up to 2019 in the field of prudential supervision, on both a microprudential and macroprudential basis, where pre-coordination via the Bank for International Settlements is worth considering. So far, the dimensions of Brexit for the UK and Europe, as well as the global economy, have generally only been visible to a certain extent, thus those in positions of responsibility at banks, firms and even economic policy actors should inform and prepare themselves for the diverse manifestations of Brexit using scenario analyses and on the basis of scientific studies. Furthermore, one can pose the question of why so many people, politicians and academics were surprised by the Brexit-majority in the UK's 2016 referendum to begin with. This question is not unlike that of Queen Elizabeth II during a 2008 visit to the London School of Economics when she asked the assembled body of academics why nobody had seen the financial crisis coming. A possible answer to both this question and indeed the question of the pro-Brexit majority is that in the West a system has developed which appears too complex for, occasionally not very professional, economic policy; the simplification of structures and institutions, as well as increased transparency and improved incentive schemes, could be part of a sensible reform of the current system. More economic analysis could provide essential in finding solutions to important issues.

References

Bazillier, R., Magris, F., & Mirza, D. (2017). Out-migration and economic cycles. *Review of World Economics, 153*, 39–70.

Müller-Graff, P. -C. (2016). Brexit–die unionsrechtliche Dimension, *Integration*, 267–282.

OECD. (2014). *Focus on Inequality and Growth—December 2014: Does Income Inequality Hurt Economic Growth?* Paris: OECD Publishing.

Popper, K. (1934). *Logik der Forschung: Zur Erkenntnistheorie der modernen Naturwissenschaft* [in English as The Logic of Scientific Discovery]. Vienna: Springer.

Ryan, C. (2016). Where does one start to make sense of Brexit. *International Economics and Economic Policy, 13*, 531–537.

Appendix—Annex 1: Knowledge Creation and Enhanced Investment Dynamics in a Europe with New Institutions

Introduction

The European Union in 2016/17 is facing an economic upswing on the continent, while the UK—after the Brexit referendum of June 23, 2016—will have modest growth and might, in fact, come close to an economic downturn in 2017. As regards the Eurozone, some progress has been achieved in terms of structural change and lower deficit-Gross Domestic Product (GDP) ratios; however, there is still an underutilization of production potential. High youth unemployment rates in many EU countries stand for a considerable economic challenge such that one has to raise the question of what long-term strategy, in Europe and the European Union—after about 2020 without the UK—respectively, could be successful in achieving higher economic growth as well as sustainable development. Within such a strategy the current Europe 2020 key elements are picked up, modified, and reinforced.

The fact that potential output paths have suffered a downward shift in many Organisation for Economic Co-operation and Development (OECD) member countries cannot be overlooked, as has been emphasized, for example, by Pichelmann (2015). From this perspective, it is

© The Editor(s) (if applicable) and The Author(s) 2017
P.J.J. Welfens, *An Accidental Brexit*,
DOI 10.1007/978-3-319-58271-9

quite important to adopt policy strategies that are growth-enhancing in the long run so that after a few years of preparation at the national and supranational levels a package of adequate measures could be implemented. The subsequent analysis developed here draws on the McKinsey Global Institute (2015) report and other recent research related to EU economic development and global economic dynamics. The basic idea is a framework for a triple pro-growth reform program— national, supranational and G20—in which several EU countries play a key role—deliverable by 2020 and which should appeal to electorates and decision-makers alike at both the national and European levels. Governments' supply-side and fiscal policy should adopt new initiatives in Europe after an extended period during which central banks, including the European Central Bank, have bought adjustment time for countries in Europe.

The July 2016 G20 meeting in Chengdu, China, has called for the UK to retain close relations to the EU27; however, this will only be possible to some extent; namely, that the United Kingdom seriously wants such cooperation despite a Brexit referendum—which is a historical step involving the withdrawing of experienced UK diplomats and experts from roughly a dozen EU institutions so that a considerable depreciation of institutional capital in the European Union will take place. This in itself weakens growth prospects for both the UK and, to some extent, the EU27. While one cannot easily anticipate the outcome of UK–EU27 negotiations about future British access to the EU27 single market, it is fairly clear that the European Union's interest to maintain strong incentives for member countries to stay within the EU implies that the UK cannot expect an easy deal with the EU27. This, however, does not exclude the possibility that the UK and EU27 could yet find a mutually beneficial arrangement and be able to define new fields of cooperation.

The EU, and individual member countries, will have to consider medium-term institutional reforms and regain credibility. An adequate vertical fiscal policy integration is still lacking in the Eurozone and an adequate policy mix is also not yet visible; growth policy and stabilization policy will have to be combined.

Since the Brexit referendum, medium-term output forecasts for many European countries, particularly the UK, have seen a downward revision by the IMF (2016a) World Economic Outlook Update of July 19, 2016. As regards the Eurozone, the IMF raised the real GDP growth forecast to 1.6%, namely by 0.1 points for 2016, but reduced it by 0.2 points—1.4% growth—for 2017. The IMF expects the UK's growth in 2016 to fall slightly to 1.7% which is 0.2 points below the April 2016 forecast of 1.9%; however, in 2017, the growth rate is expected to be 1.3% which is 0.9% points lower than the IMF forecast of April 2016. The economic growth perspectives for the EU28 thus are rather modest in 2017—compared to the April WEO forecast figures—and are expected to be below that of the US: which the IMF WEO July update left unchanged at 2.5%. These forecasts were too pessimistic for the UK in 2016. The EU27 could raise economic growth through a multi-pronged package, namely, first by focusing on the Eurozone, second by placing emphasis on Eastern European EU countries and, third, with a broad emphasis on digital Europe that would include the UK and other non-EU countries in Europe; an EU27–UK Joint European Infrastructure Bank could play a positive role for financing major infrastructure projects in an environment with negative nominal—sometimes also real—interest rates. The analytical basis is the study of the McKinsey Global Institute (2015), the knowledge production function and the empirical results, respectively, obtained in the Jungmittag/Welfens (2016) analysis for 20 EU countries and the recent IMF paper of Atoyan et al. (2016) on Eastern European emigration dynamics. The analysis of Pichelmann (2015) is also important as he emphasizes the risk of stagnation and the potential slowing down of growth through rising inequality—a related analysis with a focus on globalizationis Jaumotte et al. (2008).

The new perspective of a post-Brexit Europe has to be integrated in the subsequent analysis which looks for ways to enhance economic growth in the long run and also to consider sustainability aspects, plus the opportunities for an EU Social Market Economy that combines innovation dynamics, efficiency, and competition with the key elements of a social policy system with several layers that should make sense from the perspective of the theory of fiscal federalism. For a pro-growth policy perspective, Schumpeterian analysis as well as elements of endogenous growth analysis in open economies—with trade, FDI, and techno-globalization—should be considered. Since Europe has several policy layers, including the supranational and the national layers, it is adequate to look at the various policy layers and to also raise the question as to what extent electorates and key policy players could be motivated to support the relevant decisions and reforms to be considered. Since one may assume that the UK's leaving of the EU27 will stimulate a willingness for reform in the Community, a long-term growth perspective for Europe may include some reflections on institutional innovations after 2019 (the assumed year of the UK leaving the EU) and also the election year for the European Parliament.

Facing New Challenges and Opportunities in a Post-Brexit Europe

Migration is a useful element of adjustment in Europe, namely to the extent that it represents improving working opportunities through reduced barriers to labor mobility which actually exist in various forms, including problems with adding up entitlements from the national security systems of different countries in which workers have been active—the European Commission has encouraged labor mobility through the creation of a more consistent institutional framework, but overall EU labor mobility is still fairly low compared to Switzerland, the US or Germany (McKinsey Global Institute 2015). While very different national social security systems still impair labor mobility in Europe, one should not overlook that there also is a strong mobility from Eastern Europe to Western Europe: as the IMF has emphasized in a policy paper of Atoyan et al. (2016), Eastern European countries have experienced between 1990–2012 an emigration of about 5.4 million people to western Europe and the US. As a high share of outward migration from Eastern Europe consisted of rather young workers and skilled labor, respectively—from the perspective of emigration countries (in the receiving countries a lack of knowledge of the respective language implies that immigrants from Eastern Europe will often only find jobs as unskilled workers until a certain level of fluency in the language of the host country has been achieved)—the economic growth of source countries in certain cases was impaired and this in turn has undermined economic convergence between Eastern European countries and western EU countries to some extent; in some Eastern European EU countries the reduction of output expansion has been impaired by governments' reaction to the migration-induced increase of aging dynamics: there was a rise of social security contributions and a growing of the economic wedge between gross wage rates and net wage rates, respectively. In many OECD countries, including Eastern European countries, income inequality has increased.

Given the EU's goal of economic cohesion and the finding of the OECD (2014) that rising inequality can undermine economic growth, the EU should reconsider part of its policy framework. Lowering income inequality through adequate tax reform (formally still a competence of national policymakers), that could in part be coordinated by the governments of EU countries, could, therefore, be an element for pro-growth policy as well as new incentives for entrepreneurship in Eastern European countries: the creation of more local firms and technology-oriented small and medium enterprises (SMEs) would increase the prospects for skilled workers to find a job and in the future a certain share of EU structural funds could be assigned for this goal. Governments should encourage the training and retraining of workers as well as higher foreign direct investment (FDI) inflows in eastern EU accession countries and, if the UK has left the EU, it would be wise that western EU countries plus Norway and Switzerland and indeed the UK would contribute to an EU+ fund for the retraining of workers in Eastern Europe for a decade—this would be an impulse for intra-European economic convergence and convergence of per capita income will facilitate economic policy coordination in relevant fields as the similarity of interests is related to per capita income levels (Fig. A.1).

The EU28 has shown considerable ability to adjust to enormous shocks, including the Transatlantic Banking Crisis and the debt crisis of several Eurozone countries; at the same time, one may argue that the EU27/EU28 needs a new long-term balance of growth-enhancing policies and reforms in the context of a digital social market economy in the

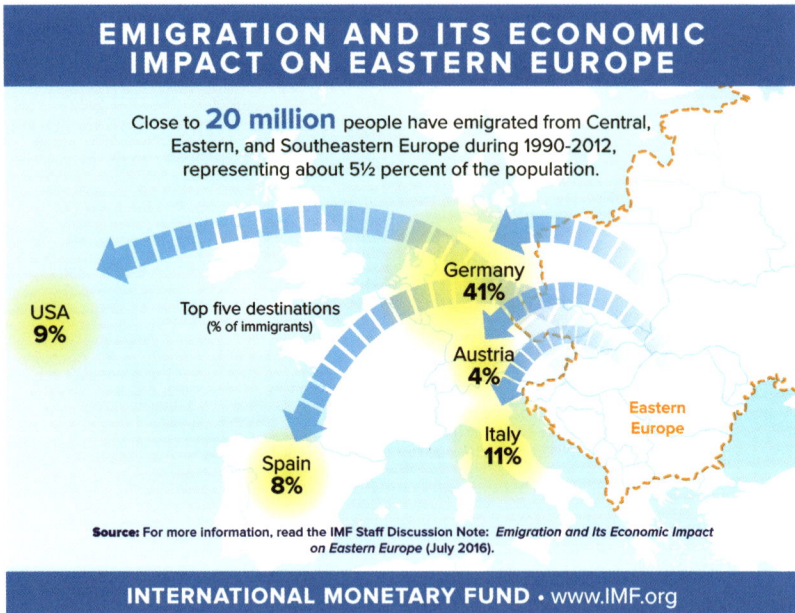

Fig. A.1   Eastern European Emigration 1990–2012. *Source* IMF (2016b)

era of economic globalization and economic interdependency. Some EU countries are facing rather strong needs in terms of structural adjustment and also need better matching processes in the labor market; e.g., the OECD (2015) has shown that if Italy's labor market matching quality was as good as the OECD top performer then labor productivity would increase by 6%. Thus, benchmarking remains important as has been emphasized by the European Commission over many years. DG ECFIN has made many calculations on a similar basis and there is no doubt that learning from other EU countries could be quite useful. At the same time, one has to consider the common challenge to adjust in a growth-enhancing way to modern globalization that will be a combination of rising trade intensity—with a rising share of intermediate technology-intensive products traded—and a higher intensity of inward FDI as well as higher outward FDI. Cumulated inward FDI can represent the ability to benefit from foreign technologies through intra-company technology transfers as well as cross-licensing among multinational companies—the latter requires adequate outward FDI as well. In the digital knowledge economy of the twenty-first century, there will be a global innovation race in which big home markets stand for a particular ability to exploit economies of scale and to combine this advantage with product differentiation that allows to fetch high export unit values which, in turn, are an important element of Schumpeterian economic rents, high real wages and adequate profit rates. The basics of modern growth theory plus integration theory and empirical findings should be considered by policymakers. Public infrastructure investment projects should also be quite important in a period in which government can finance such projects at almost zero capital cost, namely in a period of ultra-low interest rates in the Eurozone and the EU, respectively.

General Growth Drivers and Knowledge Production Function as an Analytical Basis for Pro-Growth Policy in Europe

In a study of the McKinsey Global Institute (2015), eleven main growth drivers were suggested for raising economic growth in Europe. About three-quarters of these drivers can be implemented at the national level; however, there is a particular challenge to implement these measures in a politically feasible sequence and to use benchmarking in Europe on the one hand. On the other hand, there is the question of which additional growth-enhancing elements can be mobilized at the national level and at the global level (G20). Mobilizing the workforce, boosting markets and productivity and investing for the future are three key fields that stand for eleven growth drivers identified by the McKinsey Global Institute (see Fig. A.2). As regards boosting markets and productivity, it is particularly important to reinforce the EU single market and raise public sector productivity—for the latter better use of information and communication technology in many countries is required and Industry 4.0 could indeed be picked up by both the private and the public sectors in EU countries. Further openness to trade certainly will be a natural policy element of the EU and the European Commission,

Fig. A.2 Long-term Drivers of Economic Growth in Europe. *Source* McKinsey Global Institute, 2015, A Window of Opportunity for Europe, Washington DC

respectively. Investing for the future is, of course, a key ingredient for growth and in the twenty-first century both investment in physical capital as well as human capital and in innovation will be highly relevant—new incentives for venture capital could also play a particular role and the falling real price of ICT capital has particularly reduced the barriers to entry in certain digital markets.

Combining New National and Supranational Policy Elements in Europe

After 2020, the intensified global competition will naturally lead to a more intensive focus of policymakers in Europe on the creation of new knowledge. The new world economy of the twenty-first century is one of the economic interdependencies in which there are at least five key elements: Europe–US–China–Japan–ASEAN. Since late 2015, the ASEAN has adopted its own single market program that is largely modeled on the EU single market. This implies that some pro-growth policy coordination as well as more medium-term fiscal and monetary policy coordination among these pillars of the world economy would be useful. The cyclical policy coordination could come through the OECD (including the OECD Development Centre), the pro-growth policy coordination partly through G20 which has already adopted a joint growth-enhancing framework at the Brisbane 2014 G20 summit meeting.

The study by reference Jungmittag/Welfens (2016) has shown that in the EU new knowledge (proxied by patent applications which reflect mainly industrial innovation dynamics, but manufacturing industry is still crucial for long-run growth of output in many EU countries) is basically driven by the number of researchers employed, per capita incomeand inward FDI capital stocks relative to GDP; country-fixed effects play a role as well but explain only a small part of the variance of patent applications at the European Patent Agency. The empirical panel data analysis for 20 EU countries—where data are available—suggests that this knowledge production function for the EU is highly relevant and its results can also be plugged into a macroeconomic production function so that one also gets a better idea of how raising the number of researchers and inward FDI stock–GDP ratios contribute to higher output. Indirectly, one also gets an idea about the positive feedback mechanism of international Free Trade Area Treaties; e.g., the envisaged EU–US Transatlantic Trade and Investment Partnership (TTIP) project that should bring about more transatlantic trade and foreign direct investmentwhere the Commission's TTIP study (Francois et al. 2013) suggests that trade creation effects will contribute to a rise of long-run EU output of 0.5%. With a given population, this would imply a rise of per capita output of 0.5% and, given the elasticity of patent applications with respect to per capita income of 1.82, new knowledge will be raised by 0.91%. The study also shows, in additional regression analysis for Germany, that cumulated FDI inflows do not contribute to higher output but that there is a significant indirect FDI output link that runs indeed through raising the stock of knowledge via FDI. The role of multinational companies and FDI plus innovation has indeed been emphasized as a main driver of economic growth in modern open economy macroeconomics (Welfens 2011).

These findings suggest that reinforcing inward FDI links should be emphasized more in the future by individual EU countries on the one hand—by improving locational quality of the respective country—and by the European Commission and other international policy networks on the other. At the same time, one should consider that a stronger role

of multinational companies and more two-way FDI suggests to emphasize a more international competition policy approach—and hence
cooperation in competition policy or the setting up of distinct new
competition policy institutions—in the future (except for the non-trad-
ables sector where standard competition policy approaches will work).

2018–2020 as Starting Points for Higher Growth in Europe and G20 Aspects

As a growth-enhancing strategy for Europe, one may suggest a certain
sequence and package of policy measures. The sequence should make
sure that higher economic growth is achieved in EU countries which,
in turn, is known to reinforce support for EU integration. With higher
support for EU integration, certain EU policy measures and potentially
also a discussion about a combination of less regulation from Brussels
and new steps towards a political union of the EU—or the Eurozone
as a first step—could be considered. If a new pro-growth strategy were
to be implemented in 2020, it would be wise to open a discussion of
broad elements in 2018/19, certainly prior to the 2019 elections of the
European Parliament.

G20 Prospects

Before we look at policy measures in a narrow European context, one
should also consider the international pro-growth commitment of leading EU countries in the context of the G20. The G20 Brisbane summit
of 2014 had promised to deliver an extra 2% growth by 2018 where the
OECD would monitor this process and also offered to model the growth
impact of growth policy options suggested. This OECD offer should
now—after the Brexit decision—be used extensively, as Brexit itself
implies a reduction of global GDP growth of about 0.2% in 2016–2018.
As the UK has been the direct cause of this negative effect, it would be
adequate that the UK as well as its EU27 partners consider extra efforts
to raise growth at the national and global levels; an adequate growth

strategy would consider additional opportunities for higher global green growth. As the UK will no longer contribute (on a net basis) £6.7–£7.6 billion ($8.2-$9.3 billion) annually to the EU budget as of 2019/20—assuming that this is the date for leaving the EU—the British government could contribute to a new Global Green Growth Fund that would co-finance international sustainability R&D support for firms from G20 countries: the focus would be on innovation projects with international innovation spillovers and/or international sustainability spillovers.

For reasons of political acceptability, one might consider a split of green R&D project financing of 60% in the respective country, another 25% in the respective region (e.g., for the UK, Germany, France, Italy, Spain, this would mean Europe) and 15% outside that region. There is also an economic argument behind such a split since geographical spillovers of R&D effects are rather limited; however, in the digital age there can, of course, also be some global spillover effects. If the UK would invest about £1.3/$1.6 billion in such a G20 green innovation and growth fund, the overall G20 fund could be close to £25/$31 billion. There should be a principle of additionality, namely, that national R&D programs would not be cut as a reaction to setting up a global G20 green R&D facility.

Starting Growth-Enhancing Policy Measures at the National Policy Layer

There are no real prospects for effective cyclical policy coordination through the OECD if the EU27/Eurozone countries do not better organize fiscal policy in the future. Public investment of EU countries could thus partly be organized as a virtual EU fund and, if national governments agree, the European Investment Bank (EIB) will be able to come up with part of the necessary funding. At the bottom line, the effective EU expenditures relative to GDP could be considerably increased and a new starting point for a more effective joint European counter-cyclical policy would become available. The projects to be financed should all be international intra-EU infrastructure projects—with the option for Norwayand Switzerland, as well as the UK, to join both the list of relevant projects and to become active in project financing.

For the future, there should be a list available of potentially useful European infrastructure projects which have already been considered by national parliaments such that certain projects can be earmarked as relevant in an EU context—there could be 5-year staggered and rolling time horizon and planning so that for the quarter in which a recession is identified, there is a joint list of public investment projects that could be started in an almost simultaneous way by the European Commission. The European Parliament would set up an adequate legal framework for this, as would national parliaments in EU member countries—possibly plus Norwayand Switzerland. This then allows fighting recession, while taking a rather short administrative approach, so that public infrastructure policy can make an effective contribution to stabilizing the Eurozone/EU business cycle. A typical Keynesian policy package in the US for overcoming a recession is about 0.5% of GDP and a broader package close to 1% of GDP. Hence, if the EU had a virtual public investment fund plus a basic joint defense package, on which national parliaments already had given the green light in advance, the EU could be in a position to be more effective in fiscal policy in the future. This, in turn, will reduce the risk premium in Europe and more investment will become feasible which in turn will stimulate growth.

EU member countries and the European Commission could set up a joint expert group that could look into national and supranational regulations that impair economic growth—and which could be reduced or removed without negative consequences for consumers and competition, respectively.

Sustainability: Improvements in National Green Tax Policy and R&D Promotion

For a future pro-growth agenda, it would be important to consider, at the national policy level, steps towards higher green tax–GDP revenues—perhaps with the exception of the Netherlandsand Denmark if one assumes that their green tax–GDP ratio of slightly above 4% is already reflecting an optimal internalization of negative external effects. In a pragmatic way, one may argue for splitting a higher green tax–GDP ratio into three mirror policy elements for each extra point of higher green taxation: one third could raise government promotion of private R&D; one third could imply a reduction of the income tax ratio; one third could be allocated to a multilateral EU public investment fund. Hence if the average increase of the green tax ratio would be two percentage points in the EU, one would generate a considerable increase of the R&D ratio in each member country and in the EU, respectively, as well as lower income taxes—here some emphasis could be on low-income households in order to balance supply-side elements with an impulse for higher aggregate demand. A joint public investment fund for the EU could follow up on previous European Community infrastructure initiatives and would generate demand-side effects as well as long-run supply-side and pro-competitive effects.

Global Strategy for FTA Approach of the EU

Focusing on supranational policy options for enhancing EU27 growth will be crucial: the Juncker Commission has already adopted key elements for higher growth where the digital agenda is of particular relevance—and many excellent projects have already been adopted; in addition, the politically somewhat controversial TTIP EU–USA project has been emphasized (with apparent problems in mid-2016, particularly after Brexit which is also bound to reduce the negotiation power of the EU since the UK stands for 25% of US exports to the EU). The Asian dimension of the EU's FTA policy has been neglected; the starting point in the EU–Singapore FTA (and the agreed, but not yet ratified, EU–Vietnam FTA) should become a broader EU–ASEANliberalization approach. EU member countries' Asian FTA efforts will, however, not be very credible if the EU does not arrive at implementing at least TTIP-light with the USA (assuming that the US administration would be willing to consider some aspects of Comprehensive Economic and Trade Agreement (CETA), between the EU and Canada, which seems to be a useful blueprint for a transatlantic FTA). The broader strategy of growth-enhancing policy should be a mixture of national and supranational as well as global policy elements with FTAs playing a key role from an EU perspective. In this context, it also remains clear that the

EU can obtain better FTA results than any individual EU country could normally expect to get.

While there are certain supranational policy elements that could be developed in Brussels in a long-term framework as elements contributing to higher growth and a better quality of work standards in the countries involved (see, e.g., CETA between EU countries and Canada), there are also national policy elements that can contribute to growth as well as to more sustainability—either as a purely national policy element or as part of networked policy approaches for which positive international spillovers give particular motivation.

Improving Green Tax Policy and Raising Support for R&D Projects

Taking a closer look at the revenues from environmental taxation, one finds for 2009 that amongst OECD countries the green taxrevenue relative to GDP differs considerably, from about 1.5% in Spain to about 4% in Denmark and the Netherlands (OECD 2010). It is surprising that the variation of green taxation across European OECD countries is fairly large. With respect to EU countries, this suggests that several EU countries with rather low green taxrevenue–GDP ratios could raise the respective green tax rate while raising government R&D promotion directly or indirectly if positive external effects of private innovation projects have not been adequately internalized so far. In a nutshell: if, in a given country, the green tax ratio is below the optimum while positive R&D effects are not fully internalized, then economic policy reforms that raise the green tax ratio and increase government R&D promotion will result in positive welfare effects.

Virtual Supranational Fiscal Policy

Better fiscal policy is crucial for Europe, particularly since the Eurozone has a single monetary policy while fiscal policy is not coordinated much, meaning cyclical shocks reduce consumption–GDP ratios more in the Eurozone than in the US. A key issue with respect to many policy proposals is the question of what could motivate the parliaments of EU member countries to shift part of infrastructure projects to the supranational policy layer in Brussels—beyond the simplistic argument that many economists recommend a greater role of fiscal policy at the Eurozone level in order to have more effective countercyclical policy options and a better policy mix for fighting recessions (again, the fact that IMF research is available on this will not impress national policymakers much). A key incentive could be that a combination of monetary policy, supranational policy strategy, and national policy changes would bring about a fiscal benefit for national parliaments, namely, higher revenue–GDP ratios and hence the ability to cut income tax rates or to spend some of the government budget surplus on a long-term capital fund for future payments of social security.

In a nutshell (without the supranational element), this was basically the deal between the US Federal Reserve and the Clinton administration in the 1990s. As it seems possible to achieve an EU/Eurozonepolitical union only in the long run, a first step could be the creation of a virtual infrastructure and defense budget which is an intergovernmental institutional arrangement that foreshadows a future fiscal and political union in the Eurozone; if one would set aside about 3% of national expenditures in this Fiscal Union TrUst and Resource Entity (FUTURE), it should be easier to coordinate fiscal policy. On the revenue side, one might consider setting up a joint institution that would cover the first six months of unemployment insurance in an institutional setup outside the EU Treaty—possibly without coverage of youth unemployment for which national policymakers bear the main responsibility. This could require about 0.7% of GDP—while representing some intra-Eurozone transfers—and as successful growth policy helps to bring down the unemployment rate, there could be a joint benefit in the long run as the cost of unemployment coverage would fall to as little as about 0.3% of Eurozone GDP. While the benefit to be shared in the long run seems to be rather small, the suggested mechanism is nevertheless a critical potential success story that should encourage a pro-integration spirit.

Appendix—Annex 2: UK Government Referenda Information (2014; 2016)

See Fig. A.3
See Fig. A.4

Links to HM Treasury's Studies on the Economic Impact of Brexit

HM Treasury study, "The Long-Term Economic Impact of EU Membership and the Alternatives"
https://www.gov.uk/government/uploads/system/uploads/attach-ment_data/file/517415/treasury_analysis_economic_impact_of_eu_membership_web.pdf
HM Treasury study, "The Immediate Economic Impact of Leaving the EU"
https://www.gov.uk/government/uploads/system/uploads/attach-ment_data/file/524967/hm_treasury_analysis_the_immediate_eco-nomic_impact_of_leaving_the_eu_web.pdf

© The Editor(s) (if applicable) and The Author(s) 2017
P.J.J. Welfens, *An Accidental Brexit*,
DOI 10.1007/978-3-319-58271-9

Here are five ways we'll benefit by staying in the United Kingdom.

Keep the pound.
The pound is one of the strongest and most stable currencies in the world. Staying in the UK is the only way Scotland can keep the strength of the Bank of England and the pound as we have now. Setting up a new currency for an independent Scotland would be costly and risky.

More support for public services.
Currently, Scotland benefits from public spending per person that is around 10% higher than the UK average. Taxpayers across the UK help fund the vital public services we need such as health and education. The long-term financial benefit of staying in the UK is worth up to £1,400 a year* to each person in Scotland.

One economy, more jobs.
Scotland trades more with the rest of the UK than with the rest of the world combined. Hundreds of thousands of Scottish jobs are connected to trade with the UK. A new international border and a different currency system would make trade harder and cost jobs at a time when the UK economy is recovering.

Cheaper bills.
The UK's financial standing keeps interest rates low. That means cheaper mortgages and loans. Plus our greater size makes household bills cheaper. Staying in the UK would keep future energy bills for Scottish households up to £189 a year lower.**

Best of both worlds.
The Scottish Parliament already decides important matters like health and education, and more powers for Scotland are guaranteed. And, as part of the UK family, we benefit by sharing resources and pooling risks. By staying together, we can have more decisions taken here in Scotland backed by the strength, stability and security of the UK.

Independence means Scotland will leave the UK - forever.

This is a big decision and every vote counts. Find out more at gov.uk/youdecide2014

Youdecide2014   Youdecide2014   Alternatively, you can request more information by writing to: Scotland Office, 1 Melville Crescent, Edinburgh, EH37HW.

* Source: Scotland analysis: Fiscal policy and sustainability, HM Government, May 2014 ** Source: Scotland analysis: Energy, HM Government, April 2014

Fig. A.3 UK Government Brochure Scottish Independence Referendum (2014). *Source* HM Government Information Brochure (Scottish Independence Referendum 2014)—Including long-term financial benefit per capita of staying in the EU (3-page brochure) https://www.gov.uk/government/uploads/system/uploads/attachment_data/file/340078/Make_sure_you_have_the_facts_when_you_decide_Scotland_s_future.pdf

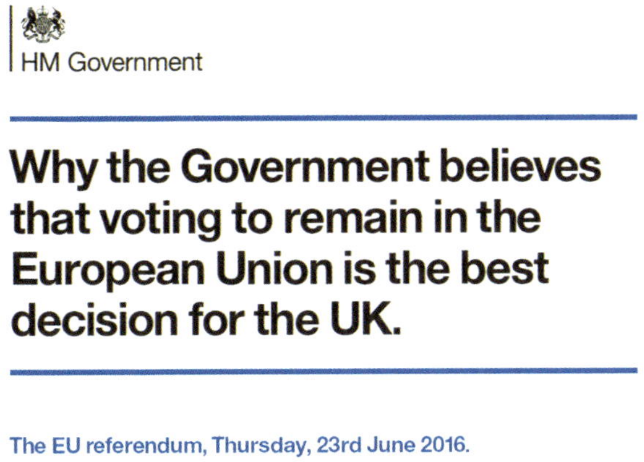

HM Government

Why the Government believes that voting to remain in the European Union is the best decision for the UK.

The EU referendum, Thursday, 23rd June 2016.

Fig. A.4 UK Government 16-page Brochure Brexit Referendum (2016). HM Government Information Brochure (Brexit Referendum 2016)—No figures included on long-term per capita benefit of staying in the EU (16-page information brochure). https://www.gov.uk/government/uploads/system/uploads/attachment_data/file/515068/why-the-government-believes-that-voting-to-remain-in-the-european-union-is-the-best-decision-for-the-uk.pdf

Appendix—Annex 3: Excerpts from the "Brexit Speech" of Prime Minister May, January 17, 2017

"A little over 6 months ago, the British people voted for change. They voted to shape a brighter future for our country. They voted to leave the European Union and embrace the world [...] And it is the job of this government to deliver it. That means more than negotiating our new relationship with the EU. It means taking the opportunity of this great moment of national change to step back and ask ourselves what kind of country we want to be. My answer is clear. I want this United Kingdom to emerge from this period of change stronger, fairer, more united and more outward-looking than ever before. I want us to be a secure, prosperous, tolerant country—a magnet for international talent and a home to the pioneers and innovators who will shape the world ahead. I want us to be a truly Global Britain—the best friend and neighbour to our European partners, but a country that reaches beyond the borders of Europe too. A country that goes out into the world to build relationships with old friends and new allies alike [...] And it is important to recognise this fact. June the 23rd was not the moment Britain chose to step back from the world. It was the moment we chose to build a truly Global Britain [...] Many in Britain have always felt that the United Kingdom's place in the European Union came at the expense of our global ties, and of a bolder embrace of free trade with

© The Editor(s) (if applicable) and The Author(s) 2017
P.J.J. Welfens, *An Accidental Brexit*,
DOI 10.1007/978-3-319-58271-9

the wider world [...] And that is why we seek a new and equal partnership—between an independent, self-governing, Global Britain and our friends and allies in the EU. Not partial membership of the European Union, associate membership of the European Union, or anything that leaves us half-in, half-out. We do not seek to adopt a model already enjoyed by other countries. We do not seek to hold on to bits of membership as we leave. No, the United Kingdom is leaving the European Union. And my job is to get the right deal for Britain as we do. So today I want to outline our objectives for the negotiation ahead. Twelve objectives that amount to one big goal: a new, positive and constructive partnership between Britain and the European Union. And as we negotiate that partnership, we will be driven by some simple principles: we will provide as much certainty and clarity as we can at every stage. And we will take this opportunity to make Britain stronger, to make Britain fairer, and to build a more Global Britain too.

1. Certainty
2. Control of our own laws
3. Strengthen the Union
4. Maintain the Common Travel Area with Ireland
5. Control of immigration
6. Rights for EU nationals in Britain, and British nationals in the EU
7. Protect workers' rights
8. Free trade with European markets
9. New trade agreements with other countries
10. The best place for science and innovation
11. Cooperation in the fight against crime and terrorism
12. A smooth, orderly Brexit

And I am confident that the objectives I am setting out today are consistent with the needs of the EU and its member states. That is why our objectives include a proposed free trade agreement between Britain and the European Union, and explicitly rule out membership of the EU's single market. Because when the EU's leaders say they believe the 4 freedoms of the single market are indivisible, we respect that position. When the 27 member states say they want to continue their journey inside the European Union, we not only respect that fact but support it. Because we do not want to undermine the single market, and we do not want to undermine the European Union. We want the EU to be a success and we want its remaining member states to prosper. And of course, we want the same for Britain. But I must be clear. Britain wants to remain a good friend and neighbor to Europe. Yet I know there are some voices calling for a punitive deal that punishes Britain and discourages other countries from taking the same path. That would be an act of calamitous self-harm for the countries of Europe. And it would not be the act of a friend. Britain would not—indeed we could not—accept such an approach. And while I am confident that this scenario need never arise—while I am sure a positive agreement can be reached—I am equally clear that no deal for Britain is better than a bad deal for Britain. Because we would still be able to trade with Europe. We would be free to strike trade deals across the world. And we would have the freedom to set the competitive tax rates and embrace the policies that would attract the world's best companies and biggest investors to Britain. And—if we were excluded from accessing the single market—we would be free to change the basis of Britain's economic model. But for the EU, it would mean new barriers to trade with one of the biggest economies in the world. It would jeopardise investments in Britain by EU companies worth more than half a trillion pounds. It would mean a loss of access for European firms to the financial services of the City of London. It would risk exports from the EU to Britain worth around £290($354) billion every year. And it would disrupt the sophisticated and integrated supply chains upon which many EU companies rely. Important sectors of the EU economy would also suffer. We are a crucial—profitable—export market for Europe's automotive industry, as well as sectors including energy, food and drink, chemicals, pharmaceuticals, and agriculture. These sectors employ millions of people around Europe. And I do not believe that the EU's leaders will seriously tell German exporters, French farmers, Spanish fishermen, the young unemployed of the Eurozone, and millions of others, that they want to make them poorer, just to punish Britain and make a political point. For all these reasons—and because of our shared values and the spirit of goodwill that exists on both sides—I am confident that we will follow a better path. I am confident that a positive agreement can be reached. It is right that the government should prepare for every eventuality—but to do so in the knowledge that a constructive and optimistic approach to the negotiations to come is in the best interests of Europe and the best interests of Britain. We do not approach these negotiations expecting failure, but anticipating success. Because we are a great, global nation with so much to offer Europe and so much to offer the world. One of the world's largest and strongest econo-mies. With the finest intelligence services, the bravest armed forces, the most effective hard and soft power, and friendships, partnerships and alliances in every continent. And another thing that's important. The essential ingredient of our success. The strength and support of 65 million people willing us to make it happen. Because after all the division and discord, the country is coming together. The referendum was divisive at times. And those divisions have taken time to heal. But one of the reasons that Britain's democracy has been such a success for so many years is that the strength of our identity as one nation, the respect we show to one another as fellow citizens, and the impor-tance we attach to our institutions means that when a vote has been held we all respect the result. The victors have the responsibility to act magnanimously. The losers have the responsibility to respect the legitimacy of the outcome. And the country comes together. And that is what we are seeing today. Business isn't calling to reverse the result, but planning to make a success of it. The House of Commons has voted overwhelmingly for us to get on with it. And the overwhelming majority of people—however they voted—want us to get on with it too. So that is what we will do. Not merely forming a new partner-ship with Europe, but building a stronger, fairer, more Global Britain too. And let that be the legacy of our time. The prize towards which we work. The destination at which we arrive once the negotiation is done. And let us do it not for ourselves, but for those who follow. For the country's children and grandchildren too. So that when future generations look back at this time, they will judge us not only by the decision that we made, but by what we made of that decision. They will see that we shaped them a brighter future. They will know that we built them a better Britain."

https://www.gov.uk/government/speeches/the-governments-negotiating-objectives-for-exiting-the-eu-pm-speech

Appendix—Annex 4: Brexit: EU27-UK Negotiations—Risk Analysis for the Euro Area and the EU27

It is unclear whether or not the EU–UK negotiations will be successful and a lot is at stake for both the UK and the EU27. One particular risk for the EU27 is related to the fact that the UK has been the banking center for the EU28 as the UK's economy had increasingly specialized on services, including financial services. Many specialized services for banks and firms in the EU27, concerning risk management on the one hand, and the launching of corporate bonds in capital markets on the other, have for decades been dominated by the UK. It is unclear whether equivalence agreements can be found in which the EU would give a green light to a broad number of financial service providers in the UK to continue offering services for EU27 countries from locations in London or elsewhere in the UK. At the end of 2012, the EU had 212 agreements with 32 countries that concerned a range of specific financial products. If there would not be a timely EU–UK agreement on key financial products by 2018—and there will be uncertainty about a successful swift ratification process—the EU27 countries will face destabilization impulses in financial markets as key services will no longer be available in traditional ways—while finding substitute services in New York, Singapore, Zurich, Tokyo or Hong Kong could be difficult and

© The Editor(s) (if applicable) and The Author(s) 2017
P.J.J. Welfens, *An Accidental Brexit*,
DOI 10.1007/978-3-319-58271-9

rather costly. It would be adequate for the EU to encourage the swift creation of critical financial services in the EU27 so that there will be no risk of financial market services disruptions; government should subsidize the provision of innovative financial services and particular advanced services since avoiding future destabilization amounts to avoiding negative external effects. Moreover, this would improve the EU27's leverage at the negotiating table.

The EU27 will initially stand together as a bloc against the UK in the EU27-UK negotiations. The broad EU27 economic upswing of 2017 will facilitate the EU27 position, not least as the EU is also facing pressure from the Trump administration in the US. At the same time, a reduction of output growth in the UK in 2017 could undermine the British position, not to mention the problem of potential Scottish independence. However, there is serious risk for the countries of the Eurozone as was already pointed out with respect to one aspect: the term premium—the change of sovereign bonds' interest rate compared to the pre-UK-referendum year (NIESER 2016a; and for a related analysis NIESER 2016b)—could increase in the Eurozone/EU27. In a broader macro simulation approach, IMK (2016) has considered three risks: a rise of the equity risk premium, a rise of the interest term premium and a rise of the investment premium (the latter is defined as the difference between the corporate bond yield and the government bond yield—for identical ratings and maturities, respectively). If all three risk effects are combined, the decline of investment in the Eurozone—relative to the baseline scenario of IMK—is small, –0.8% in 2016 and –4% the following year; the investment decline for the UK would be −0.4 and −2.8%, respectively. The much more drastic effects would occur in Italy and Greece where the effect on investment would be −2.1 and −11.8 and −12 and −25.9%, respectively; in Ireland the reduction of investment in the first year would be −1.3% and in the second year −7.5%, respectively; for Portugal the figures would be −0.9 and −5.6%, for Spain −1.2 and −8.3% (Table A.1).

Compared to the high risk scenario analysis, the CEPS report on the Brexit effects for the European Parliament (2017) shows generally rather modest negative Brexit effects for EU27 countries where two cases have been studied: (a) the UK could accede to the European Economic Area

Table A.1 Impact of a simultaneous rise of risk Premia in the context of Brexit: IMK simulations

	Change (percent) in investment in a high risk scenario (Rise of Term Premium + Equity Risk Premium + Investment Premium)[a]		Comments[b] about broader effects
UK	−0.4 (2016)	−2.8 (2017)	Response in reality delayed and much depends on EU–UK negotiations
Eurozone	−0.8	−4	Shows weak spot of EU27 in negotiation
Italy	−2.1	−11.8	Political instability?
Spain	−1.2	−8.3	Rather fast rise in unemployment
Portugal	−0.9	−5.6	Similar to Spain
Ireland	−1.3	−7.5	UK foreign direct in-vestment will help stabilizing
Greece	−12	−25.9	Expected political radicalization
Germany and France[b]	Safe haven effects imply small effects for both, the Eurozone effect thus could be smaller than line 2 suggests; Germany as a main exporter of machinery and equip-ment could face some pressure		

[a]Change vis-à-vis baseline Brexit scenario
[b]Comment by Paul JJ Welfens
Source IMK (2016), Brexit lähmt Konjunktur, IMK Report 115, June 2016, IMK/Hans-Böckler-Stiftung, Düsseldorf.

(EEA) as a non-member state like Norway or (b) the UK would not get a preferential trade relationship with the EU so that the conditions for EU market access are regulated on the basis of British membership of the World Trade Organization. While the CEPS report compiles many results from different available studies in the literature, it neglects—as the report makes clear in the introduction—foreign direct investment dynamics as well as intra-EU immigration. The CEPS report inadequately suggests that Brexit could not bring risk to the Eurozone and EU27, respectively. One should also take into account the analysis by the European Commission (2015) that shows the size of the job effects related to changes in third country exports of EU countries: in the UK, there were 720,000 jobs dependent on the third country exports of other EU countries. Here, one may anticipate that at least 15% of these jobs could be lost in the long run which means a loss of 108,000 jobs in the UK—together with multiplier effects, 150,000 jobs are likely to be lost. As intra-EU production-sharing networks involving British firms will be shrinking in the context of Brexit, even up to 30% of these jobs could be lost which means 300,000 job losses. If one assumes that reduced direct British exports to the EU27 bring job losses of about 500,000, the overall figure of job losses in the UK could approach one million.

An alternative simple supply-side view is as follows: one may argue that long-run benefits of EU membership can be assessed in the analytical context of an enhanced macroeconomic production function in which the export-GDP ratio x, the import-GDP ratio j and the degree of high-technology intensity of production h are included in addition to domestic capital K, inward cumulated foreign direct investment K^{**}, knowledge A and labor input L where ß, ß′ and ß″ as well as $v, v′$ and $v″$ all are positive parameters and $0 < ß < 1$, $0 < ß′ < 1$ and $0 < ß″ < 1$ are holding. The function suggested here is $Y = (1 + vh)(1 + v′x)(1 + v″j)K^{ß}K^{**ß′}(AL)^{1-ß-ß′}$. Thus, taking logs gives an equation that can rather easily be estimated empirically if one assumes that vh, $v′x$ and $v″j$ are close to zero (as regards the import-GDP ratio j, the relevant ratio could be defined to be intermediate imports to gross domestic product).

$$(1)\ \ln Y = vh + v′x + v″j + ß \ln K + ß′ \ln K^{**} + \left(1 - ß - ß′\right)(\ln A)$$
$$+ \left(1 - ß - ß′\right)\ln L$$

Foreign ownership of physical capital thus is directly covered by K^{**}, but one should also notice that foreign multinationals could affect the high-technology intensity h (defined as the share of high-technology output in total output) and the level of knowledge A could also be affected by cumulated inward foreign direct investment. It suffices to argue here that Brexit and hence reduced future UK access to the EU single market would be reflected by a fall of h, x, j, K^{**} (reduction through non-reinvestment over time) and A; the latter variable would, in an enhanced neoclassical growth model, affect the long-run growth rate of the UK in a negative way, while a fall of the other variables mentioned would reduce the level of the growth path. It should be mentioned that the idea that high-technology specialization matters for output in a particular way dates back to Jungmittag (2004) while the role of exports in raising output has been emphasized early by Adam Smith and more recently by Melitz (2003). The specific function for GDP suggested here allows to easily look at per capita GDP since this can be written in logarithmic terms as (with $k := K/L$ and $k^{**} := K^{**}/L$):

(2) $\ln y = vh + v'x + v''j + \beta \ln k + \beta' \ln k^{**} + (1 - \beta - \beta\prime) \ln A$

Hence if Brexit brings a reduction of x and j for the UK through weaker regional integration in Europe, while a smaller inward FDI capital intensity k^{**} and a reduction of h plus a smaller growth of knowledge is observed, the negative effect on per capita GDP will be considerable. The economically more relevant issue is per capita gross national income $z = Z/L$ (Z is real gross national output). As $Z = Y$ (GDP) plus net income from abroad, the simple asymmetric setting considered here means to additionally look at the profits of foreign subsidiaries in the UK that are transferred to the respective parent companies abroad (say in the US, EU27, Japan, Korea, China, India et cetera). In a realistic model setting for the UK, one should, of course, consider both inward foreign direct investment and outward foreign direct investment [see on this and related welfare aspects: Welfens (2017)]. An empirical implementation is rather straightforward. The supply-side concept can, of course, also be applied to EU27 countries or the Eurozone. As regards the EU27, the Brexit will reduce x, j and

h less than is the case in the UK and the reduction of k^{**} will also be rather modest; as will be the impact on knowledge generation A. This, however, should not mean to overlook considerable asymmetric effects in the Eurozone and one should also consider in addition special risk aspects that could also become relevant for the EU27 and the UK.

A new Eurozone crisis would cause new internal economic and political conflicts in the Eurozone and the EU27, respectively; and such a situation would enormously weaken the EU27 position in the EU27-UK negotiations. Such a dramatic situation for the EU27 and the Eurozone, respectively, could only be avoided if major reforms in the Eurozone/EU27 would remove that type of leverage in favor of the UK. It is thus in Germany's and indeed France's interest to push Greece, Italy and other countries to undertake quick reforms and to offer at least some special support in return for adequate reforms; this would, for example, require constitutional reforms in Greece (and possibly also in Italy) combined with a debt reduction for Greece in 2018; plus adjusting Italian framework conditions for foreign investors and the creation of Italian multinational firms—which are fairly under-represented in Italy. Additional expansionary impulses from the digital modernization of government, universities and firms are required in many EU countries. Certain joint growth-enhancing reforms could be useful in the EU in 2018/19; and here, Germany would have a special responsibility since it could reduce its high current account surplus (8% of GDP in 2016)—and thus improve the net exports of most of its Eurozone partner countries—by raising public investment and cutting the value-added tax rate. In order to avoid high deficits, Germany could raise other taxes slightly, including the income tax rate provided that the income threshold where earners enter the top income tax bracket is also raised.

If the EU27 can avoid a new crisis of the Eurozone, the EU's prospects for a favorable outcome of the EU27-UK negotiations are improved. However, one should also not overlook the potential problem that the UK walking-away from the negotiation table would trigger negative effects for the United Kingdom, but the induced higher uncertainty and risk enhancement effects in the EU27 could also present a serious challenge so that the EU27 would be wise to have adequate policy instruments readily available; part of the challenge of the EU27 is that certain financial services needed by corporate customers in EU27 countries are strongly concentrated in the UK so far. Hence it would be wise if there is sufficient Franco-German leadership—joined by other EU27 countries—to quickly encourage the broad development of comparable services in the Eurozone and the EU27, respectively. In the first quarter of 2017 no such plans had even been mentioned by leading political actors in the EU27. This points to a lack of understanding of the risks involved in the EU–UK negotiation process associated with Brexit, and a lack of risk management will carry a high price tag for the EU27. The higher this price tag is—the better the deal for the UK and the larger the incentive for other EU countries to defect in the future will be.

If Germany should stick to its traditional positions, namely to be rather inflexible vis-à-vis Greece and to maintain the argument that the German government cannot influence the country's current account position, the Eurozone and the EU27 will be heading towards considerable risk. Other Eurozone countries should also be up to the historical challenge and a broad policy package of reforms should be prepared early on by the EU27 countries and the Eurozone, respectively. There could also be a critical role for the ESM which is an important institution for the stabilization of the Eurozone. If Brexit should create instability in financial markets in the EU28, it would also be adequate that central banks, for example the ECB and the Bank of England, would cooperate in an efficient and effective manner. However, given the nature of the Brexit negotiations, that type of cooperation is rather uncertain. Both the UK and the EU27 should be aware that "disruptive negotiations" could not only destabilize the EU28 but other regions of the world economy as well—there is a joint responsibility to carefully conduct the negotiation process and to organize an adequate risk management.

Appendix—Annex 5: Top 10 Countries Ranked by GDP (Nominal and Purchasing Power Parity)

See Tables A.2 and A.3.

Table A.2 Top 10 countries ranked by nominal GDP in billions of US dollars

Ranking	Country	Nominal GDP (in Billions $US)
1	United States	18,561
2	China	11,391
3	Japan	4,730
4	Germany	3,494
5	United Kingdom	2,649
6	France	2,488
7	India	2,250
8	Italy	1,852
9	Brazil	1,769
10	Canada	1,532

Source IMF, World Economic Outlook Database, October 2016

© The Editor(s) (if applicable) and The Author(s) 2017
P.J.J. Welfens, *An Accidental Brexit*,
DOI 10.1007/978-3-319-58271-9

Table A.3   Top 10 countries ranked by GDP by purchasing power parity (PPP) in billions of current international dollars (2016)

Ranking	Country	GDP by PPP (in Billions of Current International Dollars, 2016)
1	China	21,269
2	United States	18,562
3	India	8,720
4	Japan	4,932
5	Germany	3,979
6	Russia	3,745
7	Brazil	3,134
8	Indonesia	3,027
9	United Kingdom	2,787
10	France	2,736

Source IMF, World Economic Outlook Database, October 2016

Appendix—Annex 6: Data on Gross Domestic Product and Population as Share of World Totals

See Figs. A.5, A.6 and A.7

© The Editor(s) (if applicable) and The Author(s) 2017   **407**
P.J.J. Welfens, *An Accidental Brexit*,
DOI 10.1007/978-3-319-58271-9

GDP in Percent of the World PPP (Current International Dollars)

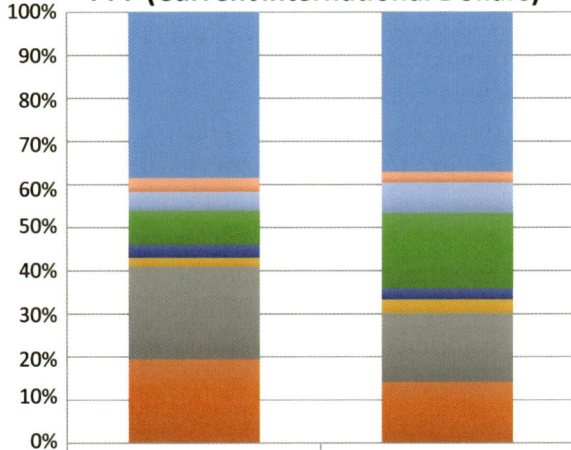

	2000	2015
■ Rest of the world	38.43%	3.70%
■ United Kingdom	3.17%	2.38%
■ India	4.35%	7.00%
■ China	7.66%	17.34%
■ Brazil	3.25%	2.80%
■ Russian Federation	2.07%	3.13%
■ United States	21.27%	15.79%
■ European Union excl. UK	19.77%	14.51%

Fig. A.5   GDP in percent of the world PPP (Current international dollars)

GDP in Percent of the World
PPP (Constant 2011 International Dollars)

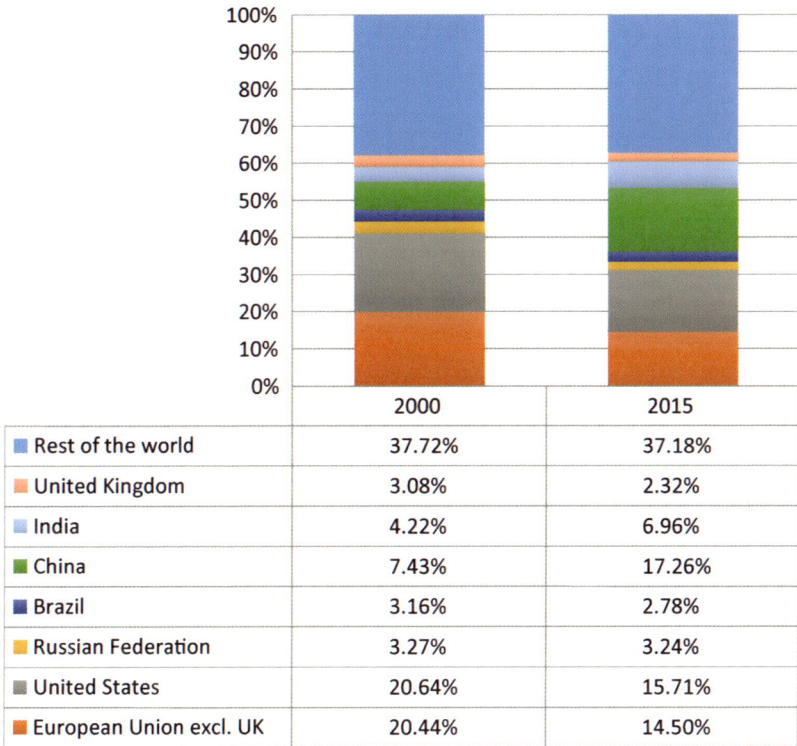

	2000	2015
■ Rest of the world	37.72%	37.18%
■ United Kingdom	3.08%	2.32%
■ India	4.22%	6.96%
■ China	7.43%	17.26%
■ Brazil	3.16%	2.78%
■ Russian Federation	3.27%	3.24%
■ United States	20.64%	15.71%
■ European Union excl. UK	20.44%	14.50%

Fig. A.6 GDP in percent of the world PPP (Constant 2011 international dollars)

Population
in Percentage of the World

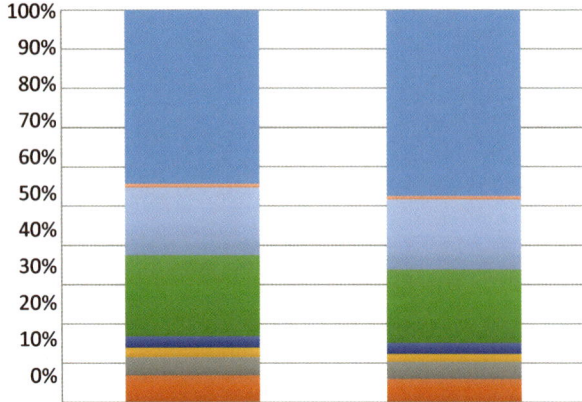

	2000	2015
■ Rest of the world	44.26%	47.38%
■ United Kingdom	0.96%	0.88%
■ India	17.22%	17.84%
■ China	20.64%	18.66%
■ Brazil	2.87%	2.82%
■ Russian Federation	2.39%	1.96%
■ United States	4.61%	4.37%
■ European Union excl. UK	7.01%	6.05%

Fig. A.7 Population in percent of the world population. *Source* World Bank, World Development Indicators, retrieved on 09.01.2017 17:08

Appendix—Annex 7: An Optimistic Medium-Term View from the Office for Budget Responsibility

The March 2017 Forecast of the Office for Budget Responsibility (OBR) is rather favorable for the UK: 2% economic growth is expected in 2017—which represents a considerable upward revision compared to the November 2016 OBR forecast. The OBR's Economic and Fiscal Outlook of March 2017 is rather optimistic in the sense that the OBR has not taken into account the bill for the exit from the EU which might amount to about £40–50 ($49–$61) billion. From this perspective, the fiscal room to maneuver claimed by Minister Hammond—he has argued that the goal of a 2% structural deficit–GDP ratio still leaves £26/$32 billion for an expansionary fiscal policy approach to absorb negative impulses from Brexit—is not as broad as suggested by the Treasury. Even if the EU exit invoice could be paid over several years, the medium-term room to maneuver will be rather restricted. The OBR's medium-term output forecast of March 2017 shows a downward revision compared to the November forecast, but it still suggests rather strong output growth for 2018–2021 as the growth rate is expected to be 1.6% in 2018, 1.7% in 2019, 1.9% in 2020, and 2% in 2021 (see Fig. A.8).

© The Editor(s) (if applicable) and The Author(s) 2017
P.J.J. Welfens, *An Accidental Brexit*,
DOI 10.1007/978-3-319-58271-9

Annual real GDP growth

Percentage change on a year earlier

3

2.2
2.2
2.1   2.0
1.8
1.4   1.6
1.7
1.7   1.9
2.1   2.1
2.0
2.0

2

1

0

2015 2016 2017 2018 2019 2020 2021

→ November
→ March

Office for
Budget
Responsibility

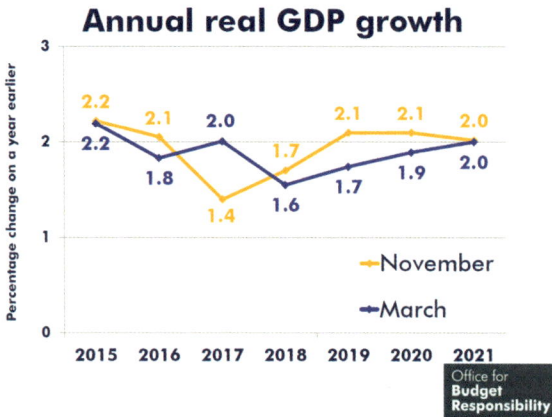

Fig. A.8 Office for budget responsibility (March 2017 annual real GP growth forecast). *Source* OBR, Economic and Fiscal Outlook, London, March, 2017

If Brexit is implemented fully, one should expect that real output growth will decline considerably in the period 2019–2021. While one may assume that the US output growth in the first half of the Trump administration will increase and thereby raise output growth in the UK and the EU27, the prospects for rising economic growth in 2020/21 in the UK could be more modest than is suggested by the OBR's March 2017 forecast. One may point out that the long-term forecast error of the OBR with respect to the deficit–GDP ratio is an underestimation of 0.5% of GDP. If one considers the UK exit invoice, one may argue that the prospects for an expansionary fiscal policy after Brexit could be more modest than seems to be suggested by the OBR.

The European Commission's European Economic Forecast Winter (2017a) forecast suggests that growth in the UK will reduce: 1.8% in 2017, 1.2% in 2018 (Fig. A.9). The growth rate of gross fixed capital formation in the UK is expected to reduce strongly in 2017/18—in 2018 only 0.2% growth is expected—and the savings rate of private households is expected to reduce by almost 2 percentage points in the period 2016–2018. With a long-run reduction of the savings rate, the level of the growth path in a neoclassical standard growth model is reduced: if Brexit brings a permanent reduction of the savings rate of

Main features of country forecast - UNITED KINGDOM

	bn GBP Curr. prices	% GDP	97-12	2013	2014	2015	2016	2017	2018
GDP	1872.7	100.0	2.0	1.9	3.1	2.2	2.0	1.5	1.2
Private Consumption	1214.7	64.9	2.4	1.6	2.2	2.4	2.8	1.9	0.9
Public Consumption	362.8	19.4	2.3	0.3	2.3	1.3	1.0	0.7	0.4
Gross fixed capital formation	317.1	16.9	1.1	3.2	6.7	3.4	1.0	1.6	0.2
of which: equipment	74.9	4.0	0.7	2.5	6.8	4.7	2.3	2.0	0.2
Exports (goods and services)	517.4	27.6	3.6	1.1	1.5	6.1	1.7	3.5	2.9
Imports (goods and services)	547.2	29.2	4.3	3.4	2.5	5.5	2.8	3.0	1.1
GNI (GDP deflator)	1847.0	98.6	2.0	1.4	2.3	2.1	1.8	1.9	1.3
Contribution to GDP growth: Domestic demand			2.2	1.6	2.9	2.3	2.2	1.6	0.7
Inventories			0.0	0.6	0.5	-0.3	-0.1	0.0	0.0
Net exports			-0.2	-0.8	-0.4	0.0	-0.3	0.1	0.5
Employment			0.8	1.2	2.4	1.8	1.3	0.5	0.3
Unemployment rate (a)			6.0	7.6	6.1	5.3	4.9	5.2	5.6
Compensation of employees / head			3.9	2.1	0.4	0.9	2.3	2.4	2.4
Unit labour costs whole economy			2.7	1.3	-0.3	0.5	1.6	1.4	1.5
Real unit labour cost			0.7	-0.6	-1.9	-0.1	0.5	-0.4	-1.0
Saving rate of households (b)			8.4	6.7	6.8	6.5	5.5	4.3	3.7
GDP deflator			2.0	1.9	1.6	0.6	1.1	1.9	2.6
Harmonised index of consumer prices			2.1	2.6	1.5	0.0	0.7	2.5	2.6
Terms of trade goods			0.0	1.4	-0.4	-1.5	0.0	-1.7	0.1
Trade balance (goods) (c)			-4.6	-6.9	-6.7	-6.4	-7.4	-8.2	-7.9
Current-account balance (c)			-2.1	-4.4	-4.7	-4.3	-5.0	-4.8	-3.9
Net lending (+) or borrowing (-) vis-a-vis ROW (c)			-2.1	-4.4	-4.7	-4.3	-5.1	-4.9	-4.0
General government balance (c)			-3.6	-5.7	-5.8	-4.4	-3.4	-2.8	-2.5
Cyclically-adjusted budget balance (d)			-3.5	-4.4	-5.5	-4.5	-3.7	-3.2	-2.6
Structural budget balance (d)			·	-4.4	-5.4	-4.5	-3.7	-3.2	-2.6
General government gross debt (c)			49.1	86.2	88.1	89.0	88.6	88.1	87.0

(a) as % of total labour force. (b) gross saving divided by adjusted gross disposable income. (c) as a % of GDP. (d) as a % of potential GDP.

Fig. A.9 Winter 2017 forecast for the UK, European Commission.
Source European Commission (2017)

2%, the level of the growth path is reduced by 1% (assuming that the output elasticity of capital is 0.33, which is a standard assumption in modern growth literature). The inflation rate in 2017/18 is expected to increase by 2 percentage points compared to 2016.

As regards the current account–GDP ratio, the EU forecast suggests that it is expected to remain around 4% of GDP in the medium term (roughly similar to the period 2013–2015), which is much higher than the average of 2.1% in 1997–2012. The implication is that the UK's foreign indebtedness-GDP would rise considerably; if the GDP trend growth rate would be 1.5% while the trend ratio of the current account deficit–GDP ratio would be 3%, the ratio of foreign indebtedness to GDP would be 200% in the long run. If the yield on investment of foreign investors were 2.5% (4%) in the UK, net factor payments going abroad would be equivalent to 5% (8%) of GDP in the long run. With Brexit, the current account–GDP ratio of the UK may be expected to rise and hence the implication for the long-run economic development in the United Kingdom is that there will be considerable negative welfare effects. Even if GDP growth would not be impaired much by Brexit, the rising current account deficit–GDP ratio implies that national income (gross national product) will increase more slowly compared to a reference scenario without Brexit. General government debt to GDP is expected to fall gradually—the peak of 89% was in 2015.

Appendix—Annex 8: UK Domestic Value-Added Content of Gross Exports

See Fig. A.10.

UK — Domestic value added content of gross exports | Gross exports (Nominal, in millions of US Dollars)

	Domestic value added content of gross exports 2005	2011	Gross exports 2005	2011
Germany	45,335	58,984	55,235	78,530
France	33,175	37,369	40,717	50,610
Italy	19,801	20,555	24,253	27,052
Spain	22,808	25,012	27,840	32,379
Ireland	28,028	31,487	33,799	40,245
Netherlands	17,070	20,652	19,350	24,833
Belgium	10,903	14,268	13,049	18,426
US	80,930	86,078	95,846	109,414
Canada	11,036	13,971	13,067	18,374
China	7,907	19,507	9,656	26,177
India	6,917	15,059	8,091	19,043
Russia	5,586	11,396	6,726	15,108
Turkey	3,912	5,780	5,028	8,229
Brazil	1,774	4,859	2,158	6,402
World	447,735	569,204	539,631	738,631
EU15	207,917	247,347	251,449	322,400
EU28	220,846	266,333	267,219	347,110
ASEAN	12,048	16,867	14,040	20,849

	2005	2011
GDP UK	2,508,000	2,609,000

UK — Domestic value added content of gross exports | Gross exports (as a percentage of GDP)

	Domestic value added content of gross exports 2005	2011	Gross exports 2005	2011
Germany	1.81%	2.26%	2.20%	3.01%
France	1.32%	1.43%	1.62%	1.94%
Italy	0.79%	0.79%	0.97%	1.04%
Spain	0.91%	0.96%	1.11%	1.24%
Ireland	1.12%	1.21%	1.35%	1.54%
Netherlands	0.68%	0.79%	0.77%	0.95%
Belgium	0.43%	0.55%	0.52%	0.71%
US	3.23%	3.30%	3.82%	4.19%
Canada	0.44%	0.54%	0.52%	0.70%
China	0.32%	0.75%	0.39%	1.00%
India	0.28%	0.58%	0.32%	0.73%
Russia	0.22%	0.44%	0.27%	0.58%
Turkey	0.16%	0.22%	0.20%	0.32%
Brazil	0.07%	0.19%	0.09%	0.25%
World	17.85%	21.82%	21.52%	28.31%
EU15	8.29%	9.48%	10.03%	12.36%
EU28	8.81%	10.21%	10.65%	13.30%
ASEAN	0.48%	0.65%	0.56%	0.80%

Fig. A.10 UK domestic value-added content of gross exports. *Source* OECD, TiVA Database

© The Editor(s) (if applicable) and The Author(s) 2017
P.J.J. Welfens, *An Accidental Brexit*,
DOI 10.1007/978-3-319-58271-9

Appendix—Annex 9: Germany's Massive Export Surplus: Questions for the Eurozone and the EU

The International Monetary Fund (IMF) has criticized the German export surplus which the country has generated for a number of years and which amounts to 8% of Gross Domestic Product (GDP). Minister of Finance in Berlin, Wolfgang Schäuble, and also Secretary of State in the Finance Ministry, Jens Spahn, have repudiated the criticisms levelled by both the IMF and certain EU partner countries. The German surplus is defended as being simply an expression of Germany's high international competitiveness. Blame has also been ascribed to the European Central Bank and its expansionary policies, which contribute to a depreciation of the Euro and high exports to the United States. That position is, however, a totally distorted view which represents a curious and contradictory playing down of the responsibility of domestic monetary and fiscal policy. On the other hand, Christine Lagarde also exceeds her mandate as Managing Director of the IMF when she suggests increased investment in the expansion of broadband networks to counter the export surplus. The supervisory function of the IMF naturally involves drawing attention to international economic imbalances, however suggesting individual policy measures to IMF member states could be regarded as a questionable interference in domestic politics. Of

© The Editor(s) (if applicable) and The Author(s) 2017
P.J.J. Welfens, *An Accidental Brexit*,
DOI 10.1007/978-3-319-58271-9

course, Germany could implement sensible policies to correct its current account position which, considering the EU's upper limit vis-à-vis net exports of 6% relative to national income, is indeed excessive—in particular through fiscal policy; here, the question of European credibility with regard to Germany is at stake—how egocentric can Germany afford to be at EU level in terms of policy? How little of a Euro-focused strategy is acceptable, particularly in the wake of the Brexit referendum in the UK?

For many years, the federal government in Berlin has emphatically argued that rules agreed at an EU level must be complied with. If Germany wishes to perennially ignore the upper 6% export surplus limit—as Schäuble suggests—then this is actually against Germany's interests in Europe, namely with respect to the demands that upper limits be respected, including regulations relating limits on deficits or debt ratios as agreed in the context of the Stability Pact. If Germany, above all, should year after year be in breach of crucial rules, then that is obviously not a smart move if one wishes to maintain a meaningful regulatory framework.

Moreover, the German current account surplus could in fact rise even further in 2017/18 as global growth increases and with it the demand for high value machinery, automobiles and chemical products from Germany. If Germany and some other countries of the world economy should continue to have ever growing surpluses, then the net imports of many trade partners will rise and thus also their foreign indebtedness. This rising foreign indebtedness is, in turn, a justifiable cause of concern for the International Monetary Fund, a body which should take global stability perspectives into consideration and relay this information to the Group of Twenty (G20). In 2017, it is Germany of all countries which holds the Presidency of the G20, while Berlin appears to be inflexible and devoid of ideas with regard to the record surpluses.

From an economic perspective, it should not of course be considered that the state would seek to limit or reduce the international competitiveness of German firms. Indeed here the Schäuble position is particularly oblique. The export surplus of a country in a macroeconomic approach is simply the difference between the production of tradable goods and the domestic demand for such goods. The federal government in Berlin could raise this domestic demand by means of two straight forward measures: on the one hand with raised public investment, for which the Finance Ministry has, carefully, paved the way. On the other hand, the desired effect can be achieved above all by way of a reduction of the value-added tax (VAT) rate by about 2%— to date, nothing has been done in Berlin with regard to this possibility. The reduction in the price of domestic tradable goods as a result of a reduction of the VAT rate raises domestic demand, and thus reduces the export surplus. The favorable current budget situation readily facilitates the undertaking of such a tax-related measure; however, somewhat raised environmental taxes could also be considered for the purposes of achieving budgetary stability and higher environmental quality.

It is imperative from the point of view of European accountability and responsibility that German surplus rates will not be passively allowed to continue and in doing so to damage the interests of Germany itself in Europe and worldwide. A land as large as Germany must consider the effects of domestic policy—and indeed the lack of political action at home—on partner countries; not to mention the ultimate feedback effects, i.e. repercussions, on Germany itself. One added advantage of reducing the surplus rate would be that it would serve to cleverly maneuver Germany out of the political firing line in Washington—although Trump has criticized Germany's export surplus without real motive, as from a transatlantic perspective it is the current account position of the Eurozone which is of primary importance and not of individual member countries. Furthermore, the latest OECD publications have shown that in international comparisons Germany's tax and contribution ratio is one of the highest. From this perspective, an expeditious reduction of the VAT rate by the federal government in Berlin is also necessary.

The West is in a period of crisis. In the United Kingdom, a referendum which did not meet the basic standards one would expect of such a vote resulted in a slight majority in favor of leaving the European Union—Prime Minister Cameron, during a period of chaotic governance in the run-up to the referendum of all times, concealed the fact that his own finance department (Her Majesty's Treasury) in a study from April 2016 found that the costs of Brexit would amount to a 10% loss of income for the UK. Had this figure been included in the 16-page government information brochure which was distributed to households across the UK before the vote, then according to well-known UK-related popularity functions regarding the relationship between growth and the popularity of the government the referendum would have resulted in a 52% majority for Remain. Why the new President of the United States, Donald Trump, regards Brexit as being a positive development, and contradicts not only reasonable and sound politics but also 70 years of US policy with regard to matters of European integration, is a mystery. That Trump was elected President of the US and seems to want to act as the protectionist leader of the Western world is curious. Rationality and economic logic have become scarce commodities in the West; the practical errors and erroneous forecasts in terms of economic policy have in many EU countries been substantial. Here, Germany is only a partial exception—France, with its national uniform minimum wage, is an economic "Absurdistan"—successive French governments are responsible for three decades with a youth unemployment rate triple that of Switzerland; in combination with the highly violent Islamist tendencies since 1979, such high unemployment rates are deadly. Since 1995, Italy has endured a massive lack of growth-promoting reforms. Moreover, there are certainly problems regarding the construction of the Eurozone and there were irresponsible Greek governments. With egoism and inadequate policies, one cannot successfully govern and develop an EU fit for the twenty-first century. Germany cannot be indifferent to the fact that 40% of the French electorate voted for radical candidates on April 23. The criticism of the German export surplus by Emmanuel Macron should also be taken seriously and considered thoughtfully in Berlin. The dwindling influence of economists of economic policy is a perilous development.

Summary

1. In the United Kingdom, there has been a lively debate on the pros and cons of EU membership. As is well known, the government successfully negotiated with the European Commission in early 2016 on some key aspects of immigration and the future deepening of the EU single

market. The government recommended that the UK should stay in the European Union, but the referendum saw a 51.9% majority vote in favor of leaving the EU. According to Opinium Research, the voters emphasized the following issues as the most important issues to them personally vis-à-vis the referendum: National Health Service problems (slightly more than 50% of respondents), economic problems, low wages, immigration (more than 20% of respondents—who could choose multiple answers), relations between the UK and the EU, housing market problems, education system problems, poverty/inequality; the relationship between the UK and the EU was not among the top four issues and, according to Bank of England research in 2015, immigration has contributed to lower wages only in the group of unskilled workers in the services sector. Hence, the referendum result was obviously mainly about rejecting the Camerongovernment and not so much the European Union which has nothing to do with the National Health Service problems, housing market problems, education system problems, and poverty/inequality. An unbiased EU referendum could only have been obtained on June 23 if there had been a separate referendum question on the performance of the Cameron government and a second separate question about British EU membership, and if the government had provided adequate information on the advantages of British EU membership and the economic costs of leaving the EU. There is also a paradox, namely that free capital flows and an unbiased referendum may be incompatible.

2. The June 2016 referendum of the Cameron government was a disorderly one: the 16-page government information brochure mailed to all households in England did not contain a single word on the Treasury Study findings showing that the long-run real income effect of Brexit is a loss of 10%. While in the run-up to the Scottish independence referendum in 2014, the Cameron government has informed voters that Scottish independence would mean a £1,400/$1,700 loss of income per capita, the much greater expected loss of per capita income due to Brexit was not communicated. Strangely, the very important UK Treasury Report (200 pages): (https://www.gov.uk/government/uploads/system/uploads/attachment_data/file/517415/

treasury_analysis_economic_impact_of_eu_membership_web. pdf) on the long-term effects of British EU membership—and thus on Brexit—was published on April 18, a week after the government's sending out of the brochure to households in England, which occurred between April 11 and 13. The rest of the UK received the brochure only after May 9—still with no info on the key findings of the Treasury Report.

3. If British households had been properly informed by the government on the long-run expected income losses and the anticipated income tax increases, the standard popularity functions for the UK imply that the result would have been 52.1% in favor of REMAIN: just the opposite of the artificial Brexit majority of 51.9% of June 23, 2016. All of the subsequent drastic historical Brexit-related decisions taken by government and the Parliament's majority therefore are doubtful and the legitimacy of the referendum is extremely weak as has been emphasized in the contribution of Welfens in the Journal *International Economics and Economic Policy* (Issue 4, 2016: http:// link.springer.com/10.1007/s10368-016-0361-3).

Since 2013, Premier Cameron has—together with his Home Secretary, Mrs. May—emphasized that EU immigration was a massive burden for government and he indeed promised to strongly reduce immigration. This has mainly served to create a scapegoat for the effects of the massive cuts in government transfers to local communities which faced reductions by the Cameron governments equivalent to 3.5% of GDP so that local public services had to be reduced: voters, impressed by the anti-immigration rhetoric of Cameron/May, then misplaced the responsibility for this under-provision of public services on the immigrants. Given the facts and analysis of OECD on EU immigration effects in the UK, however, namely that the labor market participation rate of the EU immigrants is higher than the British average and that EU immigrants stand for a positive net contribution to the government budget, one can only conclude: any anti-EU immigration rhetoric is misplaced since the net contribution of EU immigrants to the government budget implies that those immigrants had actually contributed to co-financing building of schools for their British fellow citizens. The

May government, however, writes in Chap. 5 of the White Paper 'The United Kingdom's exit from and new partnership with the European Union' (HM Govt, 2017b), titled "Immigration Control," that "… in the last decade or so, we have seen record levels of long term net migration in the UK,…and that sheer volume has given rise to public concern about pressure on public services, like schools and our infrastructure, especially housing, as well as placing downward pressure on wages for people on the lowest incomes. The public must have confidence in our ability to control immigration. It is simply not possible to control immigration overall when there is unlimited free movement of people to the UK from the EU." This view is obviously misleading in its emphasis that EU immigrants created problems regarding the building of schools and public infrastructure and the fringe of British workers facing downward wage pressure from EU immigrants is quite narrow according to the Bank of England paper. Chart 5.1 in the government's White Paper shows that it is not EU immigration dynamics that has been the main driver of immigration growth in the past decade, rather non-EU immigration has played the key role. Why is leaving the EU and the EU single market the natural answer to a rising pressure from non-EU immigration? As Francis Bacon emphasized: for every conjecture one should expect adequate evidence from the facts—evidence is missing.

The legitimacy of the British 2016 referendum is weak; the political and economic logic of the May government is opaque in the field of Brexit policy. The free trade agenda outlined by Mr. David Davis—the "Exit Minister"—is illusory since beyond a free trade agreement with the US (and Japan) not many additional free trade agreements with significant economic impact are to be expected. A free trade agreement with China is hardly feasible since it would put a large part of the British industry under extreme pressure while negotiations with India would quickly lead to the issue of additional visas for Indians. The new cooperation between Prime Minister May and the US President Trump with his broad protectionism will not work in the long run.

The White Paper of the May government (HM Govt 2017b) indicates certain inconsistencies in terms of economic policy strategy and free trade approaches. Modern free trade agreements—such as the

Trans-Pacific Partnership and the Transatlantic Trade and Investment Partnership program (EU–US project)—emphasize under the heading of "deep integration" the reduction of tariffs, but even more so the elimination of non-tariff barriers; therefore, some form of international cooperation in key economic policy fields is necessary. The EU single market project of 1993 was the first such project worldwide as it accepted some framework policy by the supranational European Commission or assumed a mutual recognition of the standards of EU countries by each other. This implies giving up some traditional national policy autonomy, but only to effectively increase the potential global outreach of the European Union: an enhanced EU power to allow shaping the rules of economic globalization as well as the imitation of EU institutions by other regional integration which creates new advantages for EU member countries (see, for example, ASEAN with its own single market; Mercosur which is a customs union—with common external tariffs—and thus similar to the EU). The new slogan of the Leave campaign that regaining traditional British policy autonomy would be an advantage is rather old-fashioned and ignores the indirect gain of power through EU membership. Brexit itself is totally in contrast to the modern concept of deep integration approaches.

Brexit will bring about a strong devaluation of the Pound Sterling—possibly by about 20%. This will raise the inflation rate which brings negative welfare effects and it will also reduce the global demand for Sterling as a reserve currency (thus "free" imports of goods and services for the UK will be reduced; the international seigniorage will fall for the UK). Moreover, the share of the British economy in world GDP falls by the same percentage as the rate of the Pound's devaluation; a lower share in the global economy means a reduction of power and political leverage in international negotiations on trade, investment treaties and so on. If one considers a 10% real income reduction due to Brexit as realistic—following the findings of the report by the UK's Treasury—the overall reduction of the UK's weight in the global economy due to Brexit could reach about 30% in the long run. Welfare losses for the UK will thus be considerable and the country may also expect to have reduced political influence. It is also obvious that foreign investors will be able to take over a larger share of the British capital stock which reduces the growth rate of real gross national income as a higher share of British profits will be transferred abroad (to MNC parent companies). It is not gross domestic product which matters for consumption but actually gross national income and hence the consumption growth rate in the UK will be negatively affected.

The real depreciation of the Pound will stimulate net exports in the medium term, but in effect this amounts to worsening terms of trade: for a given amount of imported goods, more goods have to be exported—for a given output, a real devaluation thus amounts to a tax on British citizens. To the extent that the British government will adopt a new round of excessive banking deregulation (in parallel to the US)—in an attempt to raise output growth—there is a risk of a new European banking crisis; and a repetition of the high cost of the banking crisis of 2007–2009 is quite likely to be faced by all parts of the UK and indeed by the whole of Europe and the US in the long run (for further arguments on this aspect, see also the EIIW discussion paper 238 by Welfens, forthcoming, www.eiiw.eu).

With Brexit, it will be almost impossible to maintain current sectoral market access situations for UK producers in the EU27; the fact that a sectoral UK–EU free trade arrangement will give better access to firms from third countries to the British market does change the post-Brexit trade equation for the United Kingdom. Looking at the negative sectoral current account position of the UK, one may emphasize that the future sectoral current account position will be even more negative and hence the overall current account position even more significant than previously.

Looking at the macroeconomic adjustment dynamics, one finds arguments why the first post-referendum year should be characterized primarily by a currency depreciation and a fall of relative real estate prices, while the unexpected Pound depreciation will translate into reduced real wages and some transitory employment growth in the medium-term, the long-term economic effect—once Brexit is implemented—is a fall of GDP by about 6%. This effect might, of course, be mitigated by expansionary monetary policy in the UK for some time. However, as soon as the US interest rates start rising strongly, the UK will be quickly exposed to upward pressure on interest rates.

The Leave campaign's arguments that the UK could become the new leader of a revitalized Commonwealth is unrealistic and the promise of considerable free trade gains for the UK—post-Brexit—from a series of new worldwide (but Commonwealth based) free trade agreements is illusory. The largest gain the UK can expect is from a UK–US free trade agreement. British exports to the US stood for 2.5% of the aggregate value-added of the UK in 2015, but the British exports to the EU27 represented almost 13% of the British gross domestic product. Facing restrictions in access to the EU27 after 2019, the UK will not be able to compensate market share losses in the EU27—geographically so near to the UK—by increasing US exports. That the UK could easily negotiate a free trade agreement with China is unlikely for both political reasons (that are related to US interests) and economic reasons—with much higher imports from China undermining the already low share of the manufacturing industry in total British output (and a May government eager to emphasize the goal of the reindustrialization of the UK). More free trade with India is indeed one post-Brexit option, but any Indian government will push for better visa access for Indian workers and it is unclear why the majority of British voters should be expected to be more welcoming of Indian migrants than of those EU migrants that came to the UK in the period 2004–2016.

Brexit represents a historical politico-economic turning point in the UK which can largely be explained by a disorderly referendum in a post-banking crisis period with a public that to some extent has lost confidence in broad parts of the political elite. Interestingly, the leading topics emphasized by pro-Brexit voters did not have much to do with the EU at all and largely reflected dissatisfaction with government plus some degree of anti-immigration sentiment, nevertheless the anti-EU immigration issue was indeed an artificial construct that Mr. Cameron's political rhetoric had pushed since 2013 and which was mainly concerned with creating a scapegoat for massive cuts in transfers to local communities. Anti-immigration sentiments are, however, also rhetorical elements in the broader European political picture and in Mr. Trump's US presidential campaign. The fact that Mr. Trump, as the new US president, has welcomed Brexit is a discontinuity of over 50 years of US policy in Europe and stands jointly with the Brexit for a destabilization of Western Europe and indeed the Western world.

It is obvious that the European Union has several weak points and it is unclear whether or not the EU and its member countries, respectively, will be able to solve the current problems and create, through institutional reforms, a more modern and politically attractive regional integration club. One cannot rule out that Brexit is only the beginning of a long-term EU disintegration process that could lead Europe more or less back to the late nineteenth century when fierce competition between great powers and imperialism, respectively, shaped the world—only that now, post-Brexit, there would be the US and China as two additional and indeed leading global powers. If such rivalry and a decline of multilateralism would occur, strongly reinforced by the Trump administration which in its early days appeared to be weakening the World Trade Organization and the Bank for International Settlements, the twenty-first century would be heading towards new conflicts, rising instability and reduced growth of economic prosperity.

The European Union has for decades not expended the effort sufficient to get broad political support in the UK; very few governments have engaged in campaigns to explain the functioning of the EU to the population (here, the Blair government was a notable exception) and knowledge about EU institutions remains rather weak in the UK. The half-hearted support for the EU in parts of the British political system and the idea that a mini-supranational EU budget combined with a large liberalization agenda in the European Union would be the ideal state of EU integration is quite doubtful. Voting behavior analysis in Germany shows that voters are largely aware of the key policy fields which are relevant for local, regional or national elections, while the EU activities are so unknown to voters—and actually quite small in terms of the EU budget—that they have a rather strong tendency to "experiment" at the European Parliament elections and vote for smaller radical parties: the European Parliament elections thus have become a breeding ground for the growth of fringe parties in many EU countries and this expansion of radical parties in Europe makes political consensus building rather difficult and destabilizes EU member states once these radical parties reinvest the money and reputation gained in Brussels to become larger political competitors at the national level. Maintaining this dangerous system by emphasizing the principle of subsidiarity in a naïve way has been a hallmark of several governments in Europe—all ignoring the self-radicalization dynamics from the political process in Brussels. These findings (and the assumption that voters' behavior at European Parliament elections in Germany does not significantly differ from that of voters in the UK, France, Italy, Spain and other EU countries) plus the theory of fiscal federalism clearly suggest that in the future the EU should emphasize higher government expenditures at the supranational level—mainly infrastructure projects, defense and the first six months of unemployment coverage (except for youth unemployment—the extent of which is often largely caused by national minimum wage regulations) should be key expenditure categories that should sum up to 5–6% of EU gross domestic product in the future. A full political union in the Eurozone would be useful. Policy efficiency gains at the supranational level in the context of enhanced political competition at the European Parliament elections would allow, in combination with exploitation of economies of scale, for example in a joint EU military budget, to effectively reduce the average income tax rate in a modernized EU. The current EU with its mini-budget share—1/9th of the US federal budget—is bound to implode in the medium run. A modern EU would have to face more actively the current challenges for the European Union, namely the digital economic expansion and innovation dynamics, the rising role of Asia (with the EU by 2017 having achieved a completed free trade agreement with Singapore, and an agreement with Vietnam which still has to be verified—just two of the ten ASEAN countries—and with the Republic of Korea) and the question of creating a basic political union within the EU. As regards the latter, the EU should to some extent learn from the United States—paradoxically, one cannot rule out that the anti-EU policy stance and the anti-multilateralism of the Trump administration will in fact ultimately contribute to a European Political Union.

References

Atoyan, R. et al. (2016). Emigration and its impact on Eastern Europe, IMF SDN 16/07, Washington, DC.

European Commission. (2015). EU exports to the world: Effects on employment and income, IPTS Report, Brussels.

European Commission. (2017a). European Economic Forecast, Winter 2017, DG ECFIN, Institutional Paper 048, February 2017, Brussels.

European Parliament. (2017). Directorate general for internal policies. Policy Department. CEPS Report of the IMCO Committee, Brussels, March 2017.

Francois, J., et al. (2013). *Reducing transatlantic barriers to trade and investment.* London: CEPR (for the European Commission).

HM Government. (2017a). *Prime Minister May's speech on Brexit, Lancaster House speech delivered 17th January 2017.* Available online, accessed at: https://www.gov.uk/government/speeches/the-governments-negotiating-objectives-for-exiting-the-eu-pm-speech.

HM Government. (2017b). *The United Kingdom's exit from and new partnership with the European Union, Government White Paper, London.* https://www.gov.uk/government/uploads/system/uploads/attachment_data/file/589191/The_United_Kingdoms_exit_from_and_partnership_with_the_EU_Web.pdf.

IMF. (2016). Uncertainty in the aftermath of the U.K. referendum. *World Economic Outlook Update*, July 19, 2016, Washington, DC.

IMK. (2016). *Brexit lähmt Konjunktur.* IMK Report 115, June 2016. Düsseldorf: IMK/Hans-Böckler-Stiftung.

Jaumotte, F., Lall, S., & Papageorgiou, C. (2008). *Rising income inequality: Technology, or trade and financial globalization*, IMF Working Paper WP/08/185, Washington DC.

Jungmittag, A. (2004). Innovations, technological specialisation and economic growth in the EU. *International Economics and Economic Policy, 1*, 247–273.

McKinsey Global Institute. (2015). *A window of opportunity for Europe.* Washington DC.

Melitz, M. J. (2003). The impact of trade on intra-industry reallocations and aggregate industry productivity. *Econometrica, 71*, 1695–1725.

NIESER. (2016a). *The economic consequences of leaving the EU* (Nieser Review 236). London: National Institute of Economic and Social Research.

NIESER. (2016b). *Sovereign risk and the referendum—How have bonds responded?* (NiGEM Oberservations No. 2). London: National Institute of Economic and Social Research.

OECD. (2010). *Interim report of the green growth strategy: Implementing our commitment for a sustainable future.* Meeting of the OECD Council at Ministerial Level. Paris: OECD Publishing.

Office for Budget Responsibility. (2017). *Economic and Fiscal Outlook, March 2017.* Robert Chote, Chairman, London: Briefing Slides.

Pichelmann, K. (2015). When "Secular Stagnation" Meets Piketty's Capitalism in the 21st Century. Growth and Inequality Trends in Europe Reconsidered, 12th Euroframe Conference, 12th June 2015, Vienna. DG ECFIN Working Paper.

Welfens, P. J. J. (2011). *Innovations in macroeconomics, 3rd revised/enlarged printing.* Heidelberg: Springer.

Welfens, P. J. J. (2017). *Negative welfare effects from enhanced international. M&As in the Post-Brexit-referendum UK,* EIIW Discussion Paper No. 232. www.eiiw.eu.

Index

© The Editor(s) (if applicable) and The Author(s) 2017   **431**
P.J.J. Welfens, *An Accidental Brexit*,
DOI 10.1007/978-3-319-58271-9

25738592R00261

Printed in Great Britain
by Amazon